Citizenship, Belonging, and Political Community in Africa

CAMBRIDGE CENTRE OF AFRICAN STUDIES SERIES

Series editors: Derek R. Peterson, Harri Englund, and Christopher Warnes

The University of Cambridge is home to one of the world's leading centers of African studies. It organizes conferences, runs a weekly seminar series, hosts a specialist library, coordinates advanced graduate studies, and facilitates research by Cambridge- and Africa-based academics. The Cambridge Centre of African Studies Series publishes work that emanates from this rich intellectual life. The series fosters dialogue across a broad range of disciplines in African studies and between scholars based in Africa and elsewhere.

Derek R. Peterson, ed.
Abolitionism and Imperialism in Britain, Africa, and the Atlantic

Harri Englund, ed.
Christianity and Public Culture in Africa

Devon Curtis and Gwinyayi A. Dzinesa, eds.
Peacebuilding, Power, and Politics in Africa

Ruth J. Prince and Rebecca Marsland, eds.
Making Public Health in Africa: Ethnographic and Historical Perspectives

Emma Hunter, ed.
*Citizenship, Belonging, and Political Community in Africa:
Dialogues between Past and Present*

Citizenship, Belonging, and Political Community in Africa

Dialogues between Past and Present

Edited by Emma Hunter

Ohio University Press • *Athens*

Ohio University Press, Athens, Ohio 45701
ohioswallow.com
© 2016 by Ohio University Press
All rights reserved

Printed in the United States of America
Ohio University Press books are printed on acid-free paper ⊚ ™

26 25 24 23 22 21 20 19 18 17 16   5 4 3 2 1

Library of Congress Cataloging-in-Publication Data

Names: Hunter, Emma, 1980– editor.
Title: Citizenship, belonging, and political community in Africa : dialogues
  between past and present / edited by Emma Hunter.
Other titles: Cambridge Centre of African Studies series.
Description: Athens : Ohio University Press, 2016. | Series: Cambridge centre
  of African studies series | Includes bibliographical references and index.
Identifiers: LCCN 2016024890| ISBN 9780821422564 (hc : alk. paper) | ISBN
  9780821422571 (pb : alk. paper) | ISBN 9780821445938 (pdf)
Subjects: LCSH: Citizenship—Africa. | Political rights—Africa. | Political
  Socialization—Africa.
Classification: LCC JQ1879.A2 C58 2016 | DDC 323.6096—dc23
LC record available at https://lccn.loc.gov/2016024890

Contents

Contents

Contents

Acknowledgments

This book is the result of discussions and debates made possible by the Cambridge Centre of African Studies' visiting fellows program. For several years, thanks to the generous support of Cambridge University's Isaac Newton and Smuts Memorial Trusts and the Ford, Leverhulme, and A. G. Leventis Foundations, together with hospitality from Wolfson College, the center has each year hosted a number of African academics for a six-month term. In October 2011 we welcomed as visiting fellows academics whose research interests lay in different aspects of the theme of citizenship, belonging, and political community in Africa. During the period that the visiting fellows spent in Cambridge, we explored these themes through formal and informal seminars, a workshop in Cambridge in March 2012, and a conference in Nairobi in July 2012.

The Centre of African Studies provided a wonderful environment for the discussions that led to this volume. I am particularly grateful to Megan Vaughan for her unfailing support and enthusiasm for this project. Dorian Addison and Eva Rybicki ensured that the seminar series and the workshop in Cambridge ran smoothly and efficiently, and I thank them on behalf of all the presenters and participants. The conference in Nairobi could not have happened without the generous support of Ambreena Manji and everyone at the British Institute in Eastern Africa. I am enormously grateful to Humphrey Mathenge, who ensured that the conference in Nairobi was a fantastic finale to the program.

Many people were involved in the visiting fellowship program, as well as the seminars, workshop, and conference, and thanking them all here would be impossible. But particular thanks are due to Lovise Aalen, Akoko Akech, Charles Amone, Warigia Bowman, Joel Cabrita, Geert Castryck, Dominique Connan, Marie-Aude Fouéré, Sarah Jenkins, Patience Kabamba, Edmond Keller, Miles Larmer, Baz Lecocq, Malika Rebai Maamri, Claire Mercer, Misha Mintz-Roth, Godwin Murunga, Abdul Raufu Mustapha, Hassan Mwakimako, Ridwan Osman, Tara Polzer-Ngwato, Andrea Scheibler, and Anders Sjögren. I would also like to thank former colleagues in the Centre of African Studies, particularly Florence Brisset-Foucault, Christopher Clapham, Devon

Curtis, Harri Englund, Alastair Fraser, Adam Higazi, John Lonsdale, Sharath Srinivasan, and Liz Watson, whose searching questions and contributions to our discussions helped shape the ideas developed in this volume.

The comments from the series editors and the two anonymous reviewers were enormously helpful in strengthening the volume. It has been a pleasure to work with the series editors—Derek Peterson, Harri Englund, and Chris Warnes—as well as Gillian Berchowitz, the director of Ohio University Press. Derek Peterson in particular has gone above and beyond the duties of a series editor, and I am very grateful to him for his participation in the Nairobi conference and for his insightful comments and suggestions as the volume developed.

Introduction

EMMA HUNTER

AFRICA, IT IS OFTEN SAID, IS SUFFERING FROM A CRISIS OF citizenship.[1] Since the return of multiparty politics, new dynamics of inclusion and exclusion have led to the denial of rights and privileges to those designated as "strangers."[2] In a continent where movement has always been the norm, designating particular groups as outsiders and seeking to exclude them from political rights on that basis has proved a tempting political tactic.[3] At the same time, even those who enjoy the legal status of citizenship and the political rights that flow from it face difficulties in approaching the state as active citizens engaged in ruling themselves.[4]

At the heart of contemporary debates over citizenship in Africa lie dynamic exchanges between the present and the past, between political theory and political practice, and between legal categories and lived experience. Yet studies of citizenship in Africa have often tended to foreshorten historical time and to privilege the present at the expense of the past. The very term *citizen* is often understood as relevant primarily to the postcolonial state, limiting comparative analysis of political status across space and time. As we shall see, this neglect of history poses problems, given that theories of contemporary African politics often rest heavily on readings of the past.

More broadly, a tension has emerged between the approach taken by historians and that taken by social scientists. Among the latter, it has become axiomatic that colonial states were characterized by a dichotomy between subjecthood and citizenship, representing a clear difference between the majority of the population and a privileged minority accorded full legal rights. But this focus on legal status and terminology misses the ways in which there have always been different sorts of subjects, with different sorts of rights, duties, and prerogatives negotiated on the ground as much as defined in colonial law, in ways not captured by the citizen/subject dichotomy. Still more important, the focus on legal status means that we risk losing sight of broader discursive spheres in which political membership is articulated and claims are made. We need to look beyond the normative texts of colonial and postcolonial lawmaking and more closely into the domains of history, narrative, and social practice.[5]

This is an opportune moment to survey the field and propose new ways forward. It emerges from a visiting fellowship program that brought five historians, political scientists, and sociologists from African universities to Cambridge in 2011–12 to work on the theme of citizenship, belonging, and political community in Africa. The ideas explored here were developed over a series of seminars with invited speakers, a workshop in Cambridge, and a conference in Nairobi. This volume necessarily includes only a small selection of the work presented at the Cambridge seminars and at the two conferences, but the contributions of all participants helped shape the arguments developed here.

The aim of the book is twofold. In the first place, it seeks to provide a critical reflection on citizenship in Africa by bringing together scholars working with very different case studies and with very different understandings of what is meant by citizenship. Second, by bringing historians and social scientists into dialogue in the same volume, it argues that a revised reading of the past can offer powerful new perspectives on the present.

Dialogues between Disciplines

This book brings together nine case studies that take very different approaches. But while the contributors approach the issue from the perspective of varying disciplines, the differences between them are not reducible to those disciplinary differences. Rather, they approach the issue along three thematic axes.

Civil and Civic Citizenship in Africa

If we see a legal definition of citizenship, or "civil citizenship" not as *the* definition of citizenship but as one element of a shared field, we can cast our eye back to the ways in which the governed engaged with their governors prior to, and later outwith or alongside, the institutions of the modern state.[6] This is a theme explored in more detail in

John Lonsdale's chapter, but in brief, in precolonial Africa, struggles for citizenship focused on incorporation. Jonathon Glassman's work on nineteenth-century eastern Africa has led us to appreciate the importance of struggles for inclusion. Relationships between slaves and their owners were unequal, but by employing a common language of paternalist authority, slaves could seek to defend or enhance their positions. As Glassman makes clear, they could employ an "ideological language of clientelism to express personal agendas that were aggressive and innovative."[7]

This is not surprising, for across precolonial Africa, establishing ties of personal dependence and inserting oneself into networks of authority were often more important than seeking autonomy.[8] But these relationships were fluid and unstable. Chiefs sought to build authority and attract followers, but they knew that followers could, if they wished, go elsewhere. As Cherry Leonardi writes with reference to southern Sudan, "Chiefship itself had originated in mobility and migration, in terms of both the individual acquisition of linguistic and other foreign knowledge and the subsequent attraction of adherents. But this also gave chiefs' followers their own means of holding chiefs to account by the threat and practice of further migration to alternative patrons: 'No chief wanted his people to leave him.'"[9]

While some have argued that the advent of the colonial state saw the extinguishing of older modes of interaction between governors and governed, the cases explored in this volume show clearly that in nineteenth- and twentieth-century Africa this process was never complete. Far more striking is the interaction between the new institutional forms of the state and older practices that continued to have traction.

In the Cape Colony of the seventeenth and eighteenth centuries, explored in this volume by Nicole Ulrich, Khoesan were largely excluded from the colonial legal order. This meant that they were left either to negotiate relations of dependency with frontier farmers or to bond together with other subordinated classes to better their position. The patchwork of legal statuses that characterized the seventeenth- and eighteenth-century Cape began to be extinguished from the late eighteenth century on, as colonial rulers acted to redefine sovereignty and political subjecthood and discursively to construct a relationship between the imperial state and the individual. Ulrich's chapter traces the way that this happened in the Cape with the replacement of Dutch rule with British rule. While there was institutional continuity, the British brought with them a new governing ethos underpinned by the category of the "British subject." The result was that "masters and servants were brought into the same legal framework and, in theory, came to be regarded more or less as equal before the law," a dramatic change from the Dutch East India Company (VOC) system, which was, as Ulrich reminds us, "designed to protect social hierarchies."

Colonial rulers described this relationship as reflecting a new conception of sovereignty, though at times they did so using old language, as in Zanzibar, where the term used in colonial citizenship laws was the old word for subject, *raia*.[10] New conceptions of sovereignty provided new discursive and practical resources to colonial subjects. The claim to imperial citizenship was one such discursive resource, as Ulrich shows in her chapter. Khoesan laborers "could look to the colonial state to secure limited rights and protections, especially within the realm of labor relations." In a postcolonial context, Aidan Russell's exploration of early postcolonial Burundi evocatively captures the ways in which Burundians on the border selectively employed the state's language and turned it back at state officials as a way of proving their loyalty to the state. In other contexts, legalistic forms of claim making became increasingly important. Similarly, Cherry Leonardi's informants in southern Sudan recalled going to the colonial courts "to claim one's right," as older modes of political practice were overlaid with a new juridical tone.[11]

But while colonial laws and didactic texts focused on a relationship to the imperial state, everyday political life often took place at other levels of political belonging, with rights and duties negotiated through membership of political communities smaller than the state. Individuals had different criteria for belonging, which themselves changed over time, and engaging with power often meant playing different forms of political membership off against each other. As Cherry Leonardi and Chris Vaughan show in their chapter, in 1940s and 1950s Sudan, "'local' and 'national' citizenship were interactive fields, rather than discrete spheres."

If the contributions of Ulrich, Russell, and Leonardi and Vaughan in this volume point to the need for studies that explore changing modes of engagement between governed and governors over the *longue durée*, what analytical tools might we employ to understand these? To answer this question, Aidan Russell puts forward a compelling case for destabilizing the common dichotomy between "citizen" and "subject" as a productive way forward. Modernization narratives offer an account of a gradual transition from subjecthood to universal citizenship, a narrative partially arrested in colonial Africa by the dichotomy produced by colonial states, whereby some were granted the status of citizens and others left subject to authoritarian chiefs.[12] But for Russell, "the distinction of subject and citizen is simultaneously an informative and a misleading principle of analysis." Exploring the "daily practices and expressions of people and state" in early postcolonial Burundi, Russell finds that "as the terms and obsessions of state authority shifted, the people of Burundi certainly acted the subject, yet frequently too they made the claims of active citizens, blended obedience with negotiation and loyalty with invocation, and conformed to political realities while seeking to shift them toward their interest." The focus on practice and agency, in dialogue with state discourse and legal status, comes out clearly too in Samantha Balaton-Chrimes's case study of the Nubians of Kenya, making the case, in her words, for "an account of citizenship as a multidimensional legal status and political condition that is constructed and contested by agential political subjects."

All four of these chapters thus bring out the interplay of state discourses and shifting modes of practicing citizenship from below. At the same time, they also point us to the ways in which the limits of political community, as well as who is included and excluded from any given political community, are subject to negotiation.

Deep Histories of Inclusion and Exclusion

Several of the contributors to this volume define citizenship in terms of a legal status granted or withheld by the state, which gives those holding it access to a set of rights and demands of them certain duties. Yet their contributions demonstrate that the apparent modularity of this conception of citizenship conceals historical battles over how the limits of inclusion and exclusion are defined and thus over the boundaries of political community. Far from history demonstrating a gradual but ultimately unidirectional path, there is an alternative history of institutional experiments and roads not taken. Citizenship has always been, in Luise White's words, a "slippery category."[13] In this regard, the transition from one imperial system to another and the unraveling of imperial systems in the era of decolonization were particularly important.[14]

As we have seen, the advent of British rule in the Cape gave Khoesan access to a new language of imperial citizenship. This language of imperial citizenship functioned as a weapon in argument more than settled fact, yet, as Leonardi and Vaughan point out, its appearance in the rhetoric of petitions tells us something interesting about changing conceptions of political community in the colonial era.

The same was true of the moment of decolonization, as Frederick Cooper reminds us in his postscript to this volume. Decolonizing states did not have to take an off-the-shelf model of territorial citizenship; they could experiment with alternative and more expansive models. The twists and turns taken by these experiments are brought to life in Henri-Michel Yéré's chapter, which explores Félix Houphouët-Boigny's attempt to introduce "double nationality" to early postcolonial Ivory Coast. This was not a straightforward policy of dual citizenship; rather, Houphouët-Boigny had in mind a system whereby "nationals of different West African states could benefit from the same rights and duties as citizens of their host country without being citizens." For Houphouët-Boigny, this was a political move, designed to shore up support and pursue African unity on his terms. Yet it failed, rejected by a group of elite Ivorians for whom it seemed to herald fewer jobs and opportunities. Yéré analyzes this controversy as a struggle between two alternative conceptions of citizenship: Houphouët-Boigny's reconstituted version of French imperial citizenship on the one hand and a conception of Ivorian citizenship on the other. In doing so, he demonstrates the centrality of struggles over citizenship to the decolonization process and the making of postcolonial states.

Had it succeeded, Houphouët-Boigny's model would have both destabilized and reinforced hierarchies of citizenship between Ivorians and other nationals of other West African states. The importance of hierarchies of citizenship is emphasized too in the case studies of Mauritius and Kenya. In Mauritius, as Ramola Ramtohul shows, where hierarchies of citizenship had been established historically and the purpose for which groups had originally come to the island served to define their position in Mauritius's social hierarchy, a Franco-Mauritian elite sought to use their "claim of being the 'authentic' Mauritian population that legitimately deserved to lead the country" to exclude others from political rights. Similarly, for the Nubians of Kenya, Balaton-Chrimes argues, only by tracing the history of the community within Kenya can we understand the "way in which today's Nubians are marginalized by the nation's contemporary citizenship."

More generally, the case of the Nubians reminds us, in Balaton-Chrimes's words, that "political membership has historically been negotiated in dialogue with, rather than purely determined by, colonial (and postcolonial) legal and political status," and this is as true of the present as of the past.[15] At the same time, all three of these case studies pay particular attention to the mid-twentieth century and reinforce the point, made most forcefully by Yéré, that the struggles over inclusion and exclusion that have dominated contemporary politics in much of Africa and that are often traced to the effects of political liberalization after 1989 have a much longer history than we might think.[16] That said, the political landscape has changed dramatically since 1989, and with this in mind it is to contemporary Africa that I now turn.

Multicultural Citizenship in Africa

The growing importance in contemporary Africa of struggles over autochthony or indigeneity compels us to interrogate the category of civil citizenship and reflect on the ways in which Africa has, in recent years, become a testing ground for new conceptions of multicultural citizenship. While the modernization theories of the mid-twentieth century assumed a trajectory toward the existence of homogenous nation-states, the unexpected persistence of subnational identities, particularly ethnic identities, in postcolonial Africa has led scholars and activists to consider how models of citizenship that leave space for difference might be constructed.

In this vein, some have stressed the potential for a new multicultural citizenship to open up new paths for "meaningful citizenship."[17] Peter Ekeh argued many years ago that in Africa we see the working out of a duality created by colonial rule whereby there are effectively two bases of citizenship: one "official" and determined by the state; and the other "unofficial" or "primordial," defined by local communities on the basis of birth.[18] The two publics have different norms of behavior. The civic public is, Ekeh argued, fundamentally amoral, a space in which material gains are pursued without the need to give anything back. This is a sphere of rights rather than duties. In contrast, the "primordial" public is a sphere of duties more than of rights; more important, it is a *moral* space to be contrasted with the *amorality* of the civic sphere. Thus, whereas in the West, Ekeh argues, citizenship is conceived in terms of a transactional relationship of rights and duties, in Africa rights and duties are partitioned between two separate and rival spheres of citizenship.[19] There is therefore an uncertain fit between the relationship of an individual in relation to the state and vernacular conceptions of citizenship determined locally, and in more recent work Ekeh has developed this idea further, arguing that whereas in the Hobbesian tradition individuals go to the state in search of protection, in Africa they go to ethnic kinsmen in pursuit of protection *from* the state. As a result, "[t]he bonds of mistrust between states and individuals in Africa are replaced with bonds of moral sentiments binding individuals who share a common ethnicity."[20]

But crucially, in Ekeh's work, as in more recent analyses that pursue a similar line of inquiry, there is potential for the rural domain of culture to be a space in which to develop practices of what Lahra Smith terms "meaningful citizenship."[21] This is a line of interpretation that we see in John Lonsdale's work on Kenya. In the Kenyan examples that Lonsdale explores, ethnic citizenship was not simply a domain in which individuals gave of themselves in return for protection; rather, it was a domain of moral argument, in which the proper relationship between young and old, rich and poor was worked out and in which unequal social relations were made bearable. This was, in Ekeh's terms, a domain of both rights and duties. More than that, Lonsdale shows that the development of a moral ethnic public in the colonial period did not preclude the development of other forms of citizenship, national or imperial, both in the colonial period and more recently.

Building on this argument and seeking to extend it more widely, Lahra Smith argues that "[w]hat scholars of diversity and multiculturalism theory in the west offer is a dynamic and optimistic view of the role of identity politics in supporting democratization. Adopting and modifying this theoretical approach would radically change the pessimistic and defeatist tone of what is typically studied as 'ethnic politics' in the African context."[22] For Smith, the lens of "meaningful citizenship" means that "certain kinds of claims, such as ethnic and gendered claims by citizens, can be read as liberatory and democratizing rather than atavistic or primordial, as both the western media and dominant political regimes would have us conclude."[23] Her findings lead her to be more optimistic about a process of "citizen expansion" at the local level, which she identifies in Ethiopia in the early twenty-first century, than studies of formal political institutions and quantitative measures of democratization in ethnically plural states would suggest.

These arguments are in part supported by Ramtohul's case study. In Mauritius, recognizing difference at the moment of independence allowed for the creation of a stable and durable political system. A relatively optimistic note is also struck by Eghosa Osaghae in his overview chapter. While he remains committed to a goal of equal citizenship, he argues that in contrast to earlier eras of state building when the state simply denied ethnic difference, post-1989 the "increased involvement of civil society in citizenship construction makes the process more discerning of diversity and the imperatives of equitable rights and accountability and therefore more likely to endure as a negotiated rather than a received paradigm."

But for Solomon Gofie, we should be wary of the power of recognizing ethnic identities *by itself* to make civic engagement more possible. Exploring the Ethiopian case, he argues that far from enhancing the ability of Ethiopian citizens to engage with the state through its celebration of the right to recognition of Ethiopia's "peoples," in fact "the propagation of the discourse of 'the peoples' accompanied by state control of land and the curtailment of freedom of expression and association has acted to reinforce state control and restrict the ability of Ethiopia's citizens to engage with the state." In his chapter he describes the ways in which the governing EPRDF regime in Ethiopia has used a language of recognizing group rights as a means of imposing power.

Adefemi Isumonah too sounds a cautionary note, fearing that the reification of "indigene" identities risks ignoring the fact that social change, mobility, and urbanization mean that individual rights may be becoming more important than group identities for Nigerians. In his chapter, Isumonah explores the "contradictions of the pro-ethno-territorial approaches to rights in Nigeria," arguing against the preference for group rights as the best guarantor of individual freedoms. Both Isumonah and Gofie question the idea implicit in recent thinking about multicultural citizenship that recognizing group rights is the best route to a more engaged citizenry. The discussion of colonial-era engagements with new languages of individual rights and conceptions of imperial citizenship suggests that Africans have found these languages useful in confronting authoritarian states in the past and may well do so again in the future.

The Past in the Present

Why does this matter? In the first place, asking questions about citizenship in Africa's past as well as its present is important because it helps us better understand that past. We begin to see aspects of power and its operation that we might otherwise miss, hidden beneath powerful narratives of "modernization" or "democratization." This volume therefore serves as an invitation and encouragement to historians to go further in exploring the ways in which citizenship is practiced in particular historical contexts, embracing citizenship as an analytical category not restricted to specific forms of engagement with the modern state.

But this volume also seeks to make the argument that a better understanding of the past is relevant in trying to understand our present condition and the future prospects of democracy in Africa. To see why, we return now to consider briefly the reasons that scholars have recently become so interested in the issue of citizenship.

In Africa, the return of multiparty elections in the late 1980s and early 1990s was greeted with initial enthusiasm followed by disappointment. While the model of authoritarian one-party rule that had existed since the mid-1960s rapidly became hard to defend on the international stage and new parties appeared across the continent, elections did not seem to provide an effective means of peacefully replacing incumbent parties. As scholars sought to understand the limits of elections, some turned to the political cultures that had been created in the colonial period and concluded that these political cultures militated against the creation of democratic citizenship in the postcolony. The colonial state, some scholars argued, should be understood as a regime of subjecthood and clientship, not citizenship.[24] And the persistence of patron-client relations in the postcolonial state seemed to preclude the potential for citizenship as active participation in the civic humanist tradition.

These debates were in some ways specific to Africa but were also part of a wider conversation about citizenship and democracy that had developed since the 1980s, when the forces of economic and political liberalization in an era of growing consciousness of globalization began to inspire a developing interest in the concept of citizenship. What did it mean to belong to a political community? What was the state willing to do for its citizens, and what could it do in an era when global forces seemed to be becoming more powerful than nation-states?[25] As political liberalization opened up the possibility of fundamentally reshaping the boundaries and limits of political communities, ethno-nationalist politics and the demand by minority groups for recognition of their differences returned to public political debate across the world, from Canada to Ethiopia.

In seeking to explain the apparent crisis of citizenship in contemporary Africa, many scholars have turned to the colonial past and the political culture that colonial regimes helped to create. Bruce Berman, Dickson Eyoh, and Will Kymlicka describe the colonial state as one in which "people related as subjects and clients, rather than citizens, to an authoritarian state."[26] For Mahmood Mamdani, the system of government established in the colonial era that denied citizenship rights to African subjects in rural Africa helped create the basis of postcolonial authoritarianism.[27] This, it has been suggested, helps explain why, twenty-five years after the return to multiparty democracy in much of sub-Saharan Africa, voters seldom throw incumbent governments out of office.

The colonial past has thus become crucial to understanding the present. But which colonial past? For social scientists, creating a useable past has meant ironing out many of the ambiguities and contradictions of that past and relying on a particular narrative of modernization that, in the case of Africa, is deemed to have failed. Attention has focused on the way in which colonial states simultaneously imposed a model of civil citizenship as a universal norm and at the same time denied access to the rights it offered to most of their African subjects. This is a narrative of the past in which opportunities for the governed to engage with their governors come only with the birth of the modern state and are incompatible both with precolonial modes of political authority and with colonial states that granted political rights to a few but denied them to the many.

Yet the historical case studies collected here demonstrate clearly that the governed have always sought to engage their governors, though they have done so in different ways at different times. This deeper history demands to be taken seriously, for it helped to shape the ways in which Africans engaged with their colonial and postcolonial rulers. At the same time, putting history into dialogue with contemporary social science forcefully makes the point that those concerned with policy making in the present need to be much more sensitive to local differences and to the ways in which conceptions of citizenship are worked out in different ways in different places.

Structure of the Volume

The volume begins with a chapter by John Lonsdale, making a strong argument for the importance of history in understanding citizenship in Africa. The remainder of the volume is divided into three parts, followed by a postscript. Part 1 takes the familiar distinction between "citizens" and "subjects" but destabilizes it through three historical case studies from the Cape, Burundi, and Sudan. Part 2 takes seriously the "slipperiness" of citizenship and explores three case studies from across the continent—Ivory Coast, Mauritius, and Kenya, focusing on the era of decolonization. Part 3 moves to contemporary Africa, combining an overview chapter by Eghosa Osaghae with case studies from Nigeria and Ethiopia. Finally, in his postscript Frederick Cooper offers his reflections on the volume and the issues it raises.

Taken together, the contributors to this book demonstrate some of the ways in which a revised understanding of citizenship in the colonial and early postcolonial state can help set contemporary debates in a new light and offer new avenues for creative thinking about the building of democratic cultures in Africa. While the chapters range widely in geographical and chronological focus, as well as in the debates they explore, what unites them is a desire to bring Africa's deep historical past into dialogue with the present, in ways that might also indicate new paths for the future.

Notes

I am grateful to the anonymous reviewers as well as to Frederick Cooper, Stephen McDowall, Naomi Parkinson, and Charles West for commenting on earlier drafts of this introduction. The ideas explored here have been discussed over many years with Florence Brisset-Foucault and, over recent months, with Sara Rich Dorman, and I have learned a great deal from both of them.

1. Wale Adebanwi, "Terror, Territoriality and the Struggle for Indigeneity and Citizenship in Northern Nigeria," *Citizenship Studies* 13, no. 3 (2009): 350.

2. See, in particular, Peter Geschiere and Stephen Jackson, "Autochthony and the Crisis of Citizenship: Democratization, Decentralization, and the Politics of Belonging," *African Studies Review* 49, no. 2 (2006): 1–7; and Peter Geschiere, *The Perils of Belonging: Autochthony, Citizenship and Exclusion in Africa and Europe* (Chicago: University of Chicago Press, 2009). See also John Lonsdale, "Soil, Work, Civilisation, and Citizenship in Kenya," *Journal of Eastern African Studies* 2, no. 2 (2008): 311–12. For a helpful overview, see Sara Rich Dorman, "Citizenship in Africa: The Politics of Belonging," in *Routledge Handbook of Global Citizenship Studies*, ed. Engin F. Isin and Peter Nyers (Routledge: London, 2014), 161–71.

3. Bronwen Manby, *Struggles for Citizenship in Africa* (London: Zed Books, 2009).

4. See, for example, Ebenezer Obadare and Wendy Willems, *Civic Agency in Africa: Arts of Resistance in the Twenty-First Century* (Oxford: James Currey, 2014); Steven Robins, Andrea Cornwall, and Bettina von Lieres,

"Rethinking 'Citizenship' in the Postcolony," *Third World Quarterly* 29, no. 6 (2008): 1069–86.

5. Sukanya Banerjee, *Becoming Imperial Citizens: Indians in the Late-Victorian Empire* (Durham, NC: Duke University Press, 2010), 5.

6. James Tully, "On Global Citizenship," in *On Global Citizenship: James Tully in Dialogue* (London: Bloomsbury, 2014). See also Engin F. Isin and Peter Nyers, "Introduction: Globalizing Citizenship Studies," in Isin and Nyers, *Routledge Handbook*, 2.

7. Jonathon Glassman, *Feasts and Riot: Revelry, Rebellion, and Popular Consciousness on the Swahili Coast* (Heinemann: London, 1995), 95.

8. For a powerful argument in favor of the continued importance of relationships of dependence in colonial and postcolonial Africa, see James Ferguson, "Declarations of Dependence: Labour, Personhood, and Welfare in Southern Africa," *Journal of the Royal Anthropological Institute* 19 (2013): 223–42.

9. Cherry Leonardi, *Dealing with Government in South Sudan: Histories of Chiefship, Community and State* (Woodbridge, UK: Boydell and Brewer, 2013), 113–14.

10. Jonathon Glassman, *War of Words, War of Stones: Racial Thought and Violence in Colonial Zanzibar* (Bloomington: Indiana University Press, 2011), 52, 319n; Emma Hunter, "Dutiful Subjects, Patriotic Citizens, and the Concept of 'Good Citizenship' in Twentieth-Century Tanzania," *Historical Journal* 56, no. 1 (2013): 257–77.

11. Leonardi, *Dealing with Government*, 101.

12. Mahmood Mamdani, *Citizen and Subject: Contemporary Africa and the Legacy of Late Colonialism* (Princeton: Princeton University Press, 1996).

13. Luise White, *Unpopular Sovereignty: Rhodesian Independence and African Decolonization* (Chicago: University of Chicago Press, 2015), 40.

14. On decolonization as a moment of possibility, see, for example, Gary Wilder, *Freedom Time: Negritude, Decolonization and the Future of the World* (Durham, NC: Duke University Press, 2015); Frederick Cooper, *Citizenship between Empire and Nation* (Princeton: Princeton University Press, 2014); and Emma Hunter, *Political Thought and the Public Sphere in Tanzania: Freedom, Democracy and Citizenship in the Era of Decolonization* (Cambridge: Cambridge University Press, 2015).

15. This point is developed in Samantha Balaton-Chrimes's recent book, *Ethnicity, Democracy and Citizenship in Africa: Political Marginalisation of Kenya's Nubians* (Ashgate, UK: Farnham, 2015), 10–12, 21.

16. Dorman, "Citizenship in Africa."

17. Lahra Smith, *Making Citizens in Africa: Ethnicity, Gender and National Identity in Ethiopia* (Cambridge: Cambridge University Press, 2013), 4.

18. Peter Ekeh, "Colonialism and the Two Publics in Africa: A Theoretical Statement," *Comparative Studies in Society and History* 17, no. 1 (1975): 92; Redie Bereketeab, "The Ethnic and Civic Foundations of Citizenship and Identity in the Horn of Africa," *Studies in Ethnicity and Nationalism* 11, no. 1 (2011): 63; Stephen N. Ndegwa, "Citizenship and Ethnicity: An Examination of Two

Transition Moments in Kenyan Politics," *American Political Science Review* 91, no. 3 (1997): 599–616.

19. Ekeh, "Colonialism," 106.

20. Peter Ekeh, "Individuals' Basic Security Needs and the Limits of Democratization," in *Ethnicity and Democracy in Africa*, ed. Bruce Berman, Dickson Eyoh, and Will Kymlicka (Oxford: James Currey, 2004), 36.

21. Smith, *Making Citizens in Africa*, 4.

22. Ibid., 38.

23. Ibid., 8.

24. Bruce Berman, Dickson Eyoh, and Will Kymlicka, "Introduction: Ethnicity and the Politics of Democratic Nation-Building in Africa," in Berman et al., *Ethnicity and Democracy*, 8; Robins et al., "Rethinking 'Citizenship.'"

25. Veronica Federico, *Citoyenneté et participation politique en Afrique du Sud* (Paris: L'Harmattan, 2012), 12; Charles Tilly, "Citizenship, Identity and Social History," *International Review of Social History* 40, no. 3 (1995): 1–17.

26. Berman et al., "Introduction," 8.

27. Mamdani, *Citizen and Subject*.

References

Adebanwi, Wale. "Terror, Territoriality and the Struggle for Indigeneity and Citizenship in Northern Nigeria." *Citizenship Studies* 13, no. 3 (2009): 349–63.

Balaton-Chrimes, Samantha. *Ethnicity, Democracy and Citizenship in Africa: Political Marginalisation of Kenya's Nubians*. Ashgate, UK: Farnham, 2015.

Banerjee, Sukanya. *Becoming Imperial Citizens: Indians in the Late-Victorian Empire*. Durham, NC: Duke University Press, 2010.

Bereketeab, Redie. "The Ethnic and Civic Foundations of Citizenship and Identity in the Horn of Africa." *Studies in Ethnicity and Nationalism* 11, no. 1 (2011): 63–81.

Berman, Bruce, Dickson Eyoh, and Will Kymlicka. "Introduction: Ethnicity and the Politics of Democratic Nation-Building in Africa." In *Ethnicity and Democracy in Africa*, edited by Bruce Berman, Dickson Eyoh, and Will Kymlicka, 1–21. Oxford: James Currey, 2004.

Cooper, Frederick. *Citizenship between Empire and Nation*. Princeton: Princeton University Press, 2014.

Dorman, Sara Rich. "Citizenship in Africa: The Politics of Belonging." In *Routledge Handbook of Global Citizenship Studies*, edited by Engin F. Isin and Peter Nyers, 161–71. Routledge: London, 2014.

Dorman, Sara Rich, Daniel Hammett, and Paul Nugent. "Introduction: Citizenship and Its Casualties in Africa." In *Making Nations, Creating Strangers: States and Citizenship in Africa*, edited by Sara Rich Dorman, Daniel Hammett, and Paul Nugent. Leiden: Brill, 2007.

Ekeh, Peter. "Colonialism and the Two Publics in Africa: A Theoretical Statement." *Comparative Studies in Society and History* 17, no. 1 (1975): 91–112.

———. "Individuals' Basic Security Needs and the Limits of Democratization." In *Ethnicity and Democracy in Africa*, edited by Bruce Berman, Dickson Eyoh, and Will Kymlicka, 22–37. Oxford: James Currey, 2004.

Federico, Veronica. *Citoyenneté et participation politique en Afrique du Sud*. Paris: L'Harmattan, 2012.

Ferguson, James. "Declarations of Dependence: Labour, Personhood, and Welfare in Southern Africa." *Journal of the Royal Anthropological Institute* 19 (2013): 223–42.

Geschiere, Peter. *The Perils of Belonging: Autochthony, Citizenship and Exclusion in Africa and Europe*. Chicago: University of Chicago Press, 2009.

Geschiere, Peter, and Stephen Jackson. "Autochthony and the Crisis of Citizenship: Democratization, Decentralization, and the Politics of Belonging." *African Studies Review* 49, no. 2 (2006): 1–7.

Glassman, Jonathon. *Feasts and Riot: Revelry, Rebellion, and Popular Consciousness on the Swahili Coast, 1856–1888*. Heinemann: London, 1995.

———. *War of Words, War of Stones: Racial Thought and Violence in Colonial Zanzibar*. Bloomington: Indiana University Press, 2011.

Hunter, Emma. "Dutiful Subjects, Patriotic Citizens, and the Concept of 'Good Citizenship' in Twentieth-Century Tanzania." *Historical Journal* 56, no. 1 (2013): 257–77.

———. *Political Thought and the Public Sphere in Tanzania: Freedom, Democracy and Citizenship in the Era of Decolonization*. Cambridge: Cambridge University Press, 2015.

Isin, Engin F., and Peter Nyers, "Introduction." In *Routledge Handbook of Global Citizenship Studies*, edited by Engin F. Isin and Peter Nyers, 1–11. Routledge: London, 2014.

Leonardi, Cherry. *Dealing with Government in South Sudan: Histories of Chiefship, Community and State*. Woodbridge, UK: Boydell and Brewer, 2013.

Lonsdale, John. "Soil, Work, Civilisation, and Citizenship in Kenya." *Journal of Eastern African Studies* 2, no. 2 (2008): 305–14.

Mamdani, Mahmood. *Citizen and Subject: Contemporary Africa and the Legacy of Late Colonialism*. Princeton: Princeton University Press, 1996.

Manby, Bronwen. *Struggles for Citizenship in Africa*. London: Zed Books, 2009.

Ndegwa, Stephen N. "Citizenship and Ethnicity: An Examination of Two Transition Moments in Kenyan Politics." *American Political Science Review* 91, no. 3 (1997): 599–616.

Nyamnjoh, Francis N. *Insiders and Outsiders: Citizenship and Xenophobia in Contemporary Southern Africa*. Dakar: Codesria Books, 2006.

Obadare, Ebenezer, and Wendy Willems. *Civic Agency in Africa: Arts of Resistance in the Twenty-First Century*. Oxford: James Currey, 2014.

Robins, Steven, Andrea Cornwall, and Bettina von Lieres. "Rethinking 'Citizenship' in the Postcolony." *Third World Quarterly* 29, no. 6 (2008): 1069–86.

Smith, Lahra. *Making Citizens in Africa: Ethnicity, Gender, and National Identity in Ethiopia*. Cambridge: Cambridge University Press, 2013.

Tilly, Charles. "Citizenship, Identity and Social History." *International Review of Social History* 40, no. 3 (1995): 1–17.

Tully, James. "On Global Citizenship." In *On Global Citizenship: James Tully in Dialogue,* edited by James Tully, 3–100. London: Bloomsbury, 2014.

White, Luise. *Unpopular Sovereignty: Rhodesian Independence and African Decolonization.* Chicago: University of Chicago Press, 2015.

Wilder, Gary. *Freedom Time: Negritude, Decolonization and the Future of the World.* Durham, NC: Duke University Press, 2015.

ONE

Unhelpful Pasts and a Provisional Present

JOHN LONSDALE

CITIZENSHIP HAS BEEN A FOCUS OF INTELLECTUAL DEBATE AND political conflict throughout history. Subjects and slaves have been ready to die in order to attain the more secure, free, and responsible status of citizen—whether two thousand years ago in Roman Italy,[1] in the European revolutions that began with Dutch revolt and English civil war, in the many American wars of independence, in Caribbean and West African slave revolts, in the white-settled parts of Africa half a century ago, or in the Ukraine and Syria of today. These contemporary examples remind us that would-be citizens may oppose each other as well as their state. For citizenship is a protean and dynamic condition; its rights, liberties, and obligations relate people not only to their rulers but also to fellow citizens who differ both in social class and, increasingly, in ethnic or religious culture. Competitive self-interest shapes these relations, whether vertical in terms of social class or horizontal, between cultural communities. But, as this book's subtitle suggests, self-interest commonly looks for moral support in those past precedents that come most usefully to mind. The question I ask here is whether either of two potential histories of precedent, Western and African, can help Africans to argue and resolve today's policies, strategies, and practices of citizenship.

Some questions about citizenship are in any case never settled; their contexts vary and mutate. One set of questions concerns the eligibility, costs, and benefits of citizenship. Eligibility, who is or is not qualified to be a citizen, can alter with demographic and economic change—as contemporary world history bears witness, with its rise in narrower ideas of who has local rights of "belonging" and who, by contrast, is now a "stranger."[2] The costs of citizenship in duty and loyalty also fluctuate, most obviously between times of war and peace. The depth and range of benefits in personal freedoms and public services, too, are notoriously affected by economic cycles, regional inequalities, class differentiation, and administrative (in)competence. Other questions arise from the cultural diversity typical of a global modernity. How far can or should varied loyalties, religious beliefs, and cultural practices, or a plurality of land rights, mother tongues, and family laws be tolerated, even celebrated, within one citizenry? The answer will vary with ruling ideology and partisan pressure, and both can clearly change. Fear of mutual threat can give way to trust in a shared strength, so deepening the solidarity that best enables citizens to keep an effective watch on state power. Recent history in every continent suggests that the reverse is the more likely, but the point remains: group stereotypes and prejudices, and with them the limits placed on active citizenship, are not immutable.[3]

How citizenship is imagined, secured, and performed, therefore, can only be the local and provisional outcome of continuing societal struggle from top and bottom. From above, prudent rulers aim to secure loyalty and service; but their promises of prosperity and protection can well be turned against them as tests by which their citizens may call them to account.[4] From below, subjects or the lower classes, second-class citizens, have to fight to claim and retain rights of representation, justice, and welfare. All negotiations of citizenship are, as suggested, likely to call on precedent—to encourage or to warn. Students of Africa can think of two seemingly opposed ways of interrogating possibly relevant pasts. First, print preserves what at first glance seems to be "the West's" long accumulation of universal wisdom. Secondly, while past African speech may be more mutable in memory and in its oral transmission, it does at least seem to teach local lessons. But, to answer my opening question, each history may be less helpful than it seems.

An Instructive "Western" Past?

Are "Western" print arguments about states and citizens, centuries in the making, so different from the oratory of yesterday's unlettered African elders? Both stores of political thought, canonized in print or unreliably remembered, have taken their several origins in partisan argument designed to win support in disputed times. Even when we accept the polemical nature common to both print and oral pasts, it is all too tempting to refer to supposedly superior, Western, bookish criteria when analyzing or, too often, judging African political practice. We have to remind ourselves that Western political theory is not universal, a standing rebuke to others; it is as contextually contingent and combative in local origin and purpose as the ideas orally enunciated elsewhere in the world.[5]

Intellectual historians have long abandoned the notions either that classical texts express timeless wisdom or that there has been an advance in enlightenment, with generations of political philosophers standing on their predecessors' shoulders to see more clearly. But an unwary observer may still wonder at what looks like an evolutionary teleology, from Plato to the United Nations charter, that foretells our currently hegemonic principle: which is that legitimate power rests in a liberal democracy obedient to a universal franchise exercised by citizens who know their human rights. This appearance of political progress can even be imagined as an unsleeping, critical consultation with the inexorable rise in the coercive power, bureaucratic reach, and moral ambition of the world's polities. But all that imagined history is now in question; nation-states are today said to be threatened by the blind forces of globalization, abetted by a neoliberal philosophy of individual rights that pays no heed to social obligation. As things stand (at present), therefore, the Western experience of relations between state and citizen is divided. Some states, France perhaps most obstinately, still aspire to honor an ageing social democracy, in a contract to protect citizens from the inequities of global markets.[6] More states repudiate such expensive undertakings, professing instead a neoliberal faith in the productive energies and redistributive potential that are in theory released when autonomous individuals are liberated from their former social solidarities, their citizenship. Thus divided in the lessons they draw from their particular past, Western observers are well advised to keep an open mind on how Africans work out their still-unsettled meanings of citizenship, informed and misinformed by pasts of their own.

It is in any case difficult to see any coherence in European thought and practice in the two broad fields of citizenship most discussed today, not only in Africa. These concern personal eligibility for civic status and how, if at all, cultural diversity should be publicly recognized, if all citizens are to feel equally confident in the exercise of their common rights and responsibilities.

Even the first criterion for citizenship, one's very existence, can be debated. Civic rights may be based either on one's place of birth, *jus solis*, or one's cultural genealogy, *jus sanguinis*, or on both, in changeable proportions. Other criteria change too. In the not-distant past, a Western citizen had to meet variable criteria of supposed civic responsibility: to be a man rather than a woman, to be freeborn rather than slave, to own property, to have a certain income or a specified profession, and so on. Cultural diversity, next, is a matter of concern if people are agreed to be social rather than autonomous beings. If that is so, then our public personality is privately constituted by those closest to us in language, religion, and daily custom. This intimate social formation—*subjectivation*, as our French cousins call it—is everywhere becoming more "multicultural" as historically constructed cultural majorities receive immigrant minorities. How should this and other social differences affect the mutual obligations of citizenship? Some argue that equal rights require formal respect for difference, even a promise of future cultural protection. But group and individual rights conflict: such a protected future would surely have to permit freedom of dissent, to allow members of both majority and minority groups to choose to adopt a different cultural identity.[7]

In conducting what can only be an absurdly brief inquiry into the history of Western political thought,[8] to see whether it offers guidance in such dilemmas, one is struck by both the recurrence, not evolution, of a limited repertoire of constitutional relations between states and citizens and also the dreadful ends that can result from attempts to construct culturally unified citizenries, intolerant of difference.

If one thinks, first, of the qualifications required for citizenship, our classical starting points, Athens and Rome, seem remarkably similar and equally contradictory. These slave-based polities—to which the Americas and many African kingdoms bore a marked resemblance as recently as the nineteenth century—initially restricted citizenship to freeborn, able-bodied, male family heads, men who carried private responsibility and who, being liable to military service, also had an eye to the possible cost of public decisions. In due course, both the city of Athens and the Roman Empire created a graduated citizenship by extending some, not all, rights to the free poor. But, and here was the contradiction, each polity also upheld the absolute right of wealthy family heads to rule their dependants, both slave and free. While poor citizens sought protection as clients to such powerful patrons, such submission also abridged their few civic rights. The tension between free citizenship and subservient clientage is certainly not peculiar to modern Africa, and its personal frictions can on occasion inspire what it appears designed to deter, political activism from below.[9]

The exclusion of dependent persons, including women, from full political rights has, then, been as much Western as African. Not until after the First or (in the cases of France, Greece, and Italy) the Second World War did European women gain the vote. This represented not so much constitutional evolution as a reversion to the classical connection between a citizen's liability to military risk and his or her political entitlement. Was it because they lived in a neutral country with their home front unthreatened by war that Swiss women were denied the vote until 1971, a decade after most African women? Europe cannot claim much evolutionary superiority when it comes to promoting subjects to citizenship. Today, moreover, fewer Europeans than Africans go out to vote. This idle contentment with the thinnest of citizenships, this failure in republican duty, ought to add to our reluctance to criticize others.

Nor is the European story of granting equal civic dignity to cultural diversity any better. It would be hard to think of a more dreadful history. It started well enough. Two thousand years ago, in Rome, Cicero argued that to respect a conquered people's hyphenated identity, both local and Roman, would best ensure their loyalty. The fourteenth-century Italian jurist Bartolus of Sassoferrato agreed, for the practical lawyer's reason that local customary law was more likely to be respected than distant imperial edicts. These wisdoms then seem to have been forgotten. In the eighteenth century, Jean-Jacques Rousseau persuaded revolutionary France that subordinate allegiances were conspiracies against the public interest—in terms echoed by most of Africa's postcolonial nation builders.

Learning from the French Revolution, Europe's nineteenth-century rulers set out to build unified nations out of diverse peoples, only a century before Africa's tried to do the same. In so doing, both created suspect strangers out of people whose difference was previously held, at worst, to be potentially rebellious rather than existentially treacherous.[10] Compulsory schooling and military conscription so eroded this former diversity that continued difference did indeed appear to be conspiratorial. Jews are only the best known because the most grievously oppressed of such supposed traitors to the new nations. It was in Europe that the logic of national unity was followed to the bestial lengths of the holocaust, or *shoa*, a genocidal destruction carried out in the context of two world wars, even bloodier rituals of nationhood.[11] "The West" has no cause to feel superior to Africa even when remembering Rwanda, Darfur, or Zanzibar.[12] The Universal Declaration of Human Rights, adopted by the United Nations in 1948 and an inspiration to many African activists,[13] was a reproof, not a tribute, to recent European history. Europe's pasts are no moral tutor to Africa's present—but are Africa's pasts any better equipped?

Relevant "African" Pasts?

It is even more foolish to generalize about African than European history; the continent once held more numerous polities and peoples, more varied in their means of living and governance, than early modern Europe. One generalization does, however, seem safer than others. It has two stages, demographic and political. First, before 1900 the population of sub-Saharan Africa was relatively sparse in relation to natural resources; in most regions there were limited supplies of labor and unlimited supplies of land. Second, given that land was more or less freely available, wealth and power came most economically from investment in the allegiance of scarce people, whose rational answer to any oppression would be migration rather than resistance. Africa's many internal frontiers offered asylum, opportunities to negotiate a greater self-reliance.[14] It was difficult, therefore, for Africans to build states strong enough to control the allocation of scarce resources, land especially.[15]

Three consequences of this difficulty are thought to have followed; they all question the present relevance of Africa's pasts. These are, first, the quasi-Athenian distinction between slave and free that was found in many former kingdoms; next, the vulnerability of kinless, autonomous individuals in contrast to the relative security from bondage or starvation one gained by belonging to a recognized community; and finally, the managerial authority accorded to male household heads—again like Athens or Rome.

Africa's states tended to cluster in those rare environments where peasants could practice settled rather than shifting agriculture, even at the cost of submitting themselves to the demands of power. Well-watered highland Ethiopia was one such region, the Great Lakes area of eastern Africa another, the coastal forests of West Africa a third.

Even in these favored areas, relatively ungoverned frontiers offered a refugee answer to misrule. Kings therefore had to rule with discrimination if they were to retain Africa's obstinately mobile people; to maintain a distinction between slave and free was central to statecraft. Many kingdoms sought to bind the loyalty of free householders by offloading drudgery and danger onto slaves—although slaves could also rise to high office, especially in royal armies. In some areas of West Africa, slaves might constitute one-third of the population, conscripted from among the already kinless: whether prisoners of war, convicted criminals, or famished debtors. For one to have a good chance of remaining free, it paid to surrender one's autonomy to some hierarchy of tributary belonging.[16]

The constitutional history of Africa's kingdoms—unfashionable in European studies—shows that householders had alternative ways to invest in this social capital of belonging and so win a status that could, without too much exaggeration, be called citizenship. One, a paradox found in the coastal kingdom of Dahomey, was to claim to be the property of the king, worthy of his protection. The second, more common, was to enter into client membership of—if one were not already born into—some tribute-paying group. Asante and Buganda, on opposite sides of the continent, provide well-known examples. Their kings, as elsewhere, exercised power by sharing it out among powerful subjects with useful followings—tributary "clans" that performed the ritual, administrative, and military tasks that built royal power and in so doing might also check despotism. Clan notables boosted their authority with personal clients; these could in turn try to improve their prospects by submitting to another patron whose star was rising at court: client mobility gave monarchical constitutions political histories. The benefits of something like citizenship could be acquired, then, by energetic belonging to a recognized community, by personal clientelage to a notable, or, in Dahomey, by a seemingly abject but nonetheless alert submission.[17] Several questions arise: Are these constitutional histories still useful? Are similar strategies of enlisting or taming state power still available, now reinforced by the gravitational pull of the franchise rather than the centrifugal threat of migration? Or do the social reciprocities of Africa's frontier peoples, more or less stateless as they were, offer a more relevant past?

Before 1900 most Africans probably lived stateless lives, without kings. Statelessness was not indiscipline; "republican" liberties are famously demanding. Obedience to reciprocal obligation, not easy for the poor, was the fee for social insurance—an expectation of support from one's close kin and wider community at times of domestic or natural disaster. These communities of local belonging are properly called "ethnic," culturally informed and externally defined by their expert knowledge of how to live well in a specific environment. Best seen as a mosaic of inter-active discursive arenas, they were neither the closed descent groups of the colonial imagination nor the egalitarian utopias of nationalist myth. Pastoralists were the most unequal; their poor simply ceased to be members.[18] Household management (and its productive expertise) was the peak of civic virtue, never an equal attainment. It also carried responsibility because success was never single-handed. Wealth depended on the energy of people, kin and clients who, in return, expected from their patron assets that they could then invest in married households of their own.[19] Is Africa's stateless history therefore any more helpfully instructive for today than that of its states?

An answer to that question has to reflect the memory of the dark underside of African history, that nightmare of the poor, those who failed to earn the social capital of belonging. In their marginalized experience, all power, even the power of stateless social hierarchy, was a zero-sum game; it grew by repudiating reciprocal relations of trust, not by cultivating loyalty. Africa's slave masters in particular, kings and nobles, had on this view sucked their well-fed life from out of wider society. Their European partners in the human traffic were likewise believed to prosper by employing slaves under the sea, making the goods imported in exchange for people. This terrifying vampirism betrayed the moral economy of underpopulation in which, to repeat, one earned civic virtue by supporting industrious kin and clients with the assets that offered them personal self-mastery within their community of belonging. Linguistic historians can trace such a moral premise in "long-term regional histories of durable bundles of meaning and practice."[20] But it was a fragile premise, dependent on the scarcity of labor.

The old moral economy of wealth in people, of enabling patronage, was never universal, and today labor is all too abundant; productive land has now become the scarcer factor of production. Africa's demography was revolutionized in the past century, a greater change than colonial rule and decolonization. From the 1920s to the 1950s, the population increased from around 142 million to 200 million;[21] by 2000 it had reached 700 million and today stands at one billion. Almost unlimited supplies

of labor now compete for limited resources. This reversal in value between land and people means that migrant strangers are less welcome
as clients or workers; that title to land and rights in its usage are more
narrowly defined and fiercely disputed; and that clients can expect both
a less generous endowment, if any, from a patron's domain and less freedom to choose an alternative protector.[22] In all, the poor have fewer
hopes for social mobility while rulers enjoy more unrestrained power.

For many, therefore, past meaning and practice have become menac-
ing rather than inspirational. Memory can conjure up sinister "phantoms
from different layers of time [that] flow into each other", revived by im-
ages of gluttonous elites who "eat" public assets. One common phantom
is the invisible power with which undue personal ambition consumes
the spirit of those whom it outstrips, whose envy can in turn destroy
success. These witchcraft beliefs, "the dark side of kinship," flourish on
the resentment spawned by the previously unimaginable inequalities
of wealth and power that are the fruit of political freedoms enjoyed
within a global capitalism. This "spiritual insecurity" poses obvious
problems for democracy. Politicians can appear to enjoy an invulnerable
occult power; conversely, popular fear of neighbors can provoke vigi-
lante demands for rough justice that no modern government can satisfy.
Citizens may in consequence succumb the more readily to "the ordinary
apathy of normal political life."[23]

In a world of competing beliefs, Africans struggle as much as anybody
else with their rational and existential doubts that witchcraft accusations
can ever locate moral responsibility. The anxieties that lie behind personal quests for an honorable belonging perhaps help to explain two of
today's complementary developments. First, many local communities are
ever more insistent on their exclusive rights as putative firstcomers, sons
of the soil, hostile to the immigrant strangers in their midst, even those
of several generations' standing who once added to a locality's wealth in
scarce people. Second, many urban elites, as keen to redeem their debt
to a locality that funded their education as to appease the envy of less-
fortunate kin, pay generous attention to their rural districts of origin.[24]
These communal phenomena, one of boundary making, the other of
investment in local reputation, point to what many believe to be the
chief obstacle for the sentiment and practice of full and equal African
citizenship—namely, ethnic diversity, what used to be called tribalism.

The history of ethnicity, its mutation through time—as one of a
possible set of identities, moral communities, linguistic arenas, political

constituencies, or frameworks of social action—is a contested topic in African historiography.[25] Before colonial rule, as we have seen, there were two ethnic conditions: statish and stateless. Both welcomed and assimilated strangers, often allowing mobility upward from servitude. Within kingdoms, numbers and varied skills added to a clan's political power. Elsewhere, beyond the reach of states, ethnicity, as suggested, was discursively related to the technical and managerial skills best suited to a particular ecological niche.[26] Fresh hands, often those of neighboring famine victims, could be assimilated; family strategies of insurance and accumulation often favored wives from elsewhere.

Given this dual state and nonstate history, scholars have disputed how far the need of European colonial rulers to name, map, and "read" their subjects obliged Africans to think and act within more closely defined "tribes" than before. Historians have thus far paid less attention to the likely consequences of demographic change. All that can be said with any certainty is that the internal arguments and external boundaries of community have, throughout history and all over the world, been subject to continual change, responsive to the contingencies of demographic, political, and economic context.[27]

But how does that truism clarify the question of ethnic difference and national citizenship, on which the European past has so little to boast? Colonial rule, a stronger form of state than Africans had previously known, certainly changed the competitive context and therefore tended to harden the boundaries of belonging. Ethnic membership, like past clanship, became the most accessible collective voice with which to seek both social solidarity and economic protection, and to make political claims. Local arguments about how old moral economy should accommodate social change summoned up comparative dialogues with wider pasts, thanks to a spreading knowledge of the global precedents suggested in the Qur'an or Bible, the latter in its varied vernaculars. What changed most was the character of those who led the discussion, as well as their means of communication. Wealthy elders, household heads, used to set social norms by their legal decisions, prescriptive in small localities. They began to be challenged by teachers, preachers, and clerks, whose authority came not from managing domestic production but from literacy, the magical new technology for taming the occult forces and abstruse paper of an alien state. Literacy also had a wider convening power than elders' speech, reaching along the routes taken by migrant workers and into their workplaces; it enabled one to conceive

of wider boundaries of belonging. Simplified, unified, morally uplift-
ing print histories proved that these imagined ethnic communities had
exercised civilized self-rule in the past and so were worthy of imperial
recognition.[28] Africans were claiming citizenship in the modern world
long before independence.[29]

How far colonized Africans were able to think and act in this way
as creative citizens rather than as deferential clients under the "tribal"
practices of European rule is another contested issue; it divides the
contributors to this volume.[30] But the point, surely, is that past African history had demonstrated that protective potential could lie within
different concepts of social and political belonging. The colonial era
was similarly tolerant of diverse degrees of subjecthood, as the present
volume also shows. The ideological ambiguities of the colonial rulers
themselves, both French and British, encouraged different African approaches to the possibility of political agency, of citizenship.[31]

The French found it difficult to deny their African subjects, especially salaried workers, the revolutionary promise of citizenship under
the metropolitan banner of liberty, equality, and fraternity. To evade the
costly welfare commitments to African workers implied in this promise
was one motive of French decolonization.[32] Britain found it as hard to
live up to the promises of imperial citizenship that Africans perceived in
two British claims: that the empire had abolished slavery under Good
Queen Victoria;[33] and that all imperial subjects, white and black, could
expect equal treatment—in tribute to the empire's military aid, both
Indian and African, in the First World War. Africans could in consequence employ two equally effective strategies in demanding sovereign
nationhood when imperial recognition was denied—both workers'
strikes for proletarian rights and ethnic coalitions that demanded to
assemble common citizen nationalities from out of different subject
tribespeople.

The postcolonial nationhood that followed was a greater break
with history than colonial rule had been—however much nationalist
leaders claimed to renew their links with the glories of the African
past. Much of that past (not least the civic virtue of building wealth
by the generous and demanding patronage of strangers) was in danger
of becoming irrelevant, thanks to two developments: the demographic
growth already met and the new political logic of nation building.
To aspire to global citizenship was one thing, to exercise a national
citizenship quite another.

An Unsettled Present

Independent states, unlike the colonial powers that evaded their duty to subjects by leaving, cannot escape the expectations of citizens.[34] To eradicate poverty, ignorance, and disease, as promised, were and are heavy responsibilities. Who had how much right to which scarce public goods became a pressing issue, sharpening boundaries of entitlement still further. Citizenship is not always open to all today; even second- or third-generation immigrants can be at risk. In some cases, only specified ethnicities, such as the matriclans of Asante, have secured full citizenship as firstcomers, indigenous to their new nation (*autochthones* in French). More African countries honor the rights of *jus sanguinis* than of *jus solis,* of blood rather than residence. Colonial boundaries, by contrast, had been porous; the three corners of sub-Saharan Africa (east, west, and south) had each constituted a vast migrant labor zone. In this comparatively recent past, immigrant laborers were often able to negotiate the more secure status of tenant farmer or sharecropper; today their descendants have become latecomers, unwanted foreigners (notoriously so in the Ivory Coast). Other West African countries have expelled immigrants en masse. In Africa as in nineteenth-century Europe, making new nations has created new strangers.[35]

Civic status and human rights can also come in degrees. Property ownership is nowhere in Africa a formal requirement for citizenship; nonetheless, the landless—especially new migrants to towns—and in western Africa the descendants of slaves, people said to lack self-mastery, or *possession de soi,* find it difficult to exercise rights that are legally theirs.[36] Such informal civic exclusion, consistent with past social hierarchies, is inconsistent with an impersonal rule of law, that essential condition for the full enjoyment of citizenship. The lack of secure titles to land, accordingly, is a powerful argument for tribal autochthony and its fear of strangers.[37] In the absence of such universal protection, people also seek refuge, as in the past, in clientelage. But clients today, with their ever-larger numbers, are less able to choose and check their protectors. They are more or less bound in allegiance to ethnic patrons, in the hope that these will invest their ethnic vote banks in winning a local, not private, share of state largesse.[38]

The tendency for citizens to seek safety in ethnic clientelage also raises in acute form the question of the politics of difference. European political thought has the least to offer here. Western states still possess majority cultures; their minorities can to some argued degree be publicly recognized, accommodated into a nation's past by an enlargement rather than a revision of a national story—although legacies of empire can still embarrass France and Britain. Few African states, by contrast, possess a majority culture; Somalia—not an encouraging example—Botswana, and Lesotho are among the exceptions. Others are a mosaic of anxious minorities, varied in language, social hierarchy, family authority, bodily inscription, property law, and so on. Official recognition of difference may well promote still-more-minute ethnic demarcations of dubious historical provenance, diminishing rather than enlarging freedoms. In any case, where is cultural difference produced? Is Wolof culture, for instance, created in rural Senegal, in Dakar, in Paris, or in Marseilles?[39] To add to these complexities of difference, ethnic membership still tends to demand stern "republican" standards of self-conduct and civic virtue. These, especially when interpreted by "traditional courts," do not fit well with liberal criteria of citizenship and human rights.[40]

For the West's majority cultures to practice a fraternal "multicultural" politics that respects differences in the *subjectivation*, the moral self-constitution, of minority citizens is hard enough. Africa, facing a more jealous politics of difference, has witnessed four approaches to its management: single-party despotism, "big man" manipulation of identity after the return of multiparty democracy, an educated disdain for democratic vulgarity, and the start, just possibly, of something else— elite responsibility for the diversity of nationhood.

Independent Africa's initial single-party regimes, first, appeared to tackle difference by suppressing it under synthetic cultures of national "development." As for Rousseau, so too for them difference was a conspiracy against the public interest—and, moreover, plotted by what were despised as the colonial tribalisms of yesterday. But nation-building rhetoric often masked an ethnic partiality in government; this, abetted by oppression, ensured that ethnicity did not disappear but, rather, stiffened in self-defense.[41] "Tribe" then returned as the most readily assembled interest group when the "second liberation" of the 1990s installed the forms of competitive democracy.[42] The upheaval owed much to popular outrage against life-denying dictatorships, which were so contrary to past traditions of "republican" or "moral" ethnicity, in which leadership was earned by stern but hospitable self-mastery. But democratic competition since then has too easily bent this critical moral ethnicity into a deformed, obedient clientelage as "big man" patrons have demanded a reliable vote bank with which to negotiate their entry into national politics. This political tribalism has been Africa's second, manipulative, approach to the politics of difference; it subverts the standards of public accountability that moral ethnicity demanded, and does little for the poor; it may indeed knowingly smother any discourse of class. Ethnic clientelism cannot afford to ask the critical questions that might undermine its patrons. But that is a price many are prepared to pay for inclusion in a majority parliamentary coalition of ethnic minorities, their best bet for winning for themselves what ought to be the universal entitlements of citizenship.[43]

To exercise even these conditional political rights, however, citizens need first to enjoy the social and economic rights that enable them to imagine and pay for public activity. The difficulties of the landless and those of slave descent have been mentioned. But there is now another, more subtly divisive, side to the African politics of citizenship. This is the attempt by young professionals to devise safe rules of discourse and behavior in a public sphere that was unreliably liberated in the 1990s. For lack of any local national language save in Swahili-speaking Tanzania, the consequence has been the emergence of aspirant national cultures of anglophone or francophone "politeness."[44] These admirable initiatives in active citizenship come at a cost: they are inevitably biased toward the well educated and risk disabling the citizenship of others, particularly the less educated and the poor. One can illustrate this possibility in two dimensions: one in civic society and the other in public debate.

First, many educated young people find employment in nongovernmental organizations (NGOs), often funded by overseas donors to champion the poor. But, as observed in Kenya and Malawi, they tend to act with an institutionalized paternalism that denies active debate and self-mastery to those they claim to represent.[45] One is reminded of Plato's Republic, "a tale of virtuous shepherds who manipulate the wishes and beliefs of their flock, not the operation of institutions that allow self-government by free and public-spirited, but otherwise ordinary, citizens."[46]

Second, public speech has become more free in many countries, if not yet safe from arbitrary sanctions. Radio talk shows and street parliaments attract large audiences. Their organizers and speakers show a debonair familiarity with modern technologies of communication and parliamentary procedure, a clubbable civility and fluency of literary reference. But one must doubt whether theirs is an independent public sphere, shaping the political initiatives of an independent middle class. Talk-show hosts are often trying to influence opinion in the interest of their "big man" patrons; like NGO officials, they are also impatient with, and perhaps nervous of, the clumsy, ill-spoken, excitable, and ignorant public comportment of the poor, especially women, should they dare to take the floor, *prendre la parole*.[47] This is a public sphere not yet confident in handling difference; it is designed, indeed, to silence difference as an embarrassment, at least in public discourse between politely educated elites.

That unease does not end the story of African citizenship. Some members of this new generation, self-confident and with a new sense of Africa's potential in a globalizing world, have a clear view of themselves as the citizens of the future. They can show signs of that social responsibility to which Western middle classes have long pretended, moralizing market advantage by acting as public-spirited citizens. Kenyan elites, golf-playing club members, not long ago got together to deliver famine relief to the least-regarded, least-educated ethnic group in the dry north of their country, quite independent of any state aid.[48] Again, this charitable act, this act of good citizenship, scarcely gives power to the poor—but the powerlessness, the second-class citizenship, of poverty is scarcely peculiar to Africa.

Ordinary citizens nonetheless feel corrupted by this powerlessness, by their dependence on ethnic patrons to win favors from the state. In what must have been one of Africa's most thoroughgoing inquiries into public opinion, Kenya's Constitutional Review Commission toured the country in 2002, to hear the views of *wananchi*, "the people of the country." Almost all expressed disillusion with politics. Some blamed unchecked presidential power, others venal parliamentarians. Two aspects of the proceedings strike one most. The first is that despite the politically correct exhortations of the itinerant commissioners, the men in their audiences tried to silence women. The second is the pervasive sense among speakers that while political corruption tainted all it was nonetheless unavoidable. It turned citizens into clients, not that these terms were used, and even beneficent ethnic patrons into public thieves. How far the suggested solutions—a greater religious foundation for political morality, more inclusion of marginalized ethnic groups—might change matters is open, as always, to question. But one cannot doubt the popular longing for what analysts, if not the wananchi, would call citizenship.[49]

For greater citizen responsibility and entitlement to be achieved, therefore, Africa awaits the constitutional history of its future. In these future debates, it would be unwise to ignore Western political thought, even while rejecting its universality. Half a century and more ago political activists in a Buganda kingdom still under British rule found it helpful to consult such Western—but diverse—prophets as Rousseau, John Locke, Harold Laski, and Richard Crossman as well as the Bible's prophets, to draw out comparisons with their own constitutional history. Their eclecticism avoided all teleological obedience to Western tutors. Having consulted others, these Ganda politicians could then think for themselves, in their own turbulent context, about how to revive a just monarchy or, more boldly, how to abolish Ganda social hierarchy.[50] They can stand for political thinkers all over Africa. Their own history, like the history of Western political thought, may not settle the controversies of contemporary citizenship. But cross-fertilization and comparative cautions are surely needed to stimulate fresh thought today. This book is a good example.

Notes

1. Jane Burbank and Frederick Cooper, *Empires in World History: Power and the Politics of Difference* (Princeton: Princeton University Press, 2010), 29–30.

2. Peter Geschiere, *The Perils of Belonging: Autochthony, Citizenship, and Exclusion in Africa and Europe* (Chicago: University of Chicago Press, 2009).

3. Harri Englund, "Introduction," and Francis B. Nyamnjoh, "Reconciling 'the Rhetoric of Rights' with Competing Notions of Personhood and Agency in Botswana," in *Rights and the Politics of Recognition in Africa,* ed. Harri Englund and Francis Nyamnjoh (London: Zed Books, 2004), 1–29 and 33–63, respectively.

4. John Lonsdale, "Political Accountability in African History," in *Political Domination in Africa: Reflections on the Limits of Power,* ed. Patrick Chabal (Cambridge: Cambridge University Press, 1986), 126–57.

5. Quentin Skinner, "Meaning and Understanding in the History of Ideas," *History and Theory* 8 (1969): 3–53; Skinner, "Some Problems in the Analysis of Political Thought and Action," *Political Theory* 2 (1974): 277–303.

6. Editorial, "Osons les valeurs," *Le Monde,* January 7, 2014.

7. As discussed in Charles Taylor, *Multiculturalism and "The Politics of Recognition,"* ed. Amy Gutmann (Princeton: Princeton University Press, 1992).

8. Drawn from Alan Ryan, *On Politics: A History of Political Thought from Herodotus to the Present* (London: Allen Lane, 2012); and Burbank and Cooper, *Empires in World History.*

9. See Patrick Chabal, *Africa: The Politics of Suffering and Smiling* (London: Zed Books, 2004).

10. Sara Rich Dorman, Daniel Hammett, and Paul Nugent, *Making Nations, Creating Strangers: States and Citizenship in Africa* (Leiden: Brill, 2007).

11. David Nirenberg, *Anti-Judaism: The Western Tradition* (New York: W. W. Norton, 2013).

12. Nor has Asia, after the mass murders under Mao Zedong or Pol Pot.

13. Emma Hunter, *Political Thought and the Public Sphere in Tanzania: Freedom, Democracy and Citizenship in the Era of Decolonization* (Cambridge: Cambridge University Press, 2015), 143–45, 153–54.

14. Jane Guyer and Samuel Belinga, "Wealth in People as Wealth in Knowledge: Accumulation and Composition in Equatorial Africa," *Journal of African History* 36, no. 1 (1995): 91–120.

15. See, among others, A. G. Hopkins, *An Economic History of West Africa* (London: Longman, 1973), 11–27; John Iliffe, *Africans: The History of a Continent* (Cambridge: Cambridge University Press, 2007), 133; and Shane Doyle, "Bunyoro and the Demography of Slavery Debate," in *Slavery in the Great Lakes Region of East Africa*, ed. Henri Médard and Shane Doyle (Athens: Ohio University Press, 2007), 236–37.

16. Hunter, *Political Thought*, 13, drawing on Igor Kopytoff and Suzanne Miers, "African 'Slavery' as an Institution of Marginality," in *Slavery in Africa: Historical and Anthropological Perspectives*, ed. Suzanne Miers and Igor Kopytoff (Madison: University of Wisconsin Press, 1977), 17; see also John Iliffe, *The African Poor: A History* (Cambridge: Cambridge University Press, 1987), 7, 11–12, 31, 50, 59, 68–70, 84.

17. T. C. McCaskie, *Asante Identities: History and Modernity in an African Village* (Edinburgh: Edinburgh University Press, 2000); Holly Hanson, *Landed Obligation: The Practice of Power in Buganda* (Portsmouth, NH: Heinemann, 2003); Mikael Karlström, "Civil Society and Its Presuppositions: Lessons from Uganda," in *Civil Society and the Political Imagination in Africa*, ed. John L. Comaroff and Jean Comaroff (Chicago: University of Chicago Press, 1999), 104–23; R. C. Law, "'My Head Belongs to the King': On the Political and Ritual Significance of Decapitation in Pre-colonial Dahomey," *Journal of African History* 30, no. 3 (1989): 399–415.

18. Iliffe, *African Poor*, chap. 5; David M. Anderson and Vigdis Broch-Due, *The Poor Are Not Us: Poverty and Pastoralism in Eastern Africa* (Athens: Ohio University Press, 1999).

19. Fred Hobson, "Freedom as Moral Agency: Wiathi and Mau Mau in Colonial Kenya," *Journal of Eastern African Studies* 2, no. 3 (2008): 456–70; John Iliffe, *Honour in African History* (Cambridge: Cambridge University Press, 2005), chap. 7.

20. David L. Schoenbrun, "Conjuring the Modern in Africa: Durability and Rupture in Histories of Public Healing between the Great Lakes of East Africa," *American Historical Review* 111, no. 5 (2006): 1403–39.

21. Iliffe, *Africans*, 250.

22. In *Perils of Belonging* (109–10, 216), Geschiere makes surprisingly little reference to this reversal in value between land and labor.

23. "Phantoms" quotation, Rosalind Shaw, *Memories of the Slave Trade: Ritual and the Historical Imagination in Sierra Leone* (Chicago: University of Chicago Press, 2002), 264; for kinship's dark side, see Peter Geschiere, *The Modernity of Witchcraft: Politics and the Occult in Postcolonial Africa* (Charlottesville: University of Virginia Press, 1997); "apathy" quotation, Adam Ashforth, *Witchcraft, Violence, and Democracy in South Africa* (Chicago: University of Chicago Press, 2005), 104. Luise White doubts the narrative power of past slavery; see White, *Speaking with Vampires: Rumor and History in Colonial Africa* (Berkeley: University of California Press, 2000), 15–16. For more-durable fears, see Elizabeth Isichei, *Voices of the Poor in Africa* (Rochester, NY: University of Rochester Press, 2002); and Harri Englund, "Witchcraft, Modernity and the Person: The Morality of Accumulation in Central Malawi," *Critique of Anthropology* 16 (1996): 257–79. For the eating of assets, see Jean-François Bayart, *L'État en Afrique: La politique du ventre* (Paris: Fayard, 1989). For spiritual insecurity, see Ashforth, *Witchcraft*.

24. B. E. Kipkorir, "The Educated Elite and Local Society," in *Hadith 4: Politics and Nationalism in Colonial Kenya,* ed. Bethwell A. Ogot (Nairobi: East African Publishing House, 1972), 252–69.

25. R. D. Waller, "Ethnicity and Identity," in *The Oxford Handbook of Modern African History,* ed. John Parker and Richard Reid (Oxford: Oxford University Press, 2013), 94–113.

26. Steven Feierman, *The Shambaa Kingdom: A History* (Madison: University of Wisconsin Press, 1974), 17–22.

27. John Lonsdale, "The Moral Economy of Mau Mau," in *Unhappy Valley: Conflict in Kenya and Africa,* by Bruce Berman and John Lonsdale (Athens: Ohio University Press, 1992), 266–68, 461–68; Adrian Hastings, *The Construction of Nationhood: Ethnicity, Religion and Nationalism* (Cambridge: Cambridge University Press, 1997).

28. Derek Peterson, *Creative Writing: Translation, Bookkeeping and the Work of Imagination in Colonial Kenya* (Portsmouth, NH: Heinemann, 2004); Bruce Berman and John Lonsdale, "Custom, Modernity, and the Search for *Kihooto*: Kenyatta, Malinowski, and the Making of *Facing Mount Kenya*," in *Ordering Africa: Anthropology, European Imperialism, and the Politics of Knowledge,* ed. Helen Tilley with Robert Gordon (Manchester: Manchester University Press, 2007), 173–98.

29. James Ferguson, *Global Shadows: Africa in the Neoliberal World Order* (Durham, NC: Duke University Press, 2006), chapter 6, "Of Mimicry and Membership."

30. According to how far they accept the differentiation between urban "citizens" and rural "subjects" that is asserted (too starkly in my view) in Mahmood Mamdani, *Citizen and Subject: Contemporary Africa and the Legacy of Late Colonialism* (Princeton: Princeton University Press, 1996).

31. As discussed in Emma Hunter's introduction to the present volume.

32. Frederick Cooper, *Decolonization and African Society: The Labor Question in French and British Africa* (Cambridge: Cambridge University Press, 1996).

33. John Lonsdale, "Ornamental Constitutionalism in Africa: Kenyatta and the Two Queens," *Journal of Imperial and Commonwealth History* 34, no. 1 (2006): 87–103; Derek R. Peterson, ed., *Abolitionism and Imperialism in Britain, Africa, and the Atlantic* (Athens: Ohio University Press, 2010).

34. Frederick Cooper, *Africa since 1940: The Past of the Present* (Cambridge: Cambridge University Press, 2002).

35. Jeffrey Herbst, *States and Power in Africa: Comparative Lessons in Authority and Control* (Princeton: Princeton University Press, 2000); Bruce Berman, Dickson Eyoh, and Will Kymlicka, eds., *Ethnicity and Democracy in Africa* (Athens: Ohio University Press, 2004), chaps. 1–4; Richard Kuba and Carola Lentz, eds., *Land and the Politics of Belonging in West Africa* (Leiden: Brill, 2006); Dorman et al., *Making Nations;* Geschiere, *Perils of Belonging.*

36. Emma Hunter, "Dutiful Subjects, Patriotic Citizens and the Concept of Good Citizenship in Twentieth-Century Tanzania," *Historical Journal* 56, no. 1 (2013): 257–77; Christian Lund, "Proprieté et citoyenneté: Dynamiques de reconnaissance dans l'Afrique des villes," *Politique africaine* 132 (2013): 5–25; Eric Hahonou, "Proprieté, citoyennetés et héritage de l'esclavage au Nord Bénin," *Politique africaine* 132 (2013): 73–94.

37. Morten Bøås and Kevin Dunn, *Politics of Origin in Africa: Autochthony, Citizenship and Conflict* (London: Zed Books, 2013).

38. Bruce J. Berman, "Ethnicity, Patronage and the African State: The Politics of Uncivil Nationalism," *African Affairs* 97, no. 388 (1998): 305–41; Iliffe, *Honour in African History,* chap. 18.

39. Jean-François Bayart, *The Illusion of Cultural Identity* (London: Hurst, 2005).

40. Stephen N. Ndegwa, "Citizenship and Ethnicity: An Examination of Two Transition Moments in Kenyan Politics," *American Political Science Review* 91, no. 3 (1997): 599–616.

41. Will Kymlicka, "Nation-Building and Minority Rights: Comparing Africa and the West," in Berman et al., *Ethnicity and Democracy in Africa,* 54–71.

42. A key argument in Geschiere, *Perils of Belonging.*

43. Richard Werbner, in his epilogue to Englund and Nyamnjoh, *Rights and the Politics,* 261–74, rightly called the dichotomy between moral ethnicity and political tribalism "stultifying"—as sketched in John Lonsdale, "Moral Ethnicity and Political Tribalism," in *Inventions and Boundaries: Historical and Anthropological Approaches to the Study of Ethnicity and Nationalism,* ed. Preben Kaarsholm and Jan Hultin, 131–50 (Roskilde, Denmark: Roskilde University, 1994)—but the stultification was observed in Kenya's politics, not derived from political theory.

44. For the metropolitan model, see Lawrence E. Klein, *Salisbury and the Culture of Politeness: Moral Discourse and Cultural Politics in Early Eighteenth Century England* (Cambridge: Cambridge University Press, 1994).

45. Stephen N. Ndegwa, *The Two Faces of Civil Society: NGOs and Politics in Africa* (West Hartford, CT: Kumarian Press, 1996); Harri Englund, *Prisoners of Freedom: Human Rights and the African Poor* (Berkeley: University of California Press, 2006).

46. Ryan, *On Politics*, 498.

47. Florence Brisset-Foucault, "Prendre la parole en Ouganda: Critique et citoyenneté sous l'hégémonie du Mouvement de Résistance Nationale (NRM)" (PhD diss., Université Paris 1, Panthéon-Sorbonne, 2011); Richard Banégas, Florence Brisset-Foucault, and Armando Cutelo, "Espaces publics de la parole et pratiques de la citoyenneté en Afrique," *Politique africaine* 127 (2012): 5–20.

48. Dominique Connan, "La décolonisation des clubs kényans: Sociabilité exclusive et constitution morales des élites africaines dans le Kénya contemporain" (PhD diss., Université Paris 1, Panthéon-Sorbonne, 2014), 488–538.

49. Stephanie Diepeveen, "'The Kenyas We Don't Want': Popular Thought over Constitutional Review in Kenya, 2002," *Journal of Modern African Studies* 48, no. 2 (2010): 231–58.

50. Jonathan Earle, "Political Theologies in Late Colonial Buganda" (PhD diss., University of Cambridge, 2012).

References

Anderson, David M., and Vigdis Broch-Due. *The Poor Are Not Us: Poverty and Pastoralism in Eastern Africa*. Athens: Ohio University Press, 1999.

Ashforth, Adam. *Witchcraft, Violence, and Democracy in South Africa*. Chicago: University of Chicago Press, 2005.

Banégas, Richard, Florence Brisset-Foucault, and Armando Cutelo. "Espaces publics de la parole et pratiques de la citoyenneté en Afrique." *Politique africaine* 127 (2012): 5–20.

Bayart, Jean-François. *L'État en Afrique: La politique du ventre*. Paris: Fayard, 1989.

———. *The Illusion of Cultural Identity*. London: Hurst, 2005.

Berman, Bruce J. "Ethnicity, Patronage and the African State: The Politics of Uncivil Nationalism." *African Affairs* 97, no. 388 (1998): 305–41.

Berman, Bruce J., Dickson Eyoh, and Will Kymlicka, eds. *Ethnicity and Democracy in Africa*. Athens: Ohio University Press, 2004.

Berman, Bruce J., and John Lonsdale. "Custom, Modernity, and the Search for *Kihooto:* Kenyatta, Malinowski, and the Making of *Facing Mount Kenya*." In *Ordering Africa: Anthropology, European Imperialism, and the Politics of Knowledge,* edited by Helen Tilley, with Robert Gordon, 173–98. Manchester: Manchester University Press, 2007.

Bøås, Morten, and Kevin Dunn. *Politics of Origin in Africa: Autochthony, Citizenship and Conflict*. London: Zed Books, 2013.

Brisset-Foucault, Florence. "Prendre la parole en Ouganda: Critique et citoyenneté sous l'hégémonie du Mouvement de Résistance Nationale (NRM)." PhD diss., Université Paris 1, Panthéon-Sorbonne, 2011.

Burbank, Jane, and Frederick Cooper. *Empires in World History: Power and the Politics of Difference*. Princeton: Princeton University Press, 2010.

Chabal, Patrick. *Africa: The Politics of Suffering and Smiling*. London: Zed Books, 2004.

Connan, Dominique. "La décolonisation des clubs kényans: Sociabilité exclusive et constitution morales des élites africaines dans le Kénya contemporain." PhD diss., Université Paris 1, Panthéon-Sorbonne, 2014.

Cooper, Frederick. *Africa since 1940: The Past of the Present.* Cambridge: Cambridge University Press, 2002.

———. *Decolonization and African Society: The Labor Question in French and British Africa.* Cambridge: Cambridge University Press, 1996.

Diepeveen, Stephanie. "'The Kenyas We Don't Want': Popular Thought over Constitutional Review in Kenya, 2002." *Journal of Modern African Studies* 48, no. 2 (2010): 231–58.

Dorman, Sara Rich, Daniel Hammett, and Paul Nugent. *Making Nations, Creating Strangers: States and Citizenship in Africa.* Leiden: Brill, 2007.

Doyle, Shane. "Bunyoro and the Demography of Slavery Debate." In *Slavery in the Great Lakes Region of East Africa,* edited by Henri Médard and Shane Doyle, 231–51. Athens: Ohio University Press, 2007.

Earle, Jonathan. "Political Theologies in Late Colonial Buganda." PhD diss., University of Cambridge, 2012.

Englund, Harri. "Introduction." In *Rights and the Politics of Recognition in Africa,* edited by Harri Englund and Francis B. Nyamnjoh, 1–29. London: Zed Books, 2004.

———. *Prisoners of Freedom: Human Rights and the African Poor.* Berkeley: University of California Press, 2006.

———. "Witchcraft, Modernity and the Person: The Morality of Accumulation in Central Malawi." *Critique of Anthropology* 16 (1996): 257–79.

Feierman, Steven. *The Shambaa Kingdom: A History.* Madison: University of Wisconsin Press, 1974.

Ferguson, James. *Global Shadows: Africa in the Neoliberal World Order.* Durham, NC: Duke University Press, 2006.

Geschiere, Peter. *The Modernity of Witchcraft: Politics and the Occult in Postcolonial Africa.* Charlottesville: University of Virginia Press, 1997.

———. *The Perils of Belonging: Autochthony, Citizenship, and Exclusion in Africa and Europe.* Chicago: University of Chicago Press, 2009.

Guyer, Jane, and Samuel Belinga. "Wealth in People as Wealth in Knowledge: Accumulation and Composition in Equatorial Africa." *Journal of African History* 36, no. 1 (1995): 91–120.

Hahonou, Eric. "Proprieté, citoyennetés et héritage de l'esclavage au Nord Bénin." *Politique africaine* 132 (2013): 73–94.

Hanson, Holly. *Landed Obligation: The Practice of Power in Buganda.* Portsmouth, NH: Heinemann, 2003.

Hastings, Adrian. *The Construction of Nationhood: Ethnicity, Religion and Nationalism.* Cambridge: Cambridge University Press, 1997.

Herbst, Jeffrey. *States and Power in Africa: Comparative Lessons in Authority and Control.* Princeton: Princeton University Press, 2000.

Hobson, Fred. "Freedom as Moral Agency: Wiathi and Mau Mau in Colonial Kenya." *Journal of Eastern African Studies* 2, no. 3 (2008): 456–70.

Hopkins, A. G. *An Economic History of West Africa*. London: Longman, 1973.

Hunter, Emma. "Dutiful Subjects, Patriotic Citizens and the Concept of Good Citizenship in Twentieth-Century Tanzania." *Historical Journal* 56, no. 1 (2013): 257–77.

———. *Political Thought and the Public Sphere in Tanzania: Freedom, Democracy and Citizenship in the Era of Decolonization*. Cambridge: Cambridge University Press, 2015.

Iliffe, John. *The African Poor: A History*. Cambridge: Cambridge University Press, 1987.

———. *Africans: The History of a Continent*. Cambridge: Cambridge University Press, 2007.

———. *Honour in African History*. Cambridge: Cambridge University Press, 2005.

Isichei, Elizabeth. *Voices of the Poor in Africa*. Rochester, NY: University of Rochester Press, 2002.

Karlström, Mikael. "Civil Society and Its Presuppositions: Lessons from Uganda." In *Civil Society and the Political Imagination in Africa*, edited by John L. Comaroff and Jean Comaroff, 104–23. Chicago: University of Chicago Press, 1999.

Kipkorir, B. E. "The Educated Elite and Local Society." In *Hadith 4: Politics and Nationalism in Colonial Kenya*, edited by Bethwell A. Ogot, 252–69. Nairobi: East African Publishing House, 1972.

Klein, Lawrence E. *Salisbury and the Culture of Politeness: Moral Discourse and Cultural Politics in Early Eighteenth Century England*. Cambridge: Cambridge University Press, 1994.

Kopytoff, Igor, and Suzanne Miers. "African 'Slavery' as an Institution of Marginality." In *Slavery in Africa: Historical and Anthropological Perspectives*, edited by Suzanne Miers and Igor Kopytoff, 3–85. Madison: University of Wisconsin Press, 1977.

Kuba, Richard, and Carola Lentz. *Land and the Politics of Belonging in West Africa*. Leiden: Brill, 2006.

Kymlicka, Will. "Nation-Building and Minority Rights: Comparing Africa and the West." In *Ethnicity and Democracy in Africa*, edited by Bruce J. Berman, Dickson Eyoh, and Will Kymlicka, 54–71. Athens: Ohio University Press, 2004.

Law, R. C. "'My Head Belongs to the King': On the Political and Ritual Significance of Decapitation in Pre-colonial Dahomey." *Journal of African History* 30, no. 3 (1989): 399–415.

Lonsdale, John. "The Moral Economy of Mau Mau." In *Unhappy Valley: Conflict in Kenya and Africa*, by Bruce Berman and John Lonsdale, 265–504. Athens: Ohio University Press, 1992.

———. "Moral Ethnicity and Political Tribalism." In *Inventions and Boundaries: Historical and Anthropological Approaches to the Study of Ethnicity and Nationalism*, edited by Preben Kaarsholm and Jan Hultin,

131–50. International Development Studies Occasional Paper 11. Roskilde, Denmark: Roskilde University, 1994.

———. "Ornamental Constitutionalism in Africa: Kenyatta and the Two Queens." *Journal of Imperial and Commonwealth History* 34, no. 1 (2006): 87–103.

———. "Political Accountability in African History." In *Political Domination in Africa: Reflections on the Limits of Power,* edited by Patrick Chabal, 126–57. Cambridge: Cambridge University Press, 1986.

Lund, Christian. "Proprieté et citoyenneté: Dynamiques de reconnaissance dans l'Afrique des villes." *Politique africaine* 132 (2013): 5–25.

Mamdani, Mahmood. *Citizen and Subject: Contemporary Africa and the Legacy of Late Colonialism.* Princeton: Princeton University Press, 1996.

McCaskie, T. C. *Asante Identities: History and Modernity in an African Village.* Edinburgh: Edinburgh University Press, 2000.

Ndegwa, Stephen N. "Citizenship and Ethnicity: An Examination of Two Transition Moments in Kenyan Politics." *American Political Science Review* 91, no. 3 (1997): 599–616.

———. *The Two Faces of Civil Society: NGOs and Politics in Africa.* West Hartford, CT: Kumarian Press, 1996.

Nirenberg, David. *Anti-Judaism: The Western Tradition.* New York: W. W. Norton, 2013.

Nyamnjoh, Francis B. "Reconciling 'the Rhetoric of Rights' with Competing Notions of Personhood and Agency in Botswana." In *Rights and the Politics of Recognition in Africa,* edited by Harri Englund and Francis B. Nyamnjoh, 33–63. London: Zed Books, 2004.

Peterson, Derek R., ed. *Abolitionism and Imperialism in Britain, Africa, and the Atlantic.* Athens: Ohio University Press, 2010.

———. *Creative Writing: Translation, Bookkeeping and the Work of Imagination in Colonial Kenya.* Portsmouth, NH: Heinemann, 2004.

Ryan, Alan. *On Politics: A History of Political Thought from Herodotus to the Present.* London: Allen Lane, 2012.

Schoenbrun, David L. "Conjuring the Modern in Africa: Durability and Rupture in Histories of Public Healing between the Great Lakes of East Africa." *American Historical Review* 111, no. 5 (2006): 1403–39.

Shaw, Rosalind. *Memories of the Slave Trade: Ritual and the Historical Imagination in Sierra Leone.* Chicago: University of Chicago Press, 2002.

Skinner, Quentin. "Meaning and Understanding in the History of Ideas." *History and Theory* 8 (1969): 3–53.

———. "Some Problems in the Analysis of Political Thought and Action." *Political Theory* 2 (1974): 277–303.

Taylor, Charles. *Multiculturalism and "The Politics of Recognition."* Edited by Amy Gutmann. Princeton: Princeton University Press, 1992.

Waller, R. D. "Ethnicity and Identity." In *The Oxford Handbook of Modern African History,* edited by John Parker and Richard Reid, 94–113. Oxford: Oxford University Press, 2013.

Werbner, Richard. "Epilogue: The New Dialogue with Post-liberalism." In *Rights and the Politics of Recognition in Africa,* edited by Harri Englund and Francis B. Nyamnjoh, 261–74. London: Zed Books, 2004.

White, Luise. *Speaking with Vampires: Rumor and History in Colonial Africa.* Berkeley: University of California Press, 2000.

PART ONE

Citizens and Subjects in African History

TWO

Rethinking Citizenship and Subjecthood in Southern Africa

Khoesan, Labor Relations, and the Colonial State
in the Cape of Good Hope (c. 1652–1815)

NICOLE ULRICH

THE CONCEPT OF CITIZENSHIP IN THE CAPE OF GOOD HOPE UNDER empire first became evident under the merchant colonialism of the Dutch East India Company (Verenigde Oost-Indishe Compagnie, or VOC) in 1652, and started to change with British rule beginning in 1795, marking the introduction of modern imperialism. The colonial state's approach to and the responses of indigenous Khoesan communities—who were inexorably incorporated into the colony as part of the labor force—at the Cape Colony are particularly revealing of important elements of this discussion.

Approaches to citizenship and popular claims to rights are historically and geographically constituted and dynamic, which means that citizenship varies across regions and changes over time.[1] Globally, the ideological and social contestations surrounding notions of legitimate political authority in the seventeenth and eighteenth centuries, especially during the "Age of Revolutions," laid the foundations for modern notions of citizenship and democracy.[2] An examination of citizenship and forms of belonging at the Cape at this time not only challenges the notion that the people of Africa were somehow absent from the making of the modern world and of its key universalistic political ideas but also seeks to contribute to a deeper political history of the continent that enriches our view of rule, rights, and political identities.

What can we learn from examining citizenship and political belonging at the Cape of Good Hope? There was not always a direct relationship between social class, racial designation, and political access. Nevertheless, issues related to labor control played a key part in shaping governance. Thus, while the Company awarded some inhabitants citizenship, the laboring classes (including slaves from Asia and Africa and low-ranking Company servants recruited from Europe) were denied political rights and representation and were governed through a harsh regime of labor regulation designed to terrorize and control.

The political identities and strategies of indigenous Khoesan, who were ultimately absorbed into the colony as part of the rightless laboring classes of slaves and low-ranking Company servants, were shaped by colonial conquest as well as by the experience of class exploitation. Thus, Khoesan did not reduce their identity to that of a nation or ethnicity but also participated in broader class-based modes of popular protests that drew in others.

However, notions of citizenship at the colony were by no means static, and they were fundamentally redefined under the modern imperialism introduced by the British toward the end of the eighteenth century. The "Age of Revolutions," which changed the way in which legitimate political authority was viewed worldwide, gave rise to radical demands for political rights, representation, and republicanism, after which imperial states could no longer simply rule through force and violence.[3] In this context, labor regulation was reformed and British subjecthood could be used to make broader political claims based on an imperial "citizenship" allowing Khoesan laborers to claim a level of rights and protections.

Citizenship and Empire

For scholars interested in African politics, Mahmood Mamdani's notion of the bifurcated power of the colonial state[4]—with urban constituencies ruled as citizens (by civil law, struggling over rights and representation) and rural constituencies ruled as subjects (by "traditional" authorities and customs)—provides a point of departure for scholars of Africa to make sense of the complex interplay between ethnic identities and access to state resources, rights, and citizenship. This situation, according to Mamdani a legacy of colonialism, continues to bedevil African politics, as it lays the basis for widespread ethnic politics and the ongoing power of "traditional" authorities.

The applicability of this framework to modern South Africa can be debated both because the development of the capitalist economy broke down any neat urban/rural divide and because of the distinctive trajectory of the national liberation struggle in South Africa. Nationalist parties, with the African National Congress (ANC) being the most notable, along with communist and socialist organizations and a large trade union movement continually downplayed and opposed ethnic divisions and mobilization in favor of broader-based forms of unity, by nation or by class. Race proved a more potent force than ethnicity or a rural/urban divide, yet even then, traditions of civic nationalism and nonracial mobilization were widely promoted.[5]

Within this context, questions related to "the nation," or "the nations," within South Africa have occupied pride of place in polemics, and there is still much debate over the national question and the relationship between racial and class inequality.

In the postapartheid period, issues related to citizenship have remained topical. At one level, there have been ongoing struggles around social citizenship, with the focus falling on issues like HIV treatment, access to health care, and gender inequality; at another level, the presence of African and Asian foreign nationals living in South Africa, coupled with widespread anti-immigrant sentiment, has raised questions about the boundary of the "nation."

This does not mean that ethnicity does not or has not shaped political action in South Africa. Ethnic mobilization preexisted and was reinforced by apartheid, which placed great emphasis on African "traditional" authorities. Postapartheid the Zulu king was widely accused of inciting the wave of violence against foreign nationals that took place in 2015, combining exclusive forms of ethnicity and nationhood.

Even so, political mobilization done specifically along ethnic lines has been generally regarded as chauvinist, and therefore taboo, and political discussion over the contours of the "nation" has remained preoccupied with the constitution and contours of a *South African* nation, as opposed to ethnic factionalism and regionalist separatism.

Gary Wilder's recent book, *Freedom Time* (2015), also reminds us that responses to colonial rule were varied and complex and did not follow a single pattern. Even nationalism, now seen as a natural and inevitable response, was only one of many strands. As Wilder shows, some now seen as anticolonial heroes—such as Aimé Césaire and Léopold Sédar Senghor, theorists of *Negritude*—did not necessarily equate liberation and rights with national sovereignty and independence. Both men advocated, instead, reforming the French Empire into a federation, rather than its breakup into nation-states.

The same complexities can be seen in "black loyalism" found in South Africa. Part of a larger tradition of thought also found in British-ruled Canada and India, black loyalism—found notably among the *amakholwa* (Christian-educated) Africans and elite Coloureds and Indians—is argued to have promoted loyalty to the British Crown, which was viewed as a source of protection and a bearer of rights and entitlement.[6] Expressions of loyalty were linked to claims informed by a wider conception of *imperial* citizenship and, according to Hilary Sapire, involved appeals "against actions deemed inimical to the spirit of liberal empire and its 'civilising mission.'"[7]

In this regard, citizenship claims and subject status in the imperial framework were not necessarily as mutually exclusive as Mamdani suggests: it was precisely through accepting and asserting membership of empire, even as subject races and territories, and through paying homage to the British monarchy that rights, entitlements, and protections were often claimed.

Far less, however, is known of the place of citizenship claims and associated mobilizations in earlier colonial periods, including the early colonial period of VOC rule, followed by British rule.

At the same time, the very rich social history of the Cape of Good Hope, as well as the existing literature on the political identities and actions of the small elite of free-burghers, has been shaped by the parochialism of much work on the Cape.[8] A recent trend has challenged the tendency to view the Cape in isolation or simply as an early stage of "South Africa," locating the early colonial Cape within a broader global context and relating this history to international developments and themes. However, this trend is marked by a focus on cultural themes, such as consumption, and the bodily practices of elites.[9] A notable exception, which relates the early history of the Cape to citizenship and the nation, is David Johnson's study *Imagining the Cape Colony: History, Literature, and the South African Nation* (2012), which focuses on the Khoesan and the troubled relationship between political rights and recognition, on the one hand, and economic insecurity on the other hand.

Thus, while most of the other chapters in this volume are interested in the nation-state in postcolonial modern Africa, this chapter investigates the way in which indigenous and marginalized people conceptualized rights and political belonging (in relationship to the state) in the seventeenth, eighteenth, and early nineteenth centuries.

This chapter is divided into three main parts—the first focuses on the structure of Company power at the Cape of Good Hope and the limited political integration of Khoesan, who were primarily absorbed into the colony as laborers and seen as part of the servile, rightless, laboring classes. The second section focuses on the political identities forged by Khoesan and their free-burgher masters on the colonial frontier. The third part examines the way in which British rule fundamentally changed the political terrain by reforming labor controls and recognizing Khoesan as subjects.

Citizenship and Merchant Colonialism

Merchant colonialism is a form of colonialism that needs to be understood on its own terms. How did citizenship operate under Company rule at the Cape, and in what way did the colonial state relate to indigenous Khoesan populations? The answers to these questions lie in the structure of political power and government strategies of inclusion and exclusion.

Patrimonial Power and Labor Control

In 1652 the VOC gained a foothold on the African continent when it colonized the Cape of Good Hope. To fully comprehend the structure of VOC power at the Cape, we must consider both Dutch and VOC modes of rule.

The Dutch Republic was politically fractured and decentered. The central government, or States-General, did not have sovereign powers, and there were no central funds or central bureaucracy of any importance. The Dutch Republic was a confederation of seven sovereign provinces and was fractured further along the lines of autonomous states and cities. This decentered organization of power is confirmed by Julia Adams, who categorizes the Dutch Republic as an "estatist" (as opposed to absolutist) patrimonial state.[10] This means that the early modern Dutch state was based on the "segmentation or parcelization of sovereign power among the ruler (or rulers) and corporate elites,"[11] giving rise to complex interdependencies, underpinned by permanent tensions and competition between rulers and corporate bodies and between the corporations themselves.

The VOC—which reflected the character of the Dutch state—was established in 1602 by the States-General and held the monopoly of trade from the Dutch Republic from east of the Cape of Good Hope to west of the Straits of Magellan. The Company was never purely commercial in nature and was invested with political power—the Company was mandated to enter into diplomatic relations, to establish some form of civil administration in its factories and colonies, and to billet troops.[12]

As noted by Adams, internally, the control of the Lords XVII, the directors of the VOC, was curbed by the Company's fragmented organizational structure and also by distance, which delayed the relay of information between the Netherlands and the East Indies.[13] The intermediary position of the headquarters established in Batavia complicated arrangements, and no one actor was able to establish centrality. Thus, Adams notes, the "mutual and symmetrical dependency inscribed in the heart of the VOC's hierarchy undercut the potential power advantage of the metropole."[14]

The Company built a vast empire in the Indian Ocean. Despite the VOC's military prowess, its trade and colonial relations were shaped by intricate and shifting regional balances of power.[15] As a rule, the Company was dependent on local alliances and allies to gain economic and political advantage, and its reach was limited.

To carry out its function as a cross-continental trader, the Company relied on a large body of labor; a key aspect of Company administration, and indeed governance, included the control and regulation of labor. Much like those of other merchant companies, the VOC's labor practices were predicated on a system of physical violence and coercion and what appears to be sheer disregard of human life.

Most Company "servants" were men of low rank and worked as sailors and soldiers or general laborers.[16] Recruited from northern Europe, they were bound by four- to seven-year contracts and were subject to a regimented system of coercive control based on a hierarchy of officers, strict routine, and a set of regulations (*Artikelsbrief*) supported by a network of land-based and maritime courts.

Sailors and soldiers could be beaten by their officers for minor offenses.[17] Those suspected of more serious offenses, such as assault, would be arrested and tried by a court, which further institutionalized and entrenched violence. In addition to forced labor and imprisonment, punishments, usually carried out in public, included whipping, brand-ings, face mutilation, strangulation, drowning, running the gauntlet, and hanging. Dissidents could even be punished after death. Their corpses could be quartered, hung out in public, and left in the open to rot.

Other labor regimes that operated in the Company included the use of convict labor and slavery.[18] The institutional frameworks for these systems were developed by the Company in Batavia. Batavia was par-ticularly reliant on the labor of Chinese debtors, who built much of the Company's infrastructure, but in addition, African exiled convicts were used to assist the police and executioners with corporal punishments.

Regulations governing slaves—an institution that remained illegal in the Netherlands but was used by the VOC abroad—were codified by Batavian administrators in the Statutes of India of 1642 and 1766. As in the case of sailors and soldiers, slave codes were backed up by the criminal justice system, and more-serious offences and disorderly acts were tried by the criminal court.

Under the VOC, there was no pretence of equality under the law: the legal system was consciously and explicitly based on entrenching and maintaining hierarchies and inequalities of class and status.[19] The most gruesome and violent punishments were reserved for slaves. For instance, they could be broken on the wheel, be burnt alive, or have their heels and noses cut off.

In addition to suffering violent regimes of control and discipline, the slaves and servants of charter companies, including the VOC, had to contend with the omnipresence of death. Jan Lucassen estimates that of the roughly one million men who travelled to the East Indies with the VOC during the seventeenth and eighteenth centuries, only one-third (33.1 percent) returned.[20] High mortality can be attributed to the lack of medical knowledge, the prevalence of disease in the tropics, and the poor health of the men recruited by the VOC, but ill-treatment, abuse, malnutrition, war, and capital punishment also played key roles.

Labor had to be constantly replenished and new recruits or slaves disciplined into their new roles. As Peter Linebaugh and Marcus Re-diker indicate, such human wastage was simply part of business.[21] The constant presence of death was an important element of the emerging global system of labor, with its regimes of control that perpetuated vio-lence and terror.

The VOC reflected the character of Dutch institutions more gener-ally and was based on a fragmented arrangement of power and alliances.

However, the VOC's fragmented and partial rule should not be interpreted as benign. VOC-run factories and settlements were based on the premises of colonial conquest as well as a harsh regime of labor control.

Servant, Slave, and Citizen

Starting out as a refreshment port for VOC fleets travelling between the Netherlands and the East Indies, the Cape Colony gave rise to a relatively extensive colonial settlement that required government administration. In line with norms of the time, the Company developed a distinctive strategy of political inclusion, based on a limited form of citizenship, and exclusion, which denied large sections of the population, specifically the laboring class, access to political rights and protections.

The VOC had no plans to establish a settlement, and the colony initially consisted of a fort and garden with a basic administration. The commander, later the governor, ruled together with the Council of Policy, which met weekly to carry out "all functions of government" on land, and a Court of Justice, modelled on Batavian law supplemented with local ordinances, was created in 1656.[22]

However, the Company had some difficulty in acquiring the cattle from indigenous Khoesan communities needed to feed men and stock ships and was dependent on importing farming produce from the Netherlands and Batavia. To reduce this dependence on outside food sources, the Company established a scheme whereby Company servants could be released from their contracts to farm.[23] In return, they were awarded the status of free-burghers (or free citizens).

With European society still largely bound by feudal structures and relations, citizenship was neither widespread nor nearly as central to political processes and ideologies as it is today. Nevertheless, as Prak documents, early forms of citizenship could be found in certain cities, including some in the Dutch Republic.[24] Citizenship varied a great deal from city to city. Prak notes, for instance, that in Bois-le-Duc, the category of citizens included all those born or baptized within the town, while in Deventer only children born of citizens were assured citizenship. Yet, in general, citizenship offered membership to guilds (which monopolized the trade and production of goods) and a trial by local courts. Although citizens could be elected to office in some cities, Prak argues that the administration of municipalities was still controlled by the aristocracy and political representation was limited. In return for these privileges, citizens were expected to pay taxes and to participate in the protection and policing of the city.

Regardless of the various legal parameters, Prak notes, it was primarily the urban middle classes who honed citizenship into a distinct identity—separating them from the poor, foreigners, and Jews—and mobilized as citizens to make political claims. For instance, the obligations of burghers were construed as tasks that only those who earned a decent living and were autonomous from a lord or master could carry out. This could be seen in the case of citizen militias, a highly contested institution, which became central to the notion of citizenship in the Netherlands as the power of guilds declined.

In the colonial context of the early Cape, burgher status was conferred on more-modest men and their wives, who would not be regarded as proper citizens by the urban middle classes in the Dutch Republic. The autonomy of the Cape burghers was quite limited.[25] Although released from their Company contracts, they could be reinstated as servants at the Company's behest. Burghers were also obliged to sell their produce to the Company at fixed prices and were not permitted to trade privately with Khoesan. In addition, they were expected to provide military service.

Nevertheless, Cape burghers did gain privileged access to state and social resources. Many started as low-ranking Company servants, and the change in legal status allowed many to elevate their class position. They were provided access to land and to other people's labor, as well as an opportunity for advancement and autonomy.

Political and social rights were intricately linked, and burghers were allowed to marry, thus giving them further access to family labor, as well as access to material and social "capital" in the forms of inheritances and credit. From as early as 1658, Cape burghers were also given some political representation. Two (later three) burgher representatives were incorporated onto the Council of Policy when cases involving burghers were heard.[26]

Although dominated by the Company, the Cape economy diversified. Through the establishment of retail and small-scale manufacture, burghers added to the urban port-centered economy based on Company shipping dependent on the labor of low-ranking men, mainly sailors and soldiers under contract. As in the case of the VOC more generally, servants stationed at the Cape—estimated to be approximately three thousand men by the late 1700s—were governed through labor codes and the criminal justice system, not as citizens.[27]

The Company retained a few farms and outposts, but farming was soon taken over by burghers. Those involved in retail, manufacture, and farming usually depended on others to provide labor. At first the commander of the Cape, Jan van Riebeeck, advocated the importation of convict Chinese labor, but starting in 1658 slaves were brought into the colony.[28] Some of these slaves were retained by the Company, and together with a small number of convicts, they provided domestic labor and worked on Company farms and public works. However, the overwhelming majority became "private" slaves, who were sold to and worked for burghers.

From the 1670s on, intensive agriculture was replaced with extensive agriculture, leading to the establishment of new farming districts (Stellenbosch, Paarl, Franschhoek, Tijgerberg, Wagenmakers Valley, the Land of Waveren, and Paardeberg).[29] Farmers mostly grew grapes for wine production and grain, and there were also a few farmers engaged in mixed farming, which included cultivation and stock farming.

Government administration was extended to the new, rural districts. The *Collegie van Heemraden* served as the chief administrative body, which was headed by the *landdrost,* a VOC official.[30] The *heemraden* was able to deal with minor civil cases, involving disputes in which claims did not exceed fifty rix-dollars, and the *landdrost* was expected to prosecute those crimes committed in his district before the Court of Justice.

As farming grew, the number of slaves in the colony steadily increased. Slaveholdings remained relatively small, especially when compared to the plantation economies of the Americas, and few farmers in the Cape owned more than fifty slaves at a time.[31] Nevertheless, "private" slaves soon outnumbered Company slaves and became the most prominent form of labor in the colony. By 1770, there were approximately 8,200 slaves in the colony, outnumbering the 7,736 free-burgher inhabitants.[32]

Individual slave owners exercised direct authority over their slaves, but they were still bound by Company rules and regulations (established by the Statutes of India of 1642 and 1766, supplemented with local ordinances). Owners could punish their slaves in most instances, but the court recognized slaves as human and presided over their lives and limbs. Only the court could order restraints such as leg-irons, or the torture and death of dissidents, and slave owners who overstepped the bounds of acceptable forms of punishment for slaves could face censure.[33]

However, as noted by Wayne Dooling, the implementation of slave regulations was in practice determined by local power relations.[34] Leading slave owners, the landed gentry, resented Company restrictions. Through capturing key positions in local government, forging alliances with VOC officials, and exploiting legal ambiguities, they were able "to give specific content and particular meaning to the rule of law."[35] This meant that slave owners were not necessarily penalized by the court for violent excesses against slaves.

By the late seventeenth century, the burgher population was augmented by a small number of "free blacks," who had been emancipated from slavery or had completed their sentences as convicts.[36] Some free blacks were involved in occupations similar to those of burghers (rented rooms, ran eating houses, grew and sold vegetables, or practiced a craft), but most were involved in fishing.[37] Although "free," this section of the population was denied the same status and political rights as burghers, unless they married into burgher families. (According to Nigel Worden, Company men intent on applying for citizenship, or burgher status, often married free black women.[38] Together, both parties could be viewed as more respectable and improve their social and political standing in Cape society.)

It is important to note that there were free inhabitants, including citizens, who were unable to make an independent living. They formed part of the free poor who worked for others or as indigents relied on state aid to survive.[39]

By the early 1700s, social and political hierarchies had already taken form. A significant part of the population was free, but not all free inhabitants were granted citizenship. Although not as independent as the city-based citizens found in the Netherlands, citizens did have limited political representation and access to resources.

However, the majority of the Cape's inhabitants—low-ranking Company servants, who were contracted/indentured, and slaves—were laborers and primarily governed through harsh regimes of controls and the criminal justice system. These elements of the Cape's population had very few, if any, rights, and the courts were predicated on maintaining social hierarchies, which meant that punishments were often determined by an offender's social class rather than his or her crime.

The Company, Stock Farming, and Indigenous Khoesan

In addition to the free population and bonded laborers, indigenous Khoesan constituted a significant part of the colony. The Company's approach to indigenous communities gives much insight into the nature of colonial conquest at the Cape and the linkages between political power, the economy, and labor.

When the first commander of the VOC-Cape, Jan van Riebeeck, arrived at the Cape, he was instructed to develop trade relations with local pastoral Khoesan communities.[40] However, when Khoesan failed to trade their cattle in the numbers required by the Company, van Riebeeck petitioned the Lords XVII (the directors of the Company) for permission to enslave Khoesan.[41] He claimed that Khoesan were idle, godless savages and "a brutal gang living without any conscience."[42] Much like the native people of America, dispossessed commoners, political dissidents, and renegades, as well as rebellious women, or "Amazons," in the North Atlantic,[43] men like van Riebeeck construed the Khoesan as monstrosities worthy of destruction.

However, the Lords XVII refused van Riebeeck's request. According to Kerry Ward, who examines the banishment of convicts to the Cape, the Company instructed local officials to treat the Khoesan respectfully as a trading nation.[44] However, when placed in a context of colonial occupation, this rhetoric of benign trade quickly gave way to a reality of systematic territorial enclosure and political domination.

The VOC's station occupied territory on which Goringhaicona, or *strandlopers* (beachcombers), relied for their marine-based hunter-gathering and that also formed part of the grazing routes of pastoralists such as the Goringhaiqua and the Cochoqua.[45] Khoesan were increasingly prevented from accessing this land. At first, the Company grew hedges to keep Khoesan and their cattle out. At one stage, the Lords XVII even wondered whether it would be possible to dig a channel between the Salt and Liesbeek Rivers with a view of separating the Cape from the African continent.[46]

Concerned about the permanence and growth of the VOC outpost—from which they were excluded—peninsular Khoesan united and took up arms against the Company in 1659. After this war (referred to as the First Dutch-Khoesan War), the justification for occupation appears to have shifted, and Company officials argued that they had won the territory through war.

After the Second Khoesan-Dutch War (1673–77), territorial and political inclusion became possible for Khoesan polities but strictly on Company terms and on an indirect basis. The defeated Gonnema, leader of the Cochoqua, was expected to pay a tribute of thirty cattle a year. At about the same time, the Company asserted its right to adjudicate disputes between different clans in its territory.[47]

Governor Simon van der Stel (1679–99) also developed a practice whereby he would officially recognize loyal Khoesan chiefs or captains, bestowing on them a ceremonial staff and a classical name (such as Hercules and Hannibal).[48] Such officially sanctioned leaders were able to retain access to land and grazing in the colony. Legal pluralism accompanied institutional pluralism, and Khoesan who broke the law in the colony were handed to their communities for punishment.

At first, the Company had sought to exclude the Khoesan entirely from the small station. However, as the station expanded and became more secure, the Company established systems to deal with Khoesan indirectly through officially appointed patriarchs.

Mamdani argues that indirect rule was introduced by the British; he describes the VOC-Cape as a "a multiracial society marked by a single legal order" and claims that "the colonized were the indigenous Khoikhoi and the imported Malay slaves, forming a small minority of the Cape population."[49] However, the situation is considerably more complex than Mamdani describes. The core of Company rule based on labor and criminal codes was coercive for the majority of people, which included the "colonized" consisting of slaves and Khoesan. There was a form of indirect rule, but this took a much weaker form as seen in parts of twentieth-century colonial Africa. VOC-sanctioned patriarchal loyalists had little real power and did not form a key part of the administrative apparatus, and there was no effort to shore up "traditional" authorities or codify "custom." Company-appointed Khoesan patriarchs were, for example, rewarded by special concessions yet generally lacked coercive power, as well as the respect and loyalty of the communities that they supposedly governed.

Moreover, the Company failed to develop systematic laws and institutions for those Khoesan who were increasingly drawn into the colony, mainly as workers. Khoesan labor was particularly important for the stock-farming sector that emerged at the beginning of the 1700s when free grazing permits, or "loan farms," were made available for a small annual rent, giving potential farmers access to a minimum of 2,420 hectares.[50] Stock farming required substantially less capital and labor than arable farming. There was subsequently a rapid increase in the number of stock farmers. In 1746, there were approximately 225 stock farmers. By 1770, this number had grown to 600.[51]

More and more loan farms were taken out at ever-increasing distances from Cape Town.

Although government was extended with the establishment of new districts, the colonial borderlands, or frontier, proved much more difficult to govern. It is here that free-burghers interfaced with surrounding Khoesan and other African communities, as well as new multiracial communities constituted by fugitives and runaways from the colony and surrounding societies. No one particular group was able to establish outright political or cultural dominance.[52] Economic competition was fierce, and inhabitants resorted to violent strategies of accumulation based on illicit cattle raiding or turned to hunting to gain an advantage. There were a few rich stock farmers, but most free-burgher stock farmers were fairly modest cattle herders.[53] Some stock farmers owned one or two slaves. However, free-burghers in the borderlands were mostly dependent on the labor of Khoesan, who were skilled in handling animals.

Traditionally, Khoesan entered into relations of dependency or became clients within their own societies to acquire dogs, cattle, or weapons, but such relationships remained fluid.[54] Dependents could leave to become autonomous or to enter into another dependency relationship. Even when forced to find work in VOC-controlled territory, Khoesan attempted to retain some independence by refusing to enter into long-term contracts.[55] Because such workers often returned to their kin and communities after their contracts expired, they became migrant laborers of a sort. Communities often moved to secure the best pasturage for their animals, making Khoesan migrants doubly mobile.

Although an increasingly important source of labor for the colony, these Khoesan workers did not conform to official categories—be they Company servant, burgher, slave, or subjugated Khoesan under a loyal Company-appointed patriarch—and had no clear legal status. In the absence of any official codes for Khoesan workers, it was left to masters and servants to negotiate instruments of control. On the more-open frontier, some Khoesan workers were able to assert more-traditional Khoesan practices of dependency in relation to their burgher masters. Those who had lost their cattle and access to pasturage would attach themselves to a farmer, often adopting Christianity and the Dutch language. Such dependents, known as Oorlams, would be rewarded with a cow or two and even a horse or a gun.[56]

Stock farmers could also rely on the labor of "Bastaards," or people of mixed European-Khoesan descent, or the distinct category of

"Bastaard-Hottentots," specifically referring to people with slave fathers and Khoesan mothers. Reflecting complex racial and class hierarchies, Khoesan with European heritage tended to have a higher status and gravitated toward less menial jobs, often working as craftspeople or transport riders.[57] In many instances, frontier burghers sent trusted Khoesan dependents on commando (militia) duty as their substitutes.[58]

However, there was also room for a great deal of abuse and violence—Khoesan "orphans" (in reality children kidnapped in raids) were forced into labor, and in opposition to the flexible work arrangements preferred by Khoesan servants, masters were also known to withhold remuneration to recover debts, seize livestock, and chase runaways, as well as to hold children hostage to force their parent(s) to return to work.[59]

The first VOC attempts to regulate Khoesan workers directly, as opposed to through Khoesan patriarchs, started in the 1730s and 1740s when dissidents were tried and punished by the colony's criminal court. As noted above, the criminal justice system had long been used as a mechanism to discipline slaves and low-ranking Company servants accused of more-serious offences, and it was easily extended to include Khoesan workers.

It is important to underscore that Khoesan workers were only partially integrated into the Company's administration and primarily interfaced with its legal system as criminals. For instance, at this time, the Company did not even keep a basic census of Khoesan workers, or indeed of any Khoesan living in the colony.[60] Its loyal patriarchs had limited power and were subject to little in the way of supervision. The partial integration as criminals institutionalized Khoesan workers' servile status. Along with slaves and Company servants, Khoesan workers were constructed by the state as part of a naturally violent and deviant, indeed monstrous, laboring class.

Territorial expansion, mainly through the illicit hunter-trader-raider economy, took its toll. Khoesan lost their independent way of life; they were proletarianized and forced into labor. Only in 1775—two decades before the complete eclipse of VOC rule—were the first codes specifically for Khoesan workers introduced, when the Company approved a regulation in Stellenbosch that allowed children of Khoesan mothers and slave fathers to be "apprenticed" (indentured) up until the age of twenty-five.[61]

The Company did not respect Khoesan communities as nations in their own right, nor did it treat them as equal trading partners or as "free" people. Rather, the land that Khoesan relied on for subsistence was occupied, their leaders were defeated and subjugated, and Khoesan were integrated into the colony as laborers. Yet unlike the governance of Company servants and slaves, there were no ready-made codes through which to govern Khoesan laborers, and they occupied a relatively ambivalent legal position.

Underpinned by the conflicting imperatives of keeping Khoesan apart from the colony politically but absorbing them economically as laborers, the Company's approach moved from excluding Khoesan from the colony to a fatuous system of indirect rule, partial institutional integration to provide some form of labor control, and indenture. Much like low-ranking Company servants and slaves, Khoesan were primarily deemed to be part of the servile laboring class and were denied political rights.

Political Belongings and Imaginations of Freedom

For the majority of Khoesan in the colony, colonial enclosure, class exploitation, and violence were intimately linked and most acutely experienced on the frontier. It is there that the political identities and aspirations of Khoesan laborers and their burgher masters were forged and most keenly expressed.

The colonial borderlands were difficult for the Company to control and were characterized by violence emanating from cattle raids. Such raids did not only reflect the accumulation strategies of those who participated in the hunter-raider-trader economy but were also a central part of Khoesan resistance to colonial rule.[62]

Burghers in this part of the colony developed a distinct identity different from that of their more elite and urban counterparts.[63] Aggrieved that the Company did not provide them with enough support against raids by independent Khoesan and fugitive bands, they questioned the legitimacy of Company rule. For instance, the 1738 rebellion reflected the more humble backgrounds of frontier free-burghers and was led by a deserted Company soldier, Etienne Barbier.[64] Rebels maintained that they were easily ruined by raids and not only objected to the high cost of loan farms but also questioned the Company's control over the supply of ammunition needed to initiate cattle raids and protect themselves from retaliation.

The VOC's decline signaled that significant political and institutional changes were taking place at the Cape. Elite burghers, who were inspired by the American Revolution and by the Patriots in the Netherlands, gained in political confidence. They challenged the Company's monopolistic trade policies and demanded more representation in government.[65]

By the 1790s, political turmoil had also spread to the borderlands, by which time the anti-Company sentiments of frontier burghers had given root to republicanism.[66] Embroiled in the Anglo-Dutch War (1780–84), the VOC attempted to exact the burghers' military obligations. However, those residing in the recently established Graaff-Reinet district were reluctant to leave their farms and families, as raids by Khoesan and fugitive groups had intensified in response to expanding colonial settlement. Left to their own defenses, that is, without Company protection, they believed that they no longer owed the Company their allegiance. British spies reported that these burghers were informed by the "ridiculous notion, that like America, they could exist as an independent state."[67]

However, the republicanism of these burghers remained exclusive and narrow. They did not generalize their calls for freedom, equality, and fraternity to other sections of the population, least of all their slaves or Khoesan laborers.

For many Khoesan, participation in cattle raids was not simply motivated by cattle accumulation but was often informed by a clear political motive. According to Shula Marks, regular raids on the colony marked a shift away from the wars initially waged by Cape Peninsular Khoesan against the Company and represented a form of protest in objection to colonialism.[68] In 1739, for instance, an interpreter explained that the purpose of a particularly large raid along the Berg River was to "chase the Dutch out of their land as long as they lived on their land, and that this was but a beginning but would do the same to all the people around there."[69]

At the same time, the crimes for which Khoesan were prosecuted show that these workers did not necessarily operate only within neat national or ethnic categories and were also involved in other forms of protest action. Khoesan bands overlapped with or incorporated other fugitive groupings, or runaway slaves, sailors, and soldiers.[70] These communities served as living examples of a modest, yet autonomous, way of life for those living under their masters in the colony.

Not adequately recognized in the literature on the early colonial Cape is that Khoesan laborers also established connections with other working poor and participated in proletarian solidarities, contributing to proletarian traditions of direct action.[71]

Thus, Khoesan laborers, together with slaves and low-ranking Company servants, devised ways in which to strike back at their exploiters and oppressors or to improve their living and working conditions for the better. Through withholding labor, desertion, arson, verbal and physical assault on masters, mutiny, striking, and other forms of rebellion, the working poor took the moral codes of their masters and colonial authorities to task. In so doing, they rejected their condition of servitude, pursued a life of freedom, created their own independent class communities, questioned poor living conditions, refused to work on Sundays, developed their own understanding of fair punishment, protected their relationships with others, challenged the authority of their masters and overseers in the workplace, refused to accept high rates of mortality, and exposed corruption.

These often modest struggles need to be seen in context. In a society based on colonial conquest and on the widespread use of bonded and slave labor, military might and physical violence served as the main pillars of the power of the state and master class. Any overt challenges were met with violent repression. More often than not, the ringleaders of rebellions or mutinies were put to death, their corpses desecrated and denied proper burial.

Like the burgher elites, the Cape's popular classes were not quiescent during the "Age of Revolutions" and also challenged their masters and the Company. Marks notes that from the 1770s onward, Khoesan laborers deserted in large numbers to join armed bands that raided frontier farms.[72] By the 1780s, Marks notes, some bands were several hundred strong, and in the 1790s there was one report of a band that had grown to almost a thousand. In line with the growing republicanism as well as the nationalist sentiment of the age, they wanted to govern themselves and buck the yoke of colonial rule. By that time, their anticolonial aspirations had begun to increasingly converge with their labor grievances.

By the 1780s, the anticolonial action of the Khoesan, often with the support of others, started to take on new forms. Most notable was the movement in the Overburg led by the prophet Jan Parel, who combined millenarianism with a vision of revolution.[73] Parel predicted that the world would end on October 25, 1788 (a year before the French Revolution), ushering in an era of utopian bliss and the end of colonial rule. To prepare, his followers (consisting of four hundred Khoesan servants, free blacks, and slaves) were urged to burn their European clothing and to erect new straw huts with two doors. Once these rituals were complete, they were to attack the Swellendam Drosty and kill all "Christians." However, predictably, this spiritual-political protest did not translate into widespread protest, nor did it deliver the colony from colonial or class rule.

Toward the end of the 1700s, republicanism, which grew out of the violence that characterized life on the frontier, had become a key political idea. While free-burghers developed an exclusive form of republicanism, seeking more self-rule in a society in which most people were to remain servile, rebellious Khoesan laborers attempted to make sense of both their political dispossession and class exploitation. Anticolonial resistance in the form of raids was most fierce on the colonial frontier, where the threat to their political and economic independence was most immediate. Ethnic and national identities were complicated by the experiences of the Khoesan as laborers. They often identified with others who were marginalized, exploited, and oppressed and also participated in modes of class-based resistance.

Imperial Citizenship

When the British took control of the Cape in 1795, the colony was gripped by social and political conflict. The British (and Batavian Republic, the new revolutionary Dutch government) reorganized the structure of power, introducing new strategies of inclusion and exclusion. Partly in a response to the radical political ideologies associated with the "Age of Revolutions," the British state's approach to Khoesan laborers provided new opportunities for different kinds of political engagements and identities.

Drawing on the practice adopted for other new colonies taken during the Napoleonic Wars, the British War Office decided to keep most of the institutions inherited from the Company in place,[74] which is probably why scholars have tended to stress the continuity between Dutch and British rule at the Cape.[75] However, the British administration was underpinned by a different, and increasingly modern, ethos. The British state introduced two hugely significant changes that redefined the national question at the Cape as well as the terrain of popular political engagement.

First, the British War and Colonial Office used the category of "British subject" as a key organizing principle as well as a tool of state legitimation.

Frontier farmers (who then came to be referred to as "Boers") lost their privileged status as citizens. Together with their Khoesan laborers, they were incorporated into the category of British subject. In so doing, masters and servants were brought into the same legal framework and, in theory, were regarded more or less as equal before the law. The legal system, then, differed from that of the VOC, which included explicit measures designed to protect social hierarchies often further reinforced through the public display of physical punishment.

In the second instance, the British colonial state was sensitive to the changes in elite and official conceptions of acceptable forms of labor across the British Empire and much of the globe. Largely because of an international campaign against slavery in the late eighteenth century, as well as slave revolts across the Atlantic, some forms of unfree labor had become morally repugnant to "Enlightened" men and women, and existing forms of labor were reformed.

The Cape's new imperial rulers promoted a paternalistic rather than a liberal attitude toward labor. Un-freedom would be retained, but the brutality of the system would be limited by the state, which was represented as a neutral arbitrator and intruded more forcefully into the regulation of masters and servants.

Most notably, the criminal justice system, a key tool of labor control under the VOC, was reformed. The British War and Colonial Office and local officials expressed particular concern over the court's blatant impartiality and the use of torture to exact confessions and to punish.[76] The use of terror was tempered, while the introduction of an appeals court and circuit courts extended mechanisms for legal redress.[77] These did not simply address broader political concerns regarding the provision of rights and protections; such measures also altered the operation of the criminal justice system and, in so doing, reformed a central aspect of labor control.

Nevertheless, the slave question proved difficult to resolve—although reforms were introduced to ameliorate the conditions in which slaves lived and worked. When the British first arrived at the Cape, some of the elites believed that slaves would be encouraged to rise up and revolt.[78] However, the slave owners were quickly placated by promises of free trade, the protection of private property (including slaves), and limited taxes. Perhaps keen to consolidate state–upper-class relations and cognizant of the continued reliance on slave labor for agricultural production, the new administration focused attention instead on the unruly eastern frontier and on the Khoesan labor question.[79]

In addition to securing the territorial boundary of the colony and keeping the Xhosa out, authorities sought to discipline both masters and their Khoesan servants into what was viewed as their correct class and legal roles. British officials depicted their Boer subjects as indolent, unsophisticated, and cruel masters in need of state regulation, while their Khoesan subjects were viewed as an "innocent and oppressed race of men" that required "countenance and protection" from government.[80]

No sooner had rebellious republican Boers been defeated by the military and brought under British rule in April 1799 than Khoesan, including those regarded as the most loyal workers, deserted en masse to join large bands on the frontier, giving rise to the "Servant Rebellion" (1799–1803).

Once again, Khoesan drew attention to the link between their colonial and class oppression, and their rebellion was against the colonial state as much as against the master class. In the words of the rebel Captain Stuurman, the best remedy to the violent abuse Khoesan had suffered at the hands of their masters was to reclaim "the country of which [their] fathers were despoiled by the Dutch" and to fight for their independence from their Boer masters.[81]

The rebellion has been documented by Susan Newton-King and V. C. Malherbe.[82] After briefly courting the Cape's new British rulers, rebel Khoesan instead chose to ally with members of fugitive Xhosa communities who also sought refuge on the frontier. The growing rebel forces raided outlying farms, plundering arms, ammunition, and horses. Farmers fled the area, and by the end of July 1799, Khoesan bands were in control of the whole southeastern portion of the Graaff-Reinet district. They not only had succeeded in halting the latest colonial encroachments but also had managed to push the colonial border back.

Doubtful that a military campaign against the rebel Khoesan Confederacy would be successful, British authorities adopted two strategies to quell the rebellion. First, as noted by Susan Newton-King, any claim to territory east of the Sundays River to the Zuurveld was relinquished, and so the alliance between Xhosa fugitives and the confederacy became destabilized.[83] This was part of a broader strategy of extending state authority over complex border relations, by drawing a clear boundary between the Xhosa lands and the colony. This was to be done by establishing a direct relationship with Xhosa communities, instead of relying on frontier Boers as intermediaries, by prohibiting Boers from using Xhosa as laborers, and by preventing Xhosa from entering the colony without a pass.[84]

Secondly, authorities focused on regulating master-servant relations and by extending basic protections to Khoesan.[85] In 1801, the Fiscal urged that formal contracts be made with Khoesan workers and be registered with the court. This system was designed to bind Khoesan workers to their masters by preventing them from deserting, but it was also meant to stop farmers beating their servants "*ad libitum.*"[86]

In 1801, Governor Young reported that "the Boers [were] becoming less Savage Masters, under the Eye of Government, and the poor Hottentots [were] returning to their masters under the Protection of the Government, and by a Strict administration of Justice, more useful servants, & more peaceable."[87]

The Servant Rebellion dissipated by 1803 under the brief period of Batavian rule. Soon after the British regained the Cape, the slave trade within the British Empire was abolished. The stabilization and regulation of Khoesan labor became even more urgent. The rudimentary existing measures to regulate Khoesan workers were extended by the 1809 Caledon Code (the "Hottentot Regulation") and by apprenticeship legislation in 1812.[88] In addition, from 1812 onward, Khoesan had access to the so-called "black" circuit courts, which investigated abuses and ill-treatment.

These protections were minimal. Nevertheless, as subjects with limited protections, Khoesan were able to negotiate rights and obligations with the state. For the first time, a reformist political strategy became viable, and with the help of missionaries, Khoesan lobbied the government and used the courts to win further legal reforms.[89]

Under the British, limited labor reform together with the incorporation of Khoesan—and their free-burgher masters—into the category of "British subject" fundamentally redefined the limits of political possibility. With the basis of a form of imperial citizenship laid, Khoesan laborers could look to the colonial state to secure limited rights and protections, especially within the realm of labor relations. It is at this point that the earliest manifestation of "black loyalism" in what would become South Africa may be found. The new imperial power, in codifying rights and protections as part of its larger project of administrative reform at the Cape—and in line with the new global necessity of ruling, not simply by brute force but as a "legitimate" protector of its subject races and classes—opened space for a new type of politics. Under the VOC, popular dissent was met with terror and repression; un-freedom was affirmed at every turn; spectacular and brutal reprisals were the norm. The new British order, by contrast, enabled claims to be made for the protection of the British Crown, even by its most subject groups, and, to the extent that this really did expand the rights and protections of the most downtrodden classes, made the possibility of a reformist and a loyalist politics real for the first time.

Generally, VOC rule was fragmented yet still brutal in that it was predicated on colonial conquest and a harsh regime of labor control. At the Cape, the Company introduced a unique form of citizenship, but a large proportion of inhabitants were servants or slaves governed through harsh labor codes and subject to a criminal justice system based on upholding social and political inequalities.

A significant part of colonial governance dealt with the indigenous Khoesan population. The Company's approach to Khoesan was shaped by the conflicting imperatives of political exclusion and separation of Khoesan polities from the colony, giving rise to a very weak form of indirect rule, and the absorption of Khoesan as laborers, which led to their partial institutional integration, mainly into the criminal justice system, and eventually to the development of labor codes that legalized their indenture. Like Company servants and slaves, they were part of the servile laboring class and denied the same political rights and protections awarded to their free burgher masters.

The political identities and aspirations of Khoesan laborers and frontier free-burgher masters were formed in relation to one another. For Khoesan, colonial conquest and class exploitation were intimately linked. This could be seen in both their anticolonial action and their participation in broader forms of class-based resistance.

Both state and popular articulations of citizenship changed significantly beginning in 1795 under British rule. Reflecting broader global shifts associated with the "Age of Revolutions," labor conditions were ameliorated, and Khoesan were incorporated as British subjects. This allowed Khoesan to claim rights and protections from the colonial state, laying the basis for different kinds of engagements and political belonging.

A direct line cannot be drawn between the governmental categories or political relations that emerged in the early colonial Cape and the practices and meanings attached to national citizenship in postapartheid South Africa. Nevertheless, this deeper political history can still shed light on how we may understand the state, as well as the construction of political identities and aspirations.

First, by focusing on the early modern period, this chapter shows that there is not just one standard or continuous narrative of colonial rule in Africa.

Second, the "native question,"[90] or the way in which a foreign minority rules an indigenous majority, was not simply determined by the organization of power, as Mamdani claims. Rather, government strategies of inclusion and exclusion as well as political identities and strategies were also closely tied to issues of labor exploitation, as well as class-based connections, solidarities, and aspirations.

Finally, neat distinctions cannot be drawn between notions of the citizen and the subject. Under British rule, Khoesan were able to draw on a broader notion of imperial citizenship to make demands on the colonial state, suggesting that early manifestations of "black loyalism" had a significant popular component.

Notes

1. Rogers Brubaker and Frederick Cooper, "Beyond 'Identity,'" *Theory and Society* 29 (2000): 1–47.

2. C. A. Bayly, *The Birth of the Modern World* (Malden, MA: Blackwell Publishing, 2004), 9–21.

3. Ibid., 86–120.

4. Mahmood Mamdani, *Citizen and Subject: Contemporary Africa and the Legacy of Late Colonialism* (Princeton: Princeton University Press, 1996), 16–18.

5. Edward Webster, ed., *The Unresolved National Question in Left Thinking* (Johannesburg: University of the Witwatersrand Press, 2016).

6. Hilary Sapire, "African Loyalism and Its Discontents: The Royal Tour of South Africa, 1794," *Historical Journal* 54, no. 1 (2011): 215–40.

7. Ibid., 217.

8. For instance, see Hermann Giliomee, *The Afrikaners: Biography of a People* (Charlottesville: University of Virginia Press, 2003).

9. Nicole Ulrich, "Time, Space and the Political Economy of Merchant Colonialism in the Cape of Good Hope and VOC World," *South African Historical Journal* 63, no. 3 (2010): 571–88.

10. Julia Adams, "Trading States, Trading Places: The Role of Patrimonialism in Early Modern Dutch Development," *Comparative Studies in Society and History* 36, no. 2 (1994): 319–55.

11. Ibid., 326.

12. J. Israel, *The Dutch Republic: Its Rise, Greatness and Fall, 1477–1806* (Oxford: Clarendon Press, 1995), 23.

13. Julia Adams, "Principals and Agents, Colonialists and Company Men: The Decay of Colonial Control in the Dutch East Indies," *American Sociological Review* 61, no. 1 (1996): 12–28.

14. Ibid., 25.

15. This point is made by numerous authors. See, for instance, Israel, *Dutch Republic;* and, more recently, Kerry Ward, *Networks of Empire: Forced Migration in the Dutch East India Company* (Cambridge: Cambridge University Press, 2009).

16. For an overview of VOC labor, see Jan Lucassen, "A Multinational and Its Labor Force: The Dutch East India Company, 1595–1795," *International Labor and Working-Class History* 66 (2004): 12–39.

17. A personal account of the brutality on ships is given in Roelof Van Gelder, *Naporra's Omveg: Het Leven van een VOC-Matroos (1731–1793)* (Amsterdam: Atlas, 2003). For the treatment and regulation of VOC sailors and soldiers in the East Indies, see P. A. McVay, "'I Am the Devil's Own': Class and Identity in the Seventeenth Century Dutch East Indies" (PhD diss., University of Illinois, 1995).

18. For a detailed discussion of convicts, see Ward, *Networks of Empire.*

19. For a discussion of the workings of the Cape court, see Nigel Worden and Gerald Groenewald, eds., *Trials of Slavery: Selected Documents Concerning Slaves from the Criminal Records of the Council of Justice at the Cape of Good Hope, 1705–1794* (Cape Town: Van Riebeeck Society, 2005).

20. Lucassen, "Multinational and Its Labor Force," 14–15.

21. Peter Linebaugh and Marcus Rediker, *The Many-Headed Hydra: Sailors, Slaves, Commoners, and the Hidden History of the Revolutionary Atlantic* (Boston: Beacon Press, 2000), 1–7, 143–73.

22. Nigel Worden, Elizabeth van Heyningen, and Vivian Bickford-Smith, *Cape Town: The Making of a City, an Illustrated History* (Cape Town: David Philips, 2004), 29.

23. Leonard Guelke, "Freehold Farmers and Frontier Settlers, 1657–1780," in *The Shaping of South African Society, 1652–1840,* ed. Richard Elphick and Hermann Giliomee, 2nd ed. (Cape Town: Maskew, Miller and Longman, 1989), 66–108, esp. 70; Worden, van Heyningen, and Bickford-Smith, *Cape Town,* 20.

24. Maarten Prak, "Burghers into Citizens: Urban and National Citizenship in the Netherlands during the Revolutionary Era (c. 1800)," *Theory and Society* 26, no. 4 (1997): 405.

25. Guelke, "Freehold Farmers," 70; Gerrit Shutte, "Company and Colonists at the Cape, 1652–1795," in Elphick and Giliomee, *Shaping of South African Society,* 284–323, esp. 298–303.

26. Worden and Groenewald, *Trials of Slavery,* xxxi.

27. Worden et al., *Cape Town,* 49.

28. For a detailed discussion of slavery in the Cape, see Robert Shell, *Children of Bondage: A Social History of the Slave Society at the Cape of Good Hope, 1652–1838* (Johannesburg: University of the Witwatersrand Press, 2001); and

Nigel Worden, *Slavery in Dutch South Africa* (Cambridge: Cambridge University Press, 1985).

29. Guelke, "Freehold Farmers," 73–75.

30. Worden and Groenewald, *Trials of Slavery*, xii; Schutte, "Company and Colonists," 296.

31. James Armstrong and Nigel Worden, "The Slaves, 1652–1834," in Elphick and Giliomee, *Shaping of South African Society*, 136; Worden, *Slavery in Dutch South Africa*, 31.

32. Richard Elphick and Hermann Giliomee, "The Origins and Entrenchment of European Domination at the Cape, 1652–c. 1840," in Elphick and Giliomee, *Shaping of South African Society*, 524.

33. Worden, *Slavery in Dutch South Africa*, 11.

34. Wayne Dooling, "'The Good Opinion of Others': Law, Slavery and Community in the Cape Colony, c. 1760–1830," in *Breaking the Chains: Slavery and Its Legacy in the Nineteenth-Century Cape Colony*, ed. Nigel Worden and Clifton Crais, 25–44 (Johannesburg: University of the Witwatersrand Press, 1994).

35. Wayne Dooling, *Slavery, Emancipation and Colonial Rule in South Africa* (Scottsville: University of KwaZulu Natal Press, 2007), 45.

36. Worden et al., *Cape Town*, 64.

37. Ibid.

38. Nigel Worden, "Artisan Conflicts in a Colonial Context: The Cape Town Blacksmith Strike of 1752," *Labor History* 46, no. 2 (2005): 161.

39. Worden et al., *Cape Town*, 68.

40. Richard Elphick and V. C. Malherbe, "The Khoisan to 1828," in Elphick and Giliomee, *Shaping of South African Society*, 10.

41. Ibid., 11.

42. Henry Trotter, "Sailors as Scribes: Travel Discourse and the (Con)textualisation of the Khoisan at the Cape of Good Hope, 1649–90," *Journal of African Travel Writing*, nos. 8 and 9 (2001): 33.

43. Linebaugh and Rediker, *Many-Headed Hydra*, 39.

44. Kerry Ward, "'The Bounds of Bondage': Forced Migration from Batavia to the Cape of Good Hope during the Dutch East India Company Era, c. 1652–1795" (PhD diss., University of Michigan, 2002), 6.

45. Worden et al., *Cape Town*, 21.

46. Ibid., 25.

47. Elphick and Malherbe, "Khoisan to 1828," 14.

48. Ibid.

49. Mamdani, *Citizen and Subject*, 65–66.

50. Guelke, "Freehold Farmers," 78.

51. Ibid., 85.

52. Martin Legassick, "The Northern Frontier to c. 1840: The Rise and Decline of the Griqua People," in Elphick and Giliomee, *Shaping of South African Society*, 367.

53. Guelke, "Freehold Farmers," 89.

54. Legassick, "Northern Frontier," 367.

55. Elphick and Malherbe, "Khoisan to 1828," 31. See also characterizations of Khoesan in O. F. Mentzel, *Geographical and Topographical Description of the Cape of Good Hope*, part 3, vol. 2, German ed., trans. G. V. Marias and J. Hoge (Cape Town: Van Riebeeck Society, 1944), 264; P. Thunberg, *Travels at the Cape of Good Hope, 1777–1775*, ed. V. S. Forbes, trans. J. Rudner and I. Rudner (Cape Town: Van Riebeeck Society, 1986), 316; and A. Sparrman, *A Voyage to the Cape of Good Hope, towards the Antarctic Polar Circle, around the World and to the Country of the Hottentots and the Caffers from the Year 1772–1776*, vols. 1 and 2, ed. V. S. Forbes, trans. J. Rudner and I. Rudner, Reprint Series (Cape Town: Van Riebeeck Society, 2007), 1:209.

56. Legassick, "Northern Frontier," 368.

57. Ibid., 370.

58. Ibid.

59. Elphick and Malherbe, "Khoisan to 1828," 10.

60. Worden, *Slavery in Dutch South Africa*, 11.

61. Elphick and Malherbe, "Khoisan to 1828," 32.

62. Shula Marks, "Khoisan Resistance to the Dutch in the Seventeenth and Eighteenth Centuries," *Journal of African History* 13, no. 1 (1972): 55–80.

63. See recent discussions of burgher identity in Laura Mitchell, *Belongings: Property and Identity in Colonial South Africa, an Exploration of Frontiers, 1725–c. 1830* (New York: Columbia University Press, 2009); and Gerald Groenewald, "Kinship, Entrepreneurship and Social Capital: Alcohol *Pachters* and the Making of a Free-Burgher Society in Cape Town, 1652–1795" (PhD diss., University of Cape Town, 2009).

64. Nigel Penn, *Rogues, Rebels and Runaways: Eighteenth-Century Cape Characters* (Cape Town: David Philip Publishers, 2003), 101.

65. Worden et al., *Cape Town*, 82.

66. David Johnson, *Imagining the Cape Colony: History, Literature and the South African Nation* (Claremont: UCT Press, 2012), 116–39.

67. Memorandum on the Condition of the Colony, F. Kersteins, n/d, in the Records of the Cape Colony in G. M. Theal, ed., *Records of the Cape Colony*, vols. 1–7, 1793–1811 (Manuscript Documents in the Public Record Office, London, printed for the Government of the Cape Colony, 1897–99), 1:168. Hereafter cited as *RCC*.

68. Marks, "Khoisan Resistance," 55–80.

69. Cited in ibid., 71.

70. Ibid.

71. For a detailed discussion of popular identity and resistance, see Nicole Ulrich, "Counter Power and Colonial Rule in the Eighteenth-Century Cape of Good Hope: Belongings and Protest of the Labouring Poor" (PhD thesis, University of the Witwatersrand, 2011), 100–177. See also Nicole Ulrich, "Popular Community in 18th-Century Southern Africa: Family, Fellowship, Alternative Networks, and Mutual Aid at the Cape of Good Hope, 1652–1795," *Journal of Southern African History* 40, no. 6 (2014): 1139–57.

72. Marks, "Khoisan Resistance," 73–74.

73. Russel Viljoen, "'Revelation of a Revolution': The Prophecies of Jan Parel, Alias Onse Liewe Heer," *Kronos* 21 (1994): 5.

74. See also Instructions to our Right Trusty and Right well Beloved Cousin and Councillor George Earl of Macartney, K.B. Our Commander in Chief and over the Settlement of Cape of Good Hope in South Africa— Given Our Court at St. James the Thirteenth Day of December, one thousand seven hundred and ninety-six, in the Thirty seventh year of our Reign, *RCC,* 2:3–20.

75. William Freund, "The Cape under the Transitional Governments, 1795–1814," in Elphick and Giliomee, *Shaping of South African Society,* 324–57.

76. Instructions to . . . Macartney, *RCC,* 3–20, esp. 6.

77. Timothy Keegan, *Colonial South Africa and the Origins of the Racial Order* (Cape Town: David Philip, 1996), 55–56; Freund, "Cape under the Transitional Governments," 324–57, esp. 347. See also Proclamation by His Excellency George Earl of Macartney, July 17, 1797, *RCC,* 2:124; Proclamation by His Excellency George Earl of Macartney, July 24, 1797, *RCC,* 2:126–28.

78. Address of Sir George Keith Elphinstone, K.B., and Major General Craig to the Governor, Council Magistrates, and Inhabitants of the Settlement and Town of the Cape of Good Hope, June 24, 1795, *RCC,* 1:74–75.

79. See especially the narrative written by imperial spy and ideologue John Barrow, *Travels into the Interior of Southern Africa,* vols. 1 and 2, 2nd ed. (London: T. Cadell and W. Davies, 1806).

80. Ibid., 1:375.

81. Susan Newton-King, "Part I: The Rebellion of the Khoesan," in *The Khoikhoi Rebellion in the Eastern Cape (1977–1803),* by Susan Newton-King and V. C. Malherbe (Cape Town: Centre for African Studies, UCT, 1981), 20.

82. Susan Newton-King and V. C. Malherbe, *The Khoikhoi Rebellion in the Eastern Cape (1977–1803)* (Cape Town: Centre for African Studies, UCT, 1981).

83. Newton-King, "Rebellion of the Khoesan," 28–30. See also instructions of the Landdrost of the Colony of Graaff Reinet, Frans Reinherd Bresler, according to which he is to act in present circumstances of Affairs in the Said Colony, June 20, 1797, *RCC,* 2:95–101; and Proclamation by His Excellency George Earl Macartney, June 27, 1797, *RCC,* 2:107.

84. Instructions of . . . Bresler, June 20, 1797, *RCC,* 2:95–101; Proclamation by . . . Macartney, June 27, 1797, *RCC,* 2:107.

85. Newton-King, "Rebellion of the Khoesan," 28–29.

86. Dooling, *Slavery, Emancipation,* 66.

87. Letter from Sir George Yonge to the Right Honourable Henry Dundas, Cape Town, January 5, 1801, *RCC,* 3:368–89, esp. 369.

88. Elphick and Malherbe, "Khoisan to 1828," 40–41; Freund, "Cape under the Transitional Governments," 335.

89. See Elphick and Malherbe, "Khoisan to 1828," 40–58.

90. An expression used by Mamdani in *Citizen and Subject,* 16.

References

Adams, Julia. "Principals and Agents, Colonialists and Company Men: The Decay of Colonial Control in the Dutch East Indies." *American Sociological Review* 61, no. 1 (1996): 12–28.

———. "Trading States, Trading Places: The Role of Patrimonialism in Early Modern Dutch Development." *Comparative Studies in Society and History* 36, no. 2 (1994): 319–55.

Armstrong, James, and Nigel Worden. "The Slaves, 1652–1834." In Elphick and Giliomee, *Shaping of South African Society*, 109–83.

Barrow, John. *Travels into the Interior of Southern Africa.* Vols. 1 and 2. 2nd ed. London: T. Cadell and W. Davies, 1806.

Bayly, C. A. *The Birth of the Modern World.* Malden, MA: Blackwell Publishing, 2004.

Brubaker, Rogers, and Frederick Cooper. "Beyond 'Identity.'" *Theory and Society* 29 (2000): 1–47.

Dooling, Wayne. "'The Good Opinion of Others': Law, Slavery and Community in the Cape Colony, c. 1760–1830." In *Breaking the Chains: Slavery and Its Legacy in the Nineteenth-Century Cape Colony*, edited by Nigel Worden and Clifton Crais, 25–55. Johannesburg: University of the Witwatersrand Press, 1994.

———. *Slavery, Emancipation and Colonial Rule in South Africa.* Scottsville: University of KwaZulu Natal Press, 2007.

Elphick, Richard, and Hermann Giliomee. "The Origins and Entrenchment of European Domination at the Cape, 1652–c. 1840." In Elphick and Giliomee, *Shaping of South African Society*, 521–26.

———, eds. *The Shaping of South African Society, 1652–1840.* 2nd ed. Cape Town: Maskew, Miller and Longman, 1989.

Elphick, Richard, and V. C. Malherbe. "The Khoisan to 1828." In Elphick and Giliomee, *Shaping of South African Society*, 3–65.

Freund, William. "The Cape under the Transitional Governments, 1795–1814." In Elphick and Giliomee, *Shaping of South African Society*, 324–57.

Giliomee, Hermann. *The Afrikaners: Biography of a People.* Charlottesville: University of Virginia Press, 2003.

Groenewald, Gerald. "Kinship, Entrepreneurship and Social Capital: Alcohol *Pachters* and the Making of a Free-Burgher Society in Cape Town, 1652–1795." PhD diss., University of Cape Town, 2009.

Guelke, Leonard. "Freehold Farmers and Frontier Settlers, 1657–1780." In Elphick and Giliomee, *Shaping of South African Society*, 66–108.

Israel, J. *The Dutch Republic: Its Rise, Greatness and Fall, 1477–1806.* Oxford: Clarendon Press, 1995.

Johnson, David. *Imagining the Cape Colony: History, Literature and the South African Nation.* Claremont: UCT Press, 2012.

Keegan, Timothy. *Colonial South Africa and the Origins of the Racial Order.* Cape Town: David Philip, 1996.

Legassick, Martin. "The Northern Frontier to c. 1840: The Rise and Decline of the Griqua People." In Elphick and Giliomee, *Shaping of South African Society*, 358–420.

Linebaugh, Peter, and Marcus Rediker. *The Many-Headed Hydra: Sailors, Slaves, Commoners, and the Hidden History of the Revolutionary Atlantic.* Boston: Beacon Press, 2000.

Lucassen, Jan. "A Multinational and Its Labor Force: The Dutch East India Company, 1595–1795." *International Labor and Working-Class History* 66 (2004): 12–39.

Mamdani, Mahmood. *Citizen and Subject: Contemporary Africa and the Legacy of Late Colonialism.* Princeton: Princeton University Press, 1996.

Marks, Shula. "Khoisan Resistance to the Dutch in the Seventeenth and Eighteenth Centuries." *Journal of African History* 13, no. 1 (1972): 55–80.

McVay, P. A. "'I Am the Devil's Own': Class and Identity in the Seventeenth Century Dutch East Indies." PhD diss., University of Illinois, 1995.

Mentzel, O. F. *Geographical and Topographical Description of the Cape of Good Hope.* Part 3, vol. 2 of the German edition. Translated by G. V. Marias and J. Hoge. Cape Town: Van Riebeeck Society, 1944.

Mitchell, Laura. *Belongings: Property and Identity in Colonial South Africa, an Exploration of Frontiers, 1725–c. 1830.* New York: Columbia University Press, 2009.

Newton-King, Susan. "Part I: The Rebellion of the Khoesan." In Newton-King and Malherbe, *Khoikhoi Rebellion in the Eastern Cape (1977–1803)*, 12–65.

Newton-King, Susan, and V. C. Malherbe. *The Khoikhoi Rebellion in the Eastern Cape (1977–1803).* Cape Town: Centre for African Studies, UCT, 1981.

Penn, Nigel. *Rogues, Rebels and Runaways: Eighteenth-Century Cape Characters.* Cape Town: David Philip Publishers, 2003.

Prak, Maarten. "Burghers into Citizens: Urban and National Citizenship in the Netherlands during the Revolutionary Era (c. 1800)." *Theory and Society* 26, no. 4 (1997): 403–20.

Sapire, Hilary. "African Loyalism and Its Discontents: The Royal Tour of South Africa, 1794." *Historical Journal* 54, no. 1 (2011): 215–40.

Shell, Robert. *Children of Bondage: A Social History of the Slave Society at the Cape of Good Hope, 1652–1838.* Johannesburg: University of the Witwatersrand Press, 2001.

Shutte, Gerrit. "Company and Colonists at the Cape, 1652–1795." In Elphick and Giliomee, *Shaping of South African Society*, 284–323.

Sparrman, A. *A Voyage to the Cape of Good Hope, towards the Antarctic Polar Circle, around the World and to the Country of the Hottentots and the Caffers from the Year 1772–1776.* Vols. 1 and 2. Edited by V. S. Forbes and translated by J. Rudner and I. Rudner. Reprint Series. Cape Town: Van Riebeeck Society, 2007.

Theal, G. M., ed. *Records of the Cape Colony.* Vols. 1–7, 1793–1811. Manuscript Documents in the Public Record Office, London, printed for the Government of the Cape Colony, 1897–99.

Thunberg, P. *Travels at the Cape of Good Hope, 1771–1775*. Edited by V. S. Forbes and revised translation by J. Rudner and I. Rudner. Cape Town: Van Riebeeck Society, 1986.

Trotter, Henry. "Sailors as Scribes: Travel Discourse and the (Con)textualisation of the Khoisan at the Cape of Good Hope, 1649–90." *Journal of African Travel Writing*, nos. 8 and 9 (2001): 30–44.

Ulrich, Nicole. "Counter Power and Colonial Rule in the Eighteenth-Century Cape of Good Hope: Belongings and Protest of the Labouring Poor." PhD diss., University of the Witwatersrand, 2011.

———. "Popular Community in 18th-Century Southern Africa: Family, Fellowship, Alternative Networks, and Mutual Aid at the Cape of Good Hope, 1652–1795." *Journal of Southern African History* 40, no. 6 (2014): 1139–57.

———. "Time, Space and the Political Economy of Merchant Colonialism in the Cape of Good Hope and VOC World." *South African Historical Journal* 63, no. 3 (2010): 571–88.

Van Gelder, Roelof. *Naporra's Omveg: Het Leven van een VOC-Matroos (1731–1793)*. Amsterdam: Atlas, 2003.

Viljoen, Russel. "Revelation of a Revolution": The Prophecies of Jan Parel, Alias Onse Liewe Heer." *Kronos* 21 (1994): 3–15.

Ward, Kerry. "'The Bounds of Bondage': Forced Migration from Batavia to the Cape of Good Hope during the Dutch East India Company Era, c. 1652–1795." PhD diss., University of Michigan, 2002.

———. *Networks of Empire: Forced Migration in the Dutch East India Company*. Cambridge: Cambridge University Press, 2009.

Webster, Edward, ed. *The Unresolved National Question in Left Thinking*. Johannesburg: University of the Witwatersrand Press. Forthcoming.

Wilder, Gary. *Freedom Time: Negritude, Decolonization, and the Future of the World*. Durham, NC: Duke University Press, 2015.

Worden, Nigel. "Artisan Conflicts in a Colonial Context: The Cape Town Blacksmith Strike of 1752." *Labor History* 46, no. 2 (2005): 155–84.

———. *Slavery in Dutch South Africa*. Cambridge: Cambridge University Press, 1985.

Worden, Nigel, and Gerald Groenewald, eds. *Trials of Slavery: Selected Documents Concerning Slaves from the Criminal Records of the Council of Justice at the Cape of Good Hope, 1705–1794*. Cape Town: Van Riebeeck Society, 2005.

Worden, Nigel, Elizabeth van Heyningen, and Vivian Bickford-Smith. *Cape Town: The Making of a City, an Illustrated History*. Cape Town: David Philips, 2004.

THREE

"We Are Oppressed and Our Only Way Is to Write to Higher Authority"

The Politics of Claim and Complaint in the
Peripheries of Condominium Sudan

CHERRY LEONARDI AND CHRIS VAUGHAN

IN LATE 1954, AS SUDAN MOVED RAPIDLY TOWARD SELF-GOVERNMENT, a letter was sent to one of the members of the new national legislative assembly, Benjamin Lwoki, by one or some of his constituents. Signed "Yei citizens" and immediately beneath this "Chief Modi Baraba," the letter complained about the behavior of northern Sudanese merchants and officials "bullying us here," about the quality of the Yei hospital and doctor, and about the transfer of a southern Sudanese official away from Yei. The letter exhorted Lwoki to "stand firm": "Our Parliament Representative and others please note that we the Yei citizens are now grieved badly and are very anxious to put our complaints forward to you in order that you have to raise them up before the house of representatives." The letter was headed with the political constituency number (62), and was copied to "Juba citizens" as well as to the Equatoria Province governor.[1]

Precisely who actually wrote the letter is not clear, but the two-line appellation "Yei citizens Chief Modi Baraba" is intriguing. Was Chief Modi, the most senior chief in Yei District (or his scribe), claiming to be writing on behalf of the people of his chiefdom? Or were other people using the name of the chief to define their political community or to add authority to their complaints? Did "Yei citizens" refer to the townspeople of Yei or to the wider citizenry of Yei District or of the political constituency? Who was included in this category?

The letter is revealing of the new political language of the late colonial period, when the Condominium government was promoting ideas and discourses of representative government and national citizenship. These ideas were to be realized first through mechanisms of local government, which may help to explain why "Yei"—as district headquarters—had become a salient political unit. In this chapter, however, we explore the deeper context behind the "local citizenship" that was being promoted by the Condominium government in the 1940s and 1950s, and we examine the ways in which it was asserted or debated by a range of people in southern and western Sudan. We argue that the local state was indeed the primary arena in which discourses and practices of citizenship emerged but that these ideas and practices also helped to produce a translocal idea of the state, to which people increasingly appealed in the course of local struggles and politics. The letter from the Yei citizens demonstrates that "local" and "national" citizenship were interactive fields rather than discrete spheres.

We also suggest in this chapter that the salience of such ideas of citizenship in the late colonial period did not appear out of a vacuum and was not solely the product of a new state-led agenda. If citizenship was a language and imaginary taken up with vigor from below in the final years of colonial rule, this was because a central aspect of this imaginary had been well established in the preceding decades: the notion of an abstracted, translocal state law that governed rulers as well as subjects. So, even when the state was trying to repress any ideas of national citizenship in the earlier years of "Indirect Rule," the workings of local politics produced demands from below that a universal state law should guarantee individual and collective rights. However, such claims were sometimes highly instrumentalized and coexisted with various other very different kinds of political claims. The extent to which the contentious politics of Indirect Rule was productive of citizenship is therefore a difficult question to answer.

For James Tully, such assertion of political rights would be a recognizable variety of "diverse citizenship"—in which groups formally denied rights by distant, unaccountable structures of power nonetheless find avenues to claim rights as members of various kinds of political community (perhaps at a very local level), often in the face of opposition from those larger structures.[2] Nonetheless, as Frederick Cooper reminds us in the postscript to this book, such a flexible approach to defining citizenship risks obscuring the particular analytical value of the term. For Cooper, citizenship posits "a collective body of equivalent citizens who have a common relationship to the state"—and the broad-based horizontal claim of equivalence is precisely what gives citizenship its particular potential and significance as a means of limiting the impositions of the state. This is quite a different form of political community and conception of rights—based on horizontal relationships of equivalence—from that created by patrimonial systems defined by vertical relationships of inequality.[3] In the case studies under examination here, the imaginary of a broad-based community of equivalent citizens definitely had traction for those making claims on the state in the period of later colonial rule (examined in the final part of this chapter), as evidenced in the explicit communication mentioned above between "Yei citizens" and "Juba citizens" in 1954. During the preceding years of Indirect Rule in the 1920s and 1930s, such an imaginary is harder to detect. Nonetheless, even in these earlier years, complaints that drew attention to breaches of the law by individuals in authority and claims made to individual or collective rights that were guaranteed by law *did* implicitly draw on an idea of equivalency—that all were subject to the rule of the law, both elites and ordinary people, and that the law guaranteed rights even as it subjected people to power. To this extent, the law did mediate an embryonic sense of citizenship, even if this was not yet as fully articulated, imagined, or indeed effective in limiting state power as would sometimes be the case in the years leading up to independence.

Our emphasis on an active local politics of citizenship in the colonial era is at odds with the prevailing scholarly emphasis on the political exclusion and denied rights of colonial subjects in such peripheral regions as southern and western Sudan. The dominant scholarly model of Sudan's political geography suggests a long-established divide in terms of political and social rights between the hyperdominant riverine core of the state and multiple peripheries that have been neglected in developmental terms and excluded from political influence. The argument has been made that this dysfunctional core-periphery relationship was not necessarily created by colonial rule but was certainly reinforced by it, and that it lay at the roots of Sudan's postcolonial civil wars.[4] These wars might themselves be understood in part as a series of struggles for full citizenship, rights, and entitlements by various peripheral populations.

The core-periphery model also fits rather well with Mahmood Mamdani's claims about the "bifurcated" character of the colonial state.[5] Condominium Sudan would appear to epitomize his depiction of a colonially constructed customary order of rural communities subjected to their chiefs and insulated from urban concepts of civil rights: from the 1920s, government policy famously sought to create rural "compartments," bounded ethnic units of population, protected from the "septic germs" of urban political activism.[6] But the quarantine was never effective: in many areas the colonial government continually struggled to keep people out of the towns and to handle the volume of complaints, appeals, and petitions with which district officials were presented. Indeed, the very category "Yei citizens" reveals the political salience of colonial towns and administrative units (rather than necessarily tribal units) as the focus of struggles over rights and relations with the state. The connection of this category to a chief demonstrates the blurring of Mamdani's dichotomies of urban and rural, rights and custom, civil society and community, citizenship and subjecthood. Despite colonial imaginaries of rural chiefship, chiefs in areas like Yei had always been closely connected to the small towns, their authority traversing any urban-rural divide.[7]

Peripheral regions may have indeed been neglected and subordinated; but our evidence that local populations in the peripheries of Sudan persistently engaged with state power and tried to turn it to their advantage, or to limit its excesses, reminds us that people from even the most marginalized regions were making claims on the state and seeking the recognition of their rights in a way that adds complexity to the core-periphery model. And the languages that people used in these endeavors also demonstrate the unbounded character of political imagination in the apparently remote peripheries of Condominium Sudan. Mamdani describes two entirely distinct languages of authority: "Urban power spoke the language of civil society and civil rights, rural power of community and culture."[8] But in late colonial southern and western Sudan, multiple registers of political language were being spoken simultaneously or alternately, as people sought to assert both collective and individual rights, to make claims on an often personalized imaginary of the state, and to regulate the behavior of state agents and intermediaries through the law. The practice of "complaining," or putting "complaints forward" as this letter did in 1954, had become a well-established means of communicating with the state. However limited the efficacy of such complaint, the practice demonstrates an expectation that the state should listen to its subjects and address their grievances—and of course sometimes it did. Claims on the state could be asserted on the basis of patrimonial relationships or rights of citizenship—often simultaneously, in ways that produced tensions for colonial officials and exposed some of the contradictions of colonial rule.

The first part of this chapter looks at the interwar heyday of indirect rule in Sudan, to trace how these multiple languages emerged and were deployed to demand political recognition and/or legal rights. We then focus on the shift in Condominium policy to a modernizing vision of local government and the largely conservative way it was implemented in the south and west from the late 1930s onwards. Finally, we look at how this limited change nevertheless generated new political and legal languages, and we explore examples of claim making, petitioning, complaint, and appeal, which increasingly took a written form in this later period. The rhetoric of rights and citizenship was intertwined with older discourses of genealogy, personalized and paternalist rule, and patrimonial obligation, demonstrating that these political languages were never mutually exclusive or confined to discrete spheres but rather inhabited what Tully terms a broader "field of citizenship."[9]

Becoming *Mazalim:* Contesting Oppression under Indirect Rule

In the 1920s, the Condominium government moved to consolidate its alliances with local leaders in the southern and western provinces, following the conquest of the Darfur sultanate and the military defeat of local uprisings or resistance elsewhere. Pax Britannica was to be enforced through the "native administration," and the judicial and coercive power of chiefs was deliberately constructed or strengthened. Local elites became adept at deploying the language of genealogy, history, and ethnicity to gain recognition from and make claims upon the state. But the colonial government's receptiveness to such discourse also opened up space for complaints and disputes over chiefship itself, as well as for the articulation of the rights and duties of rulers and subjects within the native administration units. At the same time, though, many of the chiefs' subjects seized every opportunity to appeal beyond the confines of these units to state law and justice and to assert individual as well as communal rights.

In both Darfur and the southern provinces, colonial officials encountered multiple forms of authority that they could not easily order into the neat "tribal" units envisaged in native administration policy. In Darfur, various kinds of chiefship had already been institutionalized under the Fur Sultanate and/or Turco-Egyptian and Mahdist governments in the nineteenth century, sometimes with administrative responsibilities and jurisdictions defined quite clearly by the state. But particularly in the pastoralist peripheries of the sultanate, British colonial rule brought an unprecedented concentration and centralization of authority in the hands of chiefs.[10] In the southern provinces, among mainly stateless societies, chiefship was a new form of authority and a new unit of jurisdiction: the native administration geography often mapped awkwardly onto existing smaller political communities and the wider influence of precolonial spiritual authorities like rain chiefs, spear-masters, and prophets.[11] "Tribes" were not political or territorial entities, as colonial officials quickly realized, and chiefs were appointed not as heads of tribes but as heads of smaller (sometimes multiethnic) territorial units. Many of the early colonial chiefs in southern Sudan were junior sons or dependents of more powerful families or were interpreters or soldiers in the colonial army; there is evidence that the position was initially seen as dangerous or demeaning. But as chiefs became more powerful and their position more lucrative, disputes over chiefly positions and complaints about chiefly abuses increasingly reached the attention of government.[12] And while the history of chiefship was quite different between Darfur and the south, it is strikingly clear that complaints against chiefs in both regions employed a similar combination of genealogical argument and criticism of chiefly misrule, responding to an equally similar opportunity structure created by a common (and contradictory) colonial ideology.

It is important, if obvious, to note that in this period people did not use the language of national citizenship to make their claims on government. They did not directly assert membership in a broad-based horizontal collective of equivalent citizens—rather, they mobilized on the basis of their membership in local political communities. These were communities explicitly and inherently defined by inequality, even if that inequality was itself the subject of debate and mechanisms of accountability. Often those who directed protest to government were able to do so because of their elite standing in these communities and did not necessarily make their claims explicitly on the grounds of solidarity with a wider ethnic citizenry, let alone any broader definition of political community. Nonetheless, they addressed their complaints to a state that was understood to govern these various communities and was imagined to have the obligation to hear and respond to the complaints of the people. Claims made to the state on this basis were not always successful—but they did consistently, implicitly or explicitly, assert *rights:* especially the rights of peoples to be governed by chiefs who behaved in accordance with local moralities of rule and who came from and therefore represented the local community. Definitions of such communities were therefore also at the heart of these struggles, which often rhetorically centered on dissatisfaction with a chief imposed by the government on a people not his own. This claim making was precisely the stuff of active citizenship politics—defining political communities and holding leaders to account—and while many claims remained directed to local state officials, a willingness to engage officials at higher levels in the hierarchy demonstrated that a political relationship with rulers beyond the local was also being imaginatively constructed. In making these claims, people also drew the attention of officials to ways in which chiefs contravened the law of the state, implicitly asserting that the law should apply to those who ruled as well as those who were governed.[13] Colonial and local discourses of probity and proper rule thus interacted in the course of contentious chieftaincy politics, and subjects claimed the right to be heard by their rulers as members of rights-bearing communities governed by the state.

Mamdani suggests that the power of chiefs was "unrestrained" by any law, since chiefs themselves determined the customary law that prevailed in rural areas.[14] Certainly in the 1920s, highly authoritarian versions of "customary law" were being recorded by some southern district commissioners (DCs) seeking to enforce the obedience of subjects to their chiefs.[15] The judicial and police power of chiefs that the colonial government sanctioned was unprecedented in both Darfur and the south. Indeed, by the 1930s, greater administrative introspection and ethnographic enquiry were generating concern among officials in the southern provinces that colonial policy had invented and entrenched chiefly despotism. Administrators became more open in their recognition that many chiefs had been appointed by government without any of the traditional authority or genealogical claim on which the native administration was supposedly based.[16] In fact, "custom" did not trump administrative expediency; administrators tended to stick to their choice of chiefs and policies of amalgamating smaller units into larger chiefdoms, even when this clearly had no basis in history or tradition. Chiefs were more likely to be removed from their position for contravening colonial laws (particularly hunting regulations and the remittance of taxes and court income) or for failing to meet administrative requirements for taxation and labor.

But the fact that chiefs *were* on occasion removed and replaced nevertheless demonstrated to their subjects the potential efficacy of complaining against chiefs or reporting their misdemeanors to government. Complaints and disputes over chiefship often came to the attention of colonial officials because they were orchestrated by rival claimants among local elites, who knew enough of the government to articulate their grievances most effectively. Such disputes were often factional, lineage based, or even fraternal, and complainants thus exploited the colonial concern with heredity and descent. In southern Darfur, complainants in the 1920s suggested that a Ta'aisha *nazir* (paramount chief), Zubayr Sam, "was not a Ta'aishi but half a Salami, a mule they called him in their fury."[17] A mixed family heritage here left the chief vulnerable to claims of ethnic inauthenticity, claims that also served to reassert the importance of local political community and the expectation that those in authority belonged to that community. Files on chiefs from both the south and Darfur contain detailed family trees to illustrate and explain conflicts among rival claimants and families, and the quest for the "rightful" chief was a perennial problem for officials. But in practice, administrators were often prepared to live with the knowledge that many of their most useful and cooperative chiefs were by no means "rightful" in hereditary terms. Genealogical arguments were therefore most effective when combined with complaints about chiefly misrule or illegal behavior, and this ensured that elite struggles over chiefship also opened up the potential for broader negotiations of subject rights and state law.

Chiefs of course sought to prevent complaints against them from reaching government ears. One DC in southern Darfur, Dudley Lampen, was particularly keen to get around chiefly gatekeepers to communicate with the *nas,* or ordinary people, a desire exploited by the subjects of Zubayr Sam: "Zubayr took care to lodge me in his house where I should not hear much of his extortions and bullyings, but the Taaisha were not to be denied and lay in wait for me on my strolls out. . . . He (Zubayr) was smooth-tongued and talked much to impress me, but his administration was really too corrupt to stand."[18] Some time after Lampen had heard these initial complaints, Zubayr came to

Kubbe, the subdistrict headquarters, where Lampen found him "shaking in fright"; Lampen noted, "[W]hen I told him to precede me back to his *dar* (land/territory) he said he would be killed if he went back, so I took him with me." Upon return to Dar Ta'aisha, Lampen's attention was occupied by a very successfully organized public protest against the nazir's rule: "A large crowd had gathered in the Nazir's village to listen with obvious sympathy to the complaints of a few more vocal Ta'aishi. The complaints proceeded on two lines: definite complaints of criminal action, he had robbed persons taken into quarantine against relapsing fever, he had underlisted his tribe but collected a surplus on a private listing, his administration of justice was determined by bribery. Apart from these open complaints came a number of prominent men to see me secretly and protest against his selfish leadership of the tribe."[19]

It is striking that in the public arena, complaints were articulated largely in the language of the law and state regulation. Such language was perhaps rather instrumentalized: the allegations of bribery that speakers made in Lampen's presence would likely have had little resonance among the local community. In neighboring Kordofan, Ian Cunnison noted of the Baqqara Humr that bribery incurred no shame within Humr society but allegations of bribery were frequently made against leaders to get government attention.[20] This could be a highly effective strategy: when officials had their attention drawn to particular wrongdoings that obviously contravened colonial legal norms, it was difficult for them to simply do nothing. Such pressure was heightened in the example here by the public nature of the hearing: Lampen sat for a week listening to complaints in Zubayr Sam's village, where "rows upon rows of interested spectators watched the *meglis* [council] from neighbouring trees, drawing near and having to be expelled."[21] Instrumentalized or not, the use of this language implied that people had the right to expect government to regulate the illegal misbehaviors of their chiefs and in doing so simultaneously address grievances that were perhaps more deeply felt by local people but also more difficult or dangerous to communicate to officials. This was an implicit assertion of rights shared by all those governed by the state and its laws (even as the apparatus of native courts created a landscape of great variation in local legal cultures). Yet while the public discussion focused on law and corruption, certain elite men obviously had the confidence to approach Lampen privately to express their grievances in what seems to have been a rather different idiom of good government (frustratingly underreported here), to which Lampen was also receptive in his quest to access popular opinion. Zubayr was subsequently dismissed.

A similar example of a successful complaint, voiced in multiple idioms, comes from Juba District in southern Sudan. The long-serving DC of Juba, Captain Cooke, had intervened in several chiefdoms in the 1930s to appoint his favored candidates as chiefs, regardless of their hereditary claim. In 1937, however, he proved unusually receptive to complaints against the chief of Gondokoro, Tongun Modi, for taking livestock and beating people, on the grounds that "his father Modi Shoka had no claim to the chiefship."

> I think Tongun Modi tried to carry out the wishes of Government but his people refused to obey him on many occasions because of his oppressiveness.... A complaint was made to me and I decided that a meeting should be held at Ilibari, and that it should be attended by all the headmen, elders and any who had complaints.... It was very orderly and all who spoke did so with restraint and fairness. There were complaints as to Tongun Modi's taking chickens and one or two cows—Beating two others without a proper trial, making another man sit in the sun with a heavy chain around his neck. Even allowing for certain exaggerations I am sure these complaints were based on a certain amount of fact and all, both elders and young men, appeared definitely to wish for the removal of Tongun Modi....
>
> Tongun having made himself unpopular—his people complained and stated quite correctly that he should not really be chief, but that Lako Bureng is the rightful heir according to Bari custom.

Cooke was candid in spelling out the particular combination of factors that led him to remove Tongun. Had Tongun proved as good a chief as his father, his lack of hereditary claim might have been ignored; conversely, a chief with a hereditary right to the chiefship might be tolerated even if tyrannical: "[T]hough the people may accept certain things from the man who is their rightful chief, they would not necessarily do so from one who has no claim." Cooke went on to make clear the clinching factor: "Even so one might have been prepared to keep him as Chief after taking disciplinary action if he had proved satisfactory on Government grounds, but he has not done so."[22]

In many other cases, of course, complainants failed to dislodge chiefs who were liked by the DC and gained a good reputation with government. The nazir of the Habbania in southern Darfur, El Ghaali Taj el Din, was described by one British official as "a most outrageous *zalim* [oppressor]," yet he remained in his role for fifteen years, despite persistent and forceful protest.[23] A large part of El Ghaali's success lay in forming good relations with (male) officials: immediately before he gained office; reports noted that he was "honest, loyal, hospitable and above all a Man."[24] By the 1940s El Ghaali was under increasing pressure from accusations of illegal dues collection and bribe taking, but the district and provincial staff remained supportive of him as nazir. The DC of southern Darfur put it most clearly: "As long as we support him we are making Native Administration a synonym for maladministration. But there is no denying the fact that his age and personality have given him much prestige within his tribe and he has taken care that no one else will have any at all."[25]

Custom and genealogy was thus only one of the languages in which complaints against chiefs were articulated to government, and it was not necessarily the clinching factor in administrative decisions; chiefs' ability to meet government demands and build a positive reputation among colonial officials was more crucial. While this shows that chiefs were, of course, much more vulnerable to the whims of the state than they were to their own subjects, the pragmatic emphasis on the effectiveness of chiefly authority also created an opportunity for local populations. By refusing to obey chiefs' orders and demands, their people could precipitate the kind of inquiries detailed above, which in turn opened an arena for the expression of wider grievance.

The discourse of "oppression" by chiefs was particularly prominent in such arenas, as the accounts of Chief Tongun and Nazir El Ghaali show. The Arabic term *zulm/mazlum* (oppression/oppressed) was widely used, particularly in Darfur, to complain against chiefly tyranny. It evoked deeper historical ideas about the rights and duties of rulers and their subjects.[26] In the case of Darfur, there was considerable precedent for using this discourse: under the sultanate, subjects had at times successfully appealed to the authority of the sultan against their chiefs. In a dramatic example of this, Sultan Umar Lel in the 1730s "received complaints of *zulm* [oppression against thirty leading chiefs; he had fifteen executed by the men's gate and fifteen by the women's gate of the *fashir* [royal residence]."[27] *Zulm* was endemic in sultanic governance—royal charters addressed chiefs and officials as "all those oppressive [officials] who are overbearing with the rights of the Muslims."[28] But equally people expected their rulers to act against the excesses of their local representatives.

British colonial officials in the twentieth century—and some English-speaking Sudanese—frequently used these Arabic terms in otherwise English-language texts, as well as using the English term *oppression*. Justin Willis argues that the use of other such Arabic terms by Condominium officials hints at the untranslatability of the novel governance by colonial chiefs into either the vernacular or the British languages of authority and morality.[29] Yet this very uncertainty gave room for the negotiation of what *zulm* (or its English translation) meant in the colonial context. And the invocation of the Arabic term by colonial officials implied a degree of receptivity to the culture and practice of complaint from below. *Zulm* might thus be defined as a criticism of governance that was recognized by the government (even if not necessarily acted upon). Most importantly, we might argue that the act of complaining and petitioning transformed people from *nas* ("those without authority of any sort—the 'subjects,' in the full sense in which Mahmood Mamdani uses the word"[30]) into *al-Mazlumiin* (the oppressed) in the colonial record and that the category of *Mazlumiin* therefore did not connote the passive status of subjection to oppression so much as the active contestation of this oppression and, indeed, the assertion of a form of political community based on a shared experience of chiefly wrongdoing. Paradoxically, then, those who asserted that they were *mazlum* were in fact the most active participants in the negotiation of political authority: in both precolonial Darfur and colonial Sudan they claimed the right as oppressed subjects to have their complaints heard by their rulers.

The *Mazlumiin* appropriated the colonial language of law and bureaucratic regulation to define and highlight "oppressive" behavior by chiefs. It is striking that the complaints against Chief Tongun recorded by Cooke stressed his "illegal actions" and his infliction of beatings and fines *without proper trial*, just as the complaints against Nazir Zubayr had highlighted his "criminal actions." The law was beginning to be used to regulate the behavior of chiefs rather than simply to enforce their power. And such appeals implied membership in a political community defined by that law, both subject to its control and bearing rights guaranteed by it. In 1938 a man appealed to a higher chiefs' "B court," because his own chief had sentenced him to more lashes than the "A court" warrant allowed. Many chiefs and policemen were prosecuted in the B courts for unfair or illegal activities.[31] People used the appeal hierarchy to access the state itself, as an elder in Rumbek recalled in 2006: "The village chiefs were working with the whites. If the chief did not give you your right, you went to the white man in charge of the court until you got your right, even though the village chief had denied it."[32]

From the earliest years of colonial rule, the language of law and individual rights had been deployed to petition colonial officials, often by individual subjects coming in person to the towns and government offices or directly approaching officials on trek. Even before the 1920s, officials in Rumbek in southern Sudan reported two to three thousand complaints a year being brought directly to the district headquarters to be heard by the British inspector or a *mamur* (junior official).[33] In Darfur, DC Lampen described how numerous petitioners would come to see him in the afternoons, to discuss matters that "could not be reached over the hustle and bustle of the office, but only after an introduction of several cups of syrupy tea." Indeed so many of these complainants came outside the hours of business that Lampen had to "build a rest-house to lodge them at the side of [his] compound and even hire an ex-slave girl to cook for them."[34] Officials on trek in the south were also constantly pestered by litigants, "each bent on the direct approach to the DC as the quickest means of getting what he thought was justice."[35] One DC complained of having court papers waved in his face throughout the day and even at night: "I have even had them brought to me when in bed in a rest house on the road."[36] People clearly imagined that by virtue of being ruled they possessed rights as individuals as well as communities: this was the implicit and unwritten bargain struck with government, an unwritten bargain that some also imagined to be guaranteed by the written law.

One paramount chief in southern Darfur similarly complained of the incessant demands of litigants and complainants,[37] and the chiefs' courts too became important arenas for the assertion of individual or collective rights. Chiefs also clearly sought to deter appeals and to control the recording and reporting of court cases. But people nevertheless found ways to appeal to higher authorities, whether in writing or in person or in collective protest. In doing so, they sought to establish and prevail upon personal relations with colonial officials. But they also expressed their claims and grievances in languages that were clearly known to be most efficacious in communicating with "government," the *hakuma*, more broadly, and were in part appropriated from the public discourse of colonial officials. In making their complaints, individual subjects were both recognizing the authority of the state and seeking its recognition of their rights. One official noted this quest for recognition among protesters in Dar Habbania: "[T]he individual Habbani pushing himself forward simply to be known to Government."[38] In the late colonial period, the government would promote ideas of individual rights and relations with government through new political languages of citizenship and institutions of political representation. But appeals to the law to assert such rights and relations had already been occurring within the native administration units of the interwar years and would continue to find expression in the practices of complaint against oppression and making claims on the state.

Local Government, Local Citizenship

By the late 1930s, the Condominium government was shifting away from the emphasis of native administration policies on tradition toward the modernizing, developmental rhetoric of local government reforms, with new emphasis on ideas of representation and citizenship. The institutions and practices of late colonial government in Sudan created new opportunities, particularly for the literate. But there was also considerable continuity in the composition and role of local elites, many of whom swiftly learned to speak the new language of local government and claimed to represent "their" people in order to maintain their monopoly on relations and communication with government. The Condominium government claimed to be promoting new kinds of transethnic and translocal political community, but in fact local government was intended as a means of containing politics in local arenas and limiting the potency of nationalism.[39]

The localized citizenship envisaged by the government was articulated at a "study camp" for northern Sudanese officials and intelligentsia in 1952: "Effective Local Government can in fact assert the rights of the Citizen in some ways better than he can assert them himself." The theme of the study camp was "The state versus the citizen: the problem of freedom in the modern state"; and the report also suggested that local government could "soften the impact on any individual of an all-powerful, yet remote and perhaps unsympathetic Central Authority."[40] Perhaps reflecting the perennial tension between provincial officials and the central government or recognizing the narrow composition of the Sudanese elites assuming control of the state by this time, the political elites of the late Condominium thus advocated local government as an arena in which the rights and freedoms of citizens could be protected from state tyranny.

The new local councils established in the 1940s were therefore treated as arenas in which to educate Sudanese in proper civic behavior and representative government. Local citizenship was in effect the latest disciplinary project of the state, even as it was intended to maintain (or create) the liberties of local peoples, and once again chiefs were at the forefront of this project, just as they had been the targets of educational and cash-cropping initiatives. The idea seemed to be that if chiefs could be made to perform as good citizens then "their" people would naturally enough follow their example. In the southern provinces, district officials simply turned the existing "B court" panels of chiefs into "councils," having long treated the B courts as arenas of (limited) consultation and discussion.[41] In Darfur, new "combined courts" were established for the Baggara and Zaghawa chiefs, respectively, to encourage more horizontal connections between chiefs. Disputes over chiefships were increasingly handed over to other chiefs to settle, and chiefs were prosecuted for misconduct by their peers.[42] Government officials thus sought to inculcate a sense of shared civic responsibility and statesmanship among chiefs.

In the late 1940s and early 1950s, formal rural and town councils were established, often largely composed of and elected by chiefs. At the same time, new province councils and a national legislative assembly were constituted; in the south, members were elected by the B court chiefs, and these councils and the legislative assembly included many (literate) chiefs again.[43] Chiefs were thus being turned into political representatives not just of their own chiefdoms but of district constituencies. Given that government education in Darfur had been targeted exclusively at the sons of chiefs, it is no surprise that chiefs and their families utterly dominated councils in Darfur. In the south, chiefs sometimes faced new competition from teachers and government employees: in an election for a new district education council in Juba, an ex-soldier, the only literate candidate, was elected rather than one of the three chiefs standing: "Literacy won, clan heads murmuring as they cast their votes 'because he reads,' for fear of reprisals from their chiefs."[44]

But chiefs succeeded in retaining a favored position in "representing" their people to the government. This was the context in which Chief Modi Baraba or his supporters wrote such a commanding letter to their representative in the national legislative assembly, the teacher Benjamin Lwoki. Modi was the most prominent Yei chief and had already exhorted Lwoki to "speak firmly" for his constituency in the legislative assembly when he was elected in 1948.[45] Chiefs could, it seemed, speak for those who had recently become defined as citizens, just as they had spoken for subjects in the preceding decades. One might argue, therefore, that the introduction of a discourse of citizenship had done little to displace existing political relationships and status. But the letter is also revealing of the broader ideas and expectations of the state that had emerged by the 1950s. It complained that the northern administrators in Yei were transferring the new southern mamur, or junior official, to Yambio: "[W]e should like him to work in Yei here for at least 2 years officially in order . . . to study his behaviour towards the people and watch how he carries his duty forward." This reflects both the desire to personalize government by getting to know individual officials, as chiefs always had, and the notion of administrators as public servants with a "duty" to citizens. Similarly the letter complained of bad conditions at Yei Hospital and the transfer away of a good doctor, complaints that had already been made to the Ministry of Health and the province medical inspector, indicating that the letter's author had a good knowledge of government institutions (the letter also made reference to the public service committee responsible for selecting district officials).[46] The strong sense of entitlement in the letter reflects a growing expectation that the state should provide services in return for taxes, an idea that a British missionary also reported was prevalent in nearby Moru District: "Fees for Outpatients (2 ½ d. a year) and Inpatients (2 ½ d a day) were introduced in June, and emptied the hospital, which is looked on as a Government one, which should therefore give free treatment. . . . They look on it as their right, since they pay taxes."[47]

The administrative and political reforms of the late colonial period contributed to heightening expectations of the state and provided a new language in which to make claims upon it in the name of "citizens," adding to existing repertoires of claim making and protest. But there was also considerable continuity in the way that people sought to contract with chiefs and government officials and to appeal to state justice as a resource in disputes and conflicts. In Darfur, some of the councils were reportedly seen by ordinary people as the latest addition to the native courts system, in which chiefs of a district sat together to decide on cases, not as fundamentally new administrative decision-making bodies. This was not an unreasonable view: the Northern Darfur District (NDD) Council was indeed the supreme court of appeal in the district, hearing cases from all the native courts and any petitions brought by the inhabitants of northern Darfur.[48] The DC in 1949 expressed concern at this: "[P]etitioners imagine the NDD council takes place in order that their cases may be heard and they cannot understand that the Council's primary task is to sit as a council to discuss affairs of the district." The council building at Kuttum was "often surrounded by a mob of vociferous mazalim [oppressed subjects]," and the DC foresaw that any future attempt to remove the judicial aspect of the council's role would cause problems.[49]

As this suggests, the longstanding discourse of oppression continued to be channeled into the assertion of rights in the courts and councils. But "vociferous" complainants were also finding new languages and methods for expressing grievances and claiming rights in the later colonial period.

"Petitions Are This Country's Chosen Music of Liberty": Appealing to the State

While the Condominium government promoted local government as a mechanism for safeguarding the rights of citizens from the dangers of an "all-powerful" central government, many citizens reversed this equation, appealing to central government in protest of local misrule or injustice. British officials and the northern Sudanese elite might argue that local government was the solution to "the problem of freedom in the modern state," but colonial subjects in southern and western Sudan also found their own means of addressing this problem, as the penultimate British governor of Darfur declared: "Petitions are this country's chosen music of liberty."[50] A range of colonial subjects spoke or wrote petitions and appeals to the state authorities, using the language of the law and the government's own regulatory orders to protest the behavior of chiefs or the decisions of courts and to make claims on the state. Petitions to central government were not a novel development of the late colonial period, nor was their language necessarily innovative. They continued to employ the multiple languages of colonial governance, speaking alternately or simultaneously of patrimonial obligation, personalized and paternalistic relations, genealogical and historical structure, and the force of state law. However, their authors did increasingly and explicitly also appeal to government on the grounds of their rights as citizens. Moreover, the chances of such petitions being acted upon by agents of central government were considerably greater in the politically uncertain years leading up to independence. As nationalist politics became more assertive, so government felt less able to deny the rights of those who demanded its intervention in local politics: conceding rights at a local level might be a means to preempt efforts by nationalists to link local political issues to broader conceptions of rights and freedoms. In a sense—and as with the local government reforms discussed above—granting local citizenship might stave off the advance of nationalist citizenship. The net result, however, was that the state and its agents were increasingly limited by the conceptions of political rights they themselves were promoting.

The most striking aspect of the practice of petitioning and appealing is the obvious awareness among colonial subjects of government hierarchies and central state authorities. Individuals and groups appealed to the highest authorities in Khartoum to complain against the decisions of provincial and district government officials or the local courts: this was true in the 1920s as well as the 1940s and '50s. Most of these petitions took a written form, though determining exactly who wrote them is difficult: prisoners, for example, must have had access to a prison clerk to produce their appeals, which helps to explain why they tended to follow standard stylistic tropes. Some Darfuri elites who felt poorly treated by the provincial administration traveled all the way to the capital: some of these stayed with Sayyed Abd el-Rahman al-Mahdi, the Mahdist leader and politician, in Omdurman while they wrote out formal petitions to the Sudan government protesting against their treatment. Petitions were made out to the director of intelligence or "the secretary for Native Affairs" (this ended up in the civil secretary's hands).[51] In northern Darfur, during the 1940s, the Awlad Deggain lineage of the Zaghawa people simultaneously petitioned the Northern Darfur District Council, the governor of Darfur, the civil secretary, and Sayyed Abd al-Rahman al-Mahdi in protest against the behavior of their chief, *Melik* Mohammedein.[52]

Most of these petitions did not achieve their aims: subjects often asserted rights that government refused to recognize, reminding us of the limits to the politics of citizenship being discussed here. Sending petitioners "around the block" to different levels of government was a useful way of exhausting their demands, as officials explicitly stated in correspondence.[53] The state could thus absorb such protest in a manner that did no harm to its capacity for rule. However, petitioners were sometimes remarkably persistent in their efforts, perhaps because of the "uncertainty which prevail[ed] as to the government's reception" of these petitions.[54] Especially after 1945, claims to rights expressed in petitions became more likely to be acknowledged by the state because central government was increasingly wary of the potential for local chieftaincy politics to become entwined with the wider ambitions of nationalist politicians. In the instance of the Awlad Deggain protest, by appealing to the authority of Sayyed Abd al-Rahman (SAR), alongside the authority of government, the Deggain had raised the possibility that their local demands might become entwined with the national political agenda of SAR, exactly the outcome feared by colonial government. The civil secretary in Khartoum therefore pressured the provincial administration to make concessions to their demands.[55] More generally, colonial officials believed that growing chieftaincy protests in 1950s Darfur were indeed encouraged by wider moves toward self-government and independence in Sudanese national politics. In this context, petitions that appealed to the law as a means of protecting collective or individual rights were more difficult to dismiss. Increasingly, practices among chiefs that would previously have been tolerated as part of the routine culture of local governance were viewed—by government officials as well as petitioners—as contravening an idea of the law that set limits to the power of those in authority. In the case of *Melik* Mohammedein, the chief's involvement in what the state perceived as camel theft—and his failure to deal adequately with camel theft as a crime in court—eventually precipitated his dismissal.[56] Appeals to the law—and drawing attention to the illegal misdeeds of chiefs—was an increasingly rewarding way of demanding redress.

Chiefs or ex-chiefs might in turn petition in protest at their deposition, as in the case of Lako Bureng, the chief who was appointed in Gondokoro when DC Cooke removed Tongun Modi in 1937. Lako Bureng was in turn removed two years later for "misappropriating tribute money and favoring his own relations when ordering work parties for Juba etc," and the Gondokoro chiefdom was amalgamated under the neighboring Belinian chiefdom.[57] Lako wrote to the civil secretary in Khartoum: "Why should an independent tribe be made compelled [*sic*] to go under another tribe against their wish—I write this to you seeking justice. The Local Government refused my appeal and we feel that we are oppressed and our own [*sic*] way is to write to higher authority and request that you ask for the case to see. . . . Your Excellency is the agent of the good God and if I am not justified by you I feel the gates of justice are finally closed."[58]

Lako was clearly drawing here on his Roman Catholic mission schooling as well as on the rhetoric of justice and oppression that was so often prominent in petitions to government. But strikingly, other individual petitioners began to attempt to exercise imagined rights of membership in much wider imperial communities in protests against the judgments of their chief. "As the country is subject to Union Jack I expect my right to be given in this case if found," wrote a medical assistant in Akot, complaining at the failure of a chiefs' court to enforce the return of cattle awarded to him.[59] "Therefore I suffered to come and fall under your feet being a representative of the King of England," declared a man in Torit to the governor of Equatoria, protesting the heavy punishments for adultery inflicted on his relatives by a chiefs' court.[60] The concept of imperial citizenship was here, as Emma Hunter puts it, a "weapon in argument [rather] than settled fact"—but the appearance of such rhetoric in written petitions nonetheless hints at a growing sense of political community that stretched far beyond the local, at least among those who wielded the tools to commit their claims to paper.[61]

The use of the specific term *mazlum* (oppressed) had clearly also spread to the southern provinces, despite the more limited use of Arabic there than in Darfur. Like British officials, some literate southerners deployed the Arabic term in the midst of English texts: a man imprisoned in Juba for allegedly harming another man with an herbal remedy complained, "I am *mazalum* because I have been punished heavily by imprisonment and a fine of one cow." This appellant also requested mitigation because he was the sole provider for his elderly stepmother and young brother.[62] Such personal circumstances were often heeded by courts and colonial officials, reflecting the more paternalistic characteristics of colonial government, to which petitioners also appealed: "You are my father, all people [direct] their eyes to you," wrote another deposed chief to the governor-general of Sudan.[63]

Petitioners thus continued to approach and imagine the government as a hierarchy of individuals who had personal obligations to their subjects, especially to those with whom they had built relationships of alliance and patronage. But increasingly in the late colonial period, people also imagined government as the source of an abstracted and universal law, which guaranteed the rights of citizens as well as subordinating people to the control of the state. Petitions and appeals were frequently written in a more legalistic language of rights and injustices: "I was dealt with on my rights falsely and not accordingly. . . . I wish you to investigate . . . in order that I might have my rights."[64] Appellants often referred to "government law" in their letters: "We want to know if there is any Government law forcing any body to be punished with out any mistake," complained a group of laborers claiming to have been wrongly arrested during a sectional fight in eastern Equatoria.[65]

As well as appeals for state recognition of individual rights, petitions and complaints also continued to focus on sectional political rights within chiefdoms. Indeed, the definition of local political communities and their rights became an issue of even sharper significance in the late colonial period as the rewards for recognition as a community by government became more obvious in the form of developmental goods of various kinds.

One of the commonest articulations of grievance against chiefs was the accusation that they were favoring their own clan or lineage group; such grievances were often traced back to the amalgamation of different chiefdoms under one chief. Often "oppressed" people simply voted with their feet and moved to other chiefs, as the governor of Equatoria noted with concern in 1948: "My file on the appointments and dismissals of chiefs in Juba District presents a sorry picture of incompetence and maladministration among many of the holders of such posts, and of continuous chopping and changing over by small groups from one chiefship to another."[66] But the more that the government tried to keep people under their chiefs, the more that internal tensions were channeled into protests and petitions.

Strikingly, such complaints were increasingly employing the language of representative government, as this petition by the subchiefs of Loggo West in Juba District in 1948 indicates:

> We the 659 (six hundred and fifty-nine) . . . protest that the appointment of Lako Kirba was not known to us and therefore against our will. We were never asked our views nor our votes were taken. A chief is not to be chosen by some other chiefs but by his subjects, we the 659 people voted for Philipo Legge whom we elect and found fit for the rank. But Lako Kirba has only 207 voters, and how is it that 207 votes win the 659 votes?
>
> We are greater in number than that of Lako Kirba. Why are we not given our right?

The subchiefs were here claiming to speak for their people, numbered very specifically in terms of taxpayers. In fact, the payment of taxes was quite central in perceptions of citizenship. The colonial government had always treated the payment of tax or tribute as a sign of obedience and encouraged the idea that it contracted state protection and services. From the late 1940s onward, in an era of increasing enumeration of the population and emphasis on political representation, the payment of taxes was beginning to be linked to an electoral franchise and the provision of services too. In the late 1950s, after Sudan's independence, amalgamations of chiefdoms continued to be promoted by Sudanese administrators on the grounds that larger populations would receive more social services: "Chief like Lolik Lado with 2715 tax payers weighs more that [sic] Aznaba with 277 tax payers. If the people of Aznaba join their neighbouring chief Phulai they will be able by their joint efforts to carry more efficiently their duties and will have the right to ask for services in return."[67]

In 1951, other petitioners argued against this primacy of numbers, but nevertheless emphasized the significance of paying taxes, in calling for the reinstatement of the formerly independent chiefdom of Sindiru, which had been amalgamated under another chief. The petition articulated a very clear set of contractual relations between government and chiefdom. The fulfillment of certain obligations to government was supposed to earn state recognition of political rights as an independent chiefdom: "Although we are few in number we are not exempted to pay Tribute, but we are paying the same rate which is approved for the whole Province, we clear our roads as other chief, we collect same rate of fees from our 'A' court cases as other 'A' courts. We do anything which is ordered by the Government in the same way the large chiefship is doing."[68]

In these debates over whether the rights and entitlements of communities should correspond to numbers of taxpayers or to their comparable rendering of services and dues to government, we begin to discern more-explicit evidence of an imagined equivalency in relations with the state that Cooper sees as central to definitions of citizenship. These might be communal rights that were being asserted, but they were argued on the logical basis of a wider horizontal equivalency of individual subjects whose rendering of taxes and labor established a common relationship to the state, regardless of whether the relative "weight" of their chiefdom was measured numerically or proportionally. The petition from Sindiru also made clear the fundamental assumption behind the practice of petitioning: "[A]s you are our Governor we humbly trust that you will listen to what we are asking."[69] Such petitions were not always or often successful, but the very process of petitioning invoked an implicit obligation: rulers must at least *hear* the complaints of their subjects. And the practice of petitioning assumed—and taught—that rulers could be prevailed on by invoking the logic and laws of their own rule to demand rights and recognition.

Citizenship in Sudan's southern and western "peripheries" was primarily negotiated within local political communities of chiefdom or district. But this local citizenship was increasingly defined in the late colonial period in terms of broader ideas about subjects' (and sometimes explicitly citizens') rights and the protection of state law, as well as through more well-established principles of patrimonial obligation and moral community. Indeed, the legalism of the colonial state had served as a resource in contentious local politics even in the earlier decades of colonial rule: differing discourses of rights and obligations had been in interaction throughout the colonial period in these local contexts. Struggles over political power and rights in local arenas were also struggles over access to the state and in turn helped to produce a translocal, hierarchical idea of the state to which people appealed in the course of their disputes. Indeed, as other recent literature has suggested, we might understand these local processes, including the politics of citizenship, as central to the very processes of state formation.[70]

The practice of complaining or claiming rights, whether in the courts or by letter or direct approach to officials, entailed the recognition of state authority, the acceptance by subjects of being governed. It might be argued further that the active promotion of citizenship by the late colonial state was also a disciplinary project that had the strengthening of state hegemony at its heart. But the politics we describe here entailed an active process of negotiating the relationship with government through protest, dispute, and complaint. As we show above, the chiefdom was not the bounded unit of government that either the colonial administration might have envisioned or Mamdani has described; chiefly subjects were continually going around or beyond their immediate chief to claim their rights and to protest oppression. But, equally, the chiefdom could also become a platform for asserting collective rights and for seeking state recognition, and citizenship might itself be imagined as both an individual and a collective identity. In the contentious politics of chiefship discussed in this chapter, the boundary between subjecthood and citizenship was continually blurred and contested, as experiences of oppression became the grounds for the active negotiation of citizenship.

Notes

1. This letter was found among the papers of J. C. N. Donald, governor of Equatoria, 1954–55: Yei Citizens Chief Modi Baraba to Sayed Benjamin Lwoki, Yei, December 2, 1954, Sudan Archive Durham (hereafter SAD) 761/7/1.

2. James Tully, "Two Meanings of Global Citizenship: Modern and Diverse," in *Global Citizenship Education: Philosophy, Theory and Pedagogy,* ed. Michael A. Peters, Alan Britton, and Harry Blee (Rotterdam: Sense Publishers, 2008), 15–41.

3. Frederick Cooper, postscript to this volume.

4. Douglas Johnson, *The Root Causes of Sudan's Civil Wars* (Oxford: James Currey, 2003).

5. Mahmood Mamdani, *Citizen and Subject: Contemporary Africa and the Legacy of Late Colonialism* (Princeton: Princeton University Press, 1996).

6. Minute by the governor-general, John Maffey, January 1, 1927, National Records Office, Khartoum (hereafter NRO), Civil Secretary 1/39/104.

7. Cherry Leonardi, *Dealing with Government in South Sudan: Histories of Chiefship, Community and State* (Oxford: James Currey, 2013).

8. Mamdani, *Citizen and Subject*, 18.

9. Tully, "Two Meanings" 15.

10. See Chris Vaughan, *Darfur: Colonial Violence, Sultanic Legacies and Local Politics, 1916–1956* (Oxford: James Currey, 2015).

11. Douglas H. Johnson, *Nuer Prophets: A History of Prophecy from the Upper Nile in the Nineteenth and Twentieth Centuries* (Oxford: James Currey, 1994); Simon Simonse, *Kings of Disaster: Dualism, Centralism, and the Scapegoat King in Southeastern Sudan* (Leiden: Brill, 1992).

12. See Leonardi, *Dealing with Government.*

13. Tully, "Two Meanings."

14. Mamdani, *Citizen and Subject,* 33.

15. DC Maynard, Opari-Yei District, to governor, "Lukiko Regulations," January 2, 1924; Mamour Mongalla, "Bari-Mandaris Habits and Laws of Legislation together with Adopted Rules for Mongalla District Chiefs Court," September 11, 1924; and "Amadi District Notes on Chiefs Courts," 1924: all NRO Mongalla Province 1/1/2.

16. E.g., Leonard Nalder, *A Tribal Survey of Mongalla Province, by Members of the Province Staff and Church Missionary Society* (London: Oxford University Press, 1937), 22.

17. Lampen diaries, SAD 739/9/44.

18. Ibid., SAD 734/8/40.

19. Ibid., SAD 739/9/44.

20. Ian Cunnison, *Baggara Arabs: Power and Lineage in a Sudanese Nomad Tribe* (Oxford: Clarendon Press, 1966), 121, 146.

21. Lampen memoirs, SAD 734/9/45.

22. R. C. Cooke, DC of Central District, to governor of Equatoria, June 19, 1937, South Sudan National Archives, Juba (hereafter SSNA), Equatoria Province (hereafter EP) 66.D.8.

23. McNeill, inspector of southern Darfur District, to governor of Darfur, October 1, 1919, NRO 2.D Fasher (A) 54/3/12.

24. Bence-Pembroke, governor of Darfur, to civil secretary, November 17, 1926, NRO 2.D Fasher (A) 54/3/14.

25. Assistant District Commissioner (hereafter ADC) Baggara report on Habbania affairs, June 1942, NRO 2.D Fasher (A) 54/3/14.

26. The duty of rulers to hear their subjects' complaints against oppressive officials was formalized in the much earlier institution of *mazalim* courts elsewhere in the Islamic world; see Albrecht Fuess, "*Zulm* by *Mazālim?* The Political Implications of the Use of *Mazālim* Jurisdiction by the Mamluk Sultans," *Mamlūk Studies Review* 13, no. 1 (2009): 121–47.

27. R. S. O'Fahey, *The Darfur Sultanate* (London: Hurst, 2008), 46.

28. Ibid, p. 191.

29. Justin Willis, "*Hukm:* The Creolization of Authority in Condominium Sudan," *Journal of African History* 46 (2005): 29–50.

30. Ibid., 30.

31. Equatoria Province Monthly Diaries, November 1938, NRO Civil Secretary (hereafter Civsec) 57/7/29, and February 1939, NRO Civsec 57/11/42; Yei District Monthly Diaries, March 1942, September 1942, March 1945, and December 1945, NRO Equatoria Province (hereafter EP) 2/24/87; Yei District Annual Report 1939, NRO EP 2/26/94.

32. Interview with two male elders in Agar Dinka, Rumbek, May 10, 2006.

33. Report on Bahr el Ghazal Province, enclosed in letter by Governor Ingleson to civil secretary, May 14, 1935, NRO Upper Nile Province 1/4/22.

34. Lampen memoirs, SAD 734/8/67.

35. P. P. Howell, "Recollections of Service in the Sudan," 1983, Howell Papers, SAD 769/5/54; Lakes District Monthly Reports, February–March 1937, SSNA EP 57.D.10.

36. DC of Eastern District to governor of Upper Nile, Lake Yirrol, "Report on Eastern District (Atwots and Dinkas), Bahr el Ghazal Province, on the Occasion of Its Transfer to the Upper Nile Province," December 1, 1927, NRO Bahr el Ghazal Province 1/5/28.

37. Lampen memoirs, SAD 734/8/25.

38. ADC Baggara to governor, December 12, 1926, NRO 2.D Fasher 54/3/12.

39. Chris Vaughan, "Reinventing the Wheel? Local Government and Neo-traditional Authority in Late Colonial Northern Sudan," *International Journal of African Historical Studies*, 43 (2010): 255–78.

40. University College of Khartoum, *The Functions of the Modern State: Report of the 1952 Erkowit Study Camp* (Khartoum: University College of Khartoum, 1952), 1, 71.

41. E.g., Equatoria Province Monthly Diary, November 1939, NRO Civsec 57/11/42; Governor Skeet, "Notes Based on Parr's Handing Over Note to Skeet of 1943," May 1945, NRO Dakhlia 57/1/1.

42. File on Habbania affairs, NRO 2.D Fasher (A) 54/3/14.

43. Minutes of the third meeting at Wau of the Bahr el Ghazal Province Council, January 25–26, 1940, SSNA EP 1.C.2.

44. Equatoria Province Monthly Diary, January 1950, NRO Dakhlia 57/9/24.

45. Equatoria Province Monthly Diary, November 1948, NRO Dakhlia 57/5/13.

46. Yei Citizens Chief Modi Baraba to Sayed Benjamin Lwoki, Yei, December 2, 1954, SAD 761/7/1.

47. Bertram, Annual Letter from Lui, September 1948, Church Missionary Society Archives, Birmingham, AF AL.

48. Northern Darfur District (hereafter NDD) Annual Report 1945, NRO Darfur 5/2/10.

49. NDD Annual Report 1949, NRO Darfur 47/6/29.

50. K. D. D. Henderson quoted in Sharif Harir, "The Politics of Numbers: Mediatory Leadership and the Political Process among the Beri Zaghawa of the Sudan" (PhD diss., Bergen University, 1986), 144.

51. Alawma petition to "HE The Secretary for Native Affairs," January 31, 1928, NRO Civsec (1) 66/12/108; governor of Kordofan to governor of Darfur, November 11, 1923; director of intelligence to governor of Darfur, November 24, 1923, NRO Darfur 31/164/13.

52. Harir, "Politics of Numbers," 100–101.

53. Ibid., 144.

54. Note on summary of Artag agitations, NRO Darfur 1/31/164/13.

55. Harir, "Politics of Numbers," 101.

56. Charles, DC of NDD, to governor, July 2, 1949; Henderson to civil secretary, July 11, 1949: both in NRO Darfur Kuttum A (41)/2/8.

57. Cooke, DC of Juba, to governor of Equatoria, November 8, 1939, SSNA EP 66.D.8.

58. Lako Bureng to civil secretary, undated, SSNA EP 66.D.8.

59. Daniel Kweirot, medical assistant at Akot Dispensary, to governor of Equatoria, September 28, 1946, SSNA EP 41.J.1.

60. Ibilisi Liali to governor of Equatoria, May 7, 1949, SSNA EP 41.J.1.

61. Hunter, introduction to this volume.

62. Lado Pitia, Prisoner no. 1727, to governor of Equatoria, March 22, 1949, SSNA EP 41.J.1.

63. Paulo Wallo to governor-general, April 17, 1950, SSNA EP 41.J.1.

64. Peter Lado to governor of Equatoria, January 4, 1951, SSNA EP 41.J.1.

65. Eight Boya prisoners to governor of Equatoria, July 14, 1952, SSNA EP 41.J.1.

66. H. A. Nicholson, governor of Equatoria, to DC of Juba, June 7, 1948, SSNA EP 66.D.8.

67. G. M. A. Bakheit, "Minutes of meeting held in Tali to discuss the future of the people of ex chief Aznaba Lokule," February 2, 1959; and "Minutes of

meeting at Sindiru on 22 January 1959 to discuss the question of Sindiru chieftainship," SSNA EP 66.D.8.

68. Francisco Lugör "for Sindiru people" to governor of Equatoria, Sindiru, November 25, 1951, SSNA EP 66.D.8.

69. Ibid.

70. Jocelyn Alexander, *The Unsettled Land: State-Making and the Politics of Land in Zimbabwe, 1893–2003* (Oxford: James Currey, 2006); Leonardi, *Dealing with Government.*

References

Alexander, Jocelyn. *The Unsettled Land: State-Making and the Politics of Land in Zimbabwe, 1893–2003.* Oxford: James Currey, 2006.

Cunnison, Ian. *Baggara Arabs: Power and Lineage in a Sudanese Nomad Tribe.* Oxford: Clarendon Press, 1966.

Harir, Sharif. "The Politics of Numbers: Mediatory Leadership and the Political Process among the Beri Zaghawa of the Sudan." PhD diss., Bergen University, 1986.

Johnson, Douglas H. *Nuer Prophets: A History of Prophecy from the Upper Nile in the Nineteenth and Twentieth Centuries.* Oxford: James Currey, 1994.

———. *The Root Causes of Sudan's Civil Wars.* Oxford: James Currey, 2003.

Leonardi, Cherry. *Dealing with Government in South Sudan: Histories of Chiefship, Community and State.* Oxford: James Currey, 2013.

Mamdani, Mahmood. *Citizen and Subject: Contemporary Africa and the Legacy of Late Colonialism.* Princeton: Princeton University Press, 1996.

Nalder, Leonard. *A Tribal Survey of Mongalla Province, by Members of the Province Staff and Church Missionary Society.* London: Oxford University Press, 1937.

O'Fahey, R. S. *The Darfur Sultanate.* London: Hurst, 2008.

Simonse, Simon. *Kings of Disaster: Dualism, Centralism, and the Scapegoat King in Southeastern Sudan.* Leiden: Brill, 1992.

Tully, James. "Two Meanings of Global Citizenship: Modern and Diverse." In *Global Citizenship Education: Philosophy, Theory and Pedagogy,* edited by Michael A. Peters, Alan Britton, and Harry Blee, 15–41. Rotterdam: Sense Publishers, 2008.

University College of Khartoum. *The Functions of the Modern State: Report of the 1952 Erkowit Study Camp.* Khartoum: University College of Khartoum, 1952.

Vaughan, Chris. *Darfur: Colonial Violence, Sultanic Legacies and Local Politics, 1916–1956.* Oxford: James Currey, 2015.

———. "Reinventing the Wheel? Local Government and Neo-traditional Authority in Late Colonial Northern Sudan." *International Journal of African Historical Studies* 43 (2010): 255–78.

Willis, Justin. "*Hukm:* The Creolization of Authority in Condominium Sudan." *Journal of African History* 46 (2005): 29–50.

FOUR

Burundi, 1960–67

Loyal Subjects and Obedient Citizens

AIDAN RUSSELL

BETWEEN 1960 AND 1966, THE STATE IN BURUNDI WAS DESTROYED and reinvented three times. At the beginning of the decade, Burundi was one-half of the territory of Ruanda-Urundi, controlled by Belgium under the terms of a UN trusteeship, and just beginning to discover electoral politics. Two years later it was an independent kingdom, desperately attempting to cling to internal unity while beset by fears of invasion from its republican neighbor, Rwanda. In 1966, a military coup abolished the monarchy and instituted a new Republic of Burundi, dressed in the trappings of a revolution but dominated by an authoritarian and ethnically minded clique of army officers. In a few short years the people of Burundi saw the fundamental identity of the state shift so rapidly that the nature of their interaction with power and the terms of citizenship in their unstable nation were continuously under question.

To some extent, whether commanded by authoritarian institutions of chieftaincy, monarchy, or military rule, or dominated by an overarching Belgian administration that neither expected nor desired any engagement from the common people, the population of Burundi seemed to have little claim on the unstable yet hegemonic forms of control that ruled over them. The "field of citizenship" appeared dominated by the performance of subjecthood.[1] Each of Engin Isin and Bryan Turner's "axes" of citizenship (its extent, content, and depth) was substantially characterized by subjection.[2] The extent of citizenship as a positional relationship—triangulating inclusion and exclusion between individual, state, and the political community of the nation—was narrowly delimited to those who accepted the uncontested domination of king, party, or military dictatorship. The content of citizenship—its rights and responsibilities—was defined more as narrow duties and obligations of obedience and loyalty owed by subjects to sovereigns. And the depth of citizenship was remarkably thin, depending almost entirely on the public performance of subjection under the simple, bare labels of orthodox nationalism. The transformations of state might change the language and parameters of such citizenship, but the expectation of subjection as its primary expression was remarkably consistent.

To echo Mahmood Mamdani's influential dichotomy, therefore, the people appeared as subjects, not citizens;[3] constrained by power, their relationship with the state took place primarily in terms of obedience and command, without recourse to the means of engagement or reciprocity that might provide them with the possibility of influencing the actions of authority. Yet the distinction of subject and citizen is simultaneously an informative and a misleading principle of analysis. On the one hand, it gives clarity in the search for patterns of behavior that may illuminate the nature of belonging within the political community of the nation, the practices that reproduce that community and mediate power within it, reflecting the agency and influence of people and state. At the same time, however, maintaining the distinction between the two concepts is impossible. The public performance of subjection offered a wealth of possibilities by which the position of the subject could be used to claim the opportunities of inclusion and manage the pressures of power; subjecthood was in part a discursive and constructive element within the field of citizenship, moderating both its extent and its content. As the terms and obsessions of state authority shifted, the people of Burundi certainly acted the subject, yet frequently too they made the claims of active citizens, blended obedience with negotiation and loyalty with invocation, and conformed to political realities while seeking to shift them toward their interest.

In short, citizenship is a moving target of analysis. Across each of the crisis states in the early 1960s, we must take the exploration of a changing field of citizenship as a goal rather than a premise and look to the daily practices and expressions of people and state under each brief regime to discern it.[4] To illustrate more clearly the complex issues at stake across such rapid change, this study focuses on one small area of Burundi, a stretch of borderland in the central north that most volubly displayed the dynamics of obedience and engagement that were present to varying degrees across the nation. The analysis begins with an overview of the premise of national political community that was exposed in the accelerated political development at the end of Belgian rule, a brief moment of internal democratic choice; the discussion then explores the transformation of such issues in an atmosphere of fear and suspicion, when the independent state faced crisis on its border. In both of these cases, the behavior of the population was substantially reactive to the state, and therefore we conclude with a glimpse at the early days of the military republic, seeing for the first time how individuals could instigate the same dynamics of citizenship in subjecthood to command the recognition and involvement of their undemocratic state. As Burundi stumbled on its way from colonial rule to independent nation, the nature of citizenship within it was molded and tested on its fractious edge. In the nature of popular engagement with each brief regime, we can see how the performances of citizen and subject can overlap and complement each other, less identities than strategies of political agency, providing both flexibility and stability in times of dangerous change.

Belgian Trusteeship: The Choice of the Subject

Burundi imagined itself as an ancient nation. In the last days of the colonial period, the actions and content of citizenship, of engagement between population and state, were partially encoded in the imagination of its extent, the recognition of identity and belonging within this time-honored nation. All the trappings of the archetypal imagined community were exerted to give substance to the identity of the "Barundi" as the corporate body of the nation, a "Murundi" being an individual member within this body. Politicians celebrated a deep, shared national history and reveled in the celebration of language, culture, and a supposed national character of peace, defined negatively against the supposed fractious violence of neighboring Rwanda.[5]

Central to this conception of the body of the nation was its relation to the head: the *mwami*, or king. The position of the sovereign over and above his people was fundamental to all political rhetoric of the time. Mwami Mwambutsa was hailed as Sebarundi, the "Father of the Barundi," the royal motto *Ganza Sabwa* exerting his ordained right to "rule and reign," and both his own sovereign right and his subjects' duty of obedience were enwrapped in the ideology of the nation. This ideology denoted the extent of inclusion within the family of the nation as subjection to the king, without consideration of political engagement with power. The content of such a citizenship of subjection was thus an obligation of obedience, reciprocated by a duty of protection from the "Father" to his children. Legal rights of citizenship did not exist; Africans under Belgian trustee authority were officially *ressortissants* of Ruanda-Urundi, a term simply denoting a territorial origin rather than the legal rights and membership of a *citoyen*, "citizen,"[6] and both Africans and Europeans dwelt instead on the concept of the Barundi as a great family, subject to the mwami.

The reality of colonial domination doubled this subjection, as throughout the daily practice of indirect rule the king was exerted as a veil for Belgian authority, "the familiar décor that permits us to act in the wings without alarming the masses," as a report from 1925 put it.[7] The attitude toward these "masses" was clear, and no engagement with power beyond the direction of the dual royal and colonial authority was expected. Alongside the mwami and the Belgian administration, the population was ruled by a third node of subjugating authority. The mwami himself reigned as an inviolable figurehead, but the state largely functioned through the division of power among the chiefs around him, even if this meant a near-constant pervasion of internal feuds that sometimes came perilously close to civil war.[8]

The most outstanding of these chiefs was the great Pierre Baranyanka, who worked so passionately for the colonial project that the Belgians permitted him unchallenged authority within his territory along the central northern border with Rwanda.[9] The archetypal "decentralised despot,"[10] empowered by a dynastic claim to rule as well as strong colonial support, Baranyanka's authority within his territory was enforced through regular assemblies and displays of power in which the people were summoned and directed to participate in forced labor, especially the cultivation of coffee as the cash crop of development. Tardiness, disobedience, or any other signs of marginal dissent were punished with physical abuse, such as the *kiboko* hippopotamus-nerve whip applied to the hands, feet, or buttocks of the disobedient subject.[11] They might glory in their subjection to the mwami, but the position of the population, firmly at the bottom of a stratified hierarchy that made the people doubly subjects of their chief, was readily apparent in the minds of the common people. "Umwansi utagira aho umuhungira uramusaba," ran the proverb: you bow to the enemy you cannot flee.[12]

For much of the colonial period, political development was confined to the adjustment and balance of authority between the Belgian administration, the chiefs, and the mwami. When Burundi finally caught up to the current of political change across Africa in 1959, however, and the Belgians hurriedly implemented a system of partial democratization, the ensuing political contest both exemplified the primacy of subjecthood within the field of citizenship and demonstrated the curious, if limited, possibilities of engagement with power that this position of subjection could, in fact, entail.

When local elections were announced in late 1959, the dynamics of the newly formed party politics adhered considerably to the preceding dynamics of state.[13] Parties were largely formed and directed by the chiefs, and coalitions of parties somewhat matched the dynastic divisions of preceding chiefly contests. Baranyanka's family formed the Parti Démocrate Chrétien (PDC), which urged internal autonomy beneath a continued European stewardship; their principal rival was Uprona, Union et Progrès National, which demanded immediate independence and was led by Prince Louis Rwagasore, the eldest son of Mwambutsa and a chief in his own right. But quite aside from the question of independence, the sovereign authority of the mwami and the loyalty of the Barundi as his subjects became the vital stake of political argument between these forces, a field of ironic consensus over which the parties fought for ownership.

For the Uprona nationalists, kingship was tied to memories of glorious history and resistance to colonization; they played obliquely on the monarchist sentiments of the population by conflating Mwambutsa with his son, implying that the loyal obligation of Barundi subjects to their monarchy was to devote themselves to Rwagasore's nationalist cause. The PDC and Baranyanka, in particular, were portrayed as traitors to the crown, enemies of the people. In response, the PDC insisted loudly and incessantly on its loyalty to the mwami, adding its voice to the political consensus of the relationship between sovereign and subjects. But it extended this argument to proclaim that the mwami was so superior as to be beyond politics, that one could be a loyal subject to Mwambutsa and still vote for whichever party one desired. All Barundi could be included as subjects to the king, while the political rights of engagement with power that were proffered by electoral democracy were limited to the state beneath him. The extent of citizenship was delimited by subjection to the sovereign, while its content encompassed the contestation and claim on the power of state.

The Belgians, fearful of Rwagasore's success, duly held popular *réunions d'information*, information and propaganda meetings that announced the mwami's position "above the parties," distributing public letters signed by Mwambutsa and bearing his photograph. So successful was the concatenation of political voices and popular imagination all devoted to royal authority that the administration soon found that the people were refusing to accept or believe any political tract distributed by the Belgians that did not carry the mwami's name or image.[14] The celebration of obedient subjecthood to the mwami was never more emphatic than during the political contest over his perceived favor.

Such electoral politics also necessitated the acknowledgment of power within the position of the subject, however. A citizenship defined by subjection still offered possibilities of rights and responsibilities in the management of power. It was indeed a central plank of Uprona's nationalist platform that the subject had the right and duty to choose his or her sovereign; the party simply relied on the fact that the choice had already been made. One Uprona tract explicitly portrayed the question of independence as a choice between the king of Burundi and the king of Belgium: "We have our king," the tract declared; "[W]e shall not be subject to theirs."[15] Uprona did not question that the Barundi would be subjects to power in the new independent order, but Uprona's conception of subjecthood required that the subjects themselves accept or reject the authority of their sovereign.

Furthermore, this necessity of consent and the possibility of choice within the position of the subject was brought even more powerfully to the fore in regard to the authority of the chiefs. Although the chieftaincy system was formally abolished at the beginning of the political contest, the chiefs themselves retained enormous political authority. With most parties strongly associated with chiefly leadership, people who had always been subjects to their local chief could find themselves in a situation of explicitly rejecting his authority by choosing to endorse a rival party. Powerful rumors passed around the country that a subject was obligated to vote for the party of his chief, rumors that were subtly endorsed by most parties within their own territory and angrily denounced in the territories of their rivals. It was a struggle over the nature of engagement between subject and state, the possibility of dissent and the endorsement of alternative authority balanced against the conceptions of duty, loyalty, and obedience that were fundamental to the position of the subject. As independence neared, the content of citizenship for a nation of proud subjects became the primary field of political contest.

Given Chief Baranyanka's great power and intense personal and political rivalry with Rwagasore, the dynamics of this contest were most fractiously fought out in Baranyanka's territory. Although the PDC portrayed itself as the champion of democracy against the supposedly "feudalist" calls of Uprona, Baranyanka reacted with fury to the possibility that his subjects might choose to reject his authority. When Uprona approached certain promising individuals within his chieftaincy, hoping to woo them toward becoming political pioneers in the PDC heartland, the men they chose were subjected to intense intimidation and threats by the local *sous-chefs*, Baranyanka's delegate agents.[16] When this failed to curtail the Uprona incursion and more and more people began to express sympathy toward and loyalty to Rwagasore's cause, Baranyanka threatened extreme violence against his subjects. "I will bring to you the Twa and the soldiers," he is said to have declared in one region that showed growing Uprona sentiment, "so that they may have intercourse with your wives and daughters."[17] He summoned individual Uprona propagandists to stand trial before him in his personal tribunal, punishing them with months in prison for failing to answer his summons.[18] While the content of an electoral citizenship as a legitimate contest of power was being shaped across the nation, it was countered by the reinforcement of terrorizing authoritarianism toward the Murundi subject.

However, in response to Baranyanka's violence, Upronists in his territory continued to view party rivalry as a matter of the subject's choice between sovereigns, between obedience to a chief and obedience to a king. Rather than precluding any acts of political agency or dissent, the violence of the "decentralised despot" instead exacerbated the engagement of his subjects with alternative political possibilities. The struggle was so intense that by 1961 it had spilled into violence, as propagandists for each party attacked each other in the streets.[19] Upronists were quickly dominant, glorying in their position as subjects to the mwami and obedient servants of Rwagasore. But this was by no means a passive stance; they had chosen this loyalty in the face of intense intimidation from their own authoritarian chief and fought to bring their desired political order into being. They were, and desired to be, subjects of sovereign authority, but this in itself required the engagement of consent and active political struggle. The extent of citizenship was delimited by subjecthood, but its content still encompassed the right and duty of powerful political agency.

Eventually the violence in the north became so dangerous that the Belgians flooded the region with metropolitan troops, arms, and helicopters to bring it under back under control. The key Uprona activists were arrested, and the authority of Belgium and Baranyanka was reestablished. Yet the PDC had lost the political war. In the 1961 national elections, Uprona achieved a massive victory across the country, Rwagasore becoming prime minister–elect with around 80 percent of the popular vote. The political contest both demonstrated the predominance of subjecthood beneath sovereign authority and illustrated the possibilities of engagement within this authoritarian relationship. Subjects were dependent on their superiors, but this was a "productive dependency";[20] the content of citizenship encompassed a competition for followers that created a degree of choice for the subject, one that he or she could, and did, fight to achieve.

This balance of engagement within subjection was exposed by the choice offered by democratic contest. Its incarnation was in direct response to the form of domination and contest that the state represented at the end of the colonial period, but while specific to this context, it also represented some of Burundi's most fundamental dynamics and assumptions of power. In 1962 the mwami's reign continued into independence, yet the choice of the subject was all but lost; the excitement of Rwagasore's campaign was brutally cut short, and in its place reigned fear and doubt. In this new political world, subjection and engagement remained in precarious balance, refined in strategy and expression to speak to a domineering yet insecure state. It is to this anxious time that we now turn.

Independent Monarchy: Defensive Loyalty

Within weeks of his triumph, Prince Rwagasore was assassinated, and the sons of Baranyanka were held ultimately responsible for his murder.[21] Independence came half a year later, on July 1, 1962, under a shroud of mourning and anxiety.

In the first turbulent postcolonial years, a climate of fear and a certain siege mentality altered the political dynamics of the nation. With the PDC destroyed by association with Rwagasore's killers, Uprona dominated Burundi almost unchallenged, although the state officially remained a multiparty system. Yet having lost its talismanic and unifying leader, Uprona began to splinter, polarized into rival factions that seriously destabilized the state. Many leading politicians began to look more and more toward ethnicity as a means of interpreting and expressing their struggles.[22]

All the while, relations with Rwanda deteriorated alarmingly as soon as the two halves of Ruanda-Urundi separated into independent nations. The last years of colonial rule had been dominated by a civil war in Rwanda, resulting in the abolition of the monarchy and the creation of a Hutu-dominated republic. The new government, controlled by the Parti du Mouvement de l'Émancipation des Bahutu (Parmehutu), implacably opposed the continuation of monarchy in Burundi, and things took a turn for the worse in late 1963, when monarchist Tutsi refugees from Rwanda used Burundi territory to launch a bloody invasion of their homeland.[23] The government of Rwanda accused Burundi of supporting these invaders, while Burundi denounced the Rwandan internal reprisals against Tutsi civilians as acts of genocide. The two countries teetered on the brink of war.

On September 1, 1964, it seemed that the anticipated catastrophe had finally arrived. Across a broad stretch of the Rwandan border, armed men appeared and attacked the local community, raiding and setting light to the thatched roofs of people's homes. "Invasion from Rwanda has burnt huts and pillaged the borderland region," reported the local governor in an urgent telegram; "Gendarmes totally spent, situation grave."[24] The initial violence lasted about a week, but repeated incursions marked much of the following two months. Rwandans and Barundi clashed in local skirmishes, more huts were burnt exactly a month after the first attacks, and in November the local authorities appealed for support when up to three hundred men invaded from across the border once again. Martial law was imposed across the borderland, and command was taken by an official *conseil de guerre*, a council of war.

The attitude of the state toward its border peoples in this crisis was immediately clear. Soldiers swept into the regions affected, but despite the common belief that Burundi had been invaded by a hostile Rwanda, the principal targets of state repression were the Barundi of the borderland. The army arrested anyone found out in the open. People traveling home from their fields or gathering in groups of more than two to share a drink in the evening were taken away for interrogation under suspicion of revolt.[25] The national population were treated not as citizens attacked by a foreign enemy and therefore owed a duty of defense by the state but as alien enemies of the state. The inclusion and exclusion of citizenship continued in much the same national terms as before but was expressed ever more negatively through political contrast with Rwanda. The notional unity of "the Barundi" was held up against "Rwandan" ethnic divisions, and in the unstable political atmosphere the state began to doubt that the borderlanders could still be counted within the national family. Inclusion meant not only subjecting oneself to the mwami but also passing a political test that displayed voluble endorsement of Upronist orthodoxy against Parmehutu contagion. Deeply suspicious of the borderlanders' proximity to and quotidian interaction with Rwandans across the border, the Upronist state believed the borderlanders to be "infected" by ethnic, republican, Rwandan politics, their loyalty to the state and their belonging in the nation fundamentally undermined. The field of citizenship presumed a national community coterminous with a political one, and in the eyes of the nervous state the rights of inclusion for a "Murundi" could be sacrificed by suspected political betrayal.

As the investigation proceeded, the state's anxiety over the possibility of internal responsibility for the attacks was revealed to be not entirely a matter of paranoia. The initial reports of Rwandan invasion soon gave way to a detailed account of a conspiracy, supposedly concocted by Barundi dissidents who were exploiting the territory of Rwanda and the border area as a resource for mobilizing their opposition to the government of Burundi.[26] Faced with an internal plot, the military urgently required the establishment of intelligence, and only the suspected local people could provide it. Civilians arrested en masse were given a chance at freedom by becoming informants for the state. It was a collaborative process; the state approached the community aggressively, intent on purging its undesirable elements, and members of the community responded by volunteering identification and evidence of these undesirables. The interdependence of two axes of citizenship, its extent and its content, was powerfully demonstrated; with their inclusion denied, members of the local community sought to engage with the state on its own terms to display their loyalty and claim the rights of recognition as obedient subjects. Naming names and telling the soldiers what they wanted to hear, confirming the suspicions and rumors the state already feared, the borderlanders could prove their doubted loyalty to Burundi, show their usefulness to the state, and regain their inclusion in the political community of the nation.

The loyalty displayed by these informants was substantially the loyalty of the subject. They had been arrested by a state that viewed them as the enemy, that denied their right to belong within the nation and suspected them of holding greater allegiance to Rwandan politics than to Burundi, and therefore their response was to show total obedience to the overbearing authority of government orthodoxy. There was no space to express the slightest hint of independent political thought; safety lay in the ability to perform loyalty, to show oneself as the obedient subject to state authority by agreeing and engaging with the state's fear and suspicion of others. Adopting the position of the subject was an effective defensive measure, taken under duress.

However, it could also be a far more active tactic, pursued by others who were not under arrest but wished to engage with the power of the state. Despite its open hostility to the local population, the army stood as a potential resource of defense against the self-evident danger of true rebel militants on the border, and emphatic statements of political loyalty proved the key to acquiring the army's protection. This political invocation was put into action by one small community that sought to exclude one of their neighbors. Named Rukushi Isaac, he was a proud member of the pro-Hutu Parti du Peuple and therefore an open opponent of the Uprona government. His arrogant political polemics terrified his neighbors, and a group of them took it into their own hands to imitate the state and place this dissident under a citizen's arrest.[27] Dragging Rukushi before the authorities, they recounted all the allegations that would most alarm the state. He visited the exiled leaders of his party in Rwanda, they said, and received Rwandans into his home; he conducted door-to-door propaganda, they claimed, in which he denigrated the mwami himself. Most venomously, according to one woman's testimony, he "declared that if ever our children should attempt to flee to him, he will take a sickle and cut off their arms and legs ... [and] he declared that it would be better to cut off the right arm, the right leg and the right breast of each woman, and in that way the women would become wise."[28] As if such violent rhetoric might be insufficient to prompt the state to take the action she desired, the woman continued with a statement of proud political loyalty to the government: "He said that because we are Upronist women." These informants positioned themselves as obedient members of the state's political order but did so to engage actively with state power toward shared objectives and against shared enemies, shaping and displaying the content of citizenship as a project of mutual dependency.

The possibilities made available by engaging with the state to confirm its own prejudices were nowhere more powerfully exemplified than in the claims made by one enterprising man, named Kabanda Samson, on the border. The conseil de guerre was looking for evidence that the attacks were a "racist" plot, concocted by the political enemies of the state to commit acts of genocide against Tutsi and overthrow the monarchy.[29] Despite the fact that the raids were characterized by arson, not by murder, and that no one else had identified ethnicity as a factor in the selection of targets, Kabanda gave the state exactly what it wanted. He claimed to have been present at repeated meetings in Rwanda, where he heard political figures such as the brilliant Hutu politician Paul Mirerekano, widely known as a passionate monarchist,[30] plot to become president of a new Republic of Burundi; in Kabanda's account, Mirerekano declared that "every Tutsi, even though he may have done good things in Burundi, must be put to the fire with his wife and children."[31] The informant seemed to be taking matters to the extreme in his active appeal to the state's prejudice, winning substantial favor by confirming all the worst fears and accusations that the government held against its enemies. Kabanda displayed the loyalty of the subject by repeating the state's own beliefs back to it, but in his remarkable testimony he showed that there was considerable potential for advancement and engagement in the adoption of the subject position. He was only able to make his claims because he routinely traveled to Rwanda, a fact that would naturally make him a person of high suspicion, yet through his bloodcurdling evidence Kabanda won a personal audience with the governor of the province and even maneuvered himself into a position to request a face-to-face meeting with the mwami. Volunteering himself as a subject loyal to king, nation, and political orthodoxy, Kabanda doggedly pursued a share in power as the reward of active citizenship.

Constrained by violence and fear and deprived of the personal authority of Rwagasore and the vibrant choice of the last colonial years, the inclusionary extent of citizenship during the independent monarchy was still defined by subjection. However, this subjection was understood not only as obedience to the king but also as political obedience to corporate Uprona party strictures. Furthermore, whereas the decolonization contest had seen subjecthood marshaled as a means of contesting power through the choice of authority, the instability of the independent state limited the content of citizenship to a complex yet binary relationship of recognition and mutual dependency between citizen and state; citizenship entailed not the contestation of power but its mediation. Individuals and communities claimed the reciprocal, protective obligations of the state toward its loyal subjects by performing the nascent actions of a political citizenship that incarnated political orthodoxy. Becoming the obedient political subject was a sensible defensive tactic when confronted by a hostile state or an aggressive, deviant enemy, but it also offered its own oblique possibilities of agency within local and national politics. "The positive content of citizenship," as James Ferguson frames it in relation to southern Africa, rested "precisely on being a rightful and deserving dependent of the state."[32] Denouncing or apprehending those who transgressed the orthodox political order allowed the population to present themselves as the active political subjects the state lacked, engaging with power by making themselves essential to the state and not simply tolerated by it.

Soon, however, the parameters of the field of citizenship would be transformed yet again. The year 1965 compounded disaster upon disaster, as the Hutu prime minister was assassinated by a Rwandan Tutsi refugee, new elections delivered a Hutu majority that was prevented from forming a government by an interfering mwami, and an abortive coup attempt was met with mass executions of Hutu politicians.[33] By 1966 the country was falling apart. Mwami Mwambutsa seemed to have abandoned his subjects, eventually taking up permanent residence in Switzerland, and his son, Rwagasore's younger brother, took his place as king. Soon enough, the army stepped in to neutralize the new mwami and declared a Republic of Burundi under the single party leadership of Uprona. The monarchy, an institution of deep authority and affection among its subjects, however diminished it had been by the preceding years of crisis, was replaced by an institution of force, albeit one that claimed to aspire to reformist and progressive politics. Choice of leadership was officially abolished, not to be achieved again for twenty-seven years. Yet even in this context of ominous military domination it is possible to find the modalities of engagement playing out within the terms of subjection, and we may finally witness how this relationship of dependency could arise not only from the imposition of the state but also from the instigation of citizens.

Republican Rule: The Vigilant Citizen

The military republic was heavily dominated by Tutsi officers from the south of the country, but one of their priorities was easing relations with the Hutu republic in Rwanda. With rapprochement in the air, the new government no longer feared invasion, and by 1967 the northern border had lost a lot of its urgency in the eyes of the state. Political contagion remained a concern, however, as rumors suggested that the borderlanders were in contact with Rwandans who spoke disparagingly of the "half-republic" that had brought the Tutsi-dominated army to power.[34]

In a relatively new development, the word *citoyen* began to creep into the state's vocabulary. Officials discussed how *nos concitoyens* (our fellow citizens) were being wooed by subversive Rwandans who wanted to see a violent revolution south of the border.[35] It was a possessive concept, the citizen imagined as an anonymous loyalist who was devoted to the propaganda of the peaceful military coup, standing in opposition to the bloodthirsty Rwandans. The latter were described ambiguously as simply *ressortissants*, "nationals" of their country; the word recalled the legal limbo of the colonial period, in contrast to the positive inclusive figure of the Murundi *concitoyen*. With the mythic sovereignty of the mwami no longer relevant, the inclusionary extent of citizenship had gained a new vocabulary but still remained defined by the negative example of the alien and continued to lack any formalized content of political engagement with the military government other than the expectation of obedient loyalty. The citizens of the republic were still subjects of an aspiring hegemonic state. However, given the necessary circumstances, the possibility of limited engagement remained within the grasp of these subjects, open to their invocation even when it appeared counter to the interests of the new politics.

It so happened that one Saturday afternoon in July 1967, a man drove his cattle along the southern bank of the river that marks the border with Rwanda, seeking better pastures in the higher ground.[36] It was his regular routine, yet as he followed the line of the border this time, he was followed. A group of Rwandan civilians had crossed the frontier and penetrated a kilometer into Burundi territory. They gave chase; he was caught and forcibly taken across the river, into Rwanda. There were Rwandan soldiers waiting on the far bank of the stream, and the man was stripped naked, dragged away to a hill at some distance from the frontier, and tied to a tree. The Barundi witnesses could not follow, and in the words of the provincial vice governor a week later, "to this day, the fate of Monsieur Nkurunziza is unknown."[37]

He shares a name with the current president of Burundi, but Nkurunziza was Rwandan. He had lived in the area for over fifteen years, first moving under Belgian rule when the border was officially just an internal administrative divide within the single territory of Ruanda-Urundi. Local authorities believed that Nkurunziza, along with members of the other six Rwandan families who lived on the same hill, had long been suspected by the Rwandan state of being spies for militants among the Tutsi refugees, who were known as *inyenzi*, "cockroaches," and had launched numerous bloody attacks back into Rwanda across the previous years.[38] "The Rwandan authorities," reported the vice governor, "have decided to liquidate systematically these seven persons."[39]

Nkurunziza was not, therefore, a Murundi, and the state's language noted that his identity partially excluded him from the national community. But for all that it may have been a largely Rwandan affair, the kidnapping of Nkurunziza was a shocking moment in the borderland. It was a violent incursion by a foreign power that disconcerted the state and terrified the local people, and despite the pressure from the government to get along with Parmehutu, the crime was sufficiently alarming to reawaken old fears. And the local people did all they could to fuel these proven paranoias. They described how they had confronted their Rwandan neighbors on the border and had been met with ominous threats: "It will not take more than nine days to achieve what we have planned to do," the Rwandans reportedly claimed. "Go and tell your leaders that we do not want *inyenzi* among the people, that Parmehutu will achieve its ends."[40]

Once again the border people were eager to present themselves as faithful subjects of the regime, and they exploited the rich possibilities of the border to illustrate this loyalty by graphic opposition to foreign politics. The republican government might still have been a little doubtful over the susceptibility of the borderlanders to Rwandan influence, but unlike in similar circumstances under the monarchy, it no longer treated its peripheral citizens with open aggression. Rather, the borderlanders themselves worked hard to rekindle the old border hostility of the state. In Dereje Feyissa's terms, they labored to show themselves as "more state than the state"; they insisted on the "rigidification" of the frontier against the particular interest of the government, "mobilizing the state in a local struggle."[41] They had long been at odds with their neighbors in Rwanda, engaged in reciprocal cattle raids that the state had done little to halt. Now they exploited Nkurunziza's abduction to paint their pains in the language of political danger that the state understood. Molested by the alien Other, Nkurunziza was retroactively incorporated within the inclusionary extent of citizenship, his neighbors utilizing Rwandan aggression to perform the necessary political orthodoxy that might invoke political recognition from the state. With the nights echoing with "cries of alarm . . . intended to create a spirit of insecurity amongst the peaceful population of Burundi," the inhabitants piqued the interest of the state by their revelation that their own Barundi political exiles, now refugees in Rwanda, were "at the base of these ploys,"[42] all the time "motived by a spirit of racism."[43] The opposition between peaceful citizens and destabilizing Others was played out just as the state conceived it, only set in striking contrast by the fear and danger conjured in the borderlanders' words. Engagement between state and society might only take place on the state's terms, but through the judicious performance of loyalty and political peril, the limited content of citizenship, the rights and responsibilities of protection against foreign hostility, could be instigated by subjects even when the state was keen to move on from the antagonistic past.

The people were no longer just borderlanders but border guards; having confronted Parmehutu militants on the frontier, they began to take the unusual step of enforcing a customs regime that they had previously flouted with little concern. The republican state had shown an increasing interest in regularizing and bureaucratizing the border regime through identity checks and border passes, all the better to control the population and gather tax revenue, but the borderlanders themselves had never ceased to cross the border wherever and whenever they felt like it. Yet three days after the abduction, "thirty pigs, three goats and a bullock coming from Rwanda were seized by the people. . . . The animals had been sent to market by six Rwandans, without a transport document and without a customs visa."[44] It was a transparent attempt to appeal to the state's interest in taxation and control, something that offered little to the borderlanders themselves. But it was a judicious act; as the state began to speak of the citizen in terms of bureaucratic recognition, tested by inspection on the border and distinction from the foreigner, the people both offered to endorse this nascent language of authority and showed themselves necessary to bring the state's desires into reality. The designation of the *citoyen* had been tentatively raised as a legalistic and possessive act of state, but the borderlanders offered to push it further and transform it into a collaborative engagement of mutual benefit to state and society. The state responded and once more flooded the borderland with soldiers, this time for the protection of its loyal citizens.

This border dynamic was the realization of a nationwide project between state and citizen. Covertly expanding the Tutsi domination of power, fearful that monarchist sentiments remained strong, and terrified of a potential Hutu political movement, the military was desperate to see stability in the faithfulness of the people. It formed the Jeunesse Révolutionnaire Rwagasore (JRR), a youth league that invoked Prince Rwagasore's name to serve the republican order, and gave as its commanding slogan the word *Vigilance*.[45] Watchfulness against political deviance, contagion, and incursion was to be the shared purpose of the state and its loyal citizens. Through universal vigilance, the reproduction of the political community of the nation could be achieved, a performance that maintained a loose link between citizens and state, kept them in contact, and confirmed the mutual ties of loyalty and obligation. To be a good citizen was to be a vigilant citizen. "Vigilance is a frontier phenomenon,"[46] and it lent itself well to performance on the border, but it was only a local representation of a national mode of engagement. By reporting the incursion of individuals or ideas, one presented oneself to the state as belonging to the nation, claiming inclusion within the positional identity of citizenship, and deserving of state endorsement, sharing in the content of citizenship as interdependent obligations of mutual defense. Citizen and state spoke to each other in shared terms of vigilant political orthodoxy, and each provided a degree of protection to the other. There could be reciprocity, mutual obligation, and mutual protection in the collaboration of citizen and state.

It was, nevertheless, a state-centered act, collaboration entirely on the state's terms. The citizen performed vigilance as service to the state's definitions of order and legitimacy. Even while the government became more and more dominated by Tutsi, few could denounce this insidious creep without falling foul of the powerful orthodox line that declared all talk of ethnic division to be a matter of Rwandan "racism and violence."[47] Displaying one's belonging within the nation, acting on behalf of the state and claiming its responsibility to protect, remained an acceptance of subjection to the state's hegemonic political orthodoxy. "Citizenship is Janus-faced,"[48] and when the state considered any other path of action or expression to be treasonous, then the duties of citizenship appeared synonymous with the obedience, even the silence, of the subject. Vigilance was a "ritual of citizenship," as described by Burgess, training a "new kind of citizen" who embodied both the political ideals and the needs of the aggressive state,[49] but it retained much of the expectations of submission from previous modes of power. The political limitations on the extent of citizenship, the restrained content of citizenship as defined by Uprona paranoia under the mwami, had been formalized and enhanced by the military state. Dissent was as prohibited as ever, the army demanding the subjection of the population to its new version of Uprona and acting swiftly to eliminate those who expressed dissatisfaction with the new path of the state. But with the emotive power of the monarchy lost, the language of political orthodoxy provided the subject with its own means of engagement with power. The state had changed, but still one had to play the subject and find means of engaging and ameliorating one's situation within the terms of subjection.

Citizenship is not about the realisation of a fully coherent and harmonious rational contract, but rather about the temporary (and never fully achieved) stabilisation of the polity around a set of participatory practices and new agreements, rooted in democratic and non-democratic contracts and rule making.

—Steven Robins, Andrea Cornwall, and Bettina von Lieres,
"Rethinking 'Citizenship'"[50]

The pace of change in early 1960s Burundi was extraordinary, evidence of a state careering out of control. The flashes of engagement between people and state were frantic, improvised attempts at stabilizing this dangerous and often violent interaction of politics and power. In this compressed period of recurrent transformation, the potential for change within the field of citizenship was demonstrated in the adjustments that individuals made to relate to the new character of the state above them, while the resiliency of the fundamental premise of subjecthood stood in stark reminder of the continuities shared by colony, monarchy, and republic. Whether faced with a choice between rival authorities in the electoral moment of decolonization, confronted with a hostile state in the crisis period that followed, or seeking to involve a martial government in local troubles, engaged and active citizens adjusted their actions and expressions to suit the time but did so within the constraints of the subject position. Loyalty and obedience were the performative language of engagement, demanded by the assumption that the state represented a dangerous, potentially violent hegemonic authority that would punish deviance, from Chief Baranyanka's fury to the suspicious postcolonial Uprona or the covert military ethnicization of the republic. Within these parameters of loyal subjecthood, however, there lay the possibility for a citizen to include him- or herself in the politics of the nation and deflect or direct the dangerous powers of the state to suit the circumstances of the subject community through the display of obedience. The fluctuating field of citizenship was delimited by political subjection and encompassed rights and duties of interdependence, but it was above all a performative act.

The willingness for the subject to embrace the definitions and preoccupations of the state and the potential for action, inclusion, negotiation, and engagement within this febrile relationship proved to be powerful tools of mutual benefit to state and society. Rather than a choice between citizenship and subjecthood, it was a matter of productive dependency, "a form of agency that seeks its own submission,"[51] a means by which people could not only include themselves in the nation but also advance their interests beneath and within the state. And it found temporary success in each incarnation because the state, too, knew itself to be partially dependent on its subjects. Each form of state needed to see subjects beneath it, subjects that accepted and endorsed its right to rule. The decade was defined by political instability, and while the fatal divisions most often emerged within the state itself, a nation of united, loyal subjects seemed to offer the only possibility of security for the aspirational hegemony. A citizenship of mutual dependency, predicated by the latent or active violence of the state yet nevertheless available to the instigation of the individual, offered a means of stabilization and marginal benefit for all concerned, most powerfully expressed in the settlement of vigilant citizenship under the republic.

In Burundi, unlike many other African states around the time of independence, the nature of the nation was relatively settled and provided the most basic parameters of citizenship; the nature of the state and of the relationship between state and people was what troubled the fleeting regimes of the 1960s, as the extent and content of citizenship were contracted and transformed. While placed under strain by the Rwandan threat in the early postcolonial years and then shriven of its royal component and redressed in modern language in the republican years, the imagination of Barundi familial unity provided a veneer of shared identity by which citizen and state could meet. Yet despite such stability, as Burundi emerged from its furious change in the early 1960s, this axis of citizenship was what would be most fundamentally transformed as ethnic divisions took the place of proclaimed familial unity. As Tutsi supremacists consolidated power in the republic, the state they dominated increasingly excluded Hutu from belonging within its ranks. When a Hutu revolt triggered a genocidal repression from this state in 1972,[52] this incarnation of Burundi's political community was fundamentally broken, extraordinary violence firmly establishing the primacy of ethnicity over nationhood and redefining the "depth" of citizenship through the unofficial, yet pervasive, triangulation of national, political, and above all ethnic identity. The rapid transformations around independence saw the performance and action of citizenship adapt to extreme instability, but the most fundamental challenge to the limits and claims of belonging and engagement between people and state was still to come.

Citizenship, as was said at the outset, is a moving target, evolving and reforming according to the pressures of the moment. But for all that greater and more disastrous changes were on the horizon, the shifting field of citizenship across the triple transformations of the Burundi state in the early 1960s illustrates the crucial potential in the behavior of citizen and subject as a spectrum, not an opposition. Emerging from colonial rule in crisis and uncertainty, with dangerous divisions within and aggressive enemies without, the Barundi in the 1960s refined a kind of citizenship that balanced the position of the dependent subject before an unstable yet hegemonic state with a degree of freedom within which citizens might engage with power, win inclusion and recognition, and somewhat mediate the political forces that raged around them. To the skillful actor, accepting the definitions of subjection could itself give access to the deflection, negotiation, and mediation of power. The subject could embrace dependency and still invoke the fruits of a citizenship of mutual obligation, if not of rights.

Notes

1. James Tully, "Two Meanings of Global Citizenship: Modern and Diverse," in *Global Citizenship Education: Philosophy, Theory and Pedagogy*, ed. Michael A. Peters, Alan Britton, and Harry Blee (Rotterdam: Sense Publications, 2008), 15–41.

2. Engin F. Isin and Bryan S. Turner, "Citizenship Studies: An Introduction," in *Handbook of Citizenship Studies*, ed. Engin F. Isin and Bryan S. Turner (London: Sage Publications, 2002), 1–10.

3. Mahmood Mamdani, *Citizen and Subject: Contemporary African States and the Legacy of Late Colonialism* (Princeton: Princeton University Press, 1996).

4. See Steven Robins, Andrea Cornwall, and Bettina von Lieres, "Rethinking 'Citizenship' in the Postcolony," *Third World Quarterly* 29, no. 6 (2008): 1069–86.

5. This imagination of national identity could also serve to exclude others who claimed membership in the Burundi nation, especially Swahili-speaking Muslims. See Geert Castryck, "The Hidden Agenda of Citizenship: African

Citizenship in the Face of the Modern Nation-State," in *Citizenship in Historical Perspective*, ed. Steven Ellis, Guðmundur Hálfdanarson, and Ann Katherine Isaacs (Pisa: Edizione Plus Pisa University Press, 2006), 189–202.

6. André Verbrugghe, "Introduction historique au problème de la nationalité au Burundi," *Revue administrative et juridique du Burundi* 6, no. 18 (1972): 5–8. This situation contrasted with that of the formal colony of Belgian Congo, where Africans could theoretically be recognized as citizens if they achieved the status of *évolué*.

7. René Lemarchand, *Rwanda and Burundi* (London: Pall Mall Press, 1970), 66.

8. See Roger Botte, "La guerre interne au Burundi," in *Guerres de lignages et guerres d'états en Afrique*, ed. Jean Bazin and Emmanuel Terray (Paris: Editions des Archives Contemporaines, 1982), 271–317.

9. Lemarchand, *Rwanda and Burundi*, 313–15, 336; Charles Ndayiziga, "Baranyanka et le chefferie Kunkiko-Mugamba" (mémoire de licence, University of Burundi, 1987); Aidan Russell, "Talking Politics and Watching the Border in Northern Burundi, c. 1960–1972" (PhD diss., Oxford University, 2013), 87–147.

10. Mamdani, *Citizen and Subject*, 37–61.

11. Russell, "Talking Politics," 89–91.

12. Ibid., 96.

13. See Lemarchand, *Rwanda and Burundi*; Christine Deslaurier, "Un monde politique en mutation: Le Burundi à la veille de l'indépendance (circa 1956–1961)" (PhD diss., Université Panthéon-Sorbonne, 2002).

14. Valère Vandenbulcke, *Rapport Hebdomadaire Ngozi*, March 5, 1960, Archives Africaines, Brussels (hereafter AAB), BUR 74 (4).

15. Uprona, *Ijwi ry'abadasigana*, n.d., AAB, BUR 65 (1).

16. *Les incidents de la région Rukecu-Busiga-Mihigo*, May 4, 1960, AAB, BUR 73 (5).

17. *Incidents Rukecu*, May 4, 1960, AAB, BUR 73 (5).

18. Pierre Ngendandumwe, *Jugement de Mparamirundi*, August 3, 1960, AAB, BUR 79 (8).

19. Russell, "Talking Politics," 97–147; Deslaurier, "Un monde politique," 1021–31.

20. See James Ferguson, "Declarations of Dependence: Labour, Personhood, and Welfare in Southern Africa," *Journal of the Royal Anthropological Institute* 19 (2013): 226.

21. For discussions of the assassination, see Ludo de Witte, "L'assassinat du Premier ministre burundais Louis Rwagasore" (2013), http://cas1.elis.ugent.be/avrug//forum_2013pdf/rwagasore_fr.pdf; Guy Poppe, *L'assassinat de Rwagasore, le Lumumba burundais* (Bujumbura: Iwacu, 2012).

22. Lemarchand, *Rwanda and Burundi*, 343–60.

23. Ibid., 197–228, 383–401; Filip Reyntjens, "Rencontres burundaises: Inyenzi du Rwanda et rebelles du Kivu," *Cahiers du CEDAF* 7–8 (1986): 123–37; Augustin Mariro, *Burundi 1965: La 1ère crise ethnique* (Paris: L'Harmattan, 2005).

24. Bizimana Septime, telegram to deputy prime minister, September 7, 1964, Archives Nationales du Burundi (hereafter ANB), BI 6.94.

25. Cyprien Ntahomereye, Interrogations: Nsabuwanka, Ntirumveko, Sebiganiro, Sebihehero, Mbitse, Kavamahanga, September 17, 1964, ANB, BI 5.19.

26. Conseil de guerre, *Audience publique*, April 10, 1965, ANB, BI 5.22.

27. Misigaro Tharcisse, Interrogation: Rukushi Isaac et al., August 29, 1964, ANB, BI 5.18.

28. Ibid.

29. Conseil de guerre, *Audience publique*, April 10, 1965, ANB, BI 5.22.

30. Lemarchand, *Rwanda and Burundi*, 306–8.

31. Kabanda Samson, *Inama y'ukuri*, October 29, 1964, ANB, BI 6.34.

32. Ferguson, "Declarations of Dependence," 237.

33. Lemarchand, *Rwanda and Burundi*, 416–22; Mariro, *Burundi 1965*, 173–94.

34. Zibakwiye Athanase, *Rapport mensuel Ijene*, April 7, 1967, ANB, B 9.

35. Sakubu Lucien, letter to Immigration, February 16, 1967, ANB, BI 6.120.

36. Paul Rusiga and Mathias Rwamo, *Situation frontalière de Kabarore*, July 24, 1967, ANB, B 11.2.

37. Ibid.

38. The word *inyenzi* later became notorious as a term of extreme hate speech against all Tutsi during the 1994 genocide. In the 1960s, however, it referred specifically to the refugee militants, who were said to embrace the name themselves.

39. Rusiga and Rwamo, *Situation frontalière*.

40. *Affaire Nkurunziza*, July 25, 1967, ANB, B 11.2.

41. Dereje Feyissa, "More State Than the State? The Anywaa's Call for the Rigidification of the Ethio-Sudanese Border," in *Borders and Borderlands as Resources in the Horn of Africa*, ed. Dereje Feyissa and Markus Virgil Hoehne (Oxford: James Currey, 2010), 43.

42. Rusiga and Rwamo, *Situation frontalière*.

43. *Affaire Nkurunziza*.

44. Ibid.

45. See Lemarchand, *Rwanda and Burundi*, 448, 458–59; Russell, "Talking Politics," 168–179.

46. Ray Abrahams, *Vigilant Citizens: Vigilantism and the State* (Cambridge: Polity Press, 1998), 24.

47. Although note the courageous and perspicacious report written by Martin Ndayahoze, minister of information and the most senior Hutu politician in government, on the pervasive ethnic rivalries that overwhelmed the state in 1968. René Lemarchand, *Burundi: Ethnic Conflict and Genocide* (Cambridge: Cambridge University Press, 1996), 85–86. He was later murdered by his rivals in 1972.

48. Robins et al., "Rethinking 'Citizenship,'" 1080.

49. Thomas Burgess, "The Young Pioneers and the Rituals of Citizenship in Revolutionary Zanzibar," *Africa Today* 51, no. 3 (2005): 3–29.

50. Robins et al., "Rethinking 'Citizenship,'" 1073.

51. Ferguson, "Declarations of Dependence," 237.

52. Jean-Pierre Chrétien and Jean-François Dupaquier, *Burundi 1972: Au bord des génocides* (Paris: Karthala, 2007); Lemarchand, *Burundi*, 76–105.

References

Abrahams, Ray. *Vigilant Citizens: Vigilantism and the State*. Cambridge: Polity Press, 1998.

Botte, Roger. "La guerre interne au Burundi." In *Guerres de lignages et guerres d'états en Afrique*, edited by Jean Bazin and Emmanuel Terray, 271–317. Paris: Editions des Archives Contemporaines, 1982.

Burgess, Thomas. "The Young Pioneers and the Rituals of Citizenship in Revolutionary Zanzibar." *Africa Today* 51, no. 3 (2005): 3–29.

Castryck, Geert. "The Hidden Agenda of Citizenship: African Citizenship in the Face of the Modern Nation-State." In *Citizenship in Historical Perspective*, edited by Steven Ellis, Guðmundur Hálfdanarson, and Ann Katherine Isaacs, 189–202. Pisa: Edizione Plus Pisa University Press, 2006.

Chrétien, Jean-Pierre, and Jean-François Dupaquier. *Burundi 1972: Au bord des genocides*. Paris: Karthala, 2007.

Deslaurier, Christine. "Un monde politique en mutation: Le Burundi à la veille de l'indépendance (circa 1956–1961)." PhD diss., Université Panthéon-Sorbonne, 2002.

de Witte, Ludo. "L'assassinat du Premier ministre burundais Louis Rwagasore." 2013. http://casi.elis.ugent.be/avrug//forum_2013pdf/rwagasore_fr.pdf.

Ferguson, James. "Declarations of Dependence: Labour, Personhood, and Welfare in Southern Africa." *Journal of the Royal Anthropological Institute* 19 (2013): 223–42.

Feyissa, Dereje. "More State Than the State? The Anywaa's Call for the Rigidification of the Ethio-Sudanese Border." In *Borders and Borderlands as Resources in the Horn of Africa*, edited by Dereje Feyissa and Markus Virgil Hoehne, 27–44. Oxford: James Currey, 2010.

Isin, Engin F., and Bryan S. Turner. "Citizenship Studies: An Introduction." In *Handbook of Citizenship Studies*, edited by Engin F. Isin and Bryan S. Turner, 1–10. London: Sage Publications, 2002.

Lemarchand, René. *Burundi: Ethnic Conflict and Genocide*. Cambridge: Cambridge University Press, 1996.

———. *Rwanda and Burundi*. London: Pall Mall Press, 1970.

Mamdani, Mahmood. *Citizen and Subject: Contemporary African States and the Legacy of Late Colonialism*. Princeton: Princeton University Press, 1996.

Mariro, Augustin. *Burundi 1965: La 1ère crise ethnique*. Paris: L'Harmattan, 2005.

Ndayiziga, Charles. "Baranyanka et le chefferie Kunkiko-Mugamba." Mémoire de licence, University of Burundi, 1987.

Poppe, Guy. *L'assassinat de Rwagasore, le Lumumba burundais*. Bujumbura: Iwacu, 2012.

Reyntjens, Filip. "Rencontres burundaises: Inyenzi du Rwanda et rebelles du Kivu." *Cahiers du CEDAF* nos. 7–8 (1986): 123–37.

Robins, Steven, Andrea Cornwall, and Bettina von Lieres. "Rethinking 'Citizenship' in the Postcolony." *Third World Quarterly* 29, no. 6 (2008): 1069–86.

Russell, Aidan. "Talking Politics and Watching the Border in Northern Burundi, c. 1960–1972." PhD diss., Oxford University, 2013.

Tully, James. "Two Meanings of Global Citizenship: Modern and Diverse." In *Global Citizenship Education: Philosophy, Theory and Pedagogy*, edited by Michael A. Peters, Alan Britton, and Harry Blee, 15–41. Rotterdam: Sense Publications, 2008.

Verbrugghe, André. "Introduction historique au problème de la nationalité au Burundi." *Revue administrative et juridique du Burundi* 6, no. 18 (1972): 5–8.

PART TWO

Citizenship and the Postcolonial State

FIVE

"Double Nationalité" and Its Discontents in Ivory Coast, 1963–66

HENRI-MICHEL YÉRÉ

SOON AFTER INDEPENDENCE IN AUGUST 1960 AND THE ADOPTION OF a citizenship law in December 1961, the president of Ivory Coast, Félix Houphouët-Boigny, introduced a new initiative, *double nationalité*, aimed at extending the scope of Ivorian citizenship. This was first publicly mentioned at a meeting held in September 1963 at the Abidjan stadium that bears his name:

> I would like to express a feeling of affection toward all our brothers—Guineans, Malians, Voltaics, Senegalese, Nigeriens, etc., who have been with us during the heroic struggle for the independence of this country and who are engaged with us in the harmonious building of our young state. We would like to confirm that this country is also theirs and that in the coming months we will open talks with the leaders of their respective countries, so as to grant them dual citizenship [*double nationalité*], in order to foster the African unity under way as we speak and to allow them to be a full party in the harmonious development of the Ivory Coast, who opens her maternal arms to them, just like the autochthonous Ivorians.[1]

In its classical understanding, double nationalité (dual citizenship) entitles an individual to bear the passports of two different countries, which was not how Houphouët was using the term. Rather, he was referring to the creation of a "supranationality" in which nationals of different West African states could benefit from the same rights and duties as citizens of their host country without being citizens.

Houphouët-Boigny presented this decision as one bringing francophone West Africa a step closer to African unity. Although he was speaking to a large constituency of African residents within Ivory Coast, the scope of this initiative was first narrowed down to the citizens of member states of the Conseil de l'Entente (Upper Volta, Niger, Dahomey, Togo, and Ivory Coast) and was finally defeated early in 1966.[2] It is crucial to understand the context of the birth of this project, its life, and most critically the reasons why it was abandoned. The history of this failed project highlights the nature of divisions over questions of nationality and citizenship within the Ivoirian leadership while also demonstrating the challenges involved in aligning domestic Ivoirian politics and the regional politics of West Africa. This also tells the story of the articulation of oppositional politics within the context of a one-party state with the ruling party in question as it engaged in the process of asserting its hegemony over different parts of Ivoirian society and within state institutions.[3]

Ivorian Nationality before Independence

Nationality can be defined as the cornerstone of international sovereignty, the marker of the distinct character of a state.[4] The history of Ivorian nationality did not start with the proclamation of independence, even though nationality is generally defined as that which sets the citizen of a country apart from another one in the international sphere. The question of the existence of an Ivorian nationality started within the framework of the Communauté.[5]

The Communauté was a new entity under which France and its African colonies came together in the 1958 constitution. Article (Titre) XII of the constitution dealt with the relationship between France and its overseas territories. It stated that France's colonies could choose to remain under France's umbrella either as *départements*, autonomous republics, or in the form they already were, as overseas territories. The colonies (except for Guinea) all became republics. A prime minister headed each of them, while the head of the Communauté remained the president of the French Republic. The Communauté republics had autonomy in all matters except for foreign affairs, defense, tertiary education, external transportation and communications, and strategic raw materials. Because the Communauté was a political organization that brought together several autonomous states, the discussions hinged on whether there would be one nationality for the whole of the Communauté or whether each of the autonomous member-states would have its own nationality. Hence, at the time, debates within the Communauté were centered not on Ivorian nationality but on the question of what the nationality of citizens from the Communauté republics would be. As early as February 1959, ahead of the Communauté's first executive council meeting, held in Paris, the heads of state of the new republics raised the question of nationality within the Communauté.[6] In their eyes, being a republic entailed numerous prerogatives, including having an independent nationality. The problem was that the 1958 constitution had not been explicit on the question of the nationality of Communauté citizens. In its Article 77, it simply stated that "il n'existe qu'une citoyenneté de la Communauté" (There shall be one citizenship within the Communauté).[7]

As if to confirm the constitution, French president Charles de Gaulle declared that the only nationality recognized within the Communauté was that of the French Republic. This decision was made only a few days after the first executive council meeting, which took place in Paris on February 3 and 4, 1959.[8] All Communauté citizens were thus French nationals. Such a state of affairs did not satisfy all of France's African partners, among them the government of Soudan. Soudan was committed to claiming an independent nationality. Not only that, for the Soudanais leadership, an independent nationality was a necessity for genuine economic development.[9] The Ivorian leadership, in contrast, had a very different conception of nationalism, whereby independence was not a political prerequisite for economic development.[10]

In September 1959 the Communauté leadership decided to hand the question over to an experts committee made up of representatives, mainly legal experts, from all Communauté governments and the French Republic.[11] After a series of meetings, the experts delivered their first conclusions in a report in December 1959. Their main proposal was a new concept of nationality, *nationalité superposée* (juxtaposed nationality).[12] This notion maintained a clear distinction between the concepts of citizenship and nationality, in keeping with the French tradition embodied in the 1946 constitution.[13] Citizenship referred to a regime of rights and duties open to every member of the political community within the entire Communauté. Nationality was a marker of a state's sovereignty, the way in which it distinguished the people under its authority from others. The experts committee proposed that each state would retain its individual nationality within the Communauté but that outside of the realm of Communauté each of these citizens would be regarded as French nationals and citizens.[14] The model of a passport proposed would indicate the nationality of the citizen according to his or her Communauté state (for example Senegal) with a footnote indicating that internationally the citizen would be regarded as French.[15] French nationality thus assumed the status of a "supranationality" within the Communauté. In addition, by being recognized as French citizens, the citizens of Communauté states stood to benefit from all the international treaties that France was party to. A Senegalese man traveling to the United States was to be regarded by the American authorities as a French citizen under the protection of French consular authorities. This formula gave a legal existence to African nationalities, a psychological win for many Communauté leaders. Nationality, as one of the reports noted, made one feel one step closer to independence.[16] Nationalité superposée ushered Ivorian nationality into the realm of the possible. In Houphouët-Boigny's perspective, Ivorian nationality could exist so long as it was reinforced and protected by French imperial citizenship, giving it international weight and making Ivorians potentially eligible for French social benefits.

But this was before August 1960 and the independence of Ivory Coast. In December 1961, the Ivorian National Assembly adopted a Nationality Code. The bill was made up of 105 articles and was divided into seven headings. Birth on Ivorian soil was the main principle for attribution of Ivoirian citizenship.[17] This decision to base citizenship on birth was for practical reasons. Given that the civil registrar (*état-civil*) was not fully operational in the early years of self-government, proving the descent of most Ivorians on the basis of administrative papers such as birth certificates would have been impossible. Most people did not have birth certificates at that time. Hence, descent could not be used as the sole basis for the establishment of Ivorian nationality as nationality of origin.[18] The bill also included the conditions for acquiring Ivorian nationality through marriage (Articles 12 to 16), for children born of foreign parents on Ivorian soil. In the case of a foreign woman who married an Ivorian, she could acquire Ivorian nationality immediately unless she explicitly renounced it. An Ivorian woman who married a foreigner, however, maintained her Ivorian nationality unless she explicitly chose her husband's nationality (Article 51). No explicit clause provided for the case of Ivorian men who married foreign women. The assumption was that men could not be affected in the same way because they were hardly expected to "follow" their foreign wives to the latter's country. Children born to foreign parents living in Ivory Coast could become Ivorians through a simple declaration once they reached age eighteen (Article 30). Furthermore, any foreigner who had resided for at least five years in Ivory Coast could acquire Ivorian nationality (Article 26). A last article, Article 106, was added to the bill just before deputies voted on it. It stated,

> The persons who have established their residence in Ivory Coast before 7 August 1960 and who do not wish to become Ivorian citizens, shall retain all the rights they enjoyed before that date, except for the right to vote and the right to be elected in a political assembly.
>
> Change of residence only shall cancel the effects of this measure.[19]

In explaining how they intended to vote, the deputies stated their pride in the fact that they were adopting a liberal code, which confirmed Ivory Coast as a country of hospitality and fraternity. Vamé Doumouya insisted that this code was in line with the ideals defended by the president of the republic, in particular the ideal of being a land of immigration.[20] Jean Thes asserted that the right to work had to be guaranteed to all those who wanted to participate in building the Ivorian nation. He added, "Demain, il ne devra plus y avoir dans ce pays que des nationaux à part entière, égaux devant la loi" (Tomorrow there shall only be nationals in this country, equal before the law).[21] Mamadou Coulibaly, who spoke on behalf of the Parti Démocratique de Côte d'Ivoire's *bureau politique* (the highest body of the ruling party, the PDCI), suggested that all naturalizations be watched over by the party, "pour ne permettre à personne d'entrer dans la communauté ivoirienne sous la forme de ce qui fut le Cheval de Troie" (so as not to allow anyone to enter the Ivorian community in the manner of a Trojan Horse).[22]

Double Nationalité against the Jeunesse du Rassemblement Démocratique Africain?

This was the backdrop against which Houphouët delivered the 1963 speech in which he announced his double nationalité initiative. The main purpose of the 1963 speech was to foster national unity, as well as to reassert his authority over the country. The speech came in the context of a year that had started with political turmoil in Ivory Coast. In January 1963, numerous people had been arrested and charged with high treason, accused of attempting to assassinate the president.[23] These individuals came from a group of Ivorian university graduates who studied in France during the late 1940s and the 1950s. Many of them had been active members of student organizations in France during the 1950s. The most important of these organizations was the Fédération des Étudiants d'Afrique Noire en France (FEANF). FEANF members represented the radical wing of the nationalist movement in French Africa.[24] This was despite the fact that many of these students "owed" their scholarships to Houphouët-Boigny, at the time a French cabinet minister.[25] Upon returning to Ivory Coast, many of these students sought positions within the PDCI, a party Houphouët had founded in 1946, which had established its political hegemony after its sweeping victory in the 1957 elections. They seized the first opportunity to get into the PDCI-RDA at its Third Congress, held in 1959 in Abidjan.[26] Many party members had eagerly awaited this congress, given that the last one had taken place in 1947.

Born in April 1946, PDCI, a section of Rassemblement Démocratique Africain (RDA), was the brainchild of the Syndicat Agricole Africain. Its initial brief had been to defend the citizenship rights of its African base, as was clearly illustrated by its founding leader's *coup d'éclat* of April 1946: an act suppressing the practice of forced labor in all French colonies. The RDA's parliamentary alliance with the French Communists pitted the colonial administration firmly against the party members, and in the years 1949 to 1951, a conflict ensued in Ivory Coast, whereby the colonial administration had decided to destroy the movement. The confrontation came to an end after Houphouët-Boigny heeded the call of the French government and broke the PDCI's alliance with the French Communists. The party then effected a move toward French interests in the colony, to the extent that after the victory of the French Socialist Party (SFIO) in the parliamentary elections of 1956, Houphouët was asked to join the French cabinet. In Ivory Coast itself, 1956 marked the PDCI's great comeback, and its crushing victory at all levels of power allowed it to summon the other parties to come into its fold. By 1957, PDCI had become the sole political party operating in the land. Thus had the one-party state been established as a system of governance in Ivory Coast.

In spite of this domination, the Third Congress can be regarded as a defeat for Houphouët-Boigny. His longtime companion Auguste Denise lost his position as secretary general of the party to Jean-Baptiste Mockey.[27] In addition, the Jeunesse du Rassemblement Démocratique Africain (JRDACI) was formed two weeks before the congress, with Amadou Koné as its secretary general. The JRDACI wanted to exist independently within the party with the freedom to criticize the party line.[28] The existence and position of the JRDACI was accepted at the congress. As a result, Houphouët-Boigny found himself in a minority within the party. His time as a cabinet minister in Paris had brought him esteem and prestige but had also given him the reputation of a remote leader not aware of local realities. Moreover, many regarded the man who had been elected to succeed Denise as one of the more radical figures within the party. Mockey was one of the eight party leaders who had been imprisoned by the colonial administration in 1949.[29] He had not agreed with Houphouët's view that the PDCI should break their parliamentary alliance with the French Communists in 1950. Now as secretary general of PDCI-RDA, deputy prime minister, minister of the interior, and mayor of Grand Bassam, Jean-Baptiste Mockey suddenly became a contender to reckon with, one of the most powerful men in the country.

In November 1959, Houphouët-Boigny employed an unexpected strategy to respond to Mockey's growing status in the party; he accused the deputy prime minister of plotting his assassination. A photo of Houphouët was allegedly found in the bowels of a dead black cat in his gardens in Yamoussoukro. The man who put it there was a marabout that Mockey had allegedly hired to put a spell on Houphouët that would cause his death. Houphouët revealed this information to a stunned audience of militants and party cadres in Yamoussoukro. Party members found it shocking that Mockey would resort to such extreme measures.[30] The strength of the accusation made it difficult for anyone to defend Mockey, as doing so would have meant supporting the idea of Houphouët's assassination. As a consequence, Mockey was discharged of all his responsibilities within the party and the republic with no sign of argument from his supporters.[31] This event came to be known as the "black cat plot" (*complot du chat noir*). Phillippe Yacé, the speaker of the legislative assembly, replaced him as secretary general. The event was a warning to the JRDACI cadres who supported Mockey that they should be careful. The possibilities on the political playing field had suddenly widened, and this left Houphouët's contenders uncertain of what his next move would be. Following this, the January 1963 arrests removed many prominent figures from JRDACI from the political scene. Most notably, Minister of Health Amadou Koné, Minister of Agriculture Charles Donwhai, Minister of Defense Jean Konan Banny, and Minister of Education Joachim Bony were arrested and jailed. JRDACI as an organization was banned, and its leaders were accused of plotting to overthrow the government of Houphouët-Boigny and plotting his assassination. Parliament created a special tribunal, *cour de sûreté de l'Etat*, with Philippe Yacé as its prosecutor. Houphouët appointed none other than Jean-Baptiste Mockey to preside over this new tribunal. A climate of suspicion took hold of the country at this time, with more than one hundred people arrested in January 1963 alone.[32] The first sentences, including five capital punishments, were passed in April. In September 1963, there were more arrests, including veteran PDCI figure and Justice Minister Germain Coffi Gadeau, Amadou Thiam, and Jean-Baptiste Mockey. In April 1964, the chief justice of the Supreme Court and one of the founding figures of JRDACI, Ernest Boka, who had resigned earlier in the year in protest against Houphouët's arbitrary manipulation of power, was found dead in his prison cell at Assabou, near Yamoussoukro. The official report stated that he had "committed suicide."[33]

Hence, the primary purpose of the president's speech in September 1963 in which he first mentioned double nationalité was to justify the repressive turn that his policy had taken. In the view of Amadou Koné and Marcel Amondji, the purpose of double nationalité was to prepare the ground for Houphouët-Boigny to create an alliance with cadres from other African countries to replace those who had been jailed.[34] For Houphouët, these new cadres would present the advantage of having no family (clan or ethnic) ties in Ivory Coast and were hence more likely to be exclusively at his beck and call. According to this view, double nationalité was primarily driven by Houphouët-Boigny's need to assert his political supremacy within Ivory Coast. The "plots'" victims were vindicated in 1970 when Houphouët-Boigny recognized that there had been no such a thing as a plot for eliminating him. He publically apologized and started reintegrating into his government some of those who had been arrested in the early 1960s.

More Than Africanization, Ivorization

As for those who had not been imprisoned during the wave of arrests following the plots, they used whatever venue they could find to pose implicit challenges to the double nationalité project. The PDCI's Fourth Congress was one such place. The 1965 congress, or party conference, was the first since independence and inaugurated the practice of defining party policy orientations for the following five years; the practice became a feature of these congresses. New faces within the party also emerged at this gathering. With his main "opponents" imprisoned, Houphouët could easily promote his clients within the political organization. These included the youngest member of PDCI's Politburo (*bureau politique*), Henri Konan Bédié (born in 1934), who had been the ambassador of Ivory Coast in Washington, DC, for the previous four years. Bédié read the closing speech at the congress and in it he spoke of the need for an acceleration of Africanization, a key theme among the young cadres of the party.[35] Africanization was the idea that first the public administration and then the private sector, both of which had been dominated by the French, should be handed over to Ivorian nationals. This had been a bone of contention between Houphouët-Boigny and the trade unions.[36] From their perspective, Africanization was a normal consequence of Ivory Coast being an independent sovereign nation. But in 1959, during a parliamentary debate with union representatives on the issue, Houphouët, then prime minister, had responded, "*Pas d'africanisation au rabais!*" (No cheap Africanization!), a phrase that became famous.[37]

The young cadres felt particularly concerned by this. Because many of them were university graduates (Bédié, for instance, was a lawyer by training), they would be the first ones to gain from Africanization. A few years later, the term "Ivoirisation" came to replace "Africanisation."[38] Commenting on the presence of numerous French *assistants techniques* within the Ivorian administration, Bédié explained that the "best French advisor or *assistant technique* is the one who will willingly train the African and who will hand over his position to his trainee without any intriguing."[39] He went on to say that private businesses should prioritize Africanizing their staff on the basis of competence. In the same breath, Bédié expressed, on behalf of the party's youths, his unconditional support for double nationalité between Entente states. Bédié was speaking more of an effective Ivorization; in effect, despite all his apparent support, he was making an implicit statement against double nationalité, which is made evident by the fact that all the arguments that were used against the French technical assistants were similar to the ones applied to the potential African newcomers within the framework of the implementation of double nationalité, as would become evident in the course of the discussion that took place after the signing of the double nationalité convention.

Support for the project also came from another one of the young leaders within PDCI, Arsène Assouan Usher, who at the time was the Ivorian representative at the United Nations in New York. Usher (1930–2007) wrote an article asserting that double nationalité was the surest way to create a genuine African union and that soon enough the entire continent would follow suit.[40] However, when I interviewed him in September 2007, the former ambassador assured me that he had actually been against the double nationalité project, because in his eyes, the risk was too great that Ivorians would be definitively held at bay when it came to accessing strategic and important positions within the state administration. In a political climate defined by suspicion and arbitrary actions, however, keeping up the appearance of support for the president's positions was important. In the face of these implicit oppositional stances, it is a fair question to ask how many among those who expressed public support for the double nationalité project from within the leaders of PDCI were sincerely committed to supporting the president's project. Through his speech on Africanization, Bédié was expressing a fear held by the younger generation of Ivorian professionals that they could not easily access positions that they deserved. It is reasonable to assume that those who had not been arrested in 1963 felt that they were especially deserving of prominent positions that had been left empty by those who were jailed. So in Bédié's words, although the French were explicitly referred to, anybody who could represent a potential barrier in the way of the local cadres effectively occupying the state apparatus was targeted. The point of double nationalité, according to the president, was to create the possibility for "a Voltaic to belong to the Ivorian or the Nigerien cabinet." On that basis, I contend that the young PDCI cadres were no different on this issue than their comrades imprisoned on account of the *complots*. They, after all, did belong to the same generation and studied at the same time in the same universities.

Double Nationalité on the African Stage

Houphouët's offer of double nationalité was consistent with his notion of the "necessary stages" that had to be taken in a gradual approach to African unity. Before the OAU was formed in May 1963, francophone African states had founded a common organization, the Union Africaine et Malgache (UAM).[41] Houphouët-Boigny introduced his double nationalité concept to his African peers at the UAM's second meeting in Dakar, Senegal, in February 1964. He wanted them to join him in creating a common position on nationality within francophone Africa. He added, however, that if the UAM did not accept double nationalité, Ivory Coast would continue the project with Niger and Upper Volta.[42] His francophone peers did not accept Houphouët's offer.

Seeing that his project could not fare well within the larger continental organizations, the Ivorian president settled for Conseil de l'Entente as his testing ground. In December 1964, during an official trip to Upper Volta, the Ivorian president defined this project in a speech dubbed the *Déclaration de Ouhahigouya*.[43] He spoke of the fraternity that linked Upper Volta, Niger, and Ivory Coast, while fixing the scope of his initiative within the framework of the Conseil de l'Entente: "Our initiative means that Voltaics in Ivory Coast and Ivorians in Upper Volta would have the same rights and the same duties without having to give up their respective national qualities. . . . Citizens of these three states (Ivory Coast, Niger, and Upper Volta) would vote and could be elected in each country, and one day an Ivorian would become a cabinet minister in Ouagadougou and a Voltaic would belong to the Ivorian or the Nigerien cabinet."[44]

Scaling down the number of countries that were part of this project can be interpreted as a strategy to focus on the Ivory Coast's immediate sphere of influence. Not only did the Entente lend itself geographically to such a project, but also geopolitically the Abidjan-Ouagadougou-Niamey axis made sense. Dahomey's absence from these initial conversations was attributable to internal political feuds, which resulted in the country being isolated internationally. As of 1965, many Entente meetings took place with Togo in attendance as a new member of the group. The extension of membership to Togo led to the postponement of the launch of the project to late 1965. Because this decision was made to appear as the future central piece of the Entente edifice, the organization needed to prepare itself to welcome new members, taking into account the changes that were going to be introduced by this future disposition.

On December 30, 1965, the heads of state of Ivory Coast, Niger, Upper Volta, Dahomey, and Togo signed the Double Nationalité Convention in Abidjan.[45] The five governments adopted the principle that when resident in any of these countries, the citizens of the member states could benefit from the same rights and duties as citizens of the state in which they resided. The actual definition of *double nationalité,* the acquisition and loss of it, and the particular cases of students, migrant workers, civil servants, and the military was to be defined in another convention developed after the first one signed in December 1965. A second article dealt with the economic aspects of the convention, which, according to Jacques Baulin, worked almost exclusively to the advantage of Ivory Coast.[46] This article recommended the harmonization of the member states' industrial and agricultural policies and their investment codes. Moreover, Article 2 suggested a "study of the external markets that each member state represents for one another in order to reach a sense of balance in the commercial exchanges between states." It concluded by affirming the principle that coastal states would grant landlocked states access to their ports to enable goods to be transported easily.

PDCI Members Bury the Project

However, on January 21, 1966, three weeks after the convention was signed, the secretary general of PDCI issued a communiqué announcing that the implementation of the Double Nationalité Convention was postponed until further notice. This suspension was explained as due to the "perhaps legitimate worries of some of [PDCI's] most dedicated activists" in relation to the agreement.[47] Houphouët-Boigny asked for a national council meeting during which he would clear up all misunderstandings with the militants, "so that the party's enemies [would] not take advantage of the situation to pursue their sad political ends."[48] The need for an explanatory session testifies that a gap existed between the perspective of the president and the bulk of party activists. During the session, the president explained that double nationalité would not be abandoned, but the project would be implemented on a continental scale only when the Organisation Commune Africaine et Malgache (successor institution to the UAM) and Organization of African Unity (OAU) countries followed suit. He emphasized that PDCI committees could decide which Africans could enjoy double nationalité privileges in the Ivory Coast. In doing so, he acknowledged the party activists' opposition to the idea of double nationalité. According to Arsène Assouan Usher, during the session, a old activist from Lakota rose and told the president, "Today is a day for frank truths. . . . If you want to sell the country off, then you must show us where to go!"[49] As Houphouët-Boigny acknowledged almost twenty years later, "I would like to say that it was on only three occasions throughout the time of my presidency that my people did not follow me. The first time was when I presented a project aiming to create a dual citizenship in this country."[50]

Houphouët also acknowledged that the young Ivorian professionals feared that double nationalité would allow cadres from places like Dahomey (notably) to occupy positions from which they could not be removed.[51] Lambert Amon Tanoh, at the time the Ivorian minister for education, confirmed that these were some of the reasons behind the local cadres' refusal of double nationalité.[52] There was a strong fear inherited from the experience of the *Bildungsrückstand* of the colony of Ivory Coast, as opposed to places like Dahomey and Senegal. In addition, in 1965–66, memories of the 1958 riot directed against the Dahomeyans and Togolese living in Ivory Coast were still fresh. The main motivation behind these riots was the perception that Dahomeyans had access to better professional situations, to the disadvantage of Ivorians, a stance voiced by the Ligue des Originaires de la Côte d'Ivoire (LOCI).[53]

Entente's Poor Consensus

The dominant assumption in Ivory Coast was that if double nationalité was approved, West Africans were likely to "invade" Ivory Coast. After 1951, Ivory Coast had become the most important economy in French-speaking West Africa.[54] In favor of the double nationalité project, Houphouët spoke of the fact that the current prosperity of Ivory Coast was the result of the collective effort of all West African populations living on Ivorian soil, especially of Voltaics.[55] What Ivorians did not know was that the project did not have a good reputation in Upper Volta either. On the contrary, in Upper Volta it was viewed as another instance of subordinating Voltaic interests to Ivorian ones, a stance that had come to define the presidency of Maurice Yaméogo. Yaméogo emerged as a key figure in Voltaic politics in the 1950s, particularly after the death of Ouezzin Coulibaly in 1958. Yaméogo's authoritarian style of ruling and his seeming insensitivity to the economic difficulties of the country made him an unpopular leader.[56] In addition to this, he spent a good deal of his time (some argued up to 40 percent) outside his country, mostly in Ivory Coast. As a result, Yaméogo was seen as Houphouët's "lackey," his "spokesman," who publicly spoke on matters of African politics in a way that Houphouët himself would not.[57] When Maurice Yaméogo returned to Ougadougou with the Double Nationalité Convention, trade unions were mobilizing protests over a recent 20 percent cut in civil servants' salaries. The convention added fuel to this in a context within which the unions felt they were not being heard by their president. Within three days, Yaméogo was forced to step down and hand over power to the military chief of staff, Lieutenant Colonel Sangoulé Lamizana, who reluctantly assumed the office of head of state.[58]

Yaméogo's fall, which came as a surprise, hit the Conseil de l'Entente hard. Deliberations within the Entente, essentially a heads-of-state organization, were based on personal relationships. Hence, the heads of state in the group referred to each other as "brothers." Upper Volta's membership in the organization was also essential, as it was the one Entente country that had borders with all the others.[59] Yaméogo's departure closely followed the departure of Sourou Migan Apithy, the president of Dahomey, who was overthrown by General Christophe Soglo in November 1965. Hence, the axis Abidjan-Ouagadougou-Niamey came to a sudden halt.

This new political situation left Houphouët and Hamani Diori of Niger as the only "historic" leaders of the Entente. Fresh evidence reveals that the Nigerien president was actually not an enthusiast of double nationalité but had agreed to it out of solidarity with the bloc.[60] He "sold" his signature on the convention in exchange for the promise of investment commitments in Niger by his Ivorian and Voltaic peers. Hamani Diori also did not want to lose control over the civil service of his country and hence ensured that in the initial template agreement, a clause was included detailing a selection process for applicants from other Entente countries.[61] The oppositions to the project inside Ivory Coast and in Upper Volta, when added to President Diori's reluctance, dashed the hopes of the remaining original authors of the project for pursuing it as they saw fit. The fact that the project ended in this way illustrates that it was a heads-of-state affair to which the rest of the population had hardly been attached. In this context, popular hostility to the project might have been a consequence of the lack of explanation of what the project entailed. In Ivory Coast, PDCI's leadership thought it useful to launch a major explanation campaign (*campagne d'explication*) only after the convention had been signed. This campaign made the authorities realize that party activists were in the main opposed to the idea.

Félix Houphouët-Boigny launched the double nationalité initiative in 1963 in a national climate heavy with suspicion (because of the plots) in an attempt to revive the spirit of nationalité superposée. Double nationalité could be regarded as a concrete step toward the ideal of African unity that had found a compromise arrangement in the same year (1963) in Addis-Ababa. It could also be seen as an instrument intended to strengthen the influence of Ivory Coast over its francophone peers.

One of the main obstacles to the realization of this vision was Ivorian cadres and youths concerned about professional Ivorians' possibility of finding employment in their own country. The cadres' acute consciousness of their fragility as an interest group—at the mercy of a presidential whim, as demonstrated by the plots—when added to the historic problem of a dearth of cadres available for the needs of the growing economy, pushed them to resist an attempt at opening the playing field. These groups were convinced that double nationalité would open the doors for African foreigners to take over positions that they saw as their righteous preserve, and they used the PDCI structure to vent their opposition. The political context of West Africa did not lend itself to a prolongation of the initiative, as Maurice Yaméogo in Upper Volta had been toppled by a coalition of trade unions. Among their many discontents was the double nationalité initiative, which they saw as a way to further undermine Upper Volta vis-à-vis Ivory Coast, the historic "older brother."

Double nationalité was a clear instance of a confrontation between two different views on nationality and citizenship in Ivory Coast. But the defeat of the project revealed a wedge between the top leadership of Ivorian politics and the party base over the meaning of independence from France. Whereas Houphouët-Boigny had only reluctantly accepted the effective break from France that the proclamation of independence in August 1960 entailed, the base of his party and its cadres had interpreted the immediate outcome of sovereignty as the possibility to assert the right of Ivorians (as opposed to the French and other Africans residing in the country) to be the primary beneficiaries of the new state of affairs. Furthermore, in subsequent reforms of the Ivorian nationality code, the tendency has been to restrict the possibilities for access to Ivorian citizenship, in the context of an important flow of incoming migration, mainly from other West African countries. Such a trend came with many implications, in a country whose cash-crop economy had since the 1930s heavily relied on a labor force imported mainly from Burkina Faso and Mali. This tension between the "liberal school" of an Ivorian citizenship opened to West Africa and a more "conservative" school centered on the interests of Ivorians first has been a feature of Ivorian political and social life ever since.

More than anyone else, the figure of Henri Konan Bédié best embodies this reality. Bédié, after his speech at the Fourth Congress of PDCI in 1965, stood to benefit immediately from Africanization as he became the first African minister of finance in the country's history in 1966, succeeding Raphaël Saller, a Frenchman. Later in life, Bédié became the second president of Ivory Coast, after Houphouët-Boigny's death in 1993. One of the first measures that he introduced during his nascent presidency was a modification of the electoral law, which stated that to be a candidate for president, a person had to "be an Ivorian, born to a mother and a father themselves Ivorian born."[62] He simultaneously launched a new concept, which he hoped was going to become the locus for the summation of what it meant to be an Ivorian in that day and age. He named this concept "*Ivoirité.*"[63] The consistency in Bédié's thinking, in a political life spanning at least three decades, allows me to assert that this way of thinking participates in the ideological landscape of Ivorian politics and, although it intervenes in a "politics of autochthony" visible in many other parts of the African continent, is not just a consequence of the acceleration of the globalization of the world economy.[64]

Notes

I would like to acknowledge the generous support of the Swiss National Centre of Competence in Research (NCCR) "North-South: Research Partnerships for Mitigating Syndromes of Global Change," cofunded by the Swiss National Science Foundation (SNF) and the Swiss Agency for Development and Cooperation (SDC).

1. "Je voudrais exprimer une pensée affectueuse pour tous nos frères non originaires de Côte d'Ivoire: Guinéens, Maliens, Voltaïques, Sénégalais, Nigériens, etc, qui ont été à nos côtés dans la lutte héroïque pour l'indépendance du pays et qui continuent avec nous cette lutte pour l'édification harmonieuse de notre jeune Etat. Nous leur confirmons qu'ils sont ici chez eux, et que, dans les mois qui viennent, nous allons engager, avec les responsables de leurs pays respectifs, des pourparlers en vue de leur accorder la double nationalité, ce qui permettrait dans le cadre de cette unité africaine que nous sommes en train de bâtir, et dans le respect de leur dignité et de leur fierté nationale, de participer au même titre que les Ivoiriens de souche à la construction harmonieuse de la Côte d'Ivoire qui leur ouvre tout grands ses bras maternels" (my translation). Marcel Amondji, "Assabou et Marcoussis: Deux tragedies ivoiriennes," *Outre-Terre* 2, no. 11 (2005): 219.

2. Conseil de l'Entente, often referred to as Entente, was founded in May 1959 and brought together Niger, Dahomey, Upper Volta, and Ivory Coast with

the purpose of fostering cooperation among these states. Its key institution was a solidarity fund for financing development projects. Ivory Coast's contribution was expected to be up to five-sixths of the fund, clearly illustrating where the balance of power lay in the organization. See "L'Entente est faite entre 4 états," *Afrique Nouvelle,* June 5, 1959.

3. This chapter rests on fresh evidence from the papers of Jacques Foccart, available at the French Archives Nationales in Paris. Jacques Foccart (1913–1997) was De Gaulle's foremost advisor on African affairs. I am indebted to Frederick Cooper, who first told me of their availability; my thanks to him.

4. Patrick Weil, *Qu'est-ce qu'un Français? Histoire de la nationalité française jusqu'à nos jours* (Paris: Gallimard, 2004).

5. For the original version of the constitution as adopted on October 4, 1958, see http://mjp.univ-perp.fr/france/co1958-0.htm; see also Gérard Peureux, *Le Conseil Exécutif de la Communauté* (Paris: Librairie de Droit et de Jurisprudence, 1960).

6. The executive council, Communauté's highest body, was where its most important decisions were taken. The council was chaired by the French president. "Note relative à la nationalité et à la citoyenneté dans la Communauté. Paris, le 22 janvier 1959," Centre d'Acceuil et de Recherche des Archives Nationales (hereafter CARAN), Fonds "Public" Jacques Foccart (hereafter FPU), AG/5, FPU 215.

7. My translation.

8. "Note relative à la nationalité. Paris, le 14 novembre 1959," CARAN, FPU 215.

9. Ibid.

10. See Katia Voltolina, "L'éclatement de la Fédération du Mali (1960): D'une fédération rêvée au choc des réalités," *RAHIA* 23 (2007): 27; Daniel Bach, "L'insertion ivoirienne dans les rapports internationaux," in *Etat et bourgeoisie en Côte d'Ivoire,* ed. Y.-A. Fauré and J.-F. Médard (Paris: Karthala, 1982), 92.

11. "Communiqué de la 5e reunion du Conseil exécutif de la Communauté, réunion des 10 et 11 septembre 1959 à Paris," CARAN, Fonds "Privé" Jacques Foccart (hereafter FPR) 104.

12. Jane Burbank and Frederick Cooper, "Empire, droits et citoyenneté de 212 à 1946," in *Annales, histoire, sciences sociales* 63, no. 3 (2008): 525.

13. "Note sur la nationalité des ressortissants des etats membres de la Communauté—initialement preparé par le Professeur Le Gonidec pour le Président Mamadou Dia, transmise par le Haut-Commissaire à Dakar au Secrétariat de la Communauté. Dakar, le 15 avril 1959," CARAN, FPU 215.

14. "Relevé des decisions adoptées en Conseil Exécutif de la Communauté, Saint Louis, 11–12 décembre 1959: Annexe 1: Comité des Experts: Relevé des decisions qui résultent de l'approbation du rapport sur la nationalité et la citoyenneté par le Conseil Exécutif," CARAN, FPR 104.

15. Ibid.

16. "Note relative à la nationalité: documents réunis par Mlle Dulery, membre du Comité des Experts. Paris, le 3 septembre 1959," CARAN, FPU 215.

17. However, merely to be born on Ivorian soil was not enough to be attributed Ivorian nationality at birth: one also had to be the child of at least one Ivorian citizen.

18. République de Côte d'Ivoire, Ministère de la Justice, *Exposé des motifs pour le projet de code de la nationalité soumis à l'Assemblée Nationale de Côte d'Ivoire* (Abidjan, November 26, 1961), 2 (6 pp.).

19. "Les personnes ayant établi leur domicile en Côte d'Ivoire antérieurement au 7 août 1960 qui n'acquièrent pas la nationalité ivoirienne, soit de plein droit, soit volontairement conservent cependant à titre personnel tous les droits acquis dont elles bénéficient avant cette date, à l'exception des droits d'électorat et d'éligibilité aux assemblées politiques. [paragraph break] Le transfert du domicile à l'étranger entraîne la perte du bénéfice des dispositions de l'alinéa précédent" (my translation). Assemblée Nationale de Côte d'Ivoire, *Séance plénière du vendredi 1er décembre 1961*, procès-verbal sommaire, 59–63.

20. Ibid., 60.

21. Ibid., 64 (my translation).

22. Ibid., 69 (my translation).

23. Samba Diarra, *Les Faux Complots d'Houphouët-Boigny: Fracture dans le destin d'une nation* (Paris: Karthala, 1997); Amadou Koné, *Houphouët-Boigny et la crise ivoirienne* (Paris: Karthala, 2003).

24. Tony Chafer, *The End of Empire in French West Africa: France's Successful Decolonisation?* (Oxford: Berg, 2002), 127–31; see also Charles Diané, *La FEANF et les grandes heures du mouvement syndical étudiant noir* (Paris: Éditions Chaka, 1990).

25. Chafer, *End of Empire*, 204; Diané, *La FEANF*, 55. As a French cabinet minister between 1956 and 1959, Houphouët had been responsible for taking care of French West Africa students' affairs.

26. Diarra, *Les faux complots*, 68–72.

27. J.-B. Mockey, secretary general of PDCI, "Notre voie est toute tracée: c'est celle du travail et de l'efficacité dont notre Congrès a précisé les desseins," *Côte d'Ivoire Informations*, April 11, 1959.

28. Le manifeste de la JRDACI, *Côte d'Ivoire Informations*, March 21, 1959.

29. See, in particular, Bernard Dadié, *Carnets de prison* (Abidjan: CEDA, 1984).

30. Interview with Paul Pépé, Abidjan, October 3, 2007.

31. Diarra, *Les faux complots*, 72–78; see also "Le Général de Gaulle admet l'évolution de la Communauté," *Afrique Nouvelle*, November 13, 1959.

32. Interview with Jules Yao, Abidjan, June 2008.

33. Diarra, *Les faux complots*, 180–90; Koné, *La crise ivoirienne*, 110.

34. Amondji, "Assabou et Marcoussis," 220–23.

35. Henri Konan Bédié would eventually succeed Houphouët-Boigny as the president of Côte d'Ivoire, after Houphouët's death in 1993.

36. Interview with Lambert Amon Tanoh, Abidjan, September 29, 2007.

37. Ibid. (my translation).

38. See Assemblée Nationale de Côte d'Ivoire, *Séance plénière du mercredi 8 novembre 1961*, procès-verbal sommaire, 9–14.

39. "Le discours de clôture de M. Konan Bédié," *Fraternité Matin*, September 27, 1965 (my translation).

40. "L'œuvre déterminante du Président Félix Houphouët-Boigny dans la décolonisation, par S. E. Arsène Assouan Usher," *Fraternité Matin*, July 28, 1965.

41. The adoption of the Charter for African Unity, which in effect created the organization in May 1963, was the result of a compromise between two loose groups of countries: the Casablanca Group, for "progressive" countries; and the Monrovia Group, for "moderate" ones. Ivory Coast belonged to the Monrovia Group—named after the African city where it had met. Each of these groups was committed to the overall goal of ending colonialism and apartheid in Africa and promoting African unity, but they diverged on what the means to reach these goals should be. The Monrovia Group favored a gradual approach, whose central tenet was an insistence that the borders inherited from the colonial era ought to remain as such. These borders would be the basis on which any intra-African political project would take place. The Casablanca Group brought together countries that wanted to accelerate unity in Africa by creating common institutions among countries. They questioned the borders inherited from the colonial division of Africa. Ghanaian president Kwame Nkrumah was the loudest voice in this group. He was committed to the creation of the United States of Africa with one continental government, parliament, and currency. See Kwame Nkrumah, *L'Afrique doit s'unir* (Paris: Présence Africaine, 1994); and Joseph Ki Zerbo, *Histoire de l'Afrique Noire* (Paris: Hatier, 1978), 653–57.

42. "Ministère des Affaires Etrangères, Télégramme à l'arrivée. Abidjan, le 27 février 1964," CARAN, FPU 557.

43. "Le Président à Bobo-Dioulasso: 'Moins que l'étiquette, le contenu.' Il faisait ainsi allusion à la forme de l'union des peuples frères," *Fraternité Matin*, December 19–20, 1964.

44. "Notre proposition signifie que les Voltaïques en Côte d'Ivoire et les Ivoriens en Haute Volta auront les mêmes droits et devoirs sans pour autant renoncer à leurs qualités respectives. . . . Les citoyens de Haute-Volta, du Niger et de Côte d'Ivoire auront les memes droits et les memes devoirs, égal accès à la fonction publique des trois Etats, égal accès à la propriété privée. Ils seront électeurs et éligibles et on verra un Ivorien ministre à Ouagadougou ou Niamey et réciproquement un voltaïque ministre à Abidjan ou à Niamey" (my translation). "Hier matin à Koudougou en Haute-Volta, le président Houphouët-Boigny précise sa pensée sur la double nationalité qui sera réalité dans le premier trimestre 1965," *Fraternité Matin*, December 17, 1964.

45. "La proclamation de la double nationalité," *Fraternité Matin*, December 31, 1965.

46. Jacques Baulin, *La politique africaine d'Houphouët-Boigny* (Paris: EURA-FOR, 1980), 159.

47. "Le Communiqué du PDCI-RDA," *Fraternité Matin*, January 21, 1966 (my translation).

48. "Le Chef de l'Etat hier au Palais présidentiel: 'La double nationalité n'est pas un passeport pour l'emploi chez nous,'" *Fraternité Matin,* January 22, 1966 (my translation).

49. Interview with Arsène Assouan Usher, Abidjan, September 26, 2007.

50. "Je voudrais dire qu'en trois fois seulement au cours de ma vie politique à la tête de ce pays, je n'ai pas été suivi par mon peuple. La première fois, c'est quand j'ai présenté au peuple de Côte d'Ivoire un projet de loi tendant à instaurer une double nationalité" (my translation). *La Conférence de presse du Président de la République, Président du PDCI-RDA: Abidjan, le 14 Octobre 1985* (Abidjan: Fraternité Hebdo Editions, 1985).

51. Bach, "Les rapports internationaux," 96.

52. Interview with Lambert Amon Tanoh, Abidjan, September 29, 2007.

53. In Abidjan, on October 22, 1958, there erupted a sudden wave of violence directed at Dahomeyans and Togolese. The violence was instigated by a hitherto unknown organization, the LOCI (Ligue des Originaires de la Côte d'Ivoire). The homes of Dahomeyans and Togolese were targeted, looted, and in some cases burned down. The violence went on for another four days. As a result, 18,000 Dahomeyans and Togolese were repatriated. See Alain Tirefort, "Octobre 1958, 'L'affaire Daho-Togo': Une fièvre de xénophobie en Côte d'Ivoire," in *Etre étranger et migrant en Afrique au XXe siècle: Enjeux identitaires et modes d'insertion,* vol. 1, ed. Catherine Coquery Vidrovitch, Odile Goerg, Issiaka Mande, and Faranirina Rajaonah (Paris: L'Harmattan, 2003), 416; Daouda Gary Tounkara, *Migrants soudanais/maliens et conscience ivoirienne: Les étrangers en Côte d'Ivoire (1903–1980)* (Paris: L'Harmattan, 2008), 262; information also comes from an interview with Paul Pépé, founder of LOCI, Abidjan, October 3, 2007.

54. Laurent Gbagbo, *Côte d'Ivoire: Economie et société à la veille de l'indépendance* (Paris: L'Harmattan, 1982), 116.

55. "Le Président à Bobo-Dioulasso: 'Moins que l'étiquette, le contenu.' Il faisait ainsi allusion à la forme de l'union des peuples frères," *Fraternité Matin,* December 19, 1964.

56. His wedding to Nathalie Monaco and their honeymoon in Brazil, his children's sports cars, and more generally his lavish lifestyle likely contributed to his unpopularity. See Sangoulé Lamizana, *Mémoires,* vol. 2: *Sur la brèche trente années durant* (Paris: Jaguar Conseil, 1999), 55–59.

57. Frédéric Guirma, *Comment perdre le pouvoir? Le cas de Maurice Yaméogo* (Paris: Chaka, 1991), 137.

58. See Lamizana, *Sur la brèche,* 81.

59. Interview with Maurice Mélégué Traoré, Geneva, October 2008.

60. "Ministère des Affaires Etrangères, télégramme à l'arrivée. Niamey, le 21 Décembre 1965," CARAN, FPU 557.

61. "Envoi depuis l'Ambassade de France en Haute-Volta à destination du Secrétaire Général de la Présidence de la République pour la Communauté et les Affaires Africaines et Malgaches du texte de projet de convention relatif à la double nationalité. Ouagadougou, le 13 décembre 1965," CARAN, FPU 559.

62. See Assemblée Nationale de Côte d'Ivoire, document no. 128H, *Projet de Code Electoral;* and *Journal Officiel de la République de Côte d'Ivoire,* no. 53, December 29, 1994, *Loi 94-642 portant Code electoral,* 1027–36 (my translation).

63. Henri Konan Bédié, "Mon Programme," *Fraternité-Matin,* August 28, 1995.

64. See Peter Geschiere and Bambi Ceuppens, "Autochthony: Local or Global? New Modes in the Struggle over Citizenship and Belonging in Africa and in Europe," *Annual Review of Anthropology* 34 (2005): 385–407; and Peter Geschiere and Stephen Jackson, "Autochthony and the Crisis of Citizenship," *African Studies Review* 49, no. 2 (2006): 1–8.

References

Amondji, Marcel. "Assabou et Marcoussis: Deux tragédies ivoiriennes." *Outre-Terre* 2, no. 11 (2005): 215–22.

Bach, Daniel. "L'insertion ivoirienne dans les rapports internationaux." In *Etat et bourgeoisie en Côte d'Ivoire,* edited by Y.-A. Fauré and J.-F. Médard, 89–124. Paris: Karthala, 1982.

Baulin, Jacques. *La Politique africaine d'Houphouët-Boigny.* Paris: EURAFOR, 1980.

Burbank, Jane, and Frederick Cooper. "Empire, droits et citoyenneté de 212 à 1946." *Annales, histoire, sciences sociales* 63, no. 3 (2008): 495–531.

Chafer, Tony. *The End of Empire in French West Africa: France's Successful Decolonisation?* Oxford: Berg, 2002.

La Conférence de presse du Président de la République, Président du PDCI-RDA: Abidjan, le 14 Octobre 1985. Abidjan: Fraternité Hebdo Editions, 1985.

Dadié, Bernard. *Carnets de prison.* Abidjan: CEDA, 1984.

de Benoist, Joseph Roger. *L'Afrique occidentale française de 1944 à 1960.* Dakar: NEA, 1983.

Diané, Charles. *La FEANF et les grandes heures du mouvement syndical étudiant noir.* Paris: Éditions Chaka, 1990.

Diarra, Samba. *Les faux complots d'Houphouët-Boigny: Fracture dans le destin d'une nation.* Paris: Karthala, 1997.

Gaillard, Philippe. *Foccart parle: Entretiens avec Philippe Gaillard.* Vols. 1 and 2. Paris: Fayard/Jeune Afrique, 1995.

Gbagbo, Laurent. *Côte d'Ivoire: Economie et société à la veille de l'indépendance.* Paris: L'Harmattan, 1982.

Geschiere, Peter, and Bambi Ceuppens. "Autochthony: Local or Global? New Modes in the Struggle over Citizenship and Belonging in Africa and in Europe." *Annual Review of Anthropology* 34 (2005): 385–407.

Geschiere, Peter, and Stephen Jackson. "Autochthony and the Crisis of Citizenship." *African Studies Review* 49, no. 2 (2006): 1–8.

Guirma, Frédéric. *Comment perdre le pouvoir? Le cas de Maurice Yaméogo.* Paris: Chaka, 1991.

Ki Zerbo, Joseph, *Histoire de l'Afrique Noire.* Paris: Hatier, 1978.

Koné, Amadou. *Houphouët-Boigny et la crise ivoirienne.* Paris: Karthala, 2003.

Lamizana, Sangoulé. *Mémoires*. Vol. 2, *Sur la brèche trente années durant*. Paris: Jaguar Conseil, 1999.

Nkrumah, Kwame. *L'Afrique doit s'unir*. Paris: Présence Africaine, 1994.

Osmanczyk, Edmund Jan, and Anthony Mango. *Encyclopedia of the United Nations and International Agreements: A to F*. New York: Routledge, 2003.

Péan, Pierre. *L'homme de l'ombre*. Paris: Fayard, 1990.

Peureux, Gérard. *Le Conseil exécutif de la Communauté*. Paris: Librairie de Droit et de Jurisprudence, 1960.

Siriex, Paul-Henri. *Félix Houphouët-Boigny, l'homme de la paix*. Abidjan: NEA, 1975.

Tirefort, Alain. "Octobre 1958, 'L'affaire Daho-Togo': Une fièvre de xénophobie en Côte d'Ivoire." In *Etre étranger et migrant en Afrique au XXe siècle: Enjeux identitaires et modes d'insertion*, vol. 1, edited by Catherine Coquery Vidrovitch, Odile Goerg, Issiaka Mande, and Faranirina Rajaonah, 415–36. Paris: L'Harmattan, 2003.

Tokpa, Jacques. *L'immigration voltaïque en Côte d'Ivoire, 1919–1960*. Abidjan: CERAP, 2006.

Tounkara, Daouda Gary. *Migrants soudanais/maliens et conscience ivoirienne: Les étrangers en Côte d'Ivoire (1903–1980)*. Paris: L'Harmattan, 2008.

Voltolina, Katia. "L'éclatement de la Fédération du Mali (1960): D'une fédération rêvée au choc des réalités." *RAHIA*, no. 23 (2007).

Weil, Patrick. *Qu'est-ce qu'un Français? Histoire de la nationalité française jusqu'à nos jours*. Paris: Gallimard, 2004.

Zolberg, Aristide. *One Party Government in the Ivory Coast*. Princeton: Princeton University Press, 1964.

SIX

The Nubians of Kenya

Citizenship in the Gaps and Margins

SAMANTHA BALATON-CHRIMES

TODAY'S KENYAN NUBIANS ARE A MARGINALIZED MINORITY, discriminated against in access to national identity cards, unrecognized (at least until 2009, and then only ambiguously) as a tribe of Kenya, and landless. The Nubians' story is more than anything else the story of a search for a home, and like all human stories, it is one of contradictions. It is a story of displacement and uneasy settlement, of shifting and divided loyalties, and of sometimes-conflicting strategies aimed at constructing themselves as citizens. Perhaps the only consistency in the Nubians' story is their status as in-between or outside the categories that dictate, in formal and informal terms, belonging in the communities in which they found themselves.

The various and often paradoxical ways in which the Nubians have successfully or unsuccessfully negotiated their status—as *askari*s,[1] de-tribalized natives, and ultimately ethnic strangers—are emblematic of ways in which political membership has historically been negotiated in dialogue with, rather than purely determined by, colonial (and post-colonial) legal and political status. This case draws attention to the ways in which categories through which colonial authorities sought to govern the colonized were unable to absolutely capture the lived realities of identity, difference, mobility, settlement, rights claiming, and belonging. Instead, colonial legal and administrative categories, and the gaps between them, gave rise to different and variable opportunities for African subjects to form identities within and (sometimes simultaneously)

149

against the colonial state and each other. In doing so, Africans actively contributed, albeit within significant constraints, to the construction of citizenship as a (limited) form of political membership and a license to make meaningful use of (some) rights and resources.[2]

The Nubians originated as an ethnic group in the quasi-slave armies of nineteenth-century Egypt and Sudan and were subsequently incorporated into the colonial East African armed forces, and later Kenya. Their role and position in colonial Kenya and around the time of independence were deeply ambiguous, and this history has had consequences for their citizenship in postcolonial Kenya as well as for our understanding of colonial and postcolonial citizenship categories. The way in which today's Nubians are marginalized by the nation's contemporary citizenship regime, which privileges indigenous and autochthonous ethnicity, can be understood only with a full appreciation of this story.

Strangers Introducing Strangers

A great deal of misunderstanding has surrounded the term *Nubian* in East Africa, often uncritically associating those communities who identify themselves with it as originating in the Nuba mountains or the ancient Nubian Kingdoms dating around 2000 BC to 1500 AD in the area that is now known as Nubia in northern Sudan and southern Egypt. In fact, the terms *Nubi* and *Sudanese* have been used at different times for different purposes, most notably to refer to slaves from Nubia, one of the major sources of slaves, prior to European imperialism.[3] In particular, today's Kenyan Nubians have their origins in the slave armies of nineteenth-century North Africa, armies composed of various tribes not only from Nubia but also from throughout the Sudan.[4] In the course of their migration, the soldiers lived in *zara'ib*, or garrisons, which were not only military but also social and economic communities of great complexity, including not only soldiers but also wives, concubines, domestic servants, and gun boys.[5] As the higher ranks of soldiers were populated with slaves captured in Muslim, Arabic-speaking areas of Egypt and northern Sudan (including Nubia), the command of these officers over the more southern Sudanese in the context of their living together accelerated their Arabization (at least in terms of language) and Islamization.[6] The Nubians of today continue to speak Kinubi in Kenya and Uganda; however, it is Islam that remains the most fundamental aspect of Nubian identity across East Africa.[7] Today's Kenyan Nubians have their origins in one particular group of soldiers and their dependents: those who were stationed in Equatoria, a province of the Sudan cut off from the Egyptian administration in 1883 during the Mahdist revolt.[8] After a two-year period of isolation, these soldiers were incorporated into the Imperial British East African Company by Frederick Lugard, and they later became the backbone of the protectorate armed forces, then of the colonial armies of Uganda and Kenya, playing a crucial role in the imperial project in East Africa.

The contemporary status of the Nubians must be understood against this background. That the Sudanese soldiers were introduced into East Africa, and their role determined by Europeans, themselves strangers, upset indigenous power structures and precluded to a large degree the possibility of hospitable incorporation into local African communities.[9] The British considered the Sudanese a martial race, not only deploying their military force against local populations but also elevating the Sudanese soldiers and their families above other Africans.[10] The military actively promoted the isolation and therefore "breeding" of this "race". Particularly in the early King's African Rifles, groups such as Nubians, but also other Muslim foreigners—Swahilis and Somalis—constituted the bulk of the armed forces because "they had no emotional ties to the East African population."[11] The influence of these ideas of a martial race on shaping the early and persistent identity of the Nubian community cannot be underestimated. Although "[i]n reality, the military orientation of these southern Sudanese communities was a vestige of military slavery and not some innate cultural characteristic,"[12] their treatment by the British as a superior, homogenous race served to promote a self-consciousness, the forming of external group boundaries, and the internalization of beliefs in their superiority to other Africans.[13] As Michelle Moyd notes in relation to askaris in German East Africa, the fiction of a martial race served the dual function of allowing colonizing forces to feel confident in their African armed forces and allowing those forces to access and justify an enhanced status vis-à-vis other Africans.[14] This mode of incorporation of the Sudanese askaris and their families into East Africa has had long-lasting consequences for the community, because the Nubians sustained this uneasy isolation from the communities that surround them for more than a century after this initial migration.

Detribalized and Landless Natives

More than any other factor, the issue of land and settlement has consistently illuminated the anomalous status of the Nubians and the limitations of colonial authorities' efforts to categorize and control subject populations. Their daily physical and social realities were messier and more demanding than the veneer of bravery and loyalty many colonial authorities chose to privilege in their interactions with the soldiers and their families.[15] Unlike the locally recruited soldiers, who were subject to "retribalization" upon retirement, the Sudanese soldiers no longer had anywhere they thought of as home to return to.[16] With land being of such paramount importance to African livelihoods and identities, and the great majority of the Nubian community being dependents rather than askaris, their plea for some land to settle on was both urgent and important.

By 1912, colonial and military authorities had decided that the soldiers and their dependents would be allowed to settle at Kibra, a forested area of 4,197.9 acres on the edge of Nairobi where the community had been settled since 1904.[17] The area was surveyed in 1917 and gazetted as a military reserve in 1918, supported by the protectorate government's thinking that the ex-soldiers needed somewhere to live, that families were a good moral influence on the soldiers, and that the descendants of the original soldiers could be called upon as reserves in the event of any future need, particularly for World War I.[18] Ex-askaris of more than twelve years' service, and their dependents, were given permission to live on a plot in the area, graze a limited number of cattle, and grow food, as long as they had a *shamba* pass issued by the military.[19] There were 291 of such passes, though many families settled without one.[20]

Recognizing the advantages of their position, the soldiers and their descendants maintained their ambivalent attitude toward other Africans, as well as a sort of voluntary isolation in terms of religion, language, and, as we shall see, urbanization, evident most tangibly through their legal and institutional separation in the military. While Kibera was a military reserve and its occupants under military rule, the Nubians enjoyed and came to identify with a relatively privileged status in the protectorate and, later, the colony, which they actively sought to protect as long as the British were there to formally sanction the status. Most notably, they were exempt from native tribunals and taxes and enjoyed a relatively higher rate of pay than civilians, as well as preferential recruitment into government jobs after retirement from the military.[21] They maintained their claim to this privileged treatment mainly on the basis of their military service but also their social system and religion, which further internalized the idea that they were superior to other Africans, an idea encouraged by the British.[22] This early period of settlement (and even up until the early days of independence) is remembered with great nostalgia as a "golden age" by the oldest living generation of Nubians. Mama "Jonuba" explained,

> Life was very good at that time. Food was plenty, yet very cheap. . . . We had no problems. We grew up in a very wonderful place, and a good life. We used to eat meat, meat was cheap, about some cents. That used to feed the whole family until we were satisfied. . . . During the white man's reign we could even buy clothes as cheap as two shillings. Enough for the elders, enough for the children. Very cheap. Even though their salary was somehow low, but life was at its best.[23]

However, before long, conflicting interpretations of the ownership of the land emerged. It was normal practice in the Anglo-Egyptian and colonial East African militaries to give land in lieu of a pension.[24] The Sudanese therefore understood that the land was given to them in perpetuity and seized on this interpretation in consistent pleas to authorities, as well as in their physical occupation of the area. The colonial (and independence) governments, however, continued to claim in all official correspondence with the Sudanese that they were only allowed to live on the land until the death of the immediate dependents of ex-askaris.

Kibera had upset town planning and the colonialists' desire for social order based on principles of racial segregation. African locations in urban areas were meant only to house Africans who had to be in towns for work purposes, and in Nairobi, Pumwani location was developed for this purpose. All other Africans were meant to live in the reserves. Kibera was the only African settlement to escape demolition in the 1920s and 1930s while the Nairobi City Council pursued its racially segregated plan for the city, primarily because it was protected by military patrons who admired the Sudanese soldiers. During the 1920s and 1930s, facing reduced military income and with a high number of widow-headed households, Nubians began, initially just on a small scale, renting out their structures or occasionally building new structures to rent out to the increasing African urban population to increase their income.[25] This further riled the British, who could barely tolerate the ex-askaris out of a sense of obligation and certainly could not stand the idea of other—less desirable—Africans living in the city.[26] In 1933, there were 251 Sudanese and 320 non-Sudanese living in Kibera.[27] The city authorities made several administrative attempts to evict the Sudanese and reclaim Kibera but had no success. By 1939, with all other options exhausted, the Sudanese were told they were allowed to stay, but the area was deliberately neglected in terms of service provision, and the land was encroached upon on all sides for the railway, settler sporting clubs, and settler residences.[28] By 1947 there were only 1,700 acres remaining.[29] Kibera had become, and remains, a highly visible manifestation of the state's incapacity to govern with the levels of control it desired, and this incapacity extended to the determination of the askari families' place in Kenya.

Throughout this protracted land battle, the economic value of the land overshadowed a far more important problem: the Sudanese soldiers were an anomalous category in the colonial system of governance and land allocation. During this period, a land tenure and administrative system was evolving that would have long-term consequences for the relationship between land and citizenship in Kenya, and in which the Nubians, and all detribalized natives, were an anomaly. As the colonial government balanced its protective and extractive imperatives, the white settlers were more or less forcibly taking over the fertile Central Highlands for agricultural purposes, while other areas of the protectorate less valuable to the Europeans were declared "native reserves," ostensibly to protect Africans' "undisturbed and exclusive" access to land forever.[30] The native reserves had the effect of, to a large extent, freezing claims of different tribes to particular pieces of land that they could call home, as well as calling an externally induced halt to the dynamic interactions that various tribes had with each other and with their land before European colonization.[31] As Sara Berry puts it, "[T]he reserves were organised on tribal lines, thus linking land rights firmly with social identity," a social phenomenon that continues to a large extent in Kenya today.[32] The social and political formations that Africans developed in close connection to land during this period would have long-term consequences for determining belonging in Kenya on the basis of indigeneity or autochthony, itself defined, explicitly or implicitly, in reference to colonial native reserves.

The "problem" of where and how to settle the Sudanese ex-askaris and their dependents, who were assertive about their privileged status and refused to move, and how to govern them in a context where all other Africans lived in native reserves made it apparent in the most tangible way that they were anomalous in the colonial social order.[33] The

Nubians pleaded, "We repeat that we find it difficult to appreciate how we can be classed as natives of Kenya. To us it seems elementary that we can only be classed as 'natives' in the place where we have native rights, where we have our tribal lands, or at any rate, certain land rights."[34]

In making this claim, the Union of Sudanese revealed an ambiguity, and indeed ambivalence on the Nubians' part, about their place in Kenya. This quotation can be simultaneously interpreted as an appeal to be recognized as superior to natives *and* an appeal for the same land rights *as natives*, a position that could only be contradictory under the colonial legal structure, distinguishing as it did between settler and native. Although the Sudanese had the esteem of the military and were thought to be the best kind of African, they were still African and as such not entitled to the same access to land as a white settler or even an Asian.[35] Without any "tribal land" or the private property rights of white settlers, the Sudanese were legally squatters in Kibera.

Despite the lack of clarification regarding landownership, in 1928 the military reserve was handed over with very little transparency to civilian rule under the district commissioner for Nairobi.[36] This marked a significant change in the special relationship between the Sudanese and the colonial government. Though the Nubians had always been classified as "detribalized natives," the government was spared the difficulty of figuring out how to govern them while they were under military jurisdiction. Once they came under civilian rule, it became obvious that the British were quite unsure what to do with this category of African. The Nubians' efforts to position themselves as legitimate, and indeed privileged, members of the political community (relative to other Africans) therefore took place in a context where they had some scope to try to define a space for themselves, less constrained by the tighter controls over "native subjects" in reserves, but also without any certainty about their legal and political status and rights.

Just as Africans were territorially segregated by ethnicity in native reserves, so too were they segregated by ethnicity administratively, with each supposedly homogenous reserve and its inhabitants governed by a "customary" native administration. The reserves acted as administrative units, and ethnic communities were governed though the characteristic indirect rule of the British Empire, that is, through "chiefs"—either appropriated, manipulated, or invented—who were under orders from the protectorate and later the colonial government.[37] Though the administration of Africans was not as tightly organized as it was made out to be, no problem was greater than that presented by those who could not be made to fit into the structure of native authorities.[38] Kibera not being a native reserve and with the Nubians not being considered an indigenous tribe in Kenya, the departure of the military as the authoritative body in the area left an authority vacuum, and Kibera became an "administrative grey area."[39]

There is no particularly clear legal or political definition of "detribalized natives." It was instead a category that absorbed a range of anomalous Africans who could "not be sent home as they either [did] not know to what reserve they belong[ed] or [had] lost all desire, and even the means, to live in the reserve to which their fathers belonged."[40] In practice the category included "(a) the retired ex-King's African Rifles or police askari; (b) Ex-employees of Europeans; (c) Natives who really have no reserve which they can call their own. These are almost invariably the offspring of town natives and the result of mixed marriages; [and] (d) the old and destitute who have spent most of their lives in towns."[41]

In short, "detribalized natives" were mostly Africans displaced with various degrees of force by the British in order to serve them, and they had developed urban lifestyles disconnected from those of their former ethnic communities. In their dealings with this category of native, the colonial civil (as opposed to military) authorities focused more on the former trait—their disconnection from their ethnic community—than the latter, their service for the colonial order. There prevailed a desire to provide such Africans with the means to serve the British in the "modern" ways they required (in this case militarily), while maintaining "traditional" forms of social order. While content to benefit from Africans' exposure to urban living, the colonial authorities did not believe Africans were morally "equipped to deal with the vicissitudes of town life" and did not yet deserve urban citizenship.[42] Whatever else the British thought of this category of people, the colonial government agreed that "we should keep tribal life as long as we can. A detribalized native is at present a menace to himself and to other people."[43] By way of justifying their position, the colonial government argued that "[t]he natives in this country with the exception of the Nubians and Swahilis and a few others have good reserves, and there should always be a home under natural and reasonable conditions for them there. Their land is a priceless asset to the natives of this country and they should not be allowed to deprive themselves of it."[44] What should be done with these select few groups without the "priceless asset" of a native reserve was a difficult problem for the authorities, to say the least.

The handover to civilian rule in 1928 marked the beginning of a period of great disorder in Kibera, doing nothing to improve the colonial authority's opinion of detribalized natives. The Nubians formally lost their privilege but continued to perceive themselves as owed special treatment, and they made use of their de facto control over Kibera, in the absence of a clear and implementable state-based governance structure, to develop economically, despite the authorities' objections. The Nubians themselves did not cause as much disturbance as other residents and visitors to Kibera, and the authorities recognized this.[45] However, the Nubians' activities did facilitate activity on the part of other Africans that colonial authorities found problematic but failed to control. A late 1940s census of the area pegged the population at 3,085, nearly half of whom were non-Sudanese, and almost all the non-Sudanese (often landless Kikuyus) were tenants of the Sudanese or worked for them in an agricultural capacity.[46] This expanding population brought with it prostitution by tenants and a market for Nubian gin, especially for the large number of Africans who visited Kibera by day but left before nightfall.[47] These activities—most of all the gin brewing—sustained a superior economic status for the Sudanese compared to other Africans, with the income from gin raising the average income of a Sudanese family to up to five times that of a particularly good salary for a Nubian and nearly twenty times the average salary for other Africans.[48]

In this context of a fragile superiority, and throughout the remainder of the colonial period, the Nubians tried but largely failed to shore up their formerly special relationship with the government as a means of securing a place and privilege in Kenya. As Britain's military needs were reduced after the cessation of hostilities, and as the military budget was similarly reduced, the sons of the Sudanese KAR soldiers were not needed as much as had been anticipated, and the period between World War II and independence was one of adjusting to a less military, more urban lifestyle for the community. During the 1930s the Sudanese marketed themselves to the government as a source of future military recruits because their special relationship with the government depended on it.[49] However, another generation of askaris never materialized. Partly this was because the British considered the upcoming generation to be undesirable "degenerates," based largely on their perception of the disorder in Kibera.[50] However, there were also other reasons. Even earlier, around the beginning of World War I, the British thought it wise to ethnically diversify their colonial armed forces, and the Sudanese had begun to face competition in this regard. Younger Nubians also declined to join the military because the rates of pay in the military had dropped, and instead took up other occupations. They increasingly earned their income as clerks, merchants, supervisors of Kikuyu sharecroppers, traders, butchers, bus drivers for the nascent Kenya Bus Service, police, and of course landlords, while others did not see the need to work at all, given the excellent income that women were making from gin.[51] Though many took government jobs, they were nevertheless a small minority within those occupations and did not have the strategic effect of their cousins in West Nile or Sudan or askaris in German East Africa in terms of creating the basis for the new colonial order by working in other coercive and administrative jobs and enacting the daily routines of colonialism.[52] Furthermore, while some families were still able to do well from rental properties, gin, or salaried employment, other families began to fall through the cracks beginning around the 1930s.[53] The reluctance of the Sudanese to educate their children in government or Christian mission schools, preferring to educate their children in madrassas,[54] contributed to longer-term economic challenges.[55]

It was, then, not only land and settlement but also issues related to day-to-day governance that illuminated the anomalous stranger status of the Nubians in the colonial legal order and underscored the peculiar quality of their political place in Kenya and the often improvised, ambiguous, and imprecise forms of colonial governance.[56] During this period, as detribalized natives, the Nubians were not subject to either settler law or any native authority. Instead, they were governed by an ambiguous and inconsistent constellation of ad hoc rules and authorities, both state and nonstate, and were subject to many general pieces of legislation governing natives, such as the Native Registration Ordinance of 1915, which ordered that all male Africans over the age of fifteen carry registration papers called *kipande*.[57] Only in 1949 was a specific set of by-laws established to govern Kibera, the "African Settlement (Kibera Settlement Area) Rules, 1949," and for technical reasons they did not become enforceable until 1957 by a European superintendent.[58]

Scholars of the Nubians, notably Timothy Parsons and Douglas H. Johnson, make a significant point of the petty privileges and the superior status the Nubians had access to as a "martial race," as well as the Nubians' attempts to hold on to it.[59] For example, Parsons argues that the preceding eighty years or so of shared military experience and life in Kibera had resulted in a sense that they "were entitled to the same official 'non-Native' status enjoyed by Asians, Ethiopians, Comorrians and certain Somali clans, even though their position in Kibera granted them roughly the same privileges while sparing them a higher rate of taxation."[60] This aspect of the Nubians' colonial self-identification is important. However, it is also important to note that their exceptional status carried with it many serious disadvantages. As Michelle Osborn explains, "In some ways, the exceptional detribalized status of the Sudanese had left them with more privileges, not having to answer directly to traditional or European authority; however, in other ways, there were few people within the government to advocate for the basic provisionary needs of Kibera residents. Kibera had been left to fend for itself."[61]

It is evident, then, that the British hoped such people, including the Sudanese, would simply fade away. As a result, the colonial authorities failed to legally protect the askaris' and ex-askaris' land or establish a secure place for them in the political community. The Nubians had to overcome those barriers to meaningful citizenship themselves.

Uhuru and Split Loyalties

If these contradictions had not already put the Nubians in a tenuous position, then *uhuru* (independence)[62] did. Decolonization presented a particular set of challenges for the Sudanese, pulling their loyalties in two directions as they navigated the difficult task of establishing themselves as Kenyans in political and not just military terms, after more than six decades of being identified, and identifying themselves, as distinct from (and superior to) African Kenyans.[63] Despite being unable to categorize and govern them absolutely, some of the colonial authorities saw the askaris as a potential ally in a context of African nationalism and in some ways continued to offer them special treatment. For example, although the 1957 version of the Kibera Rules allowed for evictions, the government resisted enforcing them systematically, out of fear that the Sudanese would be driven into the hands of the increasingly popular African politicians and the nationalist movement more generally.[64] Some government voices argued that the British government should seriously consider making moves to appease the various Sudanese grievances to maintain this loyalty in the face of the resistance being built among the African community to colonial rule. For example, Colonel La Fontaine, the welfare officer appointed to Kibera, argued,

"It would be a fine gesture for Government in its search for a settlement area, acceptable to them, to override all obstacles in the way. It would strengthen, if that were possible, a loyalty unshaken by the attempts of seditious Africans of other tribes to undermine it. It would deepen a love for the British connection, that stands out like an island in a sea of native unrest."[65] However, on balance, the 1950s was really the twilight of the era of special treatment for the Sudanese. Rather than take La Fontaine's advice, the government simply allowed the Sudanese to move even further into the background of their concern, and again their governance took on an ad hoc and neglectful, rather than intentional and effective, character.

A complex and seemingly paradoxical position emerged within the community in response, as it did in many ethnic communities in Kenya at the time, where some sustained a loyalty to the British, while others sided with the African nationalists. Members of the older generation clung to the increasingly tenuous relationship they had with the British as a matter of pride in their military history but also to preserve their privilege and even their very right to a place in Kenya, which they likely perceived that the African nationalists might be reluctant to grant.[66] As Michelle Moyd notes in relation to the askaris loyal to the German colonizers in East Africa, this was not a loyalty to the colonial project so much as a reflection of the askaris' understandings of the significance and mutual obligations of their relationships with the colonial state, often personalized in the figures of senior military men.[67] To prove their loyalty to the British, the people of the older generation made efforts to distance themselves from Mau Mau and the emerging nationalists. Worried about the government's concern that Kibera would harbor Mau Mau, they requested that the school that was built for them be restricted to Sudanese to avoid "contamination" of the students by nationalists.[68] Even earlier, the lifting of the exemption from paying the hut tax in 1940, even though the tax was not collected until 1946, prompted dramatic efforts on the part of this generation to try to secure their privileged position.[69] The older Sudanese felt strongly that because of their special relationship to the colonial government, they should not be treated like other Africans, and they pled to Lugard in London (in a likely bluff) that they "would rather pay [the] non-native poll tax than be included [in the] category indigenous natives."[70]

The older generation perceived the threat of a loss of their special status as an injustice and responded by seeking repatriation to the Sudan.

Their application for repatriation was rejected in part because of costs but also because they were deemed insufficiently Sudanese, having lost all connection with the rural Sudanese way of life.[71] The repatriation attempt and the deliberate distancing from African nationalists must therefore be understood not simply as expressions of attitudes of superiority and attempts to retain privilege but also as attempts to compel the government to recognize the intractability of their belonging to Kibera, and Kenya, and to legally protect their status and land rights, which they had by and large established of their own accord since Kibera moved to civilian rule.[72] Their attachment to the British (and associated privilege) must have appeared to these old soldiers as the only protective strategy they had for guaranteeing somewhere they could stay and continue to live with their families.[73] At this point in history, the Nubians experienced a subtle but crucial shift in the quality of their stranger status. Whereas under the colonial authorities they could continue to think of themselves as sojourners, maintaining (however vaguely) the possibility of leaving Kenya, with the departure of the British it became imperative that they seek not only residence but also membership, and not only socially but also politically.[74]

A strong sense of belonging in Kenya (albeit in a peculiar category) and aspirations, therefore, for full citizenship were taken up much less ambiguously by the younger generation.[75] This generation was beginning to identify with the African nationalist cause and rebuffed the idea of returning to the Sudan.[76] They were beginning to see that mere tolerance or social acceptance would not be enough. Instead, the postcolonial era required political integration as citizens.[77] Furthermore, they started referring to themselves as Nubians, detecting the need to adopt an identity that would be more conducive to identifying as an ethnic group *of Kenya* after independence.[78] The members of this generation take pride today in the fact that during the Mau Mau rebellion they were sympathetic to the cause of independence and even hid Jomo Kenyatta and other wanted Kikuyus in their houses, including "Nyumba Kubwa,"[79] in Kibera.[80] Ismail Ramadhan, himself a Nubian, explains in a newspaper article seeking to improve the public perception of the Nubians that "[a]fter the ... Second World War, the Nubians gradually reduced ties with the British and moved towards sharing a common vision and goals with fellow Kenyans. As the struggle for independence gathered momentum in the 1950s and peaked in the early 60s, they readily associated with themselves with the nationalist political parties—Mr James

Gichuru's Kenya African National Union (KANU), Mr Tom Mboya's People's Convention Party (PCP) and Mr Ronald Ngala's Kenyan African Democratic Union (KADU)."[81] Indeed, Mboya's Nairobi People's Convention Party in particular had taken an interest in Kibera and attempted to exploit the lack of service delivery there to convert the local population to the nationalist cause.[82]

We can see in this generational struggle, and the competing interpretations of history, the much deeper struggle for a place in Kenya. Ambiguous as the older generation's claims about Sudan may have been, the overwhelming point of the repatriation attempt was that the Sudanese really did, by that time, have nowhere else to go to. Kibera was the only home they knew, and they had deep and affective ties to Kenya whether they liked it or not. For example, some Sudanese wrote at the time that "[i]t is also common knowledge that owing to such long and continuous service we have entirely lost touch with our country of origin and have owing to such service embraced Kenya Colony as our country of adoption; We wish respectfully to emphasize that if we are forced to return to our country of origin we and our wives and children could be absolute strangers in the Sudan."[83]

At the moment of independence in 1963, despite the fact that Kenya had effectively become their home, the Nubians remained in an ambiguous position in the country. The British left in too much of a rush to resolve the status of the Sudanese community. Neither the tenure of the land in Kibera or the other Nubian settlements nor their status as Kenyans was ever clarified, and the political sensitivity of ownership of land in Kibera has perpetuated the neglect and marginalization that began after the transfer to civil rule in 1928, if not earlier. As Osborn puts it, "Somewhere between being Kenyan and non-Kenyan, nationalist and British supporter, privileged and impoverished, legal and illegal, owner and squatter, the status of the Nubian community has remained tenuous."[84] For Nubians, citizenship has been experienced in this insecure way ever since, and efforts to interpret and enact citizenship in meaningful ways have sought, above all, security of political and legal membership, as well as associated rights, resources, and recognition.

Ethnic Strangers

The decades after independence marked a rapid decline in the status and lifestyle of the Nubians in Kibera. The political landscape in Kenya changed in ways the Nubians were neither well positioned nor well equipped to handle. Kenya's first president, Jomo Kenyatta, established a highly centralized patrimonial state, which his successor, Daniel arap Moi, sustained. Both presidents stacked the upper echelons of power with their ethnic kinsmen, promoting the idea that to access resources or have any decision-making influence in Kenya, you must have "one of your own" in government or the civil service. Ethnic patrimonialism became the hallmark of Kenyan political culture, and even smaller recognized ethnic groups found it difficult to advance their interests at the national level. Despite the nationalism of the younger generations, by and large the Nubians felt lost without their former military patrons and unsure of how to proceed with claiming their rights and establishing themselves as rightful members of the Kenyan community. Not only were they too small in number to have much electoral influence, but also their colonial loyalties and activities worked against them, reinforcing their stranger status. The Nubians only became more marginalized socially, economically, politically, and on the land they perceived as their own.

Around the time of independence, the Nubian population was around 3,000 out of about 9,000 Kiberans on the remaining 1,150 acres of land.[85] Over the coming decades, the immigrant population in Kibera would increase dramatically, bringing the area's population from 20,000 in 1975 to 60,000–65,000 in 1980. At the same time, encroachment at the fringes of the area also continued, mainly for middle-class housing estates, which largely failed to benefit the Nubians.[86] The size of the land decreased from 800 acres in the mid-1970s to 700 acres by 1980 and only 550 acres by 1990.[87] Kibera is now one of Nairobi's most famous slums. Though the Nubians still claim the area to be their ancestral land, they are severely outnumbered, and though many of them make a living from renting out structures, they are but a small percentage of the landlords in Kibera. Most structures were built and are owned by patrons of previous MPs and chiefs in the area. The Nubians constitute only about 10,000–15,000 people in Kibera, out of a total population of between 200,000 and 300,000 on only 550 acres remaining of the original 4,197.9 acres.[88]

Until the last few years, the Nubian community was to a large degree socially invisible and, when visible, members of the community are often still perceived as foreigners, not Kenyan but Sudanese.[89] Johnson puts it dramatically but accurately when he says that "[t]he final irony is that the Nubis' earlier arguments [about their exceptional status] have at last been accepted by the postindependence Kenyan government, but as a way of disenfranchising them."[90] Nubians report feeling like "refugees" and being told by other Kenyans to "go back to Sudan," a land most of today's Nubians have never known. Few Kenyans think of the Nubians as part and parcel of Kenya's ethnic makeup.

From the early 1990s to the mid-2000s, Nubians faced discrimination in access to ID cards on the basis of their nonindigenous identity.[91] They would be asked to provide impossible documents such as their parents' birth certificates to prove they were born in Kenya to Kenyan parents. This is despite their constitutional right to the documents. Until 2009, the Nubians were never counted in national censuses, and although they were counted as one of 111 tribes of Kenya in 2009, popular belief maintains that Kenya is made up of "42 tribes," of which the Nubians are not one.[92] As such, the Nubians are disadvantaged by not having an electoral or administrative district considered their home and in which they can dominate decision-making and access benefits such as quotas for government employment, educational bursaries, and secondary school places. Because of their small number, the Nubians have also had difficulty electing "one of their own" to any political office above ward level and so have been unable to secure their political, social, and economic position in the country through political patronage.

Despite these barriers to recognition and inclusion of the Nubians as legitimate citizens of Kenya, the Nubians have, particularly since the opening up of democratic avenues of contestation after the return to multipartyism in 1992, continued to assert their allegiance to Kenya and their right to Kenyan citizenship. Their strategy for doing so, like the history of their negotiation of their place in Kenya, runs deep with tensions. On the one hand, in coalition with NGOs like the Centre for Minority Rights and Development, they have identified themselves as a marginalized minority and exploit the growing human rights discourse in the region. On the other hand, they have simultaneously sought to identify themselves as indigenous and autochthonous to Kibera and therefore in need of the protection of their homeland and their place in the country in the same way as Kenya's other tribes but in a way that sustains notions of ethnic territorialism.[93]

As various scholars of East Africa's Nubians have noted, a Nubian identity has always been a manipulable and strategic phenomenon.[94] The continued evolution of their identity in this way—toward indigeneity and even autochthony—can be understood as a response to the prevailing social and political norms governing belonging and mean-ingful citizenship in Kenya. Just as they adapted to slave soldiering and the colonial forces, so too do they adapt to the postcolonial polity.

Subject Race and Ethnic Strangers

The Nubian case calls for an evaluation of the way in which we under-stand the influence of colonial citizenship categories on colonial and postcolonial citizenship in practice. The distinction between settler and "native," citizen and subject, is often talked about as the paradigmatic distinction of colonial African history. According to Mahmood Mam-dani, white settlers were governed by civil law as civic citizens, while na-tives were governed by customary authorities, differentiated horizontally on the basis of ethnicity.[95] Natives were ethnic citizens but in the civic sphere only subjects. This is a binary order in which the Nubians had no place. Mamdani, in his study of the Tutsi in Rwanda, felt compelled to come up with a new category to capture groups of people who were not white colonizers or settlers but also were not straightforward "natives," subjugated where they were found. He calls them subject races.

Subject races were those who were, in colonial law, hierarchically in-ferior to white settlers but superior to natives. They were colonized, not colonizer. In this category, Mamdani includes Indians of East, central, and southern Africa; Arabs of Zanzibar; Tutsi of Rwanda and Burundi; and the "Coloureds" of southern Africa.[96] Critically, they either were nonindigenous immigrants or were constructed as nonindigenous by the colonial powers through racial theories of superiority (for example, the "Hamitic" Tutsis). Though they were (second-class) *citizens* in the sense that they were governed by civil rather than customary law, they were still oppressed peoples, the difference being in the nature of that oppression. While natives in reserves were subject to despotic customary authorities, subject races were homeless, rootless, and, though governed by civil laws, lacking in both civil and ethnic rights, notably to land.[97] In the postcolonial era, with their legal superiority over other Africans lost, they became mere ethnic strangers, with a victim consciousness like that of the native but without the newfound civil rights and sense of rightful place in the postcolony.[98]

Nubians can be considered something like a subject race turned ethnic stranger. A proper extension of the category of subject race to the Nu-bians requires some further explanation. Mamdani explains that "subject races usually performed a middleman function, in either the state or the market, and their position was marked by petty privilege economically and preferential treatment legally."[99] In the case of the Nubians, the nature of their middleman involvement was military—they were the force behind the British colonization of East Africa. This role, combined with the community's active reinforcement of their privileged place in Kenya, exacerbated the contradictions of their status, especially around independence. As such they are a more unusual kind of stranger in comparison to the economic migrants who have occupied more attention in studies of the incorporation of strangers in African societies.[100]

There was some degree of preferential legal and economic treatment, but the Nubians were not subject to civil law exclusively—first they were subject to military regulation, and they did not come under civil rule until 1928. Even then, they were categorized as "detribalized natives," subject to ad hoc locality-specific native by-laws. In this sense, the use of the term *subject race* to describe the Nubians is an important conceptual and historical extension of this broad category. However, as we have seen above, and as James R. Brennan suggests, the categories of native-subject, nonnative subject race, and settler-citizen must be understood not in terms of effectively imposed, internalized, and meaningful categories but as efforts at categorization that were, in practice, often contradictory, underresourced, challenged from within and outside the colonial apparatus, sometimes subverted, and sometimes reinforced, depending on the agential behaviors of the people they were designed to govern.[101] The Nubians' broadly conceived status as a "subject race" did not entail absolute subjection but rather denotes a particular position from which *different kinds* of negotiation, rights claims, status enactment, and daily social and economic practices become possible and sometimes desirable, compared to those available to the other very broad categories of native subject or settler citizen.[102]

Like other subject races, upon independence, the Nubians were forced to negotiate a new social and political order in which not only was their privilege lost but also they were a minority in a community they had helped pacify and had considered themselves superior to. That is, they were ethnic strangers. In postcolonial societies, equal citizenship became the marker of integration and meaningful inclusion, demanding that strangers take on political and not only social, cultural, and economic identities that would facilitate harmonious relations with the "host" political community.[103] Furthermore, being native-strangers, rather than racially distinct, put the Nubians in a particularly difficult category.[104] While Europeans could recast themselves as mere expatriates, and the economic security of Asians, the other significant strangers in Kenya, acted as something of a buffer from the host community, African strangers were in the peculiar position of being different enough to be strangers but similar enough to their hosts to preclude any of the other strategies by which other, racially different kinds of strangers got by.[105] An understanding of the background of the Nubians in Kenya is therefore essential for an understanding of their contemporary situation.

Rethinking Citizenship

The Nubians' negotiation of their legal and political status in protectorate, colonial, and postcolonial Kenya illuminates one of many citizenship conditions, discussed elsewhere in this volume, that unsettle top-down accounts of colonial citizenship as straightforward legal status effectively and absolutely constructed and conferred by colonial authorities. Instead, this case calls for an account of citizenship as a multidimensional legal status and political condition that is constructed and contested by agential political subjects.[106] The Nubian case is one in which, at least until the eve of Kenyan independence, African subjects sought to reinforce their privileged status as military middlemen as a "protective strategy," while simultaneously exploiting, albeit with various levels of success, their de facto control of Kibera with expeditious economic exploits made possible by the gaps in colonial systems of control.[107] They were not passive recipients of their relatively privileged (in some senses) status as detribalized natives. Similarly, as independence approached, the younger generation sought to redefine their political status for the same reasons, in a different political climate.

This case is an important one for enhancing our understanding of ways in which colonial encounters involved neither absolute subjectification nor fairly negotiated power relations but rather constructions of citizenship that were contributed to in different ways, at different times, in different measure, not only by colonial legal constructs but also by the political subjectivities of colonized, colonizer, and those caught in the middle.[108]

Notes

1. *Askari* is Swahili for "soldier" or sometimes "guard" or "police officer."
2. Samantha Balaton-Chrimes, *Ethnicity, Democracy and Citizenship in Africa: Marginalization of Kenya's Nubians* (Aldershot, UK: Ashgate, 2015).

3. I use the terms interchangeably in this chapter until the discussion of the postindependence era, in which I refer to the community exclusively as "Nubian." *Nubian* is the English version of *Nubi*. Because this book is written in English, I use the term *Nubian*, but *Nubi* is the Nubian-language word that Nubians use to describe themselves. Douglas H. Johnson, "Tribe or Nationality? The Sudanese Diaspora and the Kenyan Nubis," *Journal of Eastern African Studies* 3, no. 1 (2009): 113; Mark Leopold, "Legacies of Slavery in North-East Uganda: The Story of the 'One-Elevens,'" *Africa* 76, no. 2 (2006): 195–96.

4. The category of "slave" was a complex one at the time, entailing various forms of coercion and compulsion, as well as possibilities for freedom and agency we would not normally associate with slaves. As such, the contemporary Nubians of Kenya strongly resist the identification of their ancestors as slaves. Douglas H. Johnson, "Sudanese Military Slavery from the Eighteenth to the Twentieth Century," in *Slavery and Other Forms of Unfree Labour,* ed. Leonie Archer (London: Routledge, 1988), 142–56; Johnson, "The Structure of a Legacy: Military Slavery in Northeast Africa," *Ethnohistory* 36, no. 1 (1989): 72–88.

5. Johan de Smedt, "The Nubis of Kibera: A Social History of the Nubians and Kibera Slums" (PhD diss., University of Leiden, 2011), 38; Douglas H. Johnson, "Conquest and Colonisation: Soldier Settlers," *Sudan Notes and Records* 4 (2000): 59–79.

6. Zubairi B. Nasseem and Doka Wahib Marjan, "The 'Nubians' of East Africa: A Discussion," *Journal of Muslim Minority Affairs* 13, no. 1 (1992): 199; Barri A. Wanji, *A Preliminary Postgraduate Research Paper on the Nubi in East Africa,* Makerere University Sociology Working Paper 115 (Kampala: Makerere University, 1971), 46–50.

7. Omari H. Kokole, "The 'Nubians' of East Africa: Muslim Club or African 'Tribe'? The View from Within," *Journal of Muslim Minority Affairs* 6, no. 2 (1985): 420–48; Nasseem and Marjan, "'Nubians' of East Africa"; Omari H. Kokole, "Idi Amin, 'the Nubi' and Islam in Ugandan Politics, 1970–1979," in *Religion and Politics in East Africa,* ed. Hölger Bernt Hansen and Michael Twaddle (London: James Currey, 1995); Timothy Parsons, *The African Rank-and-File: Social Implications of Colonial Military Service in the King's African Rifles, 1902–1964* (Oxford: James Currey, 1999), 226; Ibrahim El-Zein Soghayroun, *The Sudanese Muslim Factor in Uganda* (Khartoum: Khartoum University Press, 1981); Wanji, *Nubi in East Africa.*

8. Johan de Smedt explains there were also two other "roads to Kibera." Sudanese soldiers directly recruited in Egypt (usually Cairo or Alexandria) were also deployed by the British in their territory in Somalia and by the Germans in their territory in East Africa (now Tanzania). Some of these soldiers and some of their dependents found their way to Kibera and other Nubian settlements in Kenya after they were demobilized, but these seem to be a small proportion of the Nubian community in Kibera. See de Smedt, "Nubis of Kibera," 53–60.

9. William A. Shack and Elliott P. Skinner, "Introduction," in *Strangers in African Societies,* ed. William A. Shack and Elliott P. Skinner (Berkeley:

University of California Press, 1979), 15; Elliott P. Skinner, "Conclusions," in Shack and Skinner, *Strangers in African Societies,* 282.

10. Through their military careers, even during the slave era, the Nubians consolidated their reputation among colonial authorities for military prowess, strength, bravery, and loyalty. There are numerous examples of this throughout the documented military history of the Sudanese soldiers. See Gaetano Casati, *Ten Years in Equatoria and the Return with Emir Pasha,* trans. J. Randolph Clay and I. Walter Savage Landor (assistant), 2 vols. (London: Frederick Warne, 1891), 62; Frederick Lugard, *The Rise of Our East African Empire,* vol. 2 (Edinburgh: William Blackwood and Sons, 1893), 219; H. Moyse-Bartlett, *The King's African Rifles: A Study in the Military History of East and Central Africa, 1890–1945* (Aldershot, UK: Gale and Polden, 1956), 86. More generally, see David Killingray, "Gender Issues and African Colonial Armies," in *Guardians of Empire: The Armed Forces of the Colonial Powers, c. 1700–1964,* ed. David Killingray and David Omissi (Manchester: Manchester University Press, 1999), 221–48; Leopold, "Legacies of Slavery," 183; W. Lloyd-Jones, *K.A.R., Being an Unofficial Account of the Origin and Activities of the King's African Rifles* (London: Arrowsmith, 1926), 229; cf. Michelle Moyd, *Violent Intermediaries: African Soldiers, Conquest, and Everyday Colonialism in German East Africa* (Athens: Ohio University Press, 2014); Parsons, *African Rank-and-File;* Timothy Parsons, "All Askaris Are Family Men: Sex, Domesticity and Discipline in the King's African Rifles, 1902–1964," in Killingray and Omissi, *Guardians of Empire* (Manchester: Manchester University Press, 1999), 157–78.

11. Parsons, *African Rank-and-File,* 61. Swahilis from the coast were "foreigners" to the populations of the interior, although they are not foreign to contemporary Kenya.

12. Ibid., 62.

13. De Smedt, "Nubis of Kibera," 40; Wanji, *Nubi in East Africa,* 23.

14. Moyd, *Violent Intermediaries.*

15. ibid., 20.

16. Parsons, *African Rank-and-File,* 226.

17. The area was originally inhabited by the Maasai, who legally relinquished it to the British in the 1904 Maasai Agreements. See Morris Carter, *Report of the Kenya Land Commission* (Nairobi: Secretary of State for the Colonies, 1933), appendix 8, "The Masai Agreements." Beyond this initial discussion, I refer to the area as Kibera, in keeping with the more commonly used term in contemporary Kenya.

18. Kenya Land Commission, *Kenya Land Commission Evidence and Memoranda* (Nairobi: HMSO, 1934), 1153; Timothy Parsons, "'Kibra Is Our Blood': The Sudanese Military Legacy in Nairobi's Kibera Location, 1902–1968," *International Journal of African Historical Studies* 30, no. 1 (1997): 90; Parsons, *African Rank-and-File;* Parsons, "All Askaris," 69.

19. *Shamba* is Swahili for "farm" or "garden."

20. Parsons, "Kibra Is Our Blood," 90; de Smedt, "Nubis of Kibera," 65.

21. Johnson, "Tribe or Nationality," 118.

22. Parsons, *African Rank-and-File*, 227; Johnson, "Tribe or Nationality," 123.

23. Mama "Jonuba" (pseudonym), interview with author, Nairobi, 2009.

24. Parsons, "Kibra Is Our Blood," 95; Johnson, "Tribe or Nationality," 119; de Smedt, "Nubis of Kibera," 64. The lack of a pension for ex-askaris and their dependents was a source of great discontent until the government agreed to take responsibility for it after World War II, too late for the Sudanese askaris, on which see Lloyd-Jones, *K.A.R.*, 249; and Killingray, "Gender Issues," 24.

25. Parsons, "Kibra Is Our Blood," 110–12. Africans were moving from rural areas to Nairobi as a result of a combination of push and pull factors. The poll and hut taxes introduced by the colonial authorities, as well as the degradation and overcrowding of reserves pushed people out of the reserves, into the labor market, and into the city, where the allure of better and higher-paid jobs in government or domestic service and the opportunity for social mobility were strong. Paul Ocobock, "'Joy Rides for Juveniles': Vagrant Youth and Colonial Control in Nairobi, Kenya, 1901–52," *Social History* 31, no. 1 (2006): 42–43.

26. See also Ocobock, "Joy Rides for Juveniles," 46.

27. Kenya Land Commission, *Evidence and Memoranda*, 1154.

28. Michelle Osborn, "From Forest to Jungle: Tracing the Evolution of Politics in Kibera" (MA diss., University of Oxford, 2006), 21.

29. Parsons, "Kibra Is Our Blood," 110; de Smedt, "Nubis of Kibera," 74.

30. See also James R. Brennan, *Taifa: Making Nation and Race in Urban Tanzania* (Athens: Ohio University Press, 2012); M. P. R. Sorrenson, *Origins of European Settlement in Kenya* (Nairobi: Oxford University Press, 1968), 210.

31. For an example of this, see Kenyatta's ethnographic description of land relations between the Kikuyu and the Maasai. Jomo Kenyatta, *Facing Mt. Kenya: The Traditional Life of the Gikuyu* (Nairobi: Kenway Publications, 1938), 20–52.

32. Sara Berry, "Hegemony on a Shoestring: Indirect Rule and Access to Agricultural Land," *Africa: Journal of the International African Institute* 62, no. 3 (1992): 340.

33. Parsons, *African Rank-and-File*, 226–27.

34. Officers of the Union of Sudanese to secretary of state for the colonies through governor of Kenya, October 14, 1940, Rhodes House Archive, University of Oxford, MSS Lugard L85/3, 25–29.

35. M. P. K. Sorrenson, "Land Policy in Kenya, 1895–1945," in *History of East Africa*, ed. Vincent Harlow, E. M. Chilver, and Alison Smith (Oxford: Clarendon Press, 1965), 672–89.

36. Kenya Land Commission, *Kenya Land Commission Evidence*, 1153. Following World War I, the military were running low on funds, and it was believed they would be able to move the Nubians to Meru the following year, when the KAR headquarters was to be moved there, though this never happened. Parsons, "Kibra Is Our Blood," 91–92.

37. Robert Tignor, *The Colonial Transformation of Kenya* (Princeton: Princeton University Press, 1976), 42–45.

38. Gabrielle Lynch, *I Say to You: Ethnic Politics and the Kalenjin in Kenya* (Chicago: University of Chicago Press, 2011), 16–17.

39. Parsons, "Kibra Is Our Blood," 92; see also Parsons, "All Askaris," 157.

40. District commissioner of Nairobi to provincial commissioner of Nyeri and commissioner for local government, lands and settlement, May 13, 1931, Kenya National Archives (hereafter KNA), PC/CP/9/15/3.

41. Kenya Land Commission, *Evidence and Memoranda*, 1125–26.

42. Andrew Burton, "Urchins, Loafers and the Cult of the Cowboy: Urbanization and Delinquency in Dar es Salaam, 1919–61," *Journal of African History* 42, no. 2 (2001): 216; Burton, "Townsmen in the Making: Social Engineering and Citizenship in Dar es Salaam, c. 1945–1960," *International Journal of African Historical Studies* 36, no. 2 (2003): 331–65.

43. Kenya Land Commission, *Evidence and Memoranda*, 1152.

44. Ibid., 1147.

45. De Smedt, "Nubis of Kibera," 159, 167; Department of Lands, Settlement and Local Government, Nairobi, to town clerk, March 26, 1945, KNA RN/7/19.

46. W. H. Kitching, superintendent of Kibera, to district commissioner of Nairobi, "Analysis of Census of Kibira Taken on August 23rd, 1948: Kenya Tribes and Sudanese," September 13, 1948, KNA MAA/7/458; Parsons, "Kibra Is Our Blood," 106; de Smedt, "Nubis of Kenya," 82–83; "Ibrahim" (pseudonym), interview with author, Nairobi, 2011.

47. Parsons, "Kibra Is Our Blood," 104–5; Johan de Smedt, "'Kill Me Quick': A History of Nubian Gin in Kibera," *International Journal of African Historical Studies* 42, no. 2 (2009): 201–20; Johnson, "Tribe or Nationality," 118; de Smedt, "Nubis of Kenya," 89.

48. De Smedt argues that gin was the most crucial factor in the shaping of Kibera. Without the combination of the space in the forest and *shambas* to hide the gin distilling equipment, and the urban market, the Nubians might have been more willing to move elsewhere, and Kibera would likely have been developed for European housing. De Smedt, "Nubis of Kibera," 146. In the many decades since then, however, the Nubians have established deeper substantive attachments to the land.

49. Parsons, "Kibra Is Our Blood," 95; Johnson, "Tribe or Nationality," 120.

50. District commissioner of Nairobi to provincial commissioner of Nyeri and commissioner for local government, lands and settlement, May 13, 1931, KNA PC.CP/9/15/3.

51. Parsons, *African Rank-and-File*, 69; Johnson, "Tribe or Nationality," 101, 118–19; de Smedt, "Nubis of Kibera," 67.

52. Cf. Johnson, "Conquest and Colonisation"; Moyd, *Violent Intermediaries.*

53. De Smedt, "Nubis of Kibera," 72.

54. Madrassas are Islamic schools.

55. Wangūhū Ng'ang'a, *Kenya's Ethnic Communities: Foundation of the Nation* (Nairobi: Gatūndū Publishers, 2006), 435.

56. See also Brennan, *Taifa*, 25–27.

57. Bruce Berman and John Lonsdale, "Crises of Accumulation, Coercion and the Colonial State: The Development of the Labor Control System," *Canadian Journal of African Studies* 14, no. 1 (1980): 55–81; Kenya National

Commission on Human Rights (hereafter KNCHR), *An Identity Crisis? A Study on the Issuance of National Identity Cards* (Nairobi: Kenya National Commission on Human Rights, 2007), 3. Nonstate, self-developed forms of authority in Kibera included unofficial *wazee wa kijiji* (in Swahili) or *majlish shu'uba* or *majlish shauri* (in Kinubi), meaning "council of elders." There may have been one or more of these, and they included representatives from each clan, who dealt with relations between the community and the government Another council also existed, made up of the same representatives, called *gombororo*, which dealt with internal community and family disputes. State sanctioned authorities included a *liwali* from 1919 until the death of the last liwali in the late 1960s. The liwali was also likely the chief of the wazee wa kijiji and the gombororo; however, the liwali had no legislative or coercive authority. David Clark, "Unregulated Housing, Vested Interest, and the Development of Community Identity in Nairobi," *African Urban Studies* 3 (1978–79): 33–46; Parsons, "Kibra Is Our Blood," 92; de Smedt, "Nubis of Kibera," 69; "Ibrahim" (pseudonym), interview with author, Nairobi, 2011; Abdallah Sebit and Said Abdul Rahman, interview with author, Nairobi, 2011.

58. Ag. secretary of african affairs to legal draftsman, Attorney General's Chambers, August 21, 1957, KNA OP/EST/1/365; Crown Lands Ordinance (Cap. 155)—The African Settlement (Kibira Settlement Area) Rules, 1957, KNA OP/EST/1/365; Parsons, "Kibra Is Our Blood," 116. Both the 1949 rules and the 1957 rules to govern Kibera refer to it as a native settlement area, though while this separated the Sudanese and other residents from the Europeans, it did not establish them under a native authority. Their administrative status was still liminal.

59. Parsons, "Kibra Is Our Blood"; Johnson, "Tribe or Nationality."

60. Parsons, "Kibra Is Our Blood," 113–14.

61. Osborn, "From Forest to Jungle," 22.

62. *Uhuru* is Swahili for "freedom" or "independence."

63. E. S. Atieno-Odhiambo, "'Cry Havoc! And Let Slip the Dogs of War': Historical Origins of the Nubian Tribe in East Africa," *Historical Association of Kenya Annual Conference* (1977): 7.

64. Parsons, "Kibra Is Our Blood," 118–19.

65. S. H. La Fontaine, "Report of an Investigation by Mr. S. H. La Fontaine, DSO, OBE, MC, into the Means for the Resettlement of the Soudanese Resident at Kibira," November 13, 1947, KNA MAA/8/117.

66. Wanji suggests that a similar generational split in loyalties occurred among Nubians in Uganda. Wanji, *Nubi in East Africa,* 22–25.

67. Moyd, *Violent Intermediaries,* 12.

68. Parsons, "Kibra Is Our Blood," 118.

69. Ibid.; Johnson, "Tribe or Nationality," 120.

70. Secretary Sudanese Union to Right Hon. Lugard, London, August 24, 1940, Rhodes House Oxford, MSS Lugard Box 8, file 3, folio 22.

71. District commissioner of Nairobi to provincial commissioner of Nyeri, April 27, 1931, KNA PC/CP.9/15/3; civil secretary to the Sudan government,

secret letter to Sudanese Association of East Africa, May 22, 1949, KNA PC/
CP.9/15/5; S. H. La Fontaine to chief native commissioner and chief secretary,
November 10, 1949, KNA PC/CP.9/15/5; officer in charge, Nairobi Extra-
provincial District, to secretary of African affairs, November 11, 1955; Parsons,
"Kibra Is Our Blood," 116; Johnson, "Tribe or Nationality," 121. The same ap-
plies to requests for repatriation by older Nubians in Uganda. Wanji, *Nubi in
East Africa,* 22.

72. Johnson, "Tribe or Nationality," 122.

73. Lonsdale, chap. 1, this volume.

74. Skinner, "Conclusions," 41; Donald N. Levine, "Simmel at a Distance:
On the History and Systematics of the Sociology of the Strangers," in *Strang-
ers in African Societies,* ed. W. Shack and E. Skinner (Berkeley: University of
California Press, 1979), 31.

75. De Smedt, "Nubis of Kibera," 85, 124.

76. Parsons, "Kibra Is Our Blood," 105.

77. Shack, "Introduction," 9–15.

78. Parsons, "Kibra Is Our Blood"; Johnson, "Tribe or Nationality"; de
Smedt, "Nubis of Kibera," 124.

79. *Nyumba kubwa* is Swahili for "big house."

80. Secretary for defence, secret letter to secretary for local government,
health and housing, October 25, 1954, KNA MAA/7/458; de Smedt, "Nubis of
Kibera," 85; interviews with author—Amadi, Nairobi, 2009; Issa Abdul Faraj,
Nairobi, 2009; Mohamed Abdulahi Mohamed, Nairobi, 2009; Zaid, Nairobi,
2009; Abbas Kenyi Suleiman, Nairobi, 2009; Makkah Yusuf Asman, Nairobi,
2009; "Fatuma" (pseudonym), Nairobi, 2009; Fatuma Abdul Rahman, Nairobi,
2009; Ismail Ramadhan, Nairobi, 2009.

81. Ismail Ramadhan, "Origins of the Kibera Land Row," *Daily Nation,*
October 4, 2004.

82. Parsons, "Kibra Is Our Blood," 119.

83. Ex-KAR soldiers, to the governor and commander-in-chief of Kenya,
May 6, 1938, KNA Microfilm Reel no. 1, section 17.

84. Osborn, "From Forest to Jungle," 23–24.

85. Philip H. Amis, "A Shanty Town of Tenants: The Commercialisation of
Unauthorised Housing in Nairobi, 1960–1980" (PhD diss., University of Kent,
1983), 115; Clark, "Unregulated Housing," 36; Kibra Land Committee, "The
Kibera Nubian Land Issue in Perspective," submission to Njonjo Land Reform
Commission, October 22, 2001 (copy on file with author).

86. De Smedt, "Nubis of Kibera," 97.

87. Ibid., 92, 100, 104.

88. The 2009 national census counted 15,463 Nubians; however, given that
it was possible to answer "Kenyan" for one's tribe, and given that the census
methodology was problematic, this cannot be taken as the final figure (Kenya
National Bureau of Statistics, *2009 Kenya Population and Housing Census,* vol.
2: *Population Distribution by Age, Sex and Administrative Units* (Nairobi: Kenya
National Bureau of Statistics, 2010); Billow Kerrow, "Census Circus and the

Need to Independently Audit Results," *The Standard (Nairobi)*, September 8, 2010. A 2009 research survey by the Open Society Justice Initiative gathered data on 18,862 individuals; however, methodological challenges prevented investigators from visiting every Nubian household (Open Society Justice Initiative, "Nubians in Kenya: Numbers and Voices," 2011, www.soros.org /initiatives/justice/articles_publications/publications/kenyan-nubians -20110412/nubians-kenya-data-sheet-20110506.pdf [accessed December 2, 2011]). The OSJI research established that approximately 50 percent of Kenya's Nubians live in Kibera (Open Society Justice Initiative, "Nationality and Discrimination: The Case of Kenyan Nubians," 2011, www.soros.org/initiatives /justice/articles_publications/publications/kenyan-nubians-20110412/kenyan -nubians-factsheet-20110412.pdf [accessed December 2, 2011]). If we take this proportion and slightly inflate the figures from the national census, we can estimate approximately 20,000–30,000 Nubians in Kenya, so 10,000–15,000 in Kibera. There is a great deal of discrepancy in the size of the population in Kibera. For a full review of the potential figures, ranging from 200,000 to 700,000, see de Smedt, "Nubis of Kibera," 107. On the size of Kibera in acres, see Kenya Ministry of Housing, *Abridged Version of the Kenya Slum Upgrading Programme (KENSUP) Strategy, 2005–2020* (Nairobi: Government of Kenya, 2007).

89. Maurice Odhiambo Makoloo, *Kenya: Minorities, Indigenous Peoples and Ethnic Diversity* (Nairobi: Minority Rights Group International and CEMI-RIDE, 2005), 19.

90. Johnson, "Tribe or Nationality," 127.

91. KNCHR, *Identity Crisis;* Kenya Human Rights Commission, *Foreigners at Home* (Nairobi: Kenya Human Rights Commission, 2009).

92. Samantha Balaton-Chrimes, "Counting as Citizens: Recognition of the Nubians in the 2009 Kenyan Census." *Ethnopolitics* 10, no. 2 (2011): 205–18; Balaton-Chrimes, "Indigeneity and Kenya's Nubians: Seeking Equality in Difference or Sameness?" *Journal of Modern African Studies* 51, no. 2 (2013): 331–45.

93. Balaton-Chrimes, *Ethnicity, Democracy.*

94. Parsons, "Kibra Is Our Blood"; Leopold, "Legacies of Slavery," 181; Johnson, "Tribe or Nationality," 113; de Smedt, "Nubis of Kibera."

95. Mahmood Mamdani, *Citizen and Subject: Contemporary Africa and the Legacy of Late Colonialism* (Princeton: Princeton University Press, 1996).

96. Mahmood Mamdani, "Beyond Settler and Native as Political Identities: Overcoming the Political Legacy of Colonialism," *Comparative Studies in Society and History* 43, no. 4 (2001): 656–57.

97. Mahmood Mamdani, *When Does a Settler Become a Native? Reflections on the Colonial Roots of Citizenship in Equatorial and Southern Africa* (Cape Town: University of Cape Town, 1998), 5–6.

98. Ibid., 5.

99. Mamdani, "Beyond Settler and Native," 657.

100. Shack and Skinner, *Strangers in African Societies.*

101. Brennan, *Taifa.*

102. Cooper, postface, this volume.

103. Brennan Kraxberger, "Strangers, Indigenes and Settlers: Contested Geographies of Citizenship in Nigeria," *Space and Polity* 9, no. 1 (2005): 9–27.

104. Sara Berry, *Chiefs Know Their Boundaries: Essays on Property, Power and the Past in Asante, 1896–1996* (Portsmouth, NH: Heinemann, 2001).

105. Cf. Skinner, "Conclusions," 285. These other stranger groups often clearly consider Africa their home, and as the expulsion of Asians from Uganda under Idi Amin demonstrated, these stranger groups are also vulnerable and face considerable challenges securing full citizenship in their African homes. The point I am trying to make here is that the racial sameness of native-strangers generates a qualitative difference in the experiences of these stranger groups related to ambiguous opportunities to position themselves as indigenous.

106. Balaton-Chrimes, *Ethnicity, Democracy.*

107. Lonsdale, chap. 2, this volume.

108. Cooper, postscript, this volume.

References

Amis, Philip H. "A Shanty Town of Tenants: The Commercialisation of Unauthorised Housing in Nairobi, 1960–1980." PhD diss., University of Kent, 1983.

Atieno-Odhiambo, E. S. "'Cry Havoc! And Let Slip the Dogs of War': Historical Origins of the Nubian Tribe in East Africa." *Historical Association of Kenya Annual Conference,* 1977.

Balaton-Chrimes, Samantha. "Counting as Citizens: Recognition of the Nubians in the 2009 Kenyan Census." *Ethnopolitics* 10, no. 2 (2011): 205–18.

———. *Ethnicity, Democracy and Citizenship in Africa: Marginalization of Kenya's Nubians.* Aldershot, UK: Ashgate, 2015.

———. "Indigeneity and Kenya's Nubians: Seeking Equality in Difference or Sameness?" *Journal of Modern African Studies* 51, no. 2 (2013): 331–54.

Berman, Bruce, and John Lonsdale. "Crises of Accumulation, Coercion and the Colonial State: The Development of the Labor Control System." *Canadian Journal of African Studies* 14, no. 1 (1980): 55–81.

Berry, Sara. *Chiefs Know Their Boundaries: Essays on Property, Power and the Past in Asante, 1896–1996.* Portsmouth, NH: Heinemann, 2001.

———. "Hegemony on a Shoestring: Indirect Rule and Access to Agricultural Land." *Africa: Journal of the International African Institute* 62, no. 3 (1992): 327–55.

Brennan, James R. *Taifa: Making Nation and Race in Urban Tanzania.* Athens: Ohio University Press, 2012.

Burton, Andrew. "Townsmen in the Making: Social Engineering and Citizenship in Dar es Salaam, c. 1945–1960." *International Journal of African Historical Studies* 36, no. 2 (2003): 331–65.

———. "Urchins, Loafers and the Cult of the Cowboy: Urbanization and Delinquency in Dar es Salaam, 1919–61." *Journal of African History* 42, no. 2 (2001): 199–216.

Carter, Morris. *Report of the Kenya Land Commission.* Nairobi: Secretary of State for the Colonies, 1933.

Casati, Gaetano. *Ten Years in Equatoria and the Return with Emir Pasha.* 2 vols. Translated by J. Randolph Clay, assisted by I. Walter Savage Landor. London: Frederick Warne, 1891.

Clark, David. "Unregulated Housing, Vested Interest, and the Development of Community Identity in Nairobi." *African Urban Studies* 3 (1978–79): 33–46.

de Smedt, Johan. "'Kill Me Quick': A History of Nubian Gin in Kibera." *International Journal of African Historical Studies* 42, no. 2 (2009): 201–20.

———. "The Nubis of Kibera: A Social History of the Nubians and Kibera Slums." PhD diss., University of Leiden, 2011.

Johnson, Douglas H. "Conquest and Colonisation: Soldier Settlers." *Sudan Notes and Records* 4 (2000): 59–79.

———. "The Structure of a Legacy: Military Slavery in Northeast Africa." *Ethnohistory* 36, no. 1 (1989): 72–88.

———. "Sudanese Military Slavery from the Eighteenth to the Twentieth Century." In *Slavery and Other Forms of Unfree Labour,* edited by Leonie Archer, 142–56. London: Routledge, 1988.

———. "Tribe or Nationality? The Sudanese Diaspora and the Kenyan Nubis." *Journal of Eastern African Studies* 3, no. 1 (2009): 112–31.

Kenya Human Rights Commission. *Foreigners at Home.* Nairobi: Kenya Human Rights Commission, 2009.

Kenya Land Commission. *Kenya Land Commission Evidence and Memoranda.* Nairobi: HMSO, 1934.

Kenya Ministry of Housing. *Abridged Version of the Kenya Slum Upgrading Programme (KENSUP) Strategy, 2005–2020.* Nairobi: Government of Kenya, 2007.

Kenya National Bureau of Statistics. *2009 Kenya Population and Housing Census.* Vol. 2: *Population Distribution by Age, Sex and Administrative Units.* Nairobi: Kenya National Bureau of Statistics, 2010.

Kenya National Commission on Human Rights. *An Identity Crisis? A Study on the Issuance of National Identity Cards.* Nairobi: Kenya National Commission on Human Rights, 2007.

Kenyatta, Jomo. *Facing Mt. Kenya: The Traditional Life of the Gikuyu.* Nairobi: Kenway Publications, 1938.

Killingray, David. "Gender Issues and African Colonial Armies." In *Guardians of Empire: The Armed Forces of the Colonial Powers, c. 1700–1964,* edited by David Killingray and David Omissi, 221–48. Manchester: Manchester University Press, 1999.

Kokole, Omari H. "Idi Amin, 'the Nubi' and Islam in Ugandan Politics, 1970–1979," in *Religion and Politics in East Africa,* edited by Hölger Bernt Hansen and Michael Twaddle, 45–58. London: James Currey, 1995.

———. "The 'Nubians' of East Africa: Muslim Club or African 'Tribe'? The View from Within." *Journal of Muslim Minority Affairs* 6, no. 2 (1985): 420–48.

Kraxberger, Brennan. "Strangers, Indigenes and Settlers: Contested Geographies of Citizenship in Nigeria." *Space and Polity* 9, no. 1 (2005): 9–27.

Leopold, Mark. "Legacies of Slavery in North-East Uganda: The Story of the 'One-Elevens.'" *Africa* 76, no. 2 (2006): 180–99.

Levine, Donald N. "Simmel at a Distance: On the History and Systematics of the Sociology of the Strangers." In Shack and Skinner, *Strangers in African Societies*, 21–36.

Lloyd-Jones, W. *K.A.R., Being an Unofficial Account of the Origin and Activities of the King's African Rifles*. London: Arrowsmith, 1926.

Lugard, Frederick. *The Rise of Our East African Empire*. Vol. 2. Edinburgh: William Blackwood and Sons, 1893.

Lynch, Gabrielle. *I Say to You: Ethnic Politics and the Kalenjin in Kenya*. Chicago: University of Chicago Press, 2011.

Makoloo, Maurice Odhiambo. *Kenya: Minorities, Indigenous Peoples and Ethnic Diversity*. Nairobi: Minority Rights Group International and CEMIRIDE, 2005.

Mamdani, Mahmood. "Beyond Settler and Native as Political Identities: Overcoming the Political Legacy of Colonialism." *Comparative Studies in Society and History* 43, no. 4 (2001): 656–57.

———. *Citizen and Subject: Contemporary Africa and the Legacy of Late Colonialism*. Princeton: Princeton University Press, 1996.

———. *When Does a Settler Become a Native? Reflections on the Colonial Roots of Citizenship in Equatorial and Southern Africa*. Cape Town: University of Cape Town, 1998.

Moyd, Michelle. *Violent Intermediaries: African Soldiers, Conquest, and Everyday Colonialism in German East Africa*. Athens: Ohio University Press, 2014.

Moyse-Bartlett, H. *The King's African Rifles: A Study in the Military History of East and Central Africa, 1890–1945*. Aldershot, UK: Gale and Polden, 1956.

Nasseem, Zubairi B., and Doka Wahib Marjan. "The 'Nubians' of East Africa: A Discussion." *Journal of Muslim Minority Affairs* 13, no. 1 (1992): 197–214.

Ng'ang'a, Wangũhũ. *Kenya's Ethnic Communities: Foundation of the Nation*. Nairobi: Gatũndũ Publishers, 2006.

Ocobock, Paul. "'Joy Rides for Juveniles': Vagrant Youth and Colonial Control in Nairobi, Kenya, 1901–52." *Social History* 31, no. 1 (2006): 39–59.

Osborn, Michelle. "From Forest to Jungle: Tracing the Evolution of Politics in Kibera." MA diss., University of Oxford, 2006.

Parsons, Timothy. *The African Rank-and-File: Social Implications of Colonial Military Service in the King's African Rifles, 1902–1964*. Oxford: James Currey, 1999.

———. "All Askaris Are Family Men: Sex, Domesticity and Discipline in the King's African Rifles, 1902–1964." In *Guardians of Empire: The Armed Forces of the Colonial Powers, c. 1700–1964*, edited by D. Killingray and D. Omissi, 157–78. Manchester: Manchester University Press, 1999.

———. "'Kibra Is Our Blood': The Sudanese Military Legacy in Nairobi's Kibera Location, 1902–1968." *International Journal of African Historical Studies* 30, no. 1 (1997): 87–122.

Shack, William A. "Introduction." In Shack and Skinner, *Strangers in African Societies*, 1–17.

Shack, William A., and Elliott P. Skinner, eds. *Strangers in African Societies.* Berkeley: University of California Press, 1979.

Skinner, Elliott P. "Conclusions." In Shack and Skinner, *Strangers in African Societies*, 279–88.

Soghayroun, Ibrahim El-Zein. *The Sudanese Muslim Factor in Uganda.* Khartoum: Khartoum University Press, 1981.

Sorrenson, M. P. R. "Land Policy in Kenya, 1895–1945." In *History of East Africa*, edited by Vincent Harlow, E. M. Chilver, and Alison Smith, 672–89. Oxford: Clarendon Press, 1965.

———. *Origins of European Settlement in Kenya.* Nairobi: Oxford University Press, 1968.

Tignor, Robert. *The Colonial Transformation of Kenya.* Princeton: Princeton University Press, 1976.

Wanji, Barri A. *A Preliminary Postgraduate Research Paper on the Nubi in East Africa.* Makerere University Sociology Working Paper 115. Kampala: Makerere University, 1971.

SEVEN

Divided Loyalties and Contested Identities

Citizenship in Colonial Mauritius

RAMOLA RAMTOHUL

CITIZENSHIP HAS LONG HELD CONTENTIOUS MEANING IN MAURITIUS, an African island nation in the Indian Ocean, because of its particular history. Unlike most of Africa, Mauritius was never a subsistence economy but instead was a plantation economy in which its inhabitants became part of the global capitalist economy from the start and were thus proletarianized at an early stage. Most of the theoretical writings on citizenship in African contexts highlight the divisions between natives and colonizers, settlers, or migrants, which led to a differentiated and unequal form of citizenship, often along racial and ethnic lines,[1] with land being a major factor that was weighed into claims for citizenship. The Mauritian experience makes an interesting case study because of the nature of its population and settlement dynamics. Mauritius did not have an indigenous population and was populated entirely by migrants during successive waves of colonization. The distinct experiences of the different population groups, which later formed communities strongly bound by ethnic and religious identities, largely affected the sense of belonging to the country and the meaning of citizenship for the people. The construction of citizenship is an integral component of state and nation building. However, the construction of community and identity in Mauritius differed from the majority of African experiences primarily because of the absence of a native population. Yet in Mauritius, as in most other African nations, colonial rule and settler colonialism emphasized race and later ethnicity as the primary source of social divisions, leading to the construction of citizenship based on ethnic and civic identities. The early divisions were largely based on the form of migration to the island. The people who were brought as cheap foreign labor suffered from the worst conditions, whereas those who were the first settlers claimed to be the "authentic" citizens of the island. The implications of the divisions in the population on the foundation of citizenship and belonging are significant in a newly independent Mauritius.

Citizenship in African Contexts

Citizenship is a highly contested concept that carries immense political value and contains within it the issues of political and social identity as well as rights and obligations. In his seminal work on citizenship and social class, Thomas H. Marshall expanded the conceptualization and theorization of citizenship in terms of rights granted to the individual by the state.[2] According to Marshall, citizenship entailed civil rights such as liberty of the person and freedom of thought or religion; political rights such as the right to participate in the exercise of political power; and social rights such as the right to economic welfare and security, to work, and to have a minimum standard of living. More recent approaches indicate that citizenship goes beyond the legal and political relationship between individual and the state, to involve participation in civil society.[3] Citizenship has also been historically linked to the privileges of membership of a particular kind of political community.[4] Yet the fact that citizenship presupposes membership in and belonging to a community also relates to identity; in this context, Redie Bereketeab stresses the pertinence of two types of citizenship: ethnic citizenship and civic citizenship.[5] Ethnic citizenship aligns with group rights, whereas civic citizenship links with individual rights. The cornerstones of civic identity and citizenship are civic institutions, whereas ethnic citizenship rests on the basis of community of descent.[6] These different forms of citizenship assume significant importance when analyzing citizenship in African contexts, including Mauritius, which has a population composed of different ethnic and religious groups.

The focus on and theorization of citizenship in African contexts is relatively recent, as classic writings have centered mainly on experiences of Western societies. Yet Western concepts of citizenship hold little relevance for African nations, largely because of the manner in which the process of state formation took place in colonial Africa.[7] Citizens were defined on the basis of their experiences as subjects in colonial states, which led to Africans being variously characterized as citizens, protected persons, or aliens in their homelands during the colonial period.[8] However, the traditional African notion of citizenship states that "no matter where you are born, you are the son or daughter of the original soil or homeland of the parent through whom you trace your descent."[9] Here, the emphasis is on land and ethnic community as determining factors for claims for citizenship. Peter Ekeh examined citizenship as an ideology of legitimation in Africa, recognizing the fact that colonial rule had bisected African attitudes toward rights and obligations.[10] Ekeh's work highlighted the emergence of "two publics," wherein the meaning of citizenship depended on whether it was conceived in terms of the "primordial public" or the "civic public." At the level of the primordial public, the individual saw his or her duties as moral obligations to benefit and sustain the primordial public of which he or she was a member. The citizenship structure of the civic public differed because there, emphasis was largely on economic value. In Ekeh's view, the differing stances toward the two publics could be explained by the ideologies of legitimation that were introduced by colonial rulers and later maintained by their African successors, giving credence to the myth that the civic public could never be impoverished whereas the primordial public needed care.[11]

The more recent theoretical writings on citizenship in African contexts also emphasize the colonial influence in African societies, highlighting the divisions that colonization caused between natives and colonizers, settlers, and migrants.[12] Colonies were largely founded on a basis of racial and ethnic distinctions that justified the gaps in standards of living and legal rights between rulers and the ruled. According to Mahmood Mamdani, the colonial state divided the population into two categories—races and ethnicities—and each existed in a different legal universe. Races were viewed as a civilizing influence, albeit at different levels, while ethnicities were considered to mark people in great need of being civilized.[13] Races were governed by civil law, whereas ethnicities were governed through customary laws. Mamdani's seminal work, *Citizen and Subject*, profoundly examines the magnitude of racial discrimination perpetuated by colonialism in Africa and the implications for citizenship.[14] Mamdani shows how colonialism created two categories of people in the African public sphere in the colonies: citizens and subjects, or the native and the citizen. This led to a differentiated or bifurcated form of citizenship that was also unequal. European settlers had full citizenship, which gave them the same rights as their relatives who lived in the colonial metropole or home country, whereas African "natives" were subjects, or subordinate beings without full rights. The colonizers controlled the domain of the central state, which was largely urban based and governed by civil laws, whereas the natives or the colonized were governed by a local state or the native authorities, which enforced customary laws. Direct rule was in the form of urban civil power, which granted rights-based privileges to citizens, whereas indirect rule signified a tribal authority that incorporated natives into a state-enforced customary order. Colonial law therefore made a fundamental distinction between the native and nonnative, or indigenous and nonindigenous, whereas postcolonial regimes failed to break the distinction between citizen and subject and retained a regime of differentiation while deracializing the colonial state.[15]

Peter Geschiere has analyzed citizenship in African contexts in terms of "belonging."[16] He uses the concept of "autochthony," which was an expression of the "local" representing the most authentic form of belonging.[17] To facilitate ruling over the population of the colonies, colonial regimes amplified the differences between natives and migrants, including racial differences and the belief that identity should be rooted in the soil.[18] Autochthony was about "having been there first," belonging to the land and therefore being the "authentic" citizens. Access to land represented citizenship at a regional level in many African societies, and anticolonial nationalism was often driven by historical grievances pertaining to the expropriation of land and the ensuing removal of legitimacy and livelihood from local populations.[19] In countries such as South Africa and Zimbabwe that experienced "settler colonialism," the public image of difference was racial, between the "white settlers," viewed as "oppressive aliens" by the "local population" and undeserving of citizenship, and the "natives," who regarded themselves as the "real" citizens.[20] The land issue therefore had a major role to play in the conflicting relations between the locals and the settlers, especially because the settlers had taken over the best land.

The above overview of the theoretical writings on citizenship in African contexts highlights the pertinence of specific factors that shaped the way citizenship was experienced by different groups of people during the colonial period. The native and nonnative or settler status led to a differentiated form of citizenship, which placed those classed as natives in a lower position. A racist ideology was also employed to justify unequal rights and inferior treatment and therefore the denial of full citizenship to the indigenous population, or "natives." Given the high significance of land as representative of citizenship in many African societies, access to land or the denial of access to land as well as expropriation of land by settlers and ancestral claims to the land were major sources of contestation with regard to citizenship in the former African colonies. Moreover, the distinct experiences of different communities shaped the strength of loyalty toward the state on the one hand and toward the community on the other. The relevance of these factors toward the construction and experience of citizenship in Mauritius is analyzed in the next sections.

Hierarchies of Citizenship in Colonial Mauritius

Mauritius is a volcanic island of about 720 square miles, in the southwest quadrant of the Indian Ocean. The island was uninhabited prior to its discovery by the Portuguese in the sixteenth century.[21] Mauritius was first colonized by the Dutch, who left in 1710, after which the French claimed the island in 1715, naming it Ile de France.[22] In 1722, the French East India Company brought colonists from the neighboring island of Bourbon (now known as Réunion), and settlers were given tracts of land and slaves.[23] Society in Ile de France was highly stratified, with extremes of wealth and poverty and the French elite largely dependent on slave labor. In the absence of a native population, the French settlers became the first landowners, permanent settlers, and citizens on the island. A combination of factors including landownership, trade, and the exploitation of slave labor enabled the French settlers to accumulate substantial wealth.

The British captured Ile de France in 1810 in the Napoleonic Wars and named the island Mauritius, which is the original name given by the Dutch after the Dutch *stadholder* Maurits van Nassau.[24] Under the capitulation agreement, the British undertook to preserve all existing rights and institutions.[25] The British held administrative rule of the country but did not settle in Mauritius. On this issue, Hugh Tinker states, "Although the Union Jack waved over Mauritius for 160 years, the island never effectively became British . . . Mauritius never ceased to be the *Ile de France*."[26]

The descendants of the French settlers came to be known as Franco-Mauritians. They owned and controlled most of the resources on the island and became the economic and political elite of the country, influencing policy making with the British governors. Following Franco-Mauritian demands for political representation, the Constitution of 1885 was instituted and limited elections to the legislative council were introduced by the governor in 1886. The 1885 constitution provided political rights to Franco-Mauritians and to a small segment of urban Coloured or light-skinned Creole elite.[27] Political participation was determined by high property and educational qualifications; access to land thus was a key factor that determined political citizenship. Because the Franco-Mauritians were the first permanent settlers and were given access to land and eventually some political rights, this set the stage for them to become the first "citizens" of Mauritius under British colonial rule, with economic, civic, and political rights, although they were still British subjects. Franco-Mauritians believed that there could be no claim of rights and entitlements prior to the French settlement because of the absence of natives and that their ancestors had spearheaded the development of the island, with the assistance of their slaves.[28] They were essentially making an argument for rights on the basis of autochthony as the first permanent inhabitants on the island, despite the fact that they were also descendants of migrants.[29] Thus, according to Tinker, the dominant economic and cultural position of the Franco-Mauritians in society was strengthened such that they claimed to be the "true" Mauritians.[30] In their efforts to cast themselves as the true "natives" of Mauritius, Franco-Mauritians also made use of "linguistic ideology," whereby French was portrayed as the true language of Mauritius.[31] French culture and language were presented as the true Mauritian nationalism because they integrated and "civilized" the other ethnic groups, with their cultural differences.[32] Today many of the island's daily newspapers are still in French, notwithstanding that the most commonly spoken language is the local Kreole.

The "Coloureds," also known as the free people of color, *gens de couleur*, or Creoles, are members of an ethnic category that emerged during French colonial rule.[33] Most free people of color were born on the island, and they emerged as a category of citizens with different status, rights, and entitlements than those of the Franco-Mauritians. Although they were perceived to be of an inferior standing compared to the Franco-Mauritians, they nonetheless had access to many privileges that the other population groups were denied, including education and the right to acquire property, especially land. Access to education enabled them to move into white-collar professions. From the beginning of British rule, the free Coloured population grew, and their social status and civil rights were enhanced after 1826, when they pressed for the removal of racial discrimination toward them.[34] The ability and right to acquire property proved to be crucial to the Coloured population's attempts to carve out a niche for themselves in colonial society.[35] They were also the first nonwhite population group to obtain political rights in the country in 1885.

Within the British Empire, the Franco-Mauritian planters found a vast market for sugar, leading to an expansion in the cultivation of sugarcane and an increased demand for cheap labor. This demand was quelled through the importation of cheap, exploitable servile labor—African slaves and, later, Indian indentured laborers. A hierarchy of citizenship developed, in which African slaves and Indian indentured laborers were dominated and exploited by the Franco-Mauritian planters. African slaves were governed by a different set of laws, which largely drew from their status as cheap labor.[36] Slavery was abolished in 1835, but former slaves were subject to a six-year apprentice system that bound them to the plantations.[37] The apprenticeship system was designed to prepare the former slaves to manage their new roles and responsibilities as free individuals. However, despite the new "freedom" obtained, vagrancy laws were established to compel apprentices to remain on estates, and they were beaten by order of the courts for infractions of the law.[38] The apprentice system was highly exploitative and became notorious, leading to its abolition by law in March 1839. While the British government offered Franco-Mauritian planters a generous financial compensation for the loss of their slaves, the former apprentices were not given any compensation to assist their transition toward life as free inhabitants of the colony.[39] Many became dejected and destitute, living a life of abject poverty.

Following the abolition of slavery, cheap labor for the cane fields was sourced from India in the form of indentured labor. The Indians brought a radical and permanent change in the ethnic composition of the population of the island, making up two-thirds of the population of the island by 1871.[40] The same prejudices of white colonial society toward African slaves and apprentices were transferred to the Indians.[41] Apart from the fact that Indian laborers were subject to racial discrimination, [42]they faced extremely harsh working conditions,[43] with minimal wages that were subjected to numerous deductions by the planters,[44] such that the indentured labor system was described as a "new system of slavery."[45] Under the terms of indenture, immigrants signed an initial contract of a mandatory five years of indenture with an additional five years of work or reindenture, at the end of which, immigrants who chose to remain in the colony as "old immigrants" became legal residents of the colony of Mauritius.[46] However, Indians suffered from additional discrimination from which non-Indians were exempt. Strict vagrancy laws that severely limited the geographic and occupational mobility of "old immigrants" were passed to enable the planters to retain Indian workers on the estates even though they were technically free to earn their living as they chose. Thus, as Tinker states, for one hundred years (1840–1940), Indians remained "[s]trangers in Mauritius."[47] Upward social mobility of the Indian community began in the 1880s when some Indians who had saved capital were able to acquire property, leading to a new class of landowners and economic power and set the stage for Indo-Mauritian demands for political rights.[48] Access to land was therefore a major factor that led to the eventual emancipation of the Indian population in Mauritius and their claim for equal citizenship.

Chinese migrants were initially brought to Mauritius as indentured workers, but in much smaller numbers, and they were also an exploited group.[49] They later became merchants and traders or shopkeepers after their period of indenture.[50] The experience of the Chinese immigrants has been less extensively documented than that of the other groups, yet they also experienced discrimination from the colonial authority and Franco-Mauritians. The emancipation of the Chinese immigrant community was hampered by an 1842 law that prevented foreigners from acquiring and inheriting property on the island. Whereas Indians had been classified as British subjects, Chinese were considered as aliens and were therefore subjected to restrictions on land- and property ownership, unless they applied for and were granted naturalization.[51] As such, Chinese traders were not able to invest their profits in property. While the Chinese community did not endure the extreme forms of exploitation that Indian indentured laborers and African slaves had experienced, they did not have the rights that the Franco-Mauritians and Coloureds were entitled to and received a differential treatment largely due to their status as migrant workers and aliens at that time.

While these different groups of migrants were not "subjects" in exactly the same terms as described by Mamdani, since neither group was native to the island, they nevertheless did not have the same rights and entitlements as the Franco-Mauritians and Coloureds, and most significantly, the law denied them access to land.[52] This law grievously affected all immigrants living in Mauritius because it prevented them from acquiring land and moving up the social ladder and, in the case of Indians, reinforced their dependency on the Franco-Mauritian planters. Access to land was also rendered difficult for the former slaves because the cost of land was deliberately raised when they expressed interest in purchasing land.[53] Moreover, these groups experienced extreme forms of exploitation including racist discrimination on the sugar plantations. Attempts were made to wipe out their ancestral cultures and convert them to Catholicism. This was successful with the descendants of the African slaves and with the Chinese to some extent, but the Indians resisted it and preserved their ancestral culture and languages.

Colonization and the politics under colonial rule largely shaped the formation of communities, the rights of the different groups, and their experiences as permanent inhabitants and British subjects on the island of Mauritius. The absence of an indigenous population implied that the native/nonnative contestation for citizenship was not relevant, as the population was entirely composed of the descendants of migrants who came to the island for specific and distinct purposes. Instead, the purpose of migration was what determined the rights, status, and entitlements of the different groups of migrants and their descendants on the island. Those who came as settlers, namely, the French, became the first "citizens" of the island, because they had access to property, education, and civil and political rights. Thus, in the absence of an indigenous population, the Franco-Mauritian elites claimed that they were the most "deserving" citizens and closest to being natives of the island. As the country moved toward independence, the hierarchies of inclusion and exclusion became increasingly unstable, especially as the deprived groups began to protest against exploitation and claimed equal rights. To preserve their privileged economic, cultural, and political position, the Franco-Mauritian elites worked hard to exclude the other groups from political rights and for their group to retain the claim of being the "authentic" Mauritian population that legitimately deserved to lead the country.

Decolonization and Citizenship

With no native population and the formation of distinct communities based on ethnicity and community, anticolonialism in Mauritius was not as clear-cut as in most other colonies in Africa, Asia, and the West Indies. While the British represented political rule imposed by the colonial power, economic and cultural domination was imposed by Franco-Mauritians, who, together with the elite Coloureds, dominated the politics of the country. Life was extremely harsh for non-Franco-Mauritians, and little was done to improve their situation.[54] The Franco-Mauritians had the support of the British and even the governor of the colony of Mauritius from 1938 to 1942, Sir Bede Clifford, who considered them to be the natives of Mauritius. In his writings, he stated, "[T]here could be no question of introducing into Mauritius a franchise that would take the rule of the colony abruptly out of the hands of the whites, who were the indigenous population and were responsible for its development, in order to transfer control over to the Indian newcomers, whose chief claim was their numbers and their unskilled labour."[55]

Given the tacit collaboration between Franco-Mauritians and the British, decolonization was the primary means for the exploited groups to gain the rights and entitlements they had thus far been denied, including political, economic, and social rights. On the one hand, those who enjoyed rights and entitlements as "citizens" did not want to relinquish their existing privileges; on the other hand, those who were on an inferior standing sought equal rights and the ability to participate in the political and economic management of the country. To preserve their dominant position, the Franco-Mauritians reinforced local ethnic and communal identities, although the short-term presence of Indian political leaders such as Mahatma Gandhi and his envoy, Manilall Doctor, also contributed to the rise in the political consciousness of Indo-Mauritians and to some extent reinforced their identity as an exploited ethnic group at that time. The growing emphasis on ethnic and communal identity fragmented the political process of decolonization and undermined the construction of a sense of national identity and belonging to the new independent Mauritian nation. The Franco-Mauritians, along with the elite Coloureds, sought ethnic citizenship, which entailed group rights, whereas the Indo-Mauritians, led by the Hindus, sought civic citizenship with individual rights. This rendered the meaning of citizenship problematic to the population of Mauritius. Seewoosagar Ramgoolam, who became the first prime minister of Mauritius, aptly described this situation: "Mauritius did not struggle for its independence from the British Colonial Government with a united voice and as one people[,] thanks . . . to the Franco-Mauritian population which long controlled power under the Colonial system and so was afraid of losing its vested interests. . . . They dreaded the approach of expropriation of their property, of loss of power and prestige, of an inevitable decline in their social and economic importance."[56]

The upper-class Coloureds were the first to challenge the dominance of the Franco-Mauritians and claim political rights. This led to their representation in the legislative council in 1907, while limited political representation was extended to Hindus in 1921 and to Muslims in 1940.[57] Although the franchise qualifications did not specify ethnicity as a criterion for inclusion, yet its correspondence with the specified class-based qualifications established the political significance of ethnicity. This helped reinforce the salience of ethnicity as a cost-effective strategic resource in Mauritian politics.[58] Calls for reform to enable a more balanced representation of the different segments of the Mauritian population in the legislative council caused Franco-Mauritians to fear the loss of their political and economic privileges to Indo-Mauritians, especially Hindus, because of their demographic numerical superiority. This fear of change also marked the beginning of communalism in Mauritian politics.[59] Communalism is the Mauritian equivalent of ethnic politics and has been described as the "scourge of contemporary Mauritius."[60] It highlights the preponderance of ethnic and religious communities in the public sphere and society.[61] Communalism also denotes the affiliation and loyalty of Mauritians first to their alleged community and then to the nation.

The political uprising of the Indo-Mauritians began in the early twentieth century, largely sparked by the severe wage crises in the 1930s.[62] During this period, political and workers' organizations emerged, with the aim of organizing the working class—the Creoles and Indo-Mauritians—to articulate their economic and political rights more effectively. One of the most prominent was the Mauritius Labour Party (MLP), founded in 1936 by Maurice Curé, a member of the elite Creoles. The MLP, which also had Indo-Mauritians in key positions, fought for political reforms, wider representation in the council of government, and better labor laws. Constitutional reform was deemed essential for any change to happen, and following agitations from the working class for political citizenship and representation in the legislative council, a new constitution was adopted in 1948. The new constitution implemented the franchise qualification of basic literacy favored by the Indo-Mauritian leaders but also introduced female suffrage, as suggested by the Franco-Mauritians, who had proposed the introduction of female suffrage subject to educational and property qualifications as a means to widen the franchise.[63] This proposal was rejected by the MLP and mainly Hindu political leaders who had campaigned for male adult suffrage. Their main point of contention was that female suffrage subject to qualifications would favor the privileged Franco-Mauritian and Coloured women, whereas the majority of Indian and Creole women were illiterate and would not qualify for the franchise.[64]

The Franco-Mauritians were disappointed with the new constitution because the British had left out most of their suggestions.[65] Constitutional reform led to a radical widening of the franchise, and many Indo-Mauritians (Muslims and Hindus) were able to vote for the first time in the 1948 election. This led to the transfer of political power from Franco-Mauritians to Hindus and signalled the end of Franco-Mauritian hegemony. This situation, Patrick Eisenlohr has argued, threatened the Franco-Mauritian claim to be the original and most authentic Mauritians; they had used the French language and the fact that most Mauritians spoke *patois créole* or Kreole, which was "corrupt" French, as the main justification for a central position in a Mauritian nation.[66] In an attempt to maintain their privileged social and economic position and delay the political rising of the working classes, the Franco-Mauritians began to employ a divisive strategy based on community, religion, and ethnicity, a strategy that eventually undermined the formation of a sense of national identity and belonging in an independent Mauritius.

Catherine Boudet uses the concept of *mythomoteurs* to examine the strategies employed by Franco-Mauritians during the decolonization process and the impacts on the formation of a Mauritian identity.[67] Mythomoteurs are constitutive myths that give an ethnic group its sense of purpose, and they often involve deliberate efforts to mobilize latent solidarities behind a political programme.[68] According to Boudet, Franco-Mauritians introduced two mythomoteurs—"foundation" and "Hindu peril." The "foundation" argument legitimized the accession of citizenship by ethnic groups based on their contribution to the development of land and therefore clearly favored Franco-Mauritians, who were the biggest landowners in the country. However, this argument did not hold for long, as the other groups also claimed to have contributed to development. Boudet contends that the "Hindu peril" argument was one of the most powerful mythomoteurs put forward by the Franco-Mauritians. It led to the forging of political alliances between

Franco-Mauritians and other minority ethnic groups against the Hindus. Whether the Hindu peril was indeed a myth or not is debatable. On the one hand, minority communities, led by the Franco-Mauritians and Coloureds, genuinely feared for their future in an independent Mauritius governed by a numerically superior Hindu population.[69] The difficult economic and social conditions prevailing in the country at that time, combined with large-scale illiteracy among the Hindus, largely contributed to this fear, especially that of a loss of economic and political privileges to the previously disadvantaged groups—mainly the Hindus. Yet, on the other hand, the "peril" never happened.

The transfer of political power to the Hindus had also made Creoles and other minority groups fear for their representation.[70] To incite further division, the Franco-Mauritian-owned newspaper *Le Cernéen* reported that eleven Indo-Mauritians, seven Coloureds, one Franco-Mauritian, and not a single Muslim had been elected in the 1948 election.[71] Following this election, Franco-Mauritians sought political allies on an ethnic basis, which they found in the Coloureds and Creoles, who were all Roman Catholic, as well as among the Chinese and Muslim minority groups. Ethnic considerations began to dominate Mauritian politics as the basis of political divisions shifted from class to community and the leadership of the MLP moved into the hands of Hindus. This prompted the three key minority groups—Franco-Mauritians, Creoles, and Muslims—to form a loose political alliance known as the Ralliement Mauricien in 1952 to combat the Hindus.[72] In 1955, it was turned into an organized political party known as the Parti Mauricien, focused on representing the interests of minority communities in the constitutional negotiations during the decolonization process. The Ralliement Mauricien, mainly financed by Franco-Mauritian planters, was led by Jules Koenig, a Franco-Mauritian lawyer. It opposed the MLP program, universal suffrage, and the shift of power from the colonial government to local officials.[73] From 1955, the Parti Mauricien began its campaign for proportional representation of the different communities in parliament while highlighting the dangers of "Hindu hegemony."[74] Jules Koenig stated, "If we want . . . a common citizenship, we must resort to what has been described. . . . We must resort to a form of government of all the people, by all the people, and for all the people by Proportional Representation."[75]

The main emphasis was on ethnic citizenship as opposed to civic citizenship. Through articles written by Franco-Mauritian journalist

Noel Marrier d'Unienville, also known as N.M.U., the newspaper *Le Cernéen* attacked Hindus, the MLP, and its leader, Seewoosagar Ramgoolam, stressing the notion of "Hindu peril" and annexation of Mauritius to India to instill fear among non-Hindus and oppose universal suffrage.[76]

Whereas the trend in most African colonies was of the local population fighting for independence from the colonial power, in the Mauritian case, the divisions in the population and a weak sense of national identity led to bitter contestation over decolonization and independence. Citizenship in an independent Mauritius was viewed as a route toward emancipation and liberation for some, but the divisive strategy initiated by the Franco-Mauritians to protect and preserve their interests led to the division of the working-class Hindus, Muslims, and Creoles. It also led to a stronger sense of belonging to one's community and fractured the formation of a sense of nationhood and national identity. The Hindu community was divided along linguistic and caste lines, and divisions between Hindus and Muslims deepened following the partition of India. In 1940, Muslims obtained limited representation in the legislative council, and after the 1952 census, Muslims and Chinese were classified as distinct and separate communities. During the process of decolonization, from 1948 to 1968, the Colonial Office gave further prominence to communalism. Here one can draw a parallel with Ekeh's "two publics" because loyalties in Mauritius became stronger toward the community, and this affected the meaning of citizenship as independence approached. The divide-and-rule strategy was not a novel one, as it had been adopted by colonial powers in other colonies in Africa and also India. Yet in Mauritius, rather than the colonial authority, Franco-Mauritians adopted this strategy to preserve their privileged position and protect their interests.

In 1955, a constitutional conference was held in London, where the MLP pleaded for universal suffrage and responsible government.[77] This increased the minority communities' fear of Hindu domination. The Parti Mauricien opposed universal adult suffrage and responsible government, arguing that the demands of MLP for universal adult suffrage and a reduction in the number of nominated members in the legislative council would lead to Hindu hegemony.[78] Jules Koenig believed that proportional representation would ensure a "common citizenship" for all Mauritians.[79] At the London conference, British authorities agreed to introduce adult suffrage and to consider minority interests for the mode of voting, while voting would be along party lines to avoid communalism. An electoral commission was set up to work on the most adequate electoral system to ensure that each ethnic group had adequate opportunity to secure representation in the legislative council and that each constituency had reasonable geographical boundaries.[80] This process led to the setting up of an electoral system based on forty single-member constituencies and up to twelve nominated members. It was believed that with the new electoral system, the Franco-Mauritians and Chinese would rely on the nominated seats to be present in parliament, whereas the other communities would be adequately represented and parties would be encouraged to present Muslim candidates where there were large concentrations of Muslims.[81] The constitution was changed in 1958, leading to the proclamation of universal adult suffrage, and the next election was scheduled for March 1959. The 1959 election witnessed a massive victory of the MLP under Hindu leadership, but following this election, communalism became the dominant force in national politics, and communal parties were formed. The Independent Forward Block (IFB) emerged under the leadership of Sookdeo Bissoondoyal to represent the interests of the poorer low-caste Hindus, whereas the MLP was dominated by the professional, middle-class, and high-caste Hindus. The Comité d'Action Musulman (CAM) was set up by Razack Mohamed to represent the interests of the Muslims. A significant issue here is that universal adult suffrage was approved only when minority communities were guaranteed some form of representation in parliament. Thus, Franco-Mauritians and their allies were partly successful in lobbying for the protection of their interests and some form of ethnic citizenship, although the gradual loss of their political power was imminent.

Another constitutional conference was held in London in 1961, to proceed to the next step in the decolonization process. By that time, seventeen former African colonies had become independent from Britain, and Franco-Mauritians panicked because it was evident that Mauritius would follow suit.[82] The Parti Mauricien focused its campaign on the opposition of independence and dividing the island into numerous minority groups that it claimed to represent and to be prepared to defend against the threat of a Hindu majority.[83] Gaëtan Duval, a charismatic Creole lawyer who later became leader of the Parti Mauricien, urged Creoles to vote for him and his party to save Mauritius from Hindu domination. Attempts were also made to divide Hindus along linguistic lines (especially the Tamil-, Telugu-, and Hindi-speaking Hindus) and to weaken CAM by encouraging one of the CAM leaders to set up a separate Muslim political party called the Muslim United Party.[84] The Chinese community, which had previously stayed away from politics, allied itself with the Parti Mauricien. According to Ramgoolam, the Catholic Church was also employed as an ideological apparatus to spread the message of the Parti Mauricien, especially anti-Hindu sentiments.[85] Thus, the Parti Mauricien was able to garner the support of the Coloureds, Chinese, Creoles, Christian Indians, and Tamil Indians. Christian unity was emphasized together with Tamil and Muslim separatism and caste divisions among Hindus. The elite and educated Coloureds who held high positions in the civil service feared the loss of their jobs to Hindus. With the financial support of Franco-Mauritian planters, the Parti Mauricien was able to entice members of other political parties to join and support its cause. Under the leadership of Jules Koenig, it proposed the integration of Mauritius into the United Kingdom. Koenig asked for separate electoral registers and stressed Hindu domination and the victimization of minority communities under Hindu political leadership in an independent Mauritius. However, the British were in favor of constitutional advance leading to independence, despite the opposition of the Parti Mauricien.

The last constitutional conference paving the way for Mauritius to achieve independence took place in 1965. Political tension unfortunately led to ethnic tension, resulting in clashes between Creoles and Hindus in May 1965 and a few deaths.[86] The constitution was amended in 1966, and a new electoral system was designed to ensure proper and adequate representation of minority communities in the legislative assembly.[87] In the mid-1960s, the Mauritian population became subdivided into the categories of general population, Sino-Mauritian (Chinese), Hindu, and Muslim. Franco-Mauritians were incorporated into the general population category along with the Coloureds, Creoles, and mixed-race groups. The MLP, IFB, and CAM formed an alliance called the Independence Party, and they campaigned in favor of independence, whereas the Parti Mauricien proposed the association of Mauritius with Britain, arguing that independence would isolate Mauritius and lead to mass unemployment, poverty, starvation, and famine. On August 7, 1967, a general election bearing close resemblance to a referendum was held to decide the independence of Mauritius. The results of these elections showed that 44 percent of the Mauritian population had voted for the Parti Mauricien, which opposed independence.[88] Following these elections, a motion was tabled by the premier of Mauritius, Seewoo-sagar Ramgoolam, requesting the secretary of state for the colonies to accede to the desire of the Mauritian population for independence; the date was set for March 12, 1968. A few weeks preceding the accession of independence, communal riots between the Creoles and Muslims broke out in Port Louis, causing about a dozen deaths. While little is known on who had orchestrated ethnic tensions in the country, these disturbances nonetheless highlight the success of the Franco-Mauritian strategy in instilling fear and amplifying existing divisions in the population along ethnic and religious lines. Apart from the fear of Hindu hegemony, there was also worry that independence was not economically sustainable for Mauritius. Many middle-class Franco-Mauritians and Coloureds emigrated to Australia, South Africa, or Europe because they feared the onset of Hindu hegemony and the loss of political power and were concerned about job prospects in an independent Mauritius.[89] Thus, independence did not lead to any form of political or national unity in Mauritius, and Mauritians remained deeply divided on this issue. The forging of a spirit of nationalism and unity was fractured, causing a weak sense of national identity in the new independent Mauritius.

This chapter traces the construction of citizenship in Mauritius, arguing that the purpose of migration to the island was a major factor that determined the status and rights of the inhabitants under colonial rule. In the absence of a native population, boundaries of inclusion and exclusion were in a flux, and the French settlers considered themselves as the "natives" of the island. Those with an inferior standing had come or were brought to the island as migrant workers, whereas those who had privileges as "citizens" were the French settlers and later the Coloureds. The process of decolonization in Mauritius highlights the complexities of nation building and citizenship in the island, as boundaries of inclusion and exclusion weakened further. Franco-Mauritians fought to preserve their political, economic, and cultural privileges, employing a racist ideology to maintain the status quo and to deny the other groups civic and political rights and access to landownership. For the former disadvantaged groups (of which Hindus were the most numerous), independence meant opening up political, economic, and educational opportunities that had previously been denied to them. For them, therefore, independence carried the promise of fuller citizenship, whereas for Franco-Mauritian and Coloured elites, it carried the possibility of a more diluted form of citizenship that offered them fewer privileges and carried the risk of erosion of existing ones. Koenig described their situation as a bourgeoisie "in peril" fighting to survive.[90] Yet the "survival" strategies adopted by the elites had significant effects on nation building and citizenship in an independent Mauritius. The Franco-Mauritian elites drew on the support of other minority groups and tried to block independence by instilling a divisive policy that fuelled communal sentiments and divisions in the population. This led to stronger allegiances to the specific ethnic and communal groups and a rather weak sense of belonging to the country and, hence, fractured citizenship. Consequently, Mauritius never developed a truly national spirit or a national independence movement.[91] Following independence, the Franco-Mauritians withdrew from active politics but maintained their elite economic position in the country, given the vast resources they still owned and controlled.[92] The damage done by the communal political campaigns during decolonization still persists today, as communal loyalties remain very strong, especially with regard to representation in positions of political and economic power. The electoral system that was instituted at the end of decolonization is still operational at present and has been criticized for misrepresenting the opposition, causing the underrepresentation of women and dividing the Mauritian nation. Successive governments, since the 1990s, have unsuccessfully attempted to introduce electoral reform, largely because of communal lobbies and opposition from minority communities because of their concern over parliamentary representation. While civic citizenship is formally acknowledged, ethnic citizenship remains strong, and therefore a true Mauritian nation is still under construction. Yet despite the contested claims over identity, citizenship, and belonging during decolonization, independent Mauritius has maintained a stable and strong democracy and has been a model for peace, stability, and economic development in the African region. The Mauritian case therefore highlights successful management of diversity in a plural society, and efforts are being made to incorporate the different identities into a wider form of national identity.

Notes

I am grateful to the anonymous reviewers, Thomas Hylland Eriksen, Tijo Salverda, and Emma Hunter for comments and feedback on an earlier draft.

1. These include Peter Ekeh, "Colonialism and the Two Publics in Africa: A Theoretical Statement," *Comparative Studies in Society and History* 17, no. 1 (1975): 91–112; Ekeh, "Colonialism and the Development of Citizenship in Africa: A Study in Ideologies of Legitimation," in *Themes in African Social and Political Thought,* ed. Onigu Odite (Enugu, Nigeria: Fourth Dimension Publishers, 1978), 101–25; Mahmood Mamdani, *Citizen and Subject: Contemporary Africa and the Legacy of Late Colonialism* (Cape Town: David Philip, 1996); Francis Nyamnjoh, *Insiders and Outsiders: Citizenship and Xenophobia in Contemporary Southern Africa* (Dakar: CODESRIA, 2006); Peter Geschiere, *The Perils of Belonging: Autochthony, Citizenship and Exclusion in Africa and Europe* (Chicago: University of Chicago Press, 2009); Sara Rich Dorman, Daniel Hammett, and Paul Nugent, "Introduction: Citizenship and Its Casualties in Africa," in *Making Nations, Creating Strangers: States and Citizenship in Africa,* ed. Sara Rich Dorman, Daniel Hammett, and Paul Nugent (Leiden: Brill, 2007), 3–26.

2. Thomas H. Marshall, *Citizenship and Social Class* (Cambridge: Cambridge University Press, 1950).

3. See Will Kymlicka, *Multicultural Citizenship: A Liberal Theory of Minority Rights* (Oxford: Oxford University Press, 1995); Engin F. Isin and Patricia K. Wood, *Citizenship and Identity* (London: Sage Publications, 1999).

4. Richard Bellamy, *Citizenship: A Very Short Introduction* (Oxford: Oxford University Press, 2008), 1.

5. Redie Bereketeab, "The Ethnic and Civic Foundations of Citizenship and Identity in the Horn of Africa," *Studies in Ethnicity and Nationalism* 11, no. 1 (2011): 63–64.

6. See ibid.; and Crawford Young, "Nation, Ethnicity, and Citizenship: Dilemmas of Democracy and Civil Order in Africa," in Dorman, Hammett, and Nugent, *Making Nations, Creating Strangers,* 241–64.

7. The fifty-five countries of Africa were divided between the European imperial states in the Berlin Conferences of 1884 and 1885, and no consideration was given to the existing cultural boundaries in these countries. See Tharailath K. Oomen, "Introduction: Conceptualizing the Linkage between Citizenship and National Identity," in *Citizenship and National Identity: From Colonialism to Globalism,* ed. Tharailath K. Oomen (New Delhi: Sage Publications, 1997); Olasope O. Oyelaran and Michael O. Adeliran, "Colonialism, Citizenship and Fractured National Identity: The African Case," in Oomen, *Citizenship and National Identity,* 173–98.

8. Oomen, "Introduction"; Oyelaran and Adeliran, "Colonialism."

9. George Nzongola-Ntalaja, "The Politics of Citizenship in the Democratic Republic of Congo," in Dorman, Hammett, and Nugent, *Making Nations, Creating Strangers,* 71.

10. Ekeh, "Colonialism and the Two Publics"; Ekeh, "Development of Citizenship."

11. Ekeh, "Colonialism and the Two Publics," 108.

12. These writings include Mamdani, *Citizen and Subject;* Nyamnjoh, *Insiders and Outsiders;* and Geschiere, *Perils of Belonging.*

13. Mahmood Mamdani, "Beyond Settler and Native as Political Identities: Overcoming the Political Legacy of Colonialism," *Comparative Studies in Society and History* 43, no. 4 (2001): 654.

14. Mamdani, *Citizen and Subject.*

15. Ibid.; Mamdani, "Beyond Settler and Native."

16. Geschiere, *Perils of Belonging.*

17. The concept of autochthony, first introduced by the French at the time of the colonial conquest of Sudan in the late nineteenth century, is believed to have played a vital role in categorizing the new subjects to facilitate administration of the colonies. See Bambi Ceuppens and Peter Geschiere, "Autochthony: Local or Global? New Modes in the Struggle over Citizenship and Belonging in African and Europe," *Annual Review of Anthropology* 34 (2005): 385–407.

18. See Peter Geschiere and Stephen Jackson, "Autochthony and the Crisis: Democratization, Decentralization, and the Politics of Belonging," *African Studies Review* 49, no. 2 (2006): 1–7.

19. See Dorman, Hammett, and Nugent, "Introduction."

20. Said Adejumobi, "Citizenship, Rights and the Problem of Internal Conflicts and Civil Wars in Africa," *African Journal of Political Science* 6, no. 2 (2001): 87.

21. Burton Benedict, *Mauritius: The Problems of a Plural Society* (London: Institute of Race Relations, 1965); Larry W. Bowman, *Mauritius: Democracy and Development in the Indian Ocean* (Boulder, CO: Westview Press, 1991); William K. Storey, "Small-Scale Sugar Cane Farmers and Biotechnology in Mauritius: The 'Uba' Riots of 1937," *Agricultural History* 69, no. 2 (1995): 163–76; Adele S. Simmons, *Modern Mauritius: The Politics of Decolonization* (Bloomington: Indiana University Press, 1982).

22. The Dutch landed in 1598 and made two attempts to settle on the island, bringing slaves from Madagascar to cut down the ebony forests. They also introduced sugarcane, cotton, tobacco, cattle, and deer on the island. See Burton Benedict, "Slavery and Indenture in Mauritius and Seychelles," in *Asian and African Systems of Slavery,* ed. James L. Watson (Berkeley: University of California Press, 1980), 135–68.

23. Most of the slaves were brought from Madagascar and Mozambique, but the French also brought some slaves from India in the eighteenth century. In 1826, there were about 2,590 Indian slaves in Mauritius. See Robert R. Kuczynski, *Demographic Survey of the British Colonial Empire,* vol. 2 (London: Oxford University Press, 1949), 771.

24. The capture took place for strategic reasons, to deprive the French of a base from which to harass British shipping or challenge the position of Britain in India. See Jean Houbert, "Mauritius: Independence and Dependence," *Journal of Modern African Studies* 19, no. 1 (1981): 75-105; Vijaya Teelock, *Bitter Sugar: Sugar and Slavery in 19th Century Mauritius* (Mauritius: Mahatma Gandhi Institute, 1998). At the time of British takeover, the population of Mauritius comprised 6,277 whites (mainly of French descent), 7,133 free nonwhites, and

55,422 slaves, on which see Teelock, *Bitter Sugar*, 21. British rule lasted from 1810 until Mauritius became independent in 1968.

25. The French legal system was retained, schools and cultural institutions remained dominated by the French language, and the position of the Roman Catholic Church was safeguarded since it continued receiving support from the state.

26. Hugh Tinker, "Between Africa, Asia and Europe: Mauritius; Cultural Marginalism and Political Control," *African Affairs* 76, no. 304 (1977): 323.

27. Under the 1885 constitution, a male was entitled to be registered as a voter and to vote provided that he had attained the age of twenty-one years, could read and/or write English, was under no legal incapacity, was a British subject, and had lived in the country during three years and fulfilled one of the stipulated conditions. The Constitution of 1885 also provided for a council of government consisting of the governor as president, eight official members, nine nominated members, and ten elected members. Hansraj Mathur, *Parliament in Mauritius* (Mauritius: Editions de L'Océan Indien, 1991), 15.

28. Noël Marrier d'Unienville, *L'île menacée* (Port-Louis: General Printing and Stationery, 1954), p. 3, quoted in Catherine Boudet, "Les Franco-Mauriciens: Une diaspora pollinisée," *Revue européenne des migrations internationales* 23, no. 7 (2007).

29. See Geschiere, *Perils of Belonging*, 2.

30. Tinker, "Africa, Asia and Europe," 322.

31. Patrick Eisenlohr, "Creole Publics: Language, Cultural Citizenship, and the Spread of the Nation in Mauritius," *Comparative Studies in Society and History* 49, no. 4 (2007): 978.

32. Catherine Boudet, "La construction politique d'une identité Franco-Mauricienne (1810–1968): Le discours identitaire comme gestion de la contradiction," *Kabaro, Revue internationale des sciences de l'homme et des sociétés* 3, nos. 3–4 (2005): 37.

33. The Coloured population was largely a mixed-race group, often the children of Franco-Mauritian plantation owners and slave women. Although they were unable to inherit property from their fathers, they nonetheless received an education as compensation. See Thomas H. Eriksen, *Common Denominators: Ethnicity, Nation-Building and Compromise in Mauritius* (Oxford: Berg, 1998), 9.

34. In the 1830s, the free Coloured population totalled 18,019, making up 19.6 percent of the population of the time. They rejected the Creole language and culture on the island and gravitated toward European cultural models, especially the French language, education, and professions. Teelock, *Bitter Sugar*, 269.

35. By the end of the first decade of the nineteenth century, the Coloured population had become an integral component of the economic landscape on the island, owning more than 7 percent of all inventoried land and nearly 15 percent of the slaves in the colony, and by 1830, they controlled about one-fifth if not more of agricultural wealth on the island. See Richard B. Allen, *Slaves,*

Freedmen and Indentured Labourers in Colonial Mauritius (Cambridge: Cambridge University Press, 1999), 104.

36. Under the Code Noir, which was the French law overseeing slavery, slaves were defined as chattel, with the legal status of transferable property, and they were entirely subject to their master's will, often experiencing extreme torture. Marc D. North-Coombes, *Studies in the Political Economy of Mauritius* (Mauritius: Mahatma Gandhi Institute, 2000), 162.

37. The legal framework of apprenticeship was established by an order in council on September 17, 1834. Under the "apprenticeship" system, all former slaves over the age of six had to work as apprentices for their former masters for a period of six years. The apprentices were to work for seven and a half hours a day, without pay, and were supposed to be trained in some skill. They were also to be paid for duties performed overtime. There were penalties such as additional work, imprisonment, hard labor, and cane strokes and flogging for those who did not perform duties assigned to them. Teelock, *Bitter Sugar,* 273–74.

38. Benedict, "Slavery and Indenture," 141–42.

39. Mauritian slave owners were awarded a sum of £2,112,632 in compensation for 7,386 claims, involving 66,343 slaves, from the total compensation fund of £20 million. See North-Coombes, *Political Economy,* 22.

40. More than 451,000 Indian men, women, and children came to Mauritius before Indian immigration formally ended in 1910; out of these immigrants, more than 294,000 remained on the island permanently. See Allen, *Slaves, Freedmen,* 16.

41. Teelock, *Bitter Sugar,* 291.

42. Amrit K. Mishra, "Indian Indentured Labourers in Mauritius: Reassessing the 'New System of Slavery' vs. Free Labour Debate," *Studies in History* 25, no. 2 (2009): 229–51.

43. Indians were expected to work six days per week and also to perform unpaid labor on Sunday. The work was physically demanding and oppressive, and Indians were subjected to severe beatings and received no justice from the magistrates, who were largely agents of the planters. See Bowman, *Mauritius;* Benedict, "Slavery and Indenture."

44. For instance, absence from work for six days in a month meant that the month did not count in terms of service. Another exploitative system set up by the planters in 1847 was the "double-cut system," whereby absence of work for one day meant the loss of two days of wages. The double-cut system reduced the wage bill on some estates by one-third and on others by half. The double-cut system remained in practice in Mauritius from 1830 to 1909. See Bowman, *Mauritius,* 22.

45. See Hugh Tinker, *A New System of Slavery: The Import of Indian Labour Overseas, 1830–1920* (London: Oxford University Press, 1974).

46. "New immigrants" were defined as laborers who had not completed their mandatory five years of "industrial residence." Allen, *Slaves, Freedmen,* 62.

47. Tinker, "Africa, Asia and Europe," 235.

48. By 1921, 93 percent of planters on the island were Indo-Mauritian, and they owned approximately 35 percent of all the land under cultivation, mostly sugarcane. See Bowman, *Mauritius*, 25.

49. In 1821, Governor Farquar introduced Chinese immigrants onto the island. See Huguette Ly Tio Fane-Pineo and Edouard Lim Fat, *From Alien to Citizen: The Integration of the Chinese in Mauritius* (Mauritius: Editions de L'Océan Indien, 2008), 81.

50. In 1901, out of a community of 3,515, 85 percent of Chinese immigrants were traders. Ibid., 80.

51. See Marina Carter and James Ng Foong Kwong, *Abacus and Majong: Sino-Mauritian Settlement and Economic Consolidation* (Leiden: Brill, 2009), 5; Ly Tio Fane-Pineo and Lim Fat, *From Alien to Citizen*, 81.

52. In June 1842, the colonial government passed a law that deprived immigrants of the right to own or inherit land or immovable property in the island. The proclamation of June 21, 1842, stated, "Whereas under the law now and henceforth enforced no restriction has been imposed on the purchase or on the acquisition or on the holding of land, buildings and other immovable property situate within the same island. It is thereby ordered that the law of England so far as it relates to the purchase or the acquisition or to the holding by aliens of lands, tenements or hereditaments situate within the realm of England shall be declared to be applicable to the purchase, acquisition or holding by aliens within the island of Mauritius and its dependencies of lands, buildings or other immovable property situated within the same island or its dependency." Ly Tio Fane-Pineo and Lim Fat, *From Alien to Citizen*, 82.

53. The Colonial and Land Emigration Commission in 1840 stated that "it is in no case desirable to offer great encouragement to the acquisition of small plots of land by those whose conditions in life places them among the class of labourers. We think it better that they should remain wholly dependent upon wages until they have saved sufficiently to purchase from the Crown." Quoted in Teelock, *Bitter Sugar*, 279.

54. See Bowman, *Mauritius*, 27.

55. Bede Clifford, *Proconsul: Being Incidents in the Life and Career of the Honourable Sir Bede Clifford* (London: Evans Brothers, 1964), 235.

56. Seewoosagar Ramgoolam, *Our Struggle: 20th Century Mauritius* (London: East-West Publications, 1982), 83.

57. In 1908 Dr. Eugene Laurent, a Creole, formed a political party called Action Libérale with the objective of fighting for an extension of the franchise and a more liberal constitution. See Vijaya Teelock, *Mauritian History: From Its Beginnings to Modern Times* (Mauritius: Mahatma Gandhi Institute, 2009), 343.

58. See S. Mozaffar, "Negotiating Independence in Mauritius," *International Negotiation* 10 (2005): 269.

59. Franco-Mauritian political leaders such as Sir Célicourt Antelme had already raised the issue of the "Indian spectre" in 1882, and Sir Henri Leclézio brought out the notion of an "Asiatic peril" in 1908. Sydney Selvon, *A New*

Comprehensive History of Mauritius from the Beginning to This Day, vol. 2, *From British Mauritius to the 21st Century* (Mauritius: privately printed with Createspace, 2012), 53; Kenneth Ballhatchet, "The Structure of British Official Attitudes: Colonial Mauritius, 1883–1968," *Historical Journal* 8, no. 4 (1995): 997.

60. See Mathieu Claveyrolas, "With or Without Roots: Conflicting Memories of Slavery and Indentured Labour in the Mauritian Public Space," in *Politics of Memory: Making Slavery Visible in the Public Space*, ed. Ana L. Araujo (New York: Routledge, 2012), 68.

61. Patrick Eisenlohr, *Little India: Diaspora, Time and Ethnolinguistic Belonging in Hindu Mauritius* (Berkeley: University of California Press, 2006), 274.

62. This economic crisis led to riots, violence, and industrial unrest in 1937 and the death of four Indo-Mauritian laborers. There was also a major strike in 1943. These events forced the British to pay attention to the Mauritian situation and created a rift between the British colonial authority and the Franco-Mauritian colonial bourgeoisie. See North-Coombes, *Political Economy*, 171.

63. The languages spoken in Mauritius at that time included English, French, Gujrati, Hindustani, Tamil, Telugu, Urdu, Mandarin, and Creole Patois.

64. Simmons, *Modern Mauritius*, 99.

65. These included separate electoral rolls for each community as well as retention of educational and property qualifications for the franchise. Ibid., 101.

66. Eisenlohr, "Creole Publics," 978–79.

67. Catherine Boudet, "Nationalisme, décolonisation et consociation à l'île Maurice: L'émergence d'un Mauricianisme stratégique (1945–1967)," *Canadian Journal of African Studies* 47, no. 3 (2014): 389.

68. John Armstrong and Anthony D. Smith have brought up the concept of mythomoteur as a "myth-building complex" used for the construction of ethnicity-centered nationalistic ideologies. John A. Armstrong, *Nations before Nationalism* (Chapel Hill: University of North Carolina Press, 1982); Anthony D. Smith, *The Ethnic Origins of Nations* (Oxford: Blackwell, 1986).

69. Tijo Salverda, *The Franco-Mauritian Elite: Power and Anxiety in the Face of Change* (New York: Berghahn Books, 2015), 60, 157.

70. See Benedict, *Mauritius;* and Stanley A. de Smith, "Mauritius: Constitutionalism in a Plural Society," *Modern Law Review* 31, no. 6 (1968): 601–22.

71. *Le Cernéen* was founded in 1832 by the Franco-Mauritian lawyer and planter Adrien d'Epinay. It represented the interests and views of the Franco-Mauritian community, especially the planters or sugar barons. See Salverda, *Franco-Mauritian Elite*, 40.

72. Simmons, *Modern Mauritius*, 113.

73. Ibid., 116.

74. See Teelock, *Mauritian History*, 391.

75. Statement of Jules Koenig in council in 1956, quoted in Jules A. Koenig, *Jules Koenig: Une vie pour la justice* (Mauritius: Editions de L'Océan Indien, 1998), 39.

76. Boudet, "La construction politique," 38.

77. The MLP requested a ministerial form of government, fewer nominees and more elected members, changes in the composition of the executive council, the appointment of a Speaker just as in the House of Commons, and for the leader of the majority party to be made prime minister.

78. Responsible government was expected to give members of the legislative council full power to manage almost all internal affairs of the country, without interference from the British colonial authority. See Moonindra N. Varma, *The Political History of Mauritius*, vol. 1, *1883–1983: Recollections and Reflections* (Quatre Bornes, Mauritius: M. N. Varma, 2011), 92 ; Benedict, *Mauritius;* Simmons, *Modern Mauritius;* Ballhatchet, "British Official Attitudes."

79. Selvon, *New Comprehensive History*, 125.

80. This commission was known as the Electoral Boundary Commission, and the report was written by Sir Malcom Trustam-Eve. Mathur, *Parliament in Mauritius*, 20.

81. Selvon, *New Comprehensive History*, 132.

82. Ramgoolam, *Our Struggle*, 91.

83. Simmons, *Modern Mauritius.*

84. Ramgoolam, *Our Struggle;* Simmons, *Modern Mauritius.*

85. Ramgoolam, *Our Struggle*, 96.

86. Selvon, *New Comprehensive History*, 149.

87. This led to the establishment of the "best loser system," which is unique to Mauritius. The island was divided into twenty three-member constituencies and one two-member constituency for Rodrigues. The best loser system provides for up to eight additional members of parliament from the minority communities who had not been elected, in order to ensure adequate parliamentary representation of these groups. Mathur, *Parliament in Mauritius*, 22–23, 34.

88. The Independence Party secured 39 seats with 54 percent of the votes, as compared to 23 seats that went to the Parti Mauricien (which was renamed Parti Mauricien Sociale Démocrate [PMSD]) with 44 percent of the votes. Ibid., 23.

89. See Klaus Neumann, "Anxieties in Colonial Mauritius and the Erosion of the White Australian Policy," *Journal of Imperial and Commonwealth History* 31, no. 3 (2004) : 1–24.

90. See Koenig, *Jules Koenig*, 105.

91. Teelock, *Mauritian History*, 384.

92. Salverda, *Franco-Mauritian Elite.*

References

Adejumobi, Said. "Citizenship, Rights and the Problem of Internal Conflicts and Civil Wars in Africa." *African Journal of Political Science* 6, no. 2 (2001): 77–96.

Allen, Richard B. *Slaves, Freedmen and Indentured Labourers in Colonial Mauritius.* Cambridge: Cambridge University Press, 1999.

Amstrong, John A. *Nations before Nationalism.* Chapel Hill: University of North Carolina Press, 1982.

Ballhatchet, Kenneth. "The Structure of British Official Attitudes: Colonial Mauritius, 1883–1968." *Historical Journal* 8, no. 4 (1995): 989–1011.

Bellamy, Richard. *Citizenship: A Very Short Introduction.* Oxford: Oxford University Press, 2008.

Benedict, Burton. *Mauritius: The Problems of a Plural Society.* London: Institute of Race Relations, 1965.

———. "Slavery and Indenture in Mauritius and Seychelles." In *Asian and African Systems of Slavery,* edited by James L. Watson, 135–68. Berkeley: University of California Press, 1980.

Bereketeab, Redie. "The Ethnic and Civic Foundations of Citizenship and Identity in the Horn of Africa." *Studies in Ethnicity and Nationalism* 11, no. 1 (2011): 63–81.

Boudet, Catherine. "La construction politique d'une identité Franco-Mauricienne (1810–1968): Le discours identitaire comme gestion de la contradiction." *Kabaro, Revue internationale des sciences de l'homme et des sociétés* 3, nos. 3–4 (2005): 23–44.

———. "Les Franco-Mauriciens: Une diaspora pollinisée." *Revue européenne des migrations internationales* 23, no. 7 (2007): 109–32.

———. "Nationalisme, décolonisation et consociation à l'île Maurice: L'émergence d'un Mauricianisme stratégique (1945–1967)." *Canadian Journal of African Studies* 47, no. 3 (2014): 385–403.

Bowman, Larry W. *Mauritius: Democracy and Development in the Indian Ocean.* Boulder, CO: Westview Press, 1991.

Carter, Marina, and James Ng Foong Kwong. *Abacus and Majong: Sino-Mauritian Settlement and Economic Consolidation.* Leiden: Brill, 2009.

Ceuppens, Bambi, and Peter Geschiere, "Autochthony: Local or Global? New Modes in the Struggle over Citizenship and Belonging in Africa and Europe." *Annual Review of Anthropology* 34 (2005): 385–407.

Claveyrolas, Mathieu. "With or Without Roots: Conflicting Memories of Slavery and Indentured Labour in the Mauritian Public Space." In *Politics of Memory: Making Slavery Visible in the Public Space,* edited by Ana L. Araujo, 54–70. New York: Routledge, 2012.

Clifford, Bede. *Proconsul: Being Incidents in the Life and Career of the Honourable Sir Bede Clifford.* London: Evans Brothers, 1964.

de Smith, Stanley. A. "Mauritius: Constitutionalism in a Plural Society." *Modern Law Review* 31, no. 6 (1968): 601–22.

Dorman, Sara, Daniel Hammett, and Paul Nugent. "Introduction: Citizenship and Its Casualties in Africa." In Dorman, Hammett, and Nugent, *Making Nations, Creating Strangers,* 3–26.

———, eds. *Making Nations, Creating Strangers: States and Citizenship in Africa.* Leiden: Brill, 2007.

Eisenlohr, Patrick. "Creole Publics: Language, Cultural Citizenship, and the Spread of the Nation in Mauritius." *Comparative Studies in Society and History* 49, no. 4 (2007): 968–96.

———. *Little India: Diaspora, Time and Ethnolinguistic Belonging in Hindu Mauritius.* Berkeley: University of California Press, 2006.

Ekeh, Peter. "Colonialism and the Development of Citizenship in Africa: A Study in Ideologies of Legitimation." In *Themes in African Social and Political Thought,* edited by Onigu Odite, 101–25. Enugu, Nigeria: Fourth Dimension Publishers, 1978.

———. "Colonialism and the Two Publics in Africa: A Theoretical Statement." *Comparative Studies in Society and History* 17, no. 1 (1975): 91–112.

Eriksen, Thomas H. *Common Denominators: Ethnicity, Nation-Building and Compromise in Mauritius.* Oxford: Berg, 1998.

Geschiere, Peter. *The Perils of Belonging: Autochthony, Citizenship, and Exclusion in Africa and Europe.* Chicago: University of Chicago Press, 2009.

Geschiere, Peter, and Stephen Jackson. "Autochthony and the Crisis: Democratization, Decentralization, and the Politics of Belonging." *African Studies Review* 49, no. 2 (2006): 1–7.

Halisi, C. R. D., Paul J. Kaiser, and Stephen N. Ndegwa. "Guest Editors' Introduction: The Multiple Meanings of Citizenship—Rights, Identity, and Social Justice in Africa." *Africa Today* 45 (1998): 337–50.

Houbert, Jean. "Mauritius: Independence and Dependence." *Journal of Modern African Studies* 19, no. 1 (1981): 75–105.

Isin, Engin F., and Bryan S. Turner. "Investigating Citizenship: An Agenda for Citizenship Studies." *Citizenship Studies* 11, no. 1 (2007): 5–17.

Isin, Engin F., and Patricia K. Wood. *Citizenship and Identity.* London: Sage Publications, 1999.

Koenig, Jean. A. *Jules Koenig: Une vie pour la justice.* Mauritius: Editions de L'Océan Indien, 1998.

Kuczynski, Robert R. *Demographic Survey of the British Colonial Empire.* Vol. 2. London: Oxford University Press, 1949.

Kymlicka, Will. *Multicultural Citizenship: A Liberal Theory of Minority Rights.* Oxford: Oxford University Press, 1995.

Ly Tio Fane-Pineo, Huguette, and Edouard Lim Fat. *From Alien to Citizen: The Integration of the Chinese in Mauritius.* Mauritius: Editions de L'Océan Indien, 2008.

Mamdani, Mahmood. "Beyond Settler and Native as Political Identities: Overcoming the Political Legacy of Colonialism." *Comparative Studies in Society and History* 43, no. 4 (2001): 651–64.

———. *Citizen and Subject: Contemporary Africa and the Legacy of Late Colonialism.* Cape Town: David Philip, 1996.

Manby, Bronwen. *Struggles for Citizenship in Africa.* London: Zed Books, 2009.

Mannick, A. R. *Mauritius: The Development of a Plural Society.* Nottingham: Spokesman, 1979.

Marshall, Thomas H. *Citizenship and Social Class.* Cambridge: Cambridge University Press, 1950.

Marshall-Fratani, Ruth. "The War of 'Who Is Who': Autochthony, Nationalism and Citizenship in the Ivorian Crisis." In Dorman, Hammett, and Nugent, *Making Nations, Creating Strangers,* 29–68.

Mathur, Hansraj. *Parliament in Mauritius.* Mauritius: Editions de L'Océan Indien, 1991.

Miles, William F. S. "The Mauritius Enigma." *Journal of Democracy* 10, no. 2 (1999): 91–104.

Mishra, Amit K. "Indian Indentured Labourers in Mauritius: Reassessing the 'New System of Slavery' vs. Free Labour Debate." *Studies in History* 25, no. 2 (2009): 229–51.

Moutou, Benjamin. *Ile Maurice: Récits de son histoire contemporaine.* Mauritius: B. Moutou, 2000.

Mozaffar, Shaheen. "Negotiating Independence in Mauritius." *International Negotiation* 10 (2005): 263–91.

Neumann, Klaus. "Anxieties in Colonial Mauritius and the Erosion of the White Australian Policy." *Journal of Imperial and Commonwealth History* 31, no. 3 (2004): 1–24.

North-Coombes, Marc D. *Studies in the Political Economy of Mauritius.* Mauritius: Mahatma Gandhi Institute, 2000.

Nyamnjoh, Francis. *Insiders and Outsiders: Citizenship and Xenophobia in Contemporary Southern Africa.* Dakar: CODESRIA, 2006.

Nzongola-Ntalaja, George. "The Politics of Citizenship in the Democratic Republic of Congo." In Dorman, Hammett, and Nugent, *Making Nations, Creating Strangers,* 69–82.

Oomen, Tharailath K. "Introduction: Conceptualizing the Linkage between Citizenship and National Identity." In *Citizenship and National Identity: From Colonialism to Globalism,* edited by Tharailath K. Oomen, 13–52. New Delhi: Sage Publications, 1997.

Oyelaran, Olasope O., and Michael O. Adeliran. "Colonialism, Citizenship and Fractured National Identity: The African Case." In *Citizenship and National Identity: From Colonialism to Globalism,* edited by Tharailath K. Oomen, 173–98. New Delhi, 1997.

Ramgoolam, Seewoosagar. *Our Struggle: 20th Century Mauritius.* London: East-West Publications, 1982.

Ramsurrun, Pahlad. *Sir Seewoosagar Ramgoolam: Battles for a Democratic Constitution of Mauritius.* Vol. 1. India: New Dawn Press, 2006.

Rutherford, Blair. "Shifting Grounds in Zimbabwe: Citizenship and Farm Workers in the New Politics of Land." In Dorman, Hammett, and Nugent, *Making Nations, Creating Strangers,* 105–22.

Salverda, Tijo. *The Franco-Mauritian Elite: Power and Anxiety in the Face of Change.* New York: Berghahn Books, 2015.

Selvon, Sydney. *A New Comprehensive History of Mauritius from the Beginning to This Day.* Vol. 2, *From British Mauritius to the 21st Century.* Mauritius: privately printed with Createspace, 2012.

Simmons, Adele S. *Modern Mauritius: The Politics of Decolonization.* Bloomington: Indiana University Press, 1982.

Smith, Anthony D. *The Ethnic Origins of Nations.* Oxford: Blackwell, 1986.

Storey, William K. "Small-Scale Sugar Cane Farmers and Biotechnology in Mauritius: The 'Uba' Riots of 1937." *Agricultural History* 69, no. 2 (1995): 163–76.

Sutton, Deborah. "The Political Consecration of Community in Mauritius, 1948–68." *Journal of Imperial and Commonwealth History* 35, no. 2 (2007): 239–62.

Teelock, Vijaya. *Bitter Sugar: Sugar and Slavery in 19th Century Mauritius.* Mauritius: Mahatma Gandhi Institute, 1998.

———. *Mauritian History: From Its Beginnings to Modern Times.* Mauritius: Mahatma Gandhi Institute, 2009.

Tinker, Hugh. "Between Africa, Asia and Europe: Mauritius; Cultural Marginalism and Political Control." *African Affairs* 76, no. 304 (1977): 321–28.

———. *A New System of Slavery: The Import of Indian Labour Overseas, 1830–1920.* London: Oxford University Press, 1974.

Varma, Moonindra N. *The Political History of Mauritius.* Vol. 1, *1883–1983: Recollections and Reflections.* Quatre Bornes, Mauritius: M. N. Varma, 2011.

Young, Crawford. "Nation, Ethnicity, and Citizenship: Dilemmas of Democracy and Civil Order in Africa." In Dorman, Hammett, and Nugent, *Making Nations, Creating Strangers,* 241–64.

PART THREE

Citizenship in Contemporary Africa

EIGHT

The Ethnic Language of Rights and the Nigerian Political Community

V. ADEFEMI ISUMONAH

IT INCREASINGLY SEEMS THAT GROUP RIGHTS DOMINATE THE thinking of Nigerians, directing their thoughts on political power, political participation, resource allocation, and the distribution of individual benefits. Among political elites, issues that affect the whole nation are often considered through the lens of group rights. As Bonnie Iwuoha, media adviser to the Abia State governor, wrote in 2011, it is common with Nigerians "to adopt positions that suit their ethnic, state and regional interests while looking at issues of national unity, integration, religion and development."[1]

Ethnic group identity is projected over national identity and "ethnic group nationality" over Nigerian nationality in the determination of the citizenship of the individual. The contradiction in Nigeria's ethnic group rights thought is the insistence of a given ethnic group on its cultural and political autonomy within its autochthonous territory, as well as free access to the resources of the autochthonous territory of another ethnic group. This is most exemplified by the demand of the predominantly Muslim northern Nigeria for political and cultural autonomy and also a larger share of the oil revenues derived from the Niger delta in the southern part of Nigeria.[2]

The main objects of group rights thought in Nigeria are revenue allocation (that is, allocation of revenues derived from crude oil production in the Niger delta); the distribution of government political offices to regions, states, and local communities; and the dispensation of government benefits.[3] The assumption is made that any benefit or advantage won in the name of the group—elective or appointive office, or infrastructure such as an educational institution or industrial establishment, is for the whole group, which, of course, is also assumed to be homogenous in composition and bound by an undivided interest. But Vernon Van Dyke, a foremost advocate of ethnic group rights, candidly admits that some group rights ultimately benefit individual members of the group and not the whole group.[4]

The narrative of Nigeria's political history is the groundswell of the argument, which derives from an essentialist view of the group, for ethnic group rights.[5] Evidence from Nigeria suggests that scholars have been misled by the pronouncements of politicians in that they have paid little attention to the ways in which individual lives no longer follow a pattern of ethnic-based exclusivity. Far from ethnic group rights being the basis of a progressive citizenship, a progressive citizenship would, I argue, be one based on individual rights. Rabid particularistic group claims have hindered the evolution of an integrated political community by inhibiting negotiation, compromise, and coalition building for peaceful coexistence among the diverse social and cultural groups in Nigeria. A group could be loyal to its ethnic identity yet universalistic by including a stake for members of other groups upon which it is making a demand for special treatment. No universal citizenship, no development! In addition, the twin assumption of homogeneity within a group and common interests or equal access to group benefits among all presumed members of the group is false. Through the case study of Nigeria, I show that group rights practice violates not only individual rights but also *group* rights—the rights of minor groups within a group—if, in practice, the rights of its major group command overriding attention.

The Roots of Divided Citizenship

Group rights, Claude Ake argues, are intrinsic to African thinking about rights. That Africans think and act as groups, not as individuals, then, predates their colonial domination.[6] Contrary to Basil Davidson's suggestion of the colonial origin of group rights, colonial rule did not originate the group rights thought of Africans but strengthened it by encouraging ethnic federations as an integral part of administrative policy, known as indirect rule.[7] Indeed, the British colonial power relied on precolonial cultural patterns of association to divide Africa into administrative areas.[8] Consequently, African states emerged from colonialism with the "communalist argument, that is, the argument that individual rights are irrelevant in a community."[9]

The observed orientation of Nigerians has been used as evidence in support of the entrenchment of "indigene-ship" or the particularistic principle of citizenship. This includes the practice of immigrants taking their dead for burial or building a house or marking festive occasions in the country home of their ethno-regional group. Based on this, Bolaji Akinyemi, a political scientist and Nigeria's former external affairs minister, claims that "indigene-ship" is rooted in Nigeria or Africa. In other words, preference for an indigene/nonindigene dichotomy is natural for Nigerians given the fact that nonindigenes look elsewhere rather than their place of abode as home. Thus, the behavior of Nigerians as described above is sufficient proof of their preference for the discrimination between indigenes and nonindigenes in the administration of rights.[10]

But there are problems with this analysis. First, what is presented as the *behavior* of Nigerians is a partial representation of evidence to the extent that it generalizes the behavior of a part of the group of Nigerians regarded as nonindigenes. The distinction that must be made is between (old) nonindigenes who are several generations removed from the place of what indigenes still regard as their homeland and (new or first-generation) nonindigenes with recent migratory history in other locations in Nigeria. Examples of the old nonindigenes are Hausas and Fulanis in the Jos area, Zango-Kataf, and other parts of northern Nigeria and Modakeke Yorubas in Ile-Ife. What is claimed as observed behavior of Nigerians is not true of this group. It is partially true of (new) first-generation—of very recent migratory history—nonindigenes (this will be returned to later). The solution suggested by Akinyemi is actually a misunderstanding of even the extent to which it is true of the new nonindigenes.

Both the understanding of behavior and the solution proffered amount to blaming the victim. The behavior of some new nonindigenes ought to be understood as defensive behavior. This is the kind of behavior that meets the various challenges occasioned by the negative attitude of the state government and so-called indigenes toward them. The so-called nonindigenes' behavior is a response to their branding as settlers or temporary residents and subsequent denial of integration by indigenes and the local political community.

Some aspects of this behavior were a product of immediate past experience. For example, the Igbo of eastern Nigeria lost lots of landed property in different parts of Nigeria especially Port Harcourt to the Nigerian civil war of 1967–70. Hence, in the few decades that followed the war, young Igbos gave priority to owning a landed property in their village in Igbo heartland in the eastern part of Nigeria. However, the observed trend is a resumption of acquisition of property even by new Igbo nonindigenes in their place of abode, that is, non-Igbo ethnic territory. Indeed, in their will, new nonindigenes have expressed their preference to be buried in their place of abode.[11] The generalization of this defensive behavior also loses sight of the observed tendency of even some new nonindigenes of wanting to stay in their abode. As Mahmood Mamdani has written, the new tendency is for those dubbed nonindigenes to stay and fight it out rather than head for "home" when there is a clash between them and indigenes.[12]

Local political communities' ethnic group–based discriminatory practices have been explained as compensations for lost ground or past losses.[13] This is a recast of the historical "disadvantage due to exclusion" argument for group rights.

Thus, pro–ethnic group rights scholars have tended to echo the continued predominance of group rights demands, exclusive claims in which groups within the same African state continue to discriminate against each other.[14] Effectively, the citizenship discourse in twenty-first-century Africa is confined to "citizenship-as-legal-status, that is, as full membership in a particular political community instead of citizenship-as-desirable-activity, where the extent and quality of one's citizenship [are] a function of one's participation in that community."[15]

New attitudes toward ethnic identification, which challenge fixed ethnic boundaries that need to be taken into account in theorizing group rights, are emerging. So-called nonindigenes are adopting the ethnic/group identity of their place of domicile and are using it to demand state benefits and privileges. But the organization and administration of various administrative areas on the basis of a fixed ethnic identity impede the evolution of an inclusive local and national political community in Africa. Scholars, for their part, have failed to perceive the impediment that the ethnic language of rights poses to political accountability in an ethnically diverse political community. In their veneration of the ethnic language of rights, they continue to propagate the view that an ethnically homogenous polity best guarantees the individual's well-being.

The premise of the extant scholarship on political community in Africa ignores the rights of new minorities in the midst of the "indigenous group." However, migration and cultural diversity are facts of life. It is their mismanagement that produces such consequences as genocide, population displacement with the attendant humanitarian crisis, and further underdevelopment, since violent ethnic conflicts cost human and material resources.

There are two basic reasons why pro–ethnic autonomy scholars cannot recognize the contradictions of the ethnic or particularistic language of rights. The first reason is the assumption of an unyielding preference of Africans for the primordial public as the administrative framework. This assumption finds the greatest rationalization in Peter Ekeh's "theory of two publics in Africa," in which he regards the primordial public as the bastion of moral purity.[16] Although the literature recognizes that the preference for the ethnic principle that underpins the preference for the primordial administrative framework has been championed by political elites mostly for their own benefit, investigation into the contradictions of ethno-territorial language of rights is not deemed necessary, because of the generalized utility of ethnic identity.[17] Consequently, there is an implicit acceptance in the extant literature of the impossibility of a socially and politically integrated African multiethnic state as the United States of America has substantially achieved, without first critically examining the political, social, and economic implications of the exclusionist policies of autonomous political units for individual well-being, group (minority) rights, and the national polity in Africa. The need for a critical examination of the primordial public is highlighted by Browne Onuoha, who shows that the attribution of moral chasteness to it is misplaced given the massive evidence of corruption within it.[18]

As I have argued elsewhere, the second reason scholars cannot recognize the problems of an ethnic language of rights is the essentialist view of ethnic group identity that is based on three assumptions:[19] that all (presumed) members of the group want to preserve the group's identity because it is only in that identity that their well-being lies; that all (presumed) members of the group regard its boundaries as sacrosanct; and that all (presumed) members of the ethno-territorial group wish to remain permanently in it and harbor no desire for membership of another group. As a consequence of this essentialist view and reification of group identity, an examination of the ethnic polity as the guarantor of individual well-being and the empirical trends that challenge or deviate from attachment to ethno-territorial boundaries is not deemed necessary. Examples of deviations worthy of examination include the mismanagement of homogenous ethnic administrative authorities and permanent migrations across Nigeria, representing increasing detachment from the culture of the point of migration and increasing cross-cultural interactions in Nigeria.

In the existing conceptual and philosophical background of scholarship on group rights, the question of the self-negating, internal and external ethnic diversity–amplifying ethno-territorial language of rights does not arise. Not surprisingly, works on the oil-based conflict in Nigeria have simply justified exclusivist remedial solutions to the grievances of ethnic minorities of the Niger delta.[20] These works are theoretically and philosophically limited, taking evidently anti-coexistence discrimination as given.

The Preference for Citizenship Rights Based on Ethnic Identities

In Nigeria, postcolonial elites have adopted a strategy of recognizing citizenship rights on the basis of ethnic group identities. Residents of northern Nigeria first demanded group rights with "guaranteed representation in political bodies, and veto rights over specific policies that affect" it, on the basis of a presumed higher population figure and a lack of Western educational qualifications, which were required for recruitment into public service institutions.[21] However, the north is largely responsible for its residents' backwardness in Western education. During British colonial rule, the Muslim leaders, because of their desire to preserve and protect their Islamic religion, prevented Western education from spreading to their domain.[22]

Thus, no ethnic group can honestly claim a historical disadvantage from exclusion in Nigeria. It is not the ethnic group but women who have suffered the historical disadvantage. While differentiated citizenship claims hold sway for the ethnic group in advocacy and practice, they remain largely feeble for women. Now, all Nigerian political communities (that is, ethnic groups)—whether in reality they are better off or worse off, politically dominant or not—engage in discriminatory practices, backed by the postcolonial Nigerian constitutions of 1979 and 1999.

The legal basis of elites' ethnic-based citizenship practices lies in the 1999 constitution, section 14, subsections 3 and 4, and section 147, subsection 3. This constitutional foundation of discrimination was replicated from the 1979 constitution. Section 14(3) of the 1999 constitution states,

> The composition of the Government of the Federation or any of its agencies and the conduct of its affairs shall be carried out in such a manner as to reflect the federal character of Nigeria and the need to promote national unity, and also to command national loyalty, thereby ensuring that there shall be no predominance of persons from a few States or from a few ethnic or other sectional groups in that Government or in any of its agencies.

Similarly, section 14(4) states,

> The composition of the Government of a State, a local government council, or any of the agencies of such Government or council, and the conduct of the affairs of the Government or council or such agencies[,] shall be carried out in such manner as to recognize the diversity of the people within its area of authority and the need to promote a sense of belonging and loyalty among all the people of the Federation.

In section 147, which is about the composition of the federal cabinet, the constitution provides in subsection 3 that

> [a]ny appointment under subsection (2) of this section by the President shall be in conformity with the provisions of section 14(3) of this Constitution:—provided that in giving effect to the provisions aforesaid the President shall appoint at least one Minister from each State, who shall be an indigene of such State.

The *state* as a constituent of the Nigerian federation or *local government* as a constituent of the state is the intended *group* of these constitutional provisions, which are better collectively known by Nigerians as the federal character principle. However, in implementation, the ethnic group is their underlying identity.

In reality, the government (federal, state, or local) and individuals define group identity differently. The government's concept of the individual's group identity, which is inspired by ethnic identity, is (ancient) paternal ancestry with the group entity shifting, depending on the context of resource sharing, between the collectivity of individuals and the territory.[23] It is simultaneously rigid and fluid: rigid in the sense that paternal ancestry remains its basis in whatever group entity it takes, but also fluid, in that the government's concept of group identity could be a state of the federation, a local government area, a territory comprising several states, a nonterritory/ethnic group, a local government, or a city or village, depending on the context in which sharing of public resources and advantages is taking place. It can also be a religious group, namely, Christianity or Islam.

Ethnic groups are proving very powerful in the government's conception of the individual's group identity and evolution of citizenship principles in Nigeria. But as the practice of ethnic citizenship moves from the smallest political community to the federal or national level, the territorial meaning or concept of ethnic group has assumed supremacy over the collectivity of individuals' meaning. Here lies the contradiction in ethnicity's termination of its role in the development of citizenship at ethnic citizenship rather than move it to the broader level of national citizenship: the ethnic group self-negation, which is the differentiation of individuals from individuals it originally defined as its members.

Mamdani undercuts this power of the culture of the ethnic group in the development of citizenship principles in the assertion that "both race and ethnicity need to be understood as political—and not cultural or even biological identities."[24] If this were a reference to the counterpart role that politics (or the political) plays in the process of ethnic identification or the determination of citizenship, he is right. He is wrong in seeing ethnic identity or race, and therefore, a citizenship definition or practice consequent upon it, entirely as a derivation of the political.

This is because both the nature and the application of law could be a matter of cultural disposition. If an existing law appears to be unconnected to a cultural norm, selective application reveals it. Individuals or groups may choose to ignore the law that sanctions ethnicity or racism depending on their cultural, including materialist, disposition. Hence, the determination of citizenship is ultimately cultural.[25] Evidence of the cultural roots of ethnicity or race (nationality) can be seen in the prior existence of a society of people bound by shared norms before the establishment of a political society held together by law and a constitution. A diverse political history, beginning at the time of the establishment of a city-state, is characterized by the use of the law to fight entrenched beliefs, habits, and practices to extend nationality and citizenship to more people—women, former slaves, non–property owners, and immigrants. The failure or partial success of the attempt to use law or the constitution to confer nationality and citizenship reflects the power of culture. Successful use of law reflects the dynamism of culture.

This is made clearer by the interaction between the moves and countermoves that produce a law. There is no gainsaying that if moves are weightier, a law is born, but not if countermoves are weightier. The outcome, whether birth or nonbirth of a law, is a reflection of the dominant cultural attitude expressed as an overriding political force. Mamdani's assertion does not recognize this contention in the making of laws.

Therefore, the rejection of universal citizenship by the political class of Nigeria is a reflection of cultural attitudes prevailing in Nigeria. The political class has led various Nigerian groups to pitch their tents with divided citizenship at one time or the other. For example, the Constituent Assembly of 1977/78 dropped the draft that proposed outlawing discrimination by the state of origin.[26] Thus, there is nothing natural about the rejection of universal citizenship; it is a choice that politicians have made.

As suggested above, group identities are more fluid than prevailing political discourse suggests. Second and succeeding generations of immigrants are claiming the nationality or ownership of the place in which they were born and reside, and thus they have not stuck to paternal ancestry for ethnic identification. In the survey (in-depth interviews) I conducted in September–October 2013 in the ethnically diverse areas of Lagos—Agege, Makoko, Ajegunle, and Obalende—Hausas and Yorubas born in these places are laying claim to them as their indigenous home (see table 9.1). As a Hausa resident in Agege put it, "I was born

TABLE 9.1. The claim or denial of the indigene-ship of the place of domicile other than the place of ancestral ethnic origin

Location/ancestral ethnic origin of respondents	Has claimed	Has not claimed
Agege		
Hausa	7	
Yoruba	4	
Makoko		
Yoruba	2	
Egun	1	
Ilaje	2	
Ajegunle		
Yoruba	4	
Hausa		2
Igbo		1
Itsekiri	1	
Obalende		
Igbo	1	
Yoruba	4	
Togolese	1	
Esan	1	1

Source: Field survey conducted by the author in September–October 2013.

here. . . . Most of my businesses are here. I understand the people. In fact, the people I know in Lagos State are more than those I know in Sokoto or Kano state. . . . It is also important to note that all the wealth my parents and I made was all made in Agege."

A Hausa male respondent born in Agege noted that he had chosen Lagos as his state of origin many times. He asserted, "Whenever I travel to Kano, the people there greet me with the saying, 'Lagosians are here.'" He added that he claims Agege because he grew up, went to school, and has his friends there. Another male respondent, fifty-three years old, whose grandmother was born in Agege, said that he normally rejects being labeled Hausa by some Yorubas, reminding them that he entered Agege with his head, a reference to his birth. A fifty-eight-year-old Hausa male respondent noted that many Yorubas and Hausas in Agege have blood ties through generations of interethnic marriages. This perhaps explains why it is so easy for Hausas to claim they hail from Agege and why Yorubas do not dispute their claims.

In the same vein, many Yoruba respondents concede that Hausas born and bred in Makoko can claim being from there. An Ajegunle Yoruba and political leader, Alhaji Kudus Nurudeen, noted that the *baale* (traditional political head) of Ajegunle recommends Hausas and Igbos for the indigene-ship certificate of Ajeromi Ifelodun, a local government area. A seventy-eight-year-old Igbo born in Obalende said he claims Lagos but if a public form requires him to state his state of origin, he would claim Enugu State. However, he noted that he feels safer in Obalende than in the Enugu State place of origin of his parents. The *seriki hausawa* (traditional political head of Hausas) of Ajegunle also informed me that the Lagos State government in 2013 told the Hausas to register themselves on a government form as indigenes of Lagos State. For these respondents, only the traditional political stool and aspiration to elective political office are not open to "immigrants."[27] Even so, according to the Honorable Bolaji Oso, the community development association chairman of Alayabiagba in Ajegunle, the vice-chairman of the local government of Ajeromi Ifelodun is an Igbo.

Only a few first-generation Igbo and Edo migrants do not claim that they are from the place of their birth or residence in Lagos State. But many of their children do claim the indigeneship of Lagos. An Esan sixty-year-old man who migrated to Obalende in 1971 noted that neither he nor his children claim Lagos State as their place of origin, for two reasons. First, the Nigerian state does not encourage or support such claims. As he declared, "If the Lagos State government pronounced that anybody who has lived in Lagos State for a defined period of time can claim Lagos State origin, my children and I are very disposed to accepting the offer." Second, his children have not been constrained to do so. Igbo respondents who are not inclined to claim Lagos origin want to maintain their state of origin in the Igbo heartland. As a sixty-seven-year-old put it, "If I deny my Igbo origins, my tribe and my language will disappear someday."

Nigerians who have exploited supportive cultural attributes to redefine their group identity talk about it in whispers. Nevertheless, ethnographic data indicate that individuals are using residency to redefine their group identity and are using paternal ancestry for their group identification when it is beneficial to them. When desirable and where possible, they are using birthplace or residency and the possibility of adopting a new residency, drawing on any cultural attributes such as personal names and fluency in the language and religion of the local community to redefine their group identity. That is why its prevalence is difficult to establish. Some young southern Nigerians seeking admission into federal universities, which maintain lower entry requirements for northerners, have admitted in confidence to me and to other researchers at the University of Ibadan in southwestern Nigeria that they redefined themselves as northerners, drawing on northern cultural attributes.[28]

A professor of medicine based at the Ahmadu Bello University Zaria, in the northwestern part of Nigeria, confessed to Professor Bola Osifo, a Yoruba woman based at the University of Ibadan, that he was born in the north of Yoruba parents but defines himself as a northerner to enhance his career.[29] Nigeria's former head of state, General Murtala Muhammed, who claimed Kano State (northern Nigeria) origin until his death at an assassin's hand in 1976, is reported to have hailed from Auchi in Edo State (southern midwestern Nigeria). So does the First Republic politician and elder statesman Alhaji Maitama Sule. Such reports draw credence from the religious and physical similarities between Auchi people and Hausas. It is instructive that Hausas and Auchi people are mostly Muslims and bear Muslim names. Similar cases of group self-reidentification for favorable consideration for recruitment into local, state, and federal government establishments are common in modern Nigeria. As noted above, some of the cases of group redefinition have been endorsed by traditional rulers.

Many so-called nonindigenes are asserting themselves differently through their quest for representative political office in the place of domicile outside their ethnic territory. Elections have been lost or won for seats on the local government council in the states where they are regarded as nonindigenes by the government's concept of groups. Some of the electoral victories have been facilitated by the preponderant population of fellow ethnics/nonindigenes. Such victories were recorded in the March 28, 2015, national assembly elections, in which three Igbo contestants, Chief Oghene Egboh, Mrs. Rita Urji, and Tony Nwoolu, won seats into the federal House of Representatives on the platform of the opposition party, the People's Democratic Party, in predominantly Yoruba-speaking Lagos State. Those electoral victories are remarkable even though the Igbo candidates defeated Yoruba candidates in the heavily populated constituencies of Lagos State. Chief Egboh so much agrees when he declared, "[M]y success . . . was very significant being a non-indigene to have won the seat for the first time in Amuwo Odofin federal constituency."[30]

So in the self-motivated individual's concept of group identification lies the possibility of building a Nigerian political community or national belonging. Unlike the government's rigid historical construction of the individual's identity, it agrees that "the identity of individuals is . . . historically constructed as well as analytically conceptualized."[31] But the way the government's concept of the individual's ethnic identity interacts with cultural attitudes continues to work against national integration and the Nigerian political community by withholding legal backing of the freedom of the individual to choose an ethnic group identity. In this regard, national constitutions and government policies are partly culpable for exclusive citizenship practices in Nigeria.[32] Contrary to the government's stance on ethnic identity, Nigerian ethnic cultures have shown the inclination to assimilate individuals of other cultural backgrounds.[33] Kate Meagher also notes "the absorption of other ethnic groups—such as Ibibio and Igala settlers—into Igbo communities, and the ease with which communities have federated into larger units when encouraged to do so by the structure of political incentives."[34]

New generations of Nigerians, especially bright and potentially successful ones, are showing no attachment to their government-"assigned" primordial roots. They are making close friends across ethnic boundaries and cultures, as can be gleaned from advertorials of well wishes and obituaries. Thus, the government is partly to blame for the refusal of some cultures (of "indigenes") to admit certain individuals (deemed "nonindigenes") into their group or ethnic identity. This is because the government acts on the definition of the ethnic identity of a person not by the person's current circumstances—birthplace or residence—but by the person's ancient paternal ancestry.

Is the Ethnic Basis of Citizenship Working?

The motive of Nigeria's federal character principle is clear from the letter of the constitution, namely, to ensure fair representation in government for all ethnic groups. Put differently, it is to prevent the domination of government establishments by individuals from a particular region. But the implementation of the principle is based on the discretion of the chief executive (president or governor), making it open to abuse. Thus, the state or local government may be represented and not its ethnic groups. The shifting basis of group identity also makes the implementation of citizenship based on it inherently discriminatory against one and all.

Nigeria is, indeed, now in a situation where everyone is in need of confirmation of their citizenship, depending on the proclivity for personal political participation or the level of personal political and administrative ambition. The acceptance of this need of confirmation of one's citizenship in Nigeria in the subconscious is complete: claimants of an ethnic group nationality, as well as ownership of a geographic area,[35] regard other Nigerians as *nonindigenes* or non–ethnic group citizens and, of course, themselves as *indigenes* or ethnic group citizens, while Nigerians regarded as nonindigenes agree, regardless of whether they were born or have lived all or most of their lives in that area. Indeed, it is striking that the term *indigene* has now replaced the term *citizen,* especially in the sense of rights in many African states. The dissatisfaction with the ethnic group basis of citizenship can be seen in the growing tendency of young Nigerians to use, wherever they can, residency or other criteria, versus the government's rigid reliance on paternal ancestry, to redefine their group identity and, consequently, citizenship in the local political community.

The appointment of ministers by the federal government from Kogi and Edo States between 1999 and 2010 illustrates the absurdity of the legal foundation of group rights practice in Nigeria. All the three ministers appointed from Kogi between 1999 and 2007, the first nine years of Nigeria's current democratic dispensation—David Jemibewon (minister of police affairs), Eyitayo Lambo (minister of health), and Bayo Ojo (justice and attorney general of the Federation)—were Okun (Yoruba), a subgroup of President Olusegun Obasanjo's Yoruba ethnic group. Some might see this as ethnic balancing, given that the governor of the state at the time was from the most populous Igala ethnic group. This rationalization crashed in 2007 when a new helmsman, President Umar Yar'Adua (a Fulani from the north), took over. Between 2007 and 2010, the two appointees to the ministerial post from Kogi State were Igala: Gabriel Aduku (minister of health, 2007–9) and Humphrey Abbah (minister of police affairs, 2007–10), while an Igala remained the governor of Kogi State.

Members of Kogi's third major ethnic group, Igbira, began having their shot at the ministerial office with the appointment of Mohammed Adoke as minister of justice and attorney general of the federation in 2011 under President Goodluck Jonathan (of Ijaw, a southern minority ethnic group). If Kogi State is also composed of smaller ethnic groups, the above clearly shows that the major groups are the ones being represented in the federal cabinet.

Edo State presents a similar graphic picture of the affirmation of existing group structures and domination. All the ministers appointed from Edo State between 1999 and 2015, a period of sixteen years, except one, that is, Godwin Abe (Bini, 2007–9) were Esans, namely, Tony Anenih, Odion Ugbesia, Chris Ogienwonyi, and Mike Onolomemen. This means that the ministerial representation of Edo State is being monopolized by the Bini and *especially* the Esan. The force behind the Esan monopoly of Edo State's slot(s) of the Federal Executive Council is Chief Tony Anenih, an Esan powerful member of the ruling People's Democratic Party (PDP) of that period. He was serving a second time as the chair of PDP's board of trustees during the period.

The foregoing illustrations of group rights practice in Nigeria by Edo and Kogi States make it clear that the state of the federation has been equated with the major ethnic group(s). In this regard, the major ethnic group enjoys a double advantage. First, it dominates representation in the establishments of the state. Second, it dominates representation of the state in federal establishments and institutions. From the ministerial representations of Edo and Kogi States, the practice of group rights based on states boils down to majority rule/representation. It defeats the goal of balkanization of Nigeria into states and local governments, that is, to grant minorities equal access to executive power. Only a minuscule number of minor groups, major groups among them, are benefiting from it. The rest of the minor groups in much larger number have been excluded. This is beside the point.

The assumption that a government of representatives of the group (state) will ensure that the interests of the group, that is, all members of the state, are protected must be proven to be true for the current state-based representation to be valid. The only valid proof is government that works for the welfare of all. If this is not the case, as the quality of life of most ordinary Nigerians indicates, then the existing practice of group representation in government is simply government of the elite for the elite. Group rights advocates may insist that such a government serves the purpose of group representation by ensuring that no one major group monopolizes executive power. However, this is not the case, because the philosophical basis of this variant of group representation, the interest of the entire group, is not being satisfied.

The variable meaning of "group" makes its use for administering rights arbitrary with regard to the underlying motive of the constitution. Consider two persons of the same ethnic group but from different states and regions. When state is the basis of group rights, the Yoruba person from Kwara or Kogi State may be favored over the one from Oyo or Ogun State, on the basis of an adjunct criterion of educational disadvantage of the former group of states. At another time, the same Yoruba person may be favored when region is the basis of group rights, for the same adjunct reason that Kwara and Kogi States are part of the north, which is adjudged as deserving preferential treatment on account of educational disadvantage compared to the south, of which Oyo and Ogun States are a part. In this regard, one can speak of a double advantage being enjoyed by certain persons in Nigeria's group rights practice. The concern for group rights was based on identifiable groups. But the identity of groups whose rights should be respected in Nigeria is becoming increasingly hazy.

The Case for Universal Citizenship

In this section, I argue for citizenship rights based on respect for individual rights. The recognition of citizenship rights based on ethnic identities in Nigeria and many other African states is often criticized but without situating group rights in history and theory. If group rights demands are masks for individual privileges (as they are shown in the preceding section to have become in Nigeria), then the subordination of the individual to the group in certain group rights advocacy, theory, and practice is in need of review. As Peter Jones has written, "[A] right is [a] group right only if it is borne by the group qua group. If the individuals who form a group hold rights as separate individuals, their several individual rights do not add up to a group right."[36] Thus, a group rights argument needs to be made for a particular type of human right if it is to be incontrovertible. The right to religion by a minority group is a good example of an incontrovertible argument to make.[37] There is the need, then, to subject group rights demands and practice to case-by-case evaluation. Group rights that benefit individuals, not groups qua groups, and at the same time deny individuals the freedom to choose their group, including ethnic identity, are the focus of the criticism in this section.

Liberal and communitarian perspectives through liberalism and nationalism, respectively, "represent two opposing extremes in the relationship between the individual and [the] group."[38] The liberal perspective treats the person as an identity sufficient for citizenship claims. It recognizes group rights if they serve the interests of individuals by insisting that the importance of the group is "a derivative of the importance of individuals."[39] Thus, it ascribes moral standing to the individual. It is criticized for being "too disembodied and atomistic to capture the actual needs and interests of human beings in the world."[40] Individuals need the group to actualize certain personal interests such as worship.

The communitarian perspective regards the identity of a group as primary for the enjoyment of citizenship by the individual. A variant of communitarian perspective, cultural pluralism, maintains that "members of certain groups would be incorporated into the political community not only as individuals but also through the group, and their rights would depend, in part, on their group membership."[41] As such, it ascribes moral standing to the group. It suggests as the corporatist approach to human rights that individuals and groups have mutual interests. Consequently, it undermines "the potential for harm arising from conflicts of interests within a group."[42] As Chandran Kukathas has noted, "[C]ultural communities are not undifferentiated wholes but associations of individuals with interests that differ to varying extents. So within such minorities are to be found other, smaller minorities. To regard the wider group as the bearer of cultural [group] rights, is to affirm the existing structures and therefore to favour existing majorities."[43] Groups, by whatever identification, are divided in terms of both interests and structure. This can be seen from the application of the federal character principle in Nigeria. Indeed, it is "affirming the existing structures in favour of existing majorities."[44]

A group rights argument has two major thrusts: inequality and past discrimination. They are said to be necessary for ensuring equality for weak groups in a multicultural state.[45] "Special status and rights should be extended to some groups to enable them to survive."[46] Vernon Van Dyke is opposed to a one-tracked individualism and majority rule because they allow the major group to oppress minor groups.[47] As Iris Young puts it, group rights are necessary for counteracting the effects of "differences in capacities, culture, values, and behavioural styles among groups."[48] In respect of past discrimination, Kim Forde-Mazrui asserts that affirmative action finds justification in the two moral principles that were used to argue against it, that is, "racial discrimination is unjust" and "corrective justice."[49]

In terms of access to power and economic benefits, the current group rights practice in Nigeria cannot be justified by inequality between groups and has never been justifiable by past discrimination against a group. Those who need recognition as citizens are not necessarily historically excluded people. In today's Nigeria, discrimination knows no limit, since it depends on the context and the "broader ethno-territorial concept of indigene." This concept is what has made "it possible for Yoruba individuals from other Yoruba states and not Igbo immigrants to enjoy full citizenship in Lagos State."[50]

People seen by outsiders and by themselves as the same ethnic group are discriminating against themselves. What is the justification for such discrimination? If the justification for discriminating against an advantaged group is its past or existing advantage, what is the justification, as can be observed in Nigeria, for members of one group discriminating against members of another group of exactly the same historical circumstances—such as political and economic conditions? The communitarian perspective on group rights shows no awareness of groups between which there are no past and present differences. This layer of group relationship needs to be recognized for progressive theorizing on group rights. The silence of ethnic group rights theory on the violation of the rights of individuals even within the group it theorizes is entitled to collective rights is its other limitation. African political leaders frequently use denial of citizenship to others on the basis of ethnic identity because they can get it to stick, to direct attention from their poor performance, and because "unless the situation reaches a level of significant upheaval, as in Cote d'Ivoire, there is unlikely to be widespread reaction."[51] President Paul Biya has successfully used the politics of ethnic belonging as a patrimonial channel to retain state power.[52]

Liberalism's rejection of "the idea of group claims as the basis of moral and political settlements primarily because groups are not fixed and unchanging entities in the moral and political universe" cannot be ignored.[53] But the argument for group rights in many parts of Africa presumes that the question of subgroup or major group membership is settled: every ethnic group's membership is frozen. This immutable view of the individual's ethnic group identity is certainly untrue of many contexts. Have individuals been observed to opt out or desire to opt out of the ethnic identity presumed by naturalists or primordial theorists of ethnic group formation to be theirs? It is not enough to argue for group rights. It is equally important to deal with the question of group membership and whether the process of group definition derogates from individual right of participation in it when (especially) group rights are intended to benefit individual members of the group. By treating the group, which is nevertheless undefined, as frozen, it is unbothered by the derogation of the rights of individuals in the course of enforcing the rights that supposedly belong to their group. Thus, proponents of group rights have no proper theory of human rights. For a proper theory of human rights, the group theory of rights must defrost the group and allow for changing membership as a fact.

The process of group identity making should include entry and exit even in an ethnic group and, in so doing, violates no rights, whether of the individual or of the group. For it allows the individual to choose to become or cease to be a member of the group within its basic membership principles. As Michael Freeman has observed, "[S]ince the moral basis of groups claiming group rights is the freedom of association, these groups have moral rights only if membership in them is voluntary."[54] The link in that process is group nationality or citizenship. The processual approach to membership of the group or group nationality postulated here serves as an important bridge between the liberal idea of an already made individual or citizen for whom there are duties and rights in a situation of only individual-state relationship and group theory's idea of an already made group without regard for the individual's right to association or dissociation. The possibility of the individual's desire for a new ethnic identity and the consequent rejection of the presumed ethnic identity of that individual have not featured in the thinking of group rights proponents about ethnic groups. They cannot contemplate this, because they do not regard the freedom of association with and disassociation from the ethnic group by the individual in their thinking about groups.

Kukathas has observed that cultural associations, including ethnic groups, are regarded as involuntary associations.[55] As he puts it, "[M]embership is usually determined by birth rather than by deliberate choice, and in many cases, there is no option of entry for those outside." However, limitations on admission into a new ethnic group apply to first-generation migrants of a different ethnic group. If it is considered impossible for first-generation migrants to change their ethnic group because they are thought to be rooted in the ethnic culture of their place of emigration, the same cannot be said for their children born in the new ethnic culture and territory. Which other qualifications are required of children born in and who speak the language of the new ethnic culture and territory? Consider Igbo parents—or a case in which the father is Igbo and the mother is Yoruba—who gave birth and raised their children in a Yoruba cultural community in Nigeria. If the children, by their parents' choice, grow up with Yoruba or English names and with the Yoruba language, the greatest identity marker of the Yoruba ethnic group, as their mother tongue, such children should not have problems adopting the Yoruba ethnic identity where the freedom of association and disassociation is respected. Whereas the ethnic group can change in nature or composition, the nature of the individual—the need for welfare—does not. Thus, the additional possibility of changing ethnic group identity represented by the individual's freedom of choice of ethnic association or dissociation lends further credence to foregrounding the individual in the thinking about human rights.

While advocates of ethnic (group) rights acknowledge the negative consequences of the implementation of group rights for out-group members, they have not realized that the implementation of group rights also negatively affects members of the in-group. If at all, they would consider such consequences as inconsequential or still in the interest of the individuals affected. If the current group rights practice is jeopardizing the well-being of even the in-group members for whom it is supposedly being undertaken, then there is the need to rethink it. The resolution of this contradiction cannot be achieved within the group rights theoretical framework but outside of it. In this regard, liberal theory's emphasis on "the fundamental importance of individual liberty or individual rights" recommends itself:[56] "So groups or communities have no special moral primacy in virtue of some natural priority. They are mutable historical formations—associations of individuals—whose claims are open to ethical evaluation. And any ethical evaluation must, ultimately, consider how actual individuals have been or might be affected, rather than the interests of the group in the abstract."[57]

Any maltreatment on account of group identity is borne invariably by individuals, not by the group at that given point in time. The feeling that one's group is suffering is a display of compassion, which is not unique to group members. Although a divide-and-rule tactic is a common instrument of oppressors for privileging some members of the oppressed group over their fellow citizens, not all members of the oppressed group suffer at the same time or to the same degree. It is individuals who still bear the brunt of mistreatment. Some privileged members of the oppressed group who are not compassionate may not even experience the trauma from the oppression of their group.

If individual welfare is the goal of group rights advocacy, one cannot agree more with Brian Walker:

> In most societies some ethnic groups do better than others, and thus the ethnic group that one belongs to will often determine one's statistical chances of ending up poor and culturally deprived. Yet even so, if one's goal is to address the moral difficulties involved with cultural deprivation, then the focus of analysis should be placed on issues of class. . . . Under policies which would, for example, guarantee a basic income to those worst off in society, vulnerable ethnic groups would draw a greater (that is, differentiated) benefit. If one gives all poor people access to the same basic goods, the ethnic groups who are worst treated will benefit most from the policy.[58]

Apart from this alternative approach to material inequality between ethnic groups, a rigid view of cultural boundaries amounts to denying freedom of propagation of ideas or the need to allow cultures embodied by them to compete for superiority. Those who argue for ethnic group rights and support rigid boundaries are denying the right of ethnic groups to interact and mesh. New religion and language are cultural elements that such scholars would not deny people the freedom to adopt.

Taking citizenship rights on the basis of ethnic group identities to its logical conclusion in Nigeria is producing at least three effects. First, it is becoming a barrier to the development of a larger fraternity, Nigerian political community, specifically, Nigerian nationality or citizenship in the various autonomous political and administrative areas. Second, it is encouraging a politics of difference in which leaders focus on the perception of disadvantage to become local heroes and perhaps win concessions rather than work hard to overcome the self-inflicted disadvantage by their group. Third, it is discouraging vigorous political and economic participation of those labeled nonindigenes in the local political community, thereby slowing the pace of economic development and political integration.

Besides, defending a communal approach to human rights in Africa is difficult, writes Rhoda Howard, because of the breakdown of the "ethic of communalism" in the face of industrialization and urbanization.[59] The exclusivist language of rights, which finds expression in particularistic claims, undermines the evolution of political community in Africa given its abuses of the rights of new minorities inherent in the pro-ethno-territorial approaches to ethnic minority grievances. The framing of demands in exclusivist terms by (especially) ethnic groups as a result of insecurity or past experience invariably becomes an ideology. And no matter the historical rootedness of an ideology, it is a choice. This means that the problem of exclusive citizenship lies beyond the group's position in relation to other groups in terms of political or economic power. It is a problem of the group language of rights. Either the group in control of state power or the one kept out of state power will prefer and, if in the position to do so, pursue politics of exclusion with such a language of rights if it chooses to do so. Past experience of discrimination does not point to exclusivist citizenship as a natural choice. For example, Nelson Mandela is revered worldwide for leading black South Africans to choose inclusive citizenship despite their past experience of brutal exploitative segregation at the hands of minority rule for white South Africans.

If historically there are both advantaged and disadvantaged groups that have practiced discrimination against groups with which they coexist, then discrimination must be a cultural choice rather than a defense of economic advantage. The white minority South African regime, which was economically well-off and advantaged, practiced discrimination against the economically marginal black population for decades. Similarly, in the United States of America, the white segment of the population, which was and still is economically advantaged, practiced discrimination for centuries against the economically disadvantaged

African Americans. Indeed, parochialism is often a major or dominant group syndrome because of its belief that it has enough space to pursue its interests. The dominant group tends to defend space against the legitimate quest for access by a minor group.

Concluding Remarks

The implicit preference for divided citizenship in political orientation and practice finds anchor in scholarly discourse on citizenship in Nigeria, as well as in Africa more broadly. This is the essentialist view of the group in the exposition of group rights. The changes that are taking place among individuals are being ignored by scholars of citizenship in Africa. Scholars often observe the political elite's manipulation of ethnicity and ignore the changes occurring among the nonelites. They have stuck to the assumption of permanent homeliness of the primordial home, not paying attention to the repelling factors in this home, which encourage the nonelite to embrace the nonprimordial, current place of domicile as home. The current African citizenship discourse is being misled by the closed ethnic polities' thinking to give accent to group claims at the expense of the individual's demand for inclusion or citizenship. It essentially blames underdevelopment and economic backwardness in Africa on ethnic and cultural diversity while venerating the ethnic language of rights, hence the endless demand for "self-government" by cultural groups.[60] In contrast with the past intellectual approach to group rights in Nigeria, this chapter shows that current group rights practice in Nigeria is in need of rethinking by making a case for universal citizenship.

The beneficiary of group rights practice is the political class of the major ethnic groups, not the ordinary people. An indigene-settler problem is therefore the problem of the political class. If the political class chooses to resolve the problem, the rest of the people, the nonpolitical class, will adjust to it. No protests have been heard or seen from the nonpolitical class over the appointment of those hitherto regarded as nonindigenes to positions of responsibility by some members of the political class in their states. If this class begins to see such ethnic discrimination as retrogressive and demonstrates a resistance to it in action, then the rest of its people will emulate the new attitude. The use of ethnic identity for the administration of rights for over five decades has not been very effective in addressing the issues of inequality and poverty in Nigeria. It has only created an ethnic superclass of individuals made wealthy by ethnic group rights.

Neither the demands for group rights that result in an unending pattern of discrimination against individuals nor the intellectual discourse of such citizenship demands in Africa can find an anchor in the theoretical justifications for group rights. A consensus is in sight, if not already secured, about the pitfalls of giving liberalism (individualism) free rein. Similarly, "groupism" carried too far, that is, to its logical conclusion, is antithetical to "the idea of citizenship," in which all have a stake and should acknowledge that all groups are embedded in a larger common culture.[61] This is because extreme groupism leads to discrimination of all against all, whereas citizenship is needed for the existence of the political community or, more broadly speaking, nationhood.

Notes

1. *The Nation,* Lagos, October 14, 2011, 56.

2. Nigeria's Central Bank governor at the time, Sanusi Lamido Sanusi, is one such advocate for the north who has argued that the north is not getting enough from oil revenues derived from the Niger delta. See *This Day,* Lagos, January 28, 2012, www.thisdaylive.com.

3. Government employment is mostly a distribution rather than a service delivery outlet in Nigeria.

4. Vernon Van Dyke, "Human Rights and the Rights of Groups," *American Journal of Political Science* 18, no. 4 (1974): 725–41; Van Dyke, "The Individual, the State and Communities in Political Theory," *World Politics* 29, no. 3 (1977): 343–69; Van Dyke, "Collective Entities and Moral Rights: Problems in Liberal-Democratic Thought," *Journal of Politics* 44, no. 1 (1982): 21–40.

5. Richard L. Sklar, *Nigerian Political Parties* (Princeton: Princeton University Press, 1963); James S. Coleman, *Nigeria—Background to Nationalism* (Berkeley: University of California Press, 1958); C. S. Whitaker Jr., *The Politics of Tradition: Continuity and Change in Northern Nigeria, 1946–1966* (Princeton, NJ: Princeton University Press, 1970); John Boye Ejobowah, "Political Recognition of Ethnic Pluralism: Lessons from Nigeria," *Nationalism and Ethnic Politics* 6, no. 2 (2000): 1–18; Kenneth Post and Michael Vickers, *Structure and Conflict in Nigeria, 1960–1966* (London: Heinemann, 1973); John W. Harbeson and Donald Rothchild, eds., *Africa in World Politics: Reforming Political Order* (Boulder, CO: Westview Press, 2009).

6. Claude Ake, "The African Context of Human Rights," *Africa Today* 34, nos. 1–2 (1987): 5–12.

7. Basil Davidson, *The Black Man's Burden: Africa and the Curse of the Nation-State* (New York: Times Books/Random House), 1992.

8. See K. Onwuka Dike, *Trade and Politics in the Niger Delta, 1830–1885: An Introduction to the Economic and Political History of Nigeria* (Oxford: Oxford University Press, 1956); and, particularly, Anthony D. Smith, "Culture,

Community and Territory: The Politics of Ethnicity and Nationalism," *International Affairs* 72, no. 3 (1996): 445–58.

9. Rhoda E. Howard, "Monitoring Human Rights: Problems of Consistency," *Ethics and International Affairs* 4 (1990): 162.

10. Bolaji Akinyemi, "Open Forum 1: Democracy, National Conference and Nigerian Political Science" at the Nigerian Political Science Association 24th Annual Conference, "National Conference and the Future of Nigerian Federalism," Zodiac Hotel, Enugu, August 15–18, 2005.

11. Interview with a Yoruba-speaking attorney who lived in Kaduna before the sharia riots that claimed more than 1,000 lives in 2000. Interview conducted in Abuja on January 25, 2005.

12. Mahmood Mamdani, "Beyond Settler and Native as Political Identities: Overcoming the Political Legacy of Colonialism," in *Ideology and African Development, Proceedings of the Third Memorial Programme in Honour of Professor Claude Ake*, ed. Centre for Advanced Social Science (Port Harcourt: CASS, 2000), 4–22.

13. Eghosa E. Osaghae, "Interstate Relations in Nigeria," *Publius* 24, no. 4 (1994): 83–98.

14. Vernon Van Dyke, "Human Rights"; Van Dyke, "Justice as Fairness: For Groups? A Theory of Justice by John Rawls," *American Political Science Review* 69, no. 2 (1975): 607–14; Iris Marion Young, "Polity and Group Difference: A Critique of the Ideal of Universal Citizenship," in *Theorizing Citizenship*, ed. Ronald Beiner (Albany: State University of New York Press, 1995), 175–207; Kim Forde-Mazrui, "Taking Conservatives Seriously: A Moral Justification for Affirmative Action and Reparations," *California Law Review* 92, no. 3 (2004): 683–753.

15. Will Kymlicka and Wayne Norman, "Return of the Citizen: A Survey of Recent Work on Citizenship Theory," in Beiner, *Theorizing Citizenship*, 284.

16. Peter P. Ekeh, "Colonialism and the Two Publics in Africa: A Theoretical Statement," *Comparative Studies in Society and History* 17 (1975): 91–112.

17. Okwudiba Nnoli, *Ethnic Politics in Nigeria* (Enugu, Nigeria: Fourth Dimension Press, 1978); Eghosa E. Osaghae, "A Re-examination of the Conception of Ethnicity in Africa as an Ideology of Inter-elite Competition," *African Study Monographs* (Kyoto) 12, no. 1 (1991): 43–61.

18. Browne Onuoha, "Publishing Postcolonial Africa: Nigeria and Ekeh's Two Publics a Generation After," *Social Dynamics* 40, no. 2 (2014): 322–37.

19. V. Adefemi Isumonah, "An Issue Overlooked in Nigeria's Reforms: The Continuation of Government Discriminatory Practices," *African Sociological Review* 10, no. 2 (2006): 116–32.

20. Eghosa E. Osaghae, "The Ogoni Uprising: Oil Politics, Minority Agitation and the Future of the Nigerian State," *African Affairs* 94, no. 376 (July 1995): 325–44; Claude E. Welch Jr, "The Ogoni and Self-Determination: Increasing Violence in Nigeria," *Journal of Modern African Studies* 33, no. 4 (1995): 635–50; Ben Naanen, "The Ogoni—An Endangered People," *Indigenous Affairs* 2 (1995): 18–20; Naanen, "Oil-Producing Minorities and the Restructuring of

Nigerian Federalism: The Case of the Ogoni," *Journal of Commonwealth and Comparative Politics* 33 (1995): 46–78; V. Adefemi Isumonah, "Oil and Minority Ethnic Nationalism in Nigeria: The Case of the Ogoni" (PhD diss., University of Ibadan, 1998).

21. Kymlicka and Norman, "Return of the Citizen," 303.

22. V. Adefemi Isumonah and Festus O. Egwaikhide, "Federal Presence in Higher Institutions in Nigeria and the North/South Dichotomy," *Regional and Federal Studies* 23, no. 2 (2013): 169–88.

23. Edmond J. Keller, *Identity, Citizenship, and Political Conflict in Africa* (Bloomington: Indiana University Press, 2014).

24. Mamdani, "Beyond Settler and Native," 21.

25. V. Adefemi Isumonah, "Land Tenure, Migration, Citizenship and Communal Conflicts in Africa," *Nationalism and Ethnic Politics* 9, no. 1 (Spring 2003): 1–19.

26. Gavin Williams, *State and Society in Nigeria* (Idanre, Nigeria: Afrografika Publishers, 1980).

27. Isumonah, "Issue Overlooked."

28. Isumonah and Egwaikhide, "Federal Presence."

29. Interview with Professor Osifo, Ibadan, September 12, 2014.

30. *P.M. News Nigeria,* March 31, 2015, www.pmnewsnigeria.com/tag /nigerian-newspapers.

31. Michael Freeman, "Past Wrongs and Liberal Justice," *Ethical Theory and Moral Practice* 5 (2002): 217.

32. Pita Agbese, "Managing Ethnic Relations in a Heterogeneous Society: The Case of Nigeria," in *Ethnicity and Governance in the Third World,* ed. John Mbaku, Pita Ogaba Agbese, and Mwangi S Kimenyi (Burlington, VT: Ashgate, 2001), 125–48.

33. Isumonah, "Land Tenure."

34. Kate Meagher, "Review: Axel Harneit-Sievers, *Constructions of Belonging: Igbo Communities and the Nigerian State in the Twentieth Century,* Rochester: University of Rochester Press," *African Studies Review* 50, no. 3 (2007): 154–56.

35. This can be a village, a town, or another local government area or even a state.

36. Peter Jones, "Human Rights, Group Rights, and Peoples' Rights," *Human Rights Quarterly* 21, no. 1 (1999): 82.

37. Joel E. Oestreich, "Liberal Theory and Minority Group Rights," *Human Rights Quarterly* 21, no. 1 (1999): 108–32.

38. Ronald Beiner, "Introduction: Why Citizenship Constitutes a Theoretical Problem in the Last Decade of the Twentieth Century," in Beiner, *Theorizing Citizenship,* 18.

39. Cindy L. Holder and Jeff J. Corntassel, "Indigenous Peoples and Multicultural Citizenship: Bridging Collective and Individual Rights," *Human Rights Quarterly* 24, no. 1 (2002): 131.

40. Ibid.

41. Kymlicka and Norman, "Return of the Citizen," 302.

42. Holder and Corntassel, "Indigenous Peoples," 135.

43. Chandran Kukathas, "Are There Any Cultural Rights?" *Political Theory* 20, no. 1 (1992): 114.

44. Ibid.

45. Van Dyke, "Human Rights."

46. Van Dyke, "Justice as Fairness," 612.

47. Vernon Van Dyke, *Human Rights, Ethnicity and Discrimination* (Westport, CT: Greenwood Press, 1985).

48. Young, "Polity and Group Difference," 176–77.

49. Forde-Mazrui, "Taking Conservatives Seriously," 685.

50. Isumonah, "Issue Overlooked," 124.

51. Beth Elise Whitaker, "Citizens and Foreigners: Democratization and the Politics of Exclusion in Africa," *African Studies Review* 48, no. 1 (2005): 117.

52. Sam Hickey, "Toward a Progressive Politics of Belonging? Insights from a Pastoralist 'Hometown' Association," *Africa Today* 57, no. 4 (2011): 29–47.

53. Kukathas, "Are There Any Cultural Rights?" 110.

54. Freeman, "Past Wrongs," 205.

55. Kukathas, "Are There Any Cultural Rights?" 116.

56. Ibid., 107.

57. Ibid., 112.

58. Brian Walker, "Plural Cultures, Contested Territories: A Critique of Kymlicka," *Canadian Journal of Political Science* 30, no. 2 (1997): 233.

59. Howard, "Monitoring Human Rights," 32.

60. From a three-state structure in 1954, Nigeria has been fragmented into thirty-six states, with a continuous demand for new states. The number of local government areas has also increased steadily from 301 in 1976 to 774 in 1998.

61. Beiner, "Introduction," 6.

References

Agbese, Pita. "Managing Ethnic Relations in a Heterogeneous Society: The Case of Nigeria." In *Ethnicity and Governance in the Third World,* edited by John Mbaku, Pita Ogaba Agbese, and Mwangi S. Kimenyi, 125–48. Burlington, VT: Ashgate, 2001.

Ake, Claude. "The African Context of Human Rights." *Africa Today* 34, nos. 1–2 (1987): 5–12.

Beiner, Ronald. "Introduction: Why Citizenship Constitutes a Theoretical Problem in the Last Decade of the Twentieth Century." In Beiner, *Theorizing Citizenship,* 1–28.

———, ed. *Theorizing Citizenship.* Albany: State University of New York Press, 1995.

Coleman, James S. *Nigeria—Background to Nationalism.* Berkeley: University of California Press, 1958.

Davidson, Basil. *The Black Man's Burden: Africa and the Curse of the Nation-State.* New York: Times Books/Random House, 1992.

Dike, K. Onwuka. *Trade and Politics in the Niger Delta, 1830–1885: An Introduction to the Economic and Political History of Nigeria*. Oxford: Oxford University Press, 1956.

Ejobowah, John Boye. "Political Recognition of Ethnic Pluralism: Lessons from Nigeria." *Nationalism and Ethnic Politics* 6, no. 2 (2000): 1–18.

Ekeh, Peter P. "Colonialism and the Two Publics in Africa: A Theoretical Statement." *Comparative Studies in Society and History* 17 (1975): 91–112.

Forde-Mazrui, Kim. "Taking Conservatives Seriously: A Moral Justification for Affirmative Action and Reparations." *California Law Review* 92, no. 3 (2004): 683–753.

Freeman, Michael. "Past Wrongs and Liberal Justice." *Ethical Theory and Moral Practice* 5 (2002): 201–20.

Harbeson, John W., and Donald Rothchild, eds. *Africa in World Politics: Reforming Political Order*. Boulder, CO: Westview Press, 2009.

Hickey, Sam. "Toward a Progressive Politics of Belonging? Insights from a Pastoralist 'Hometown' Association." *Africa Today* 57, no. 4 (2011): 29–47.

Holder, Cindy L., and Jeff J. Corntassel. "Indigenous Peoples and Multicultural Citizenship: Bridging Collective and Individual Rights." *Human Rights Quarterly* 24, no. 1 (2002): 126–51.

Howard, Rhoda E. "Monitoring Human Rights: Problems of Consistency." *Ethics and International Affairs* 4 (1990): 33–51.

Isumonah, V. Adefemi. "An Issue Overlooked in Nigeria's Reforms: The Continuation of Government Discriminatory Practices." *African Sociological Review* 10, no. 2 (2006): 116–32.

———. "Land Tenure, Migration, Citizenship and Communal Conflicts in Africa," *Nationalism and Ethnic Politics* 9, no. 1 (Spring 2003): 1–19.

———. "Oil and Minority Ethnic Nationalism in Nigeria: The Case of the Ogoni." PhD diss., University of Ibadan, 1998.

Isumonah, V. Adefemi, and Festus O. Egwaikhide. "Federal Presence in Higher Institutions in Nigeria and the North/South Dichotomy." *Regional and Federal Studies* 23, no. 2 (2013): 169–88.

Jones, Peter. "Human Rights, Group Rights, and Peoples' Rights." *Human Rights Quarterly* 21, no. 1 (1999): 80–107.

Keller, Edmond J. *Identity, Citizenship, and Political Conflict in Africa*. Bloomington: Indiana University Press, 2014.

Kukathas, Chandran. "Are There Any Cultural Rights?" *Political Theory* 20, no. 1 (1992): 105–39.

Kymlicka, Will, and Wayne Norman. "Return of the Citizen: A Survey of Recent Work on Citizenship Theory." In Beiner, *Theorizing Citizenship*, 283–322.

Mamdani, Mahmood. "Beyond Settler and Native as Political Identities: Overcoming the Political Legacy of Colonialism." In *Ideology and African Development, Proceedings of the Third Memorial Programme in Honour of Professor Claude Ake*, edited by Centre for Advanced Social Science (CASS), 4–22. Port Harcourt: CASS, 2000.

Meagher, Kate. "Review: Axel Harneit-Sievers, *Constructions of Belonging: Igbo Communities and the Nigerian State in the Twentieth Century,* Rochester: University of Rochester Press." *African Studies Review* 50, no. 3 (2007): 154–56.

Naanen, Ben. "The Ogoni—An Endangered People." *Indigenous Affairs* 2 (1995): 18–20.

———. "Oil-Producing Minorities and the Restructuring of Nigerian Federalism: The Case of the Ogoni." *Journal of Commonwealth and Comparative Politics* 33 (1995): 46–78.

Nnoli, Okwudiba. *Ethnic Politics in Nigeria.* Enugu, Nigeria: Fourth Dimension Press, 1978.

Oestreich, Joel E. "Liberal Theory and Minority Group Rights." *Human Rights Quarterly* 21, no. 1 (1999): 108–32.

Onuoha, Browne. "Publishing Postcolonial Africa: Nigeria and Ekeh's Two Publics a Generation After." *Social Dynamics* 40, no. 2 (2014): 322–37.

Osaghae, Eghosa E. "Interstate Relations in Nigeria." *Publius* 24, no. 4 (1994): 83–98.

———. "The Ogoni Uprising: Oil Politics, Minority Agitation and the Future of the Nigerian State." *African Affairs* 94, no. 376 (July 1995): 325–44.

———. "A Re-examination of the Conception of Ethnicity in Africa as an Ideology of Inter-elite Competition." *African Study Monographs* (Kyoto) 12, no. 1 (1991): 43–61.

Post, Kenneth, and Michael Vickers. *Structure and Conflict in Nigeria, 1960–1966.* London: Heinemann, 1973.

Sklar, Richard L. *Nigerian Political Parties.* Princeton: Princeton University Press, 1963.

Smith, Anthony D. "Culture, Community and Territory: The Politics of Ethnicity and Nationalism." *International Affairs* 72, no. 3 (1996): 445–58.

Van Dyke, Vernon. "Collective Entities and Moral Rights: Problems in Liberal-Democratic Thought." *Journal of Politics* 44, no. 1 (1982): 21–40.

———. "Human Rights and the Rights of Groups." *American Journal of Political Science* 18, no. 4 (1974): 725–41.

———. *Human Rights, Ethnicity and Discrimination.* Westport, CT: Greenwood Press, 1985.

———. "The Individual, the State and Communities in Political Theory." *World Politics* 29, no. 3 (1977): 343–69.

———. "Justice as Fairness: For Groups? A Theory of Justice by John Rawls." *American Political Science Review* 69, no. 2 (1975): 607–14.

Walker, Brian. "Plural Cultures, Contested Territories: A Critique of Kymlicka." *Canadian Journal of Political Science* 30, no. 2 (1997): 211–34.

Welch, Claude E., Jr. "The Ogoni and Self-Determination: Increasing Violence in Nigeria." *Journal of Modern African Studies* 33, no. 4 (1995): 635–50.

Whitaker, Beth Elise. "Citizens and Foreigners: Democratization and the Politics of Exclusion in Africa." *African Studies Review* 48, no. 1 (2005): 109–26.

Whitaker, C. S., Jr. *The Politics of Tradition: Continuity and Change in Northern Nigeria, 1946–1966.* Princeton, NJ: Princeton University Press, 1970.

Williams, Gavin. *State and Society in Nigeria.* Idanre, Nigeria: Afrografika Publishers, 1980.

Young, Iris Marion. "Polity and Group Difference: A Critique of the Ideal of Universal Citizenship." In Beiner, *Theorizing Citizenship,* 175–207.

NINE

The State and the "Peoples"

Citizenship and the Future of Political Community in Ethiopia

SOLOMON M. GOFIE

IN MAY 1991, THE COMBINED FORCES OF THE TIGRAYAN PEOPLE'S Liberation Front (TPLF), the Eritrean People's Liberation Front (EPLF), and the Oromo Liberation Front (OLF) overthrew the Derg regime that had ruled the country since 1974. The EPLF took control of Eritrea and turned it into an independent state. The TPLF, which had been instrumental in the formation of the Ethiopian People's Revolutionary Democratic Front (EPRDF), took power in Addis Ababa. The EPRDF consists of the TPLF, the Oromo People's Democratic Organization (OPDO), the Southern Ethiopian People's Democratic Movement (SEPDM), and the Amhara National Democratic Movement (ANDM).

Each of these EPRDF organizations took charge of one of the four regional states—Tigray; Oromia; the Southern Nations, Nationalities and Peoples Regional State (SNNPR); and the Amhara Regional State, respectively. The other five regional states continue to be run by political groups that are separate from the EPRDF and regarded as its "partner organizations." The OLF left the Ethiopian political scene early in the 1990s because of conflict with the EPRDF. The EPRDF has been in command of state power for more than two decades now, and it considers itself the dominant group destined to rule continuously and fulfil its objectives of "peace, development, and democracy" in Ethiopia.

Central to Ethiopian political dynamics since the 1990s has been the EPRDF's reconstruction of the Ethiopian state in its own image. When

it took over the state, it introduced what many considered a radical restructuring of the country along the lines of major identity groupings.
Some have termed such a formation "ethnic federalism."[1] The EPRDF
and the proponents of the post-1991 order it presides over believe that
the introduction of this form of federalism redresses long-standing
grievances of Ethiopia's constituent populations, its "nations, nationalities, and peoples," vis-à-vis successive Ethiopian rulers since the late
nineteenth century.[2] They strongly assert that the Derg regime and its
predecessors' approach to state building failed to address the problems
of domination and inequality that came about in the process of the
formation of the modern state in Ethiopia, termed by some the "Ethiopian Empire State."[3] The "constitutive inequalities" that arose in the
process prompted those who resented this phenomenon to articulate
what was termed the national question.[4] In short, this was a demand
for the right to self-determination of the "nations, nationalities,
and peoples." This became the slogan of the TPLF and others that
fought the Derg, and in the post-1991 period the EPRDF has been
working to put this into practice.[5]

In the post-1991 period, for the EPRDF and its proponents, (sub)
national groups defined mainly on the basis of language criteria have
been presented as the determinant category of belonging and the organizing principle of the Ethiopian body politic. In line with this, the
preamble of the 1995 constitution of Ethiopia begins with the statement
"we the Nations, Nationalities, and Peoples of Ethiopia have adopted
this Constitution."[6] The regional states Afar, Tigray, Amhara, Oromia,
Somalia, Benishangul-Gumuz, SNNPR, Gambella, and Harari are
recognized in the constitution as the constituent units of the federation. There are also two cities, Addis Ababa and Diredawa, directly run
from the center. The regional governments have the power to manage
the day-to-day administrative functions of the regions. The regional
states such as Oromia, Somali, and Tigray have been allowed to use the
language of the majority national groups within their respective regions
for educational and administrative purposes. The SNNPR, which is the
most diverse of all the regional states, continues to use Amharic, although some of its zonal administrations such as the Sidama zone have
been using the Sidama language for the purposes of administration and
primary education.[7]

Ethiopia thus presents us with a particularly interesting case in
the context of this volume. The continued importance of subnational

("ethnic") identities in postcolonial Africa has often been understood as a legacy of colonialism, and one that presents a significant challenge to those seeking to explain the requisites of democratic polities in contemporary Africa.[8] Yet the importance of "ethnic" identities in contemporary Ethiopia lies not in a history of European colonial rule but rather in a long history of state formation. What does this mean for the current experience of federalism and the recognition of subnational identities as the primary category of belonging in post-1991 Ethiopia?

For the political scientist Lahra Smith, students of African politics in general and Ethiopia in particular have much to learn from Western scholarship on multicultural citizenship, which, she argues, offers "a dynamic and optimistic view of the role of identity politics in supporting democratization."[9] Federalism, in this reading, has the potential to create more space for Ethiopian citizens to engage the state, as well as to engage in practices of what she terms *meaningful* citizenship. For Smith, then, the salience of "ethnic" identity in Ethiopia, and in Africa more broadly, is not a symptom of state failure but rather offers the potential to promote democratization.

This chapter raises the question of whether the introduction by the EPRDF of discourses of national self-determination for Ethiopia's constituent "peoples" as an organizing principle of the state has resulted in qualitative changes toward the improvement of the conditions of groups and individuals in the country in their relationship with the state since the fall of the Derg regime in 1991. Has it created and fostered a meaningful sense of citizenship beyond the reconfiguration of collective belonging along identity lines? I argue that while the language of self-determination as designed and employed by the EPRDF has at one level led to a modicum of cultural expression and recognition of language rights and has created a perception of local self-governance by the respective regional states, its reification as the predominant form of political belonging after 1991 went hand-in-hand with growing threats to the economic means of subsistence and the closing down of alternative spaces of association and expression, processes that seriously limited the ability of Ethiopians to practice their citizenship.

To understand contemporary political development in Ethiopia as well as in Africa more generally, we need to go beyond the focus on "ethnicity" characterizing many studies of state, society, and politics in Africa since the 1990s.[10] Politically significant issues of state-society relations in Ethiopia are not limited to "social cleavages based on identity."[11] It is doubtful whether "primordial theories of ethnicity" capture politically significant societal groupings or categories and their concerns, since the concept tends to dismiss political antagonisms as manufactured "ethnic" conflicts that pop up when authoritarian control wanes.[12] Nor does recognizing "multicultural citizenship" necessarily serve to create a society in which citizens can exercise their rights more effectively.[13]

Since 1991 Ethiopia has been ruled by a regime that has embraced the challenge of recognizing multicultural citizenship through its recognition of the self-determination of "nations, nationalities, and peoples." Yet the Ethiopian case suggests that the prospect of "meaningful citizenship" rests not just on formal recognition of "ethnic" identities but also on understanding and explaining the essence of the relationship between the state and society.

The EPRDF and the Discourse of "Revolutionary Democracy"

The apparent inconsistency between the proclaimed objectives and the actual practice of the EPRDF has a lot to do with the instrumental role it wanted to ascribe to "the peoples." Augmented with its ideology of "revolutionary democracy," during the EPRDF's early years in power it argued for the curtailment of the rights of certain elements within society, even as it claimed partisanship with "the peoples." This was a recurrent theme during the early 1990s in the EPRDF's publications such as *Revolutionary Democracy*, its weekly magazine.[14] As Jean-Nicholas Bach has recently noted in regard to its 2010 election campaign, "The EPRDF owes its successes over the past decade in guiding the Ethiopian people under its leadership to two key instruments that define its nature; these are its partisanship to the people and [the] 'revolutionary democracy' its [*sic*] advocates."[15] What is important here is that the very idea of curtailing rights embedded in the EPRDF's discourse of "revolutionary democracy" has served to justify political actions taken against individuals and groups within society and has profoundly affected the extent to which individuals and groups in society can engage the state.

The priority given to the implementation of state policies that alienate substantial parts of the population has generated a particular form of state-society relations in Ethiopia. A relationship has developed in which the imperative of power has come to form the basis for a divergence between state interests and the interests of society, giving rise to antagonisms between the state and the society in the post-1991 period. We can see this in practice if we look in more detail at state policies in two key areas: land policy and policies relating to freedom of association and expression. While the sources of the antagonisms are varied and multiple, economic subsistence (most notably land ownership) and freedom of expression and association are among the major recurring topics and lie at the center of the tension between society and the state.

The Politics of Land and the Right to Subsistence

Various economic policies and practices have been pitting the post-1991 government against groups in rural as well as urban areas. As the primary means of economic subsistence for the overwhelming majority of the Ethiopian population, land is central to discussion of state-society relationship and citizenship in Ethiopia. The land question was one of the central political issues in Ethiopia, and it drove the resistance to imperial rule that led to the assumption of power by the Derg in 1974. The groups that led the revolution were able to mobilize the peasantry and other societal forces around the motto "Land to the Tiller." Once in power, however, the Derg nationalized the land and thus ensured its control over society for the next seventeen years.[16]

The control of land remained the prerogative of the state in the aftermath of the Derg. While the 1995 constitution maintains that land is "owned" by "the peoples" and the government of Ethiopia, in practice the EPRDF's discourse of revolutionary democracy allowed it to present itself and its partners as the embodiment of "the peoples" to attain a monopoly of control over land.[17] Neither "the peoples" nor other categories of Ethiopian societies have been allowed to participate in decisions about land as the basis of the economy.

First of all, farmers, especially those living around Addis Ababa and major regional towns, have faced dislocations as state authorities opted to free highly valued plots of land for lease to investors. Such land transfers involve a process in which farmland is taken from farmers and given to investors, with or without compensation to the farming communities who had lived on it for generations. This in effect means forcing individuals and communities away from or depriving them of their means of subsistence. In such a situation, farmers have no right of appeal, and attempts to protest and resist eviction have led to threats of imprisonment.[18]

Over the years there has been widespread dislocation of the farming communities, mainly the Oromo community, who live around Addis

Ababa. While the numbers vary, tens of thousands of families have been dislocated in recent times and their livelihood severely affected.

While the process of freeing land for investment continues to unfold, as of late the government has disclosed what it calls the Addis Ababa Integrated Master Plan, which is condemned by various sections of the Oromo population, who consider it an excuse for further land grabbing. Officially, however, the smaller towns in predominantly Oromo-inhabited areas surrounding the city need to be included in the controversial master plan for the purpose of integrated development.[19]

The plan was opposed by the Oromo People's Democratic Organization (OPDO), one of the four groups constituting the EPRDF. It led to protests among Oromo students in different universities and secondary education institutions. They vehemently opposed the plan, citing the "risk of evicting more than two million farmers from around the capital city."[20] Many people including students in the town of Ambo were killed, and several were put in jail. Since this incident, the government has put on hold the implementation of the plan.

Second, the leasing of large tracts of land in different parts of the country has become a source of conflict not only between individual farmers and the government but also between the latter and the "peoples" in several regional states. The fact that huge tracts of land were being given out to investors, without the consent of the affected people, has become a bone of contention. This was the case in Gambella, Benshingul-Gumuz, Afar, and South Omo and Oromia. The people in these regions feel that they have not been consulted when large-scale land transfers have been made. Government policy in this area seems to run directly counter to the ethos of a particular form of federal structure in Ethiopia, organized around "nations, nationalities, and peoples." This has generated tensions between the government and the populations of the regional states.

One commentator, Graham Peebles, has described the land appropriation processes as "a colonial phenomenon." In an article published in 2012 he argued that the government was behaving as if land were simply "a chip to be thrown upon the international gambling table of commercialization." He argued that this practice was due to the distorted notions of development, wherein "people, traditional lifestyles and the environment come a distant second to roads, industrialisation and the leasing of land."[21]

Other researchers have corroborated this view. The Oakland Institute, which is at the forefront of documenting this phenomenon, states in one of its reports that at least 3,619,509 hectares of land (an area close to the size of Belgium) were reserved or transferred to investors in the previous ten years. While the government often claims that the land being leased is not occupied by the local communities, information from the Oakland Institute and other sources indicates that it is being cultivated by smallholders and subsistence farmers or used by pastoralists for grazing. Those using the land have been forcefully evicted.[22] Similar accounts have been put forward by human rights organizations such as Human Rights Watch and by investigative journalists writing for international media outlets.[23] In general, the transfer of huge tracts of land by the government in Ethiopia to foreign and domestic investors for the purpose of growing food and allegedly biofuels for export has made observers skeptical about the Ethiopian government's objectives in encouraging land transfers. Dessalegn Rahmato, who has been writing on issues of land policy in Ethiopia for decades, has clearly argued that this state of affairs, when viewed from the perspective of the communities affected, constitutes nothing more than the transfer of rights belonging to individuals and communities.[24]

Third, people in the towns and the cities have felt the full weight of the government's land lease policy. Any plot of land to build a residential house or a business quarter can be obtained only by leasing it from the government. Moreover, people who have more than 500 square meters of land have to either hand it over to the authorities or pay exorbitant lease values to retain it. Nowadays, one can observe the phenomenon whereby neighborhoods are removed, the land is leased to "investors," and multistory buildings are erected in a very short period of time. In Addis Ababa, large parts of the Lideta, Arat Kilo, Kazanchis, and Tekelhaimanot areas of the city have so far been cleared during the past few years. The drama usually unfolds in such a way that the Addis Ababa city administration urges city residents in the target area to vacate their residential quarters within a short period of time. Recently the administration planned to clear about 1,200 hectares of land for redevelopment, and it was mentioned that a good portion of this would be up for leasing to investors immediately. While the government housing plans led to the building of low-cost houses, especially in the suburbs of Addis Ababa, furnishing relocated residents with condominium houses fitted with adequate facilities remained a major challenge.[25]

In general, these practices on the part of the state work against its own declaration that each farmer has an unrestricted right to land and claims of guarantees of land use and that the property rights of the urban population would not be threatened. Added to this is the recent urban land lease practice following the 2003 proclamation, which converted all urban land to leaseholds under the control of the state. This serves to strengthen doubts as to whether individuals and groups in Ethiopian society today have any right of property ownership in relation to land.[26]

Freedom of Association and Expression

Freedom of association proved to be another problematic area in the troubled relationship between the state and the society in Ethiopia. The experience of the workers' union in Ethiopia in the post-1991 period serves as an example of the challenges in this respect. In the 1990s, the EPRDF embarked on a policy of liberalization and privatization of previously state-owned enterprises. In the process it created a new mechanism for administering previously publicly owned enterprises. The main feature of the approach was the appointment of a "board of managers" of the enterprises in the process of transfer of ownership. The chairmanship positions of such a board overseeing the enterprises were invariably given to high-ranking members of the TPLF/EPRDF. The positions held not only were used to help manage the enterprises and facilitate the transfer of their ownership but also served to control trade unions so that they would not effectively resist the decisions about the future of the enterprises. Consequently, in the 1990s, the fate of thousands of workers in the manufacturing industries was decided without consulting the workers.[27]

There were widespread direct interventions in the dissolution of former trade union associations, as well as the formation of progovernment union leaderships. One of the state institutions accused by the former Confederation of Ethiopian Trade Unions (CETU) in the mid-1990s of undermining the activities of trade unions was the Ministry of Labor and Social Affairs (MOLSA). This was mainly because the ministry was responsible for the implementation of Labor Proclamation No. 42/1993. According to Article 170(2) of the proclamation, "the Ministry shall organize, coordinate, follow up and execute the labor administration system, by establishing an employment service, labor inspection services, and also a permanent advisory board." In accordance with Article 145 of the proclamation, among several of its roles, it is responsible for establishing the labor relations board. The ministry has also the power to issue certificates of registration for workers' associations (Article 118). It can also cancel the certificate of registration it issues. Cancellation of the certificate of registration would lead to dissolution of an association, in this case, workers' associations (Article 120).[28] MOLSA played a significant role on behalf of the state in cancelling the registration of many workers' unions in conflict with the management of the enterprises the state wanted to privatize. MOLSA was accused of playing a role in the formation of progovernment workers' associations at lower levels such as the workers' federations. The Ethiopian Human Rights Council (EHRCO, now HRC) through its periodic reports has requested the government to stop illegal practices against workers and their associations and has appealed to human rights organizations and religious groups in Ethiopia and abroad "who support the rule of law and human rights to use their influence to make the Ethiopian government . . . respect the human rights" of workers.[29]

The former labor union, the Confederation of Ethiopian Trade Unions (CETU), attempted to resist the move toward privatizing the enterprises without ensuring the participation and consultation of workers. In the face of heightened state interference, especially in 1994, CETU attempted to express its concerns regarding targeted and widespread dismissals of workers. One of the persistent concerns aired by a proworkers' trade union leadership before its forceful dissolution revolved around the issue of job security of employees and the lack of transparency in the process of transferring the ownership of enterprises.[30] The struggle for workers' rights failed with the ban and dismemberment of CETU in 1994 and its replacement by a new organization, generally considered docile in representing the interests of workers. The consequence has been the relegation to a secondary consideration of the right of workers to form free and independent associations and of workers' rights in general.[31] In the absence of a strong workers' organization, the vast majority of workers in Ethiopia are left to the mercy of state control and to the whim and will of so-called "developmental investors" and owners of companies.[32]

More generally, freedom of association has been a key area of antagonism between the state, on one hand, and individuals and group members of the society, on the other, over the past two decades. Besides the challenges faced by workers, other groups such as political parties continue to complain that their leaders, members, and supporters have been subjected to harassment, intimidation, and arrest. This is the case when such independent organizations are seen as mobilizing support from among society and working to organize the population around political agendas. At any rate, the hostile attitude of the state toward freedom of association and assembly has negatively affected the emergence of independent institutions and organizations.

These problems are further exacerbated by the lack of space for free expression. In the post-1991 period, the effects of curtailment of freedom of expression have not been limited to the private media and civil society organizations. Restrictions on expression have permeated the practices of state institutions, affecting individuals and groups in the society. The challenge faced by the youth in educational institutions is instructive of this situation.

In Ethiopia, students have historically been at the forefront of resistance against state policies and practices. Students were recognized as one of the primary social forces that brought to an end the imperial regime in the 1960s and 1970s. But since 1991 there has been growing state distrust of this group. State authorities see students' attempts to express themselves in higher education institutions as the works of antidemocracy and antipeace and antidevelopment forces working against the post-1991 order.[33] Student protests have met with a severe response from state authorities.[34] This has made a mockery of the idea of higher-education institutions as a space for free expression of ideas. Instead, some have talked of a pervasive sense of being controlled and monitored in public institutions and beyond, limiting the emergence of alternative forms of expression and association.[35]

Thus, since 1991, while the state has sought to address the "national question" through a discourse of "the peoples," it has clamped down on the ability of key social groups such as farmers, workers, and youths to form free associations and to express themselves politically. This has served the EPRDF's aim of consolidating their hold on power. A discourse of "the peoples" has gone hand in hand with a state policy of retaining control of land and other key resources. This has enabled the state to undertake land appropriation in rural areas and policies that have led to the dislocation of many in towns and urban areas. This situation clearly attests to the subordination of the economic means of subsistence for the many to state-driven accumulation in the interests of the few.

Similarly, while state laws, the constitution, and official pronouncements have emphasized the right to organize, the practice has been one of pervasive suppression of free association. The story of CETU, discussed above, and other associations such as the former Ethiopian Teachers Association (ETA) attest to this. The lack of trust in free and independent organizations on the part of state authorities has contributed to the weakening of existing organizations and limited the possibility of the emergence of strong autonomous organizations or institutions. Today there is a widely felt view within Ethiopian society that organizations are allowed to exist insofar as they further the interest of the state or as long as they are not perceived as threats. In regard to freedom of expression, the practice on the part of state authorities has followed a similar logic. The persistent actions of the state in using different mechanisms of undermining freedom of expression have resulted in self-censorship of speeches, as well as experiences of fear and mistrust within the society. Besides the challenges faced by the younger population in educational institutions, as already discussed, the suppression of private media and the use of state media as an instrument of propagating the advantages and the benefits that the post-1991 order brought about for "the peoples" conform to the state's understanding of free expression as a threat to its aims and objectives.

State-Society Antagonisms

The political leadership of the state in the post-1991 period has consistently ridiculed concerns and attempts to resist government policies threatening the economic means of subsistence of the population as the works of "anti-peace, anti-development and anti-democracy forces" working to derail its peace, development and democracy agendas,[36] and this is indicative of how the EPRDF understands its perceived adversaries. In general, the consequence of the state-society antagonisms described above has been the fragmentation of the Ethiopian political community and the virtual absence of social solidarity. The experiences of farming communities and workers in manufacturing industries are indicative of a pervasive sense of fear, insecurity, fragmentation, and disunity.

Experiences over the past two decades show no meaningful development of a sense of solidarity whereby the affected members of the society come together to form collective movements. Land appropriation in rural as well as urban areas does not seem to galvanize support for the affected communities. Not only were workers unable to salvage themselves, but also their suffering did not earn them support from other sections of the society. The proworkers' Confederation of the Ethiopian Labour Union (CELU), led by Dawi Ibrahim (who went into exile in 1994 because of pressures from state functionaries), protested against the dismissal of workers and curtailment of freedom of association and made repeated calls for the people to express their support to workers, to prevent the dissolution of the workers' association. It did not gain any tangible support from students, government employees, and the public at large, however, underscoring the significance of solidarity as a precondition for collective action.

This underlines the importance of having space for expression. Solidarity in itself is difficult to conceive without a space of expression necessary to form associations and build trust and confidence. The antagonistic state-society relationship described above has made the task difficult, for the legal and institutional space for discussion of political issues has been monopolized by the state, while fear, insecurity, and self-censorship of expression characterize conditions at the societal level. Attempts to create an alternative space for expression through the politics of opposition, through elections, and through the works of nongovernmental organizations (NGOs) have been repeatedly rebuffed. Little has been achieved in terms of changing the way state authorities deal with individuals and groups within the society, since actors such as NGOs continue to operate within the parameters defined by the state. Similar attempts were made through the independent media that emerged in 1991, but this was more or less shut down following the May 2005 elections.

EPRDF's project of reconstruction of the state in Ethiopia presents the rights of self-determination of nations, nationalities, and peoples as an organizing principle of the Ethiopian body politic. While the recognition of "peoples" and their rights to self-determination in Ethiopia appears to go some way toward recognizing diversity or difference, its reification by the state in post-Derg Ethiopia has served as an instrument of the political forces in command of state power since the early 1990s. Consequently, while ordinary Ethiopians of various political persuasions continue to strongly identify themselves with the country (the land and its peoples), their religion or beliefs, the region, and their identities, the unresolved issues with regard to the right to economic means of subsistence (notably, the land issue), as well as freedom of association and expression, have negatively affected the ability of Ethiopians to practice "meaningful citizenship" in the post-1991 period.

The EPRDF government over the past two decades has been emphasizing the importance of peace, democracy, and development. The state has sought to use a discourse of respect for the rights of "the peoples" but at the same time has limited the space available for solidarity, association, and expression. Therefore conceiving of citizenship in its fullest sense is difficult and the task of building a viable political community in Ethiopia remains uncertain.

Notes

1. Assefa Fiseha, "Theory versus Practice in the Implementation of Ethiopia's Ethnic Federalism," in *Ethnic Federalism: The Ethiopian Experience in Comparative Perspective,* ed. David Turton (Oxford: James Currey, 2006), 131–64.

2. Andreas Eshete, "Ethnic Federalism: New Frontiers," in *First National Conference on Federalism, Conflict and Peace Building,* ed. G. Barna, Proceeding of the Ministry of Federal Affairs and German Technical Cooperation (Addis Ababa: United Printers, 2003), 142–72.

3. Merera Gudina, *Ethiopia: Competing Ethnic Nationalism and the Quest for Democracy, 1960–2000* (Addis Ababa: Shaker Publishing, 2003).

4. Asnake Kefale, "Federalism and Self-Determination: Some Observations on the Ethiopian Experience," in *Topics in Contemporary Political Developments in Ethiopia: Towards Research Agenda in the Framework of DPSIR-NIHR Research Programme (1998–2003),* Proceedings of the Launching Workshop of the Department of Political Science and International Relations (DPSIR) and the Norwegian Institute of Human Rights (NIHR) (Addis Ababa: Department of Political Science and International Relations, Addis Ababa University, 2003), 1–21.

5. Merera, *Ethiopia.*

6. Proclamation of the Constitution of the Federal Democratic Republic of Ethiopia (Proclamation No. 1/1995, Addis Ababa, August 1995), www.wipo.int /edocs/lexdocs/laws/en/et/et007en.pdf.

7. John Merkakis, *Ethiopia: The Last Two Frontiers* (Oxford: James Currey, 2011).

8. Lahra Smith, *Making Citizens in Africa: Ethnicity, Gender, and National Identity in Ethiopia* (Cambridge: Cambridge University Press, 2013), 34.

9. Ibid., 38.

10. K. J. Holsti, "International Relations Theory and Domestic Wars in the Third World: The Limits of Relevance," in *International Relations Theory and the Third World,* ed. Stephanie Neuman (Palgrave Macmillan, 1998), 110.

11. Ibid., 109.

12. Ibid.

13. Will Kymlicka, *Multicultural Citizenship: A Liberal Theory of Minority Rights* (Oxford: Clarendon Press, 1995).

14. *Abiyotawi Demokraci* (*Revolutionary Democracy*) is a weekly newspaper written in Amharic and published by the Ethiopian Press Agency from March to April 1993 in the Gregorian calendar (Megabit–Miazia 1985 in the Ethiopian calendar).

15. Jean-Nicolas Bach, "Abyotawi Democracy: Neither Revolutionary nor Democratic, a Critical Review of EPRDF's Conception of Revolutionary Democracy in Post-1991 Ethiopia," *Journal of Eastern African Studies* 5, no. 4 (2011): 643.

16. Dessalegn Rahmato, *The Peasant and the State: Studies in Agrarian Change in Ethiopia, 1950–2000s* (Addis Ababa: Addis Ababa University Press, 2009).

17. Mulugeta Abebe Wolde, "A Critical Assessment of Institutions, Roles and Leverage in Public Policy Making: Ethiopia, 1974–2004" (PhD diss., University of Stellenbosch, 2005).

18. Workineh Kelbessa, *The Utility of Ethical Dialogue for Marginalized Voices in Africa*, Discussion Paper: IIED (London: International Institute for Environment and Development, 2005), http://pubs.iied.org/13508IIED .html.

19. "TPLF Leaders' Arrogance and Contempt Invites Further Bloodshed— Human Rights League of the Horn of Africa (HRLHA)," *Ethiopia Observatory*, February 24, 2015, http://ethiopiaobservatory.com/2015/02/24/.

20. "Ethiopia Protest: Ambo Students Killed in Oromia State," *BBC News*, May 2, 2014, www.bbc.com/news/world-africa-27251331.

21. Graham Peebles, "What's Yours Is Mine, What's Mine's My Own," *Eurasia Review*, May 30, 2012, www.eurasiareview.com/30052012-the-ethiopian -land-giveaway-oped.

22. "Understanding Land Investment Deals in Africa, Ethiopia: Country Report," Oakland Institute, www.oaklandinstitute.org/land-deals-africa/ethiopia .www.oaklandinstitute.org/sites/oaklandinstitute.org/files/OI_Ethiopa_Land _Investment_report.pdf.

23. Human Rights Watch, "Waiting Here for Death: Forced Displacement and 'Villagization' in Ethiopia's Gambella Region," report, January 16, 2012, www.hrw.org/report/2012/01/16/waiting-here-death/forced-displacement -and-villagization-ethiopias-gambella-region.

24. Dessalegn Rahmato, *Land to Investors: Large Scale Land Transfers in Ethiopia* (Addis Ababa: Forum for Social Studies, 2011).

25. "Land Robbery around Addis Ababa Intensifies," *Ethiopia Observatory*, April 27, 2014, http://ethiopiaobservatory.com/2014/04/27/land-robbery -around-addis-abeba-intensifies/.

26. Rahmato, *Land to Investors*.

27. Abebe Teferi and Admit Zerihun, *Ethiopian Privatization Program: Rational Performance, and Impact on the Labour Market* (Addis Ababa: CETU, 2001).

28. Transitional Government of Ethiopia, "Labour Proclamation No. 42/1993," *Negarit Gazeta* 52, no. 27 (January 20, 1993): 268–328.

29. Ethiopian Human Rights Council, *The Human Rights Situation in Ethiopia: Compiled Reports of EHRCO, December 1991–December 1997* (Addis Ababa: Ethiopian Human Rights Council, 1999).

30. Pers. comm., 1994, "Short Briefings of CETU Crisis."

31. "The Plight of the Laid-Off at Coca Cola," (Ethiopian) *Reporter,* August 21, 2002.

32. Pers. comm., 1994, "Trade Union Situation in Ethiopia."

33. Solomon M. Gofie, "State-Society Relationships and Human Rights in Ethiopia: A Critique of State-Centred Approach" (PhD diss., University of Manchester, 2007).

34. Ethiopian Human Rights Commission, *Human Rights Violations Committed against University Student,* Special Report no. 12 (Addis Ababa: Ethiopian Human Rights Commission, 1997); "Protest in Oromia Runs into Fifth Day," Ethiomedia, November 15, 2005, www.ethiomedia.com/fastpress /olf_111605.html.

35. Solomon Mebrie (Gofie), "An Alternative Space of Discussion on Human Rights Issues? Experience from ECSEC," *Ethiopian Journal of the Social Sciences and Humanities* 4, no. 1 (2006): 31–45.

36. See for instance Eyob Balcha, "Can 'Authoritarian Developmentalism' Be Tested at the Ballot Box?" (2015), http://blog.gdi.manchester.ac.uk /can-authoritarian-developmentalism-be-tested-at-the-ballot-box/.

References

Mulugeta Abebe. "A Critical Assessment of Institutions, Roles and Leverage in Public Policy Making: Ethiopia, 1974–2004." PhD diss., University of Stellenbosch, 2005.

Bach, Jean-Nicholas. "Abyotawi Democracy: Neither Revolutionary nor Democratic, a Critical Review of EPRDF's Conception of Revolutionary Democracy in Post-1991 Ethiopia." *Journal of Eastern African Studies* 5, no. 4 (2011): 641–63.

Andreas Eshete. "Ethnic Federalism: New Frontiers." In *First National Conference on Federalism, Conflict and Peace Building,* edited by G. Barna, 142–72. Proceeding of the Ministry of Federal Affairs and German Technical Cooperation. Addis Ababa: United Printers, 2003.

Ethiopian Human Rights Commission. *Human Rights Violations Committed against University Student.* Special Report no. 12. Addis Ababa: Ethiopian Human Rights Commission, 1997.

Ethiopian Human Rights Council. *The Human Rights Situation in Ethiopia: Compiled Reports of EHRCO, December 1991–December 1997.* Addis Ababa: Ethiopian Human Rights Council, 1999.

Fiseha, A. "Theory versus Practice in the Implementation of Ethiopia's Ethnic Federalism." In *Ethnic Federalism: The Ethiopian Experience in Comparative Perspective,* edited by David Turton, 131–64. Oxford: James Currey, 2006.

Gofie, Solomon M. "State-Society Relationships and Human Rights in Ethiopia: A Critique of State-Centred Approach." PhD diss., University of Manchester, 2007.

Gudina, Merera. *Ethiopia: Competing Ethnic Nationalism and the Quest for Democracy, 1960–2000.* Addis Ababa: Shaker Publishing, 2003.

Holsti, K. J. "International Relations Theory and Domestic Wars in the Third World: The Limits of Relevance." In *International Relations Theory and the Third World,* edited by Stephanie Neuman, 103–32. Basingstoke: Palgrave Macmillan, 1998.

Kefale, Asnake. "Federalism and Self-Determination: Some Observations on the Ethiopian Experience." In *Topics in Contemporary Political Developments in Ethiopia: Towards Research Agenda in the Framework of DPSIR-NIHR Research Programme (1998–2003),* 1–21. Proceedings of the Launching Workshop of the Department of Political Science and International Relations (DPSIR) and the Norwegian Institute of Human Rights (NIHR). Addis Ababa: Department of Political Science and International Relations, Addis Ababa University, 2003.

Kelbessa, Workineh. *The Utility of Ethical Dialogue for Marginalized Voices in Africa.* Discussion Paper: IIED. London: International Institute for Environment and Development, 2005. http://pubs.iied.org/13508IIED.html.

Keller, Edmond J. *Identity, Citizenship and Political Conflict in Africa.* Bloomington: Indiana University Press, 2014.

Kymlicka, Will. *Multicultural Citizenship: A Liberal Theory of Minority Rights.* Oxford: Clarendon Press, 1995.

Mebrie (Gofie), Solomon. "An Alternative Space of Discussion on Human Rights Issues? Experience from ECSEC." *Ethiopian Journal of the Social Sciences and Humanities* 4, no. 1 (2006): 31–45.

Merkakis, John. *Ethiopia: The Last Two Frontiers.* Oxford: James Currey, 2011.

Rahmato, Dessalegn. *Land to Investors: Large Scale Land Transfers in Ethiopia.* Addis Ababa: Forum for Social Studies, 2011.

———. *The Peasant and the State: Studies in Agrarian Change in Ethiopia, 1950–2000s.* Addis Ababa: Addis Ababa University Press, 2009.

Smith, Lahra. *Making Citizens in Africa: Ethnicity, Gender, and National Identity in Ethiopia.* Cambridge: Cambridge University Press, 2013.

Teferi, Abebe, and Admit Zerihun. *Ethiopian Privatization Program: Rational Performance, and Impact on the Labour Market.* Addis Ababa: CETU, 2001.

Transitional Government of Ethiopia. "Labour Proclamation No. 42/1993." *Negarit Gazeta* 52, no. 27 (January 20, 1993): 268–328.

TEN

Ethnicity and Contested Citizenship in Africa

EGHOSA E. OSAGHAE

LONG AGO, REINHARD BENDIX DISTINGUISHED BETWEEN TWO OPPOSING principles of citizenship: the plebiscitarian principle, which holds citizens as individuals who relate directly to the state, and the functional representation principle, in which relations between individuals and the state are mediated by the primary group(s) to which the individual belongs.[1] At the core of liberal democracy is the plebiscitarian principle, which promotes universal citizenship, whereby citizens, irrespective of ethnic origin, race, sex, or religion, are formally equal in terms of rights, duties, and opportunities.[2] The functional principle, in contrast, defines citizens and the rights they enjoy on the basis of the hierarchical groups they belong to and tends to promote unequal, exclusionary, and contested citizenship.

The coexistence of both forms of citizenship and the contradictory forces they provoke are central to the problems of citizenship in multi-ethnic states. In Africa, the prevalence of the functional principle and associated problems underlies the conundrum of John Ayoade's "states without citizens," an apt description of the fact that some so-called citizens are precluded from the rights and benefits of citizenship because of the subordinated, excluded or marginalized groups they belong to.[3] This is explained by three underlying factors. First, and the historically most fundamental, are the anomalies and structural disabilities bequeathed by colonialism and the colonial state. These mostly had to do with the artificial origins and violent character of the colonial state, which involved the forced incorporation of diverse and hostile groups and suppression of people's rights; the instrumentalities of indirect rule and ethnic inequalities, which kept groups divided and subjected some of them to domination; and the fact that the colonial state pursued the interests of the colonizer rather than those of the colonized.[4] By its very nature, the colonial regime precipitated the crises of state legitimacy and ownership, which are fundamental to the problems of citizenship today. In particular, as Mahmood Mamdani has pointed out, the colonial state had subjects and not citizens, and by restricting so-called natives to membership in tribal groups rather than the state, colonialism sowed the seeds of contested citizenship.[5]

The second underlying factor for the prevalence of the functionalist principle is the predominance of precapitalist social formations in which rights (and corresponding duties) are conceived of in organic, communitarian, collectivistic, and exclusivist terms.[6] According to Okwudiba Nnoli, "Individuals do not have any claims which may override those of the collectivity. Harmony and cooperation rather than divergence of interest, competition and conflict characterize social life. People are more inclined to think of their obligations to other members of the group than their rights. . . . Even in the urban areas a feeling of belongingness to a community is an important part of individual existence."[7]

The ethnic group and its derivatives—ethnicity and ethnic identity— are central to this conception. Citizenship is then constructed on an ethnic basis. Perhaps the best illustration of this is the indigeneity clause in the Nigerian 1999 constitution, section 25(1)a, which makes belonging to an ethnic group indigenous to the country a condition for citizenship by birth. Indigeneity makes the individual an ethnic citizen whose rights are tied to those of the ethnic group.[8] Indigene-based citizenship has serious implications, which are not only disenabling of equal citizenship but also promote conflicts. First, it makes citizenship a mutually exclusive category of "insiders" and "outsiders." According to a submission by the Plateau State government to the constitutional amendment committee in Nigeria, "Everyone comes from somewhere and therefore one can only be an indigene of one place. . . . It is culturally impossible to have dual and multiple indigeneship."[9] In effect, indigeneship separates insider-citizens (indigenes) from outsider-citizens (nonindigenes) and makes rights and privileges in the indigenous group, locality, or state the exclusive preserve of indigenes.

Although the Plateau government submission clarifies that the exclusive rights and privileges are restricted to "indigenous" or "traditional" rights mostly having to do with rights and access to land and that all citizens, irrespective of indigeneity, are entitled to the fundamental and so-called residency rights provided for in the constitution, the reality is that nonindigenes suffer discrimination and exclusion on most matters and are treated as noncitizens within the domains of the indigenous groups.[10] This has been the source of protracted indigene/nonindigene, indigene/settler conflicts in several parts of the country, especially in the Middle Belt state of Plateau and other ethnic minority domains of the north where long years of religious conflicts between powerful Muslim groups and non-Muslims have created deeply divided societies. The Plateau State submission argues that indigene-based conflicts can be resolved only if traditional and indigene rights can be abolished, but this is unlikely as long as indigenous groups exist and constitute the basis for the constitutional definition of citizenship.

There is also a problem with the determination of indigeneity: who is truly an indigene, and who does the defining and determination? Because of the arbitrary manner in which boundaries of African states were demarcated by colonizers and the long history of migrations and displacements across ethnic boundaries, the question of which groups are truly indigenous, settler, and migrant remains fiercely contested and unresolved.[11] The opening of previously closed political spaces beginning in the late 1990s rekindled contestations over the status of descendants of individual migrants and migrant groups, particularly in countries like Malawi, Zambia, and Côte d'Ivoire, where the (original) origins of incumbent presidents, former presidents, and presidential aspirants became major electoral issues. A case in point is the constitutional amendment to prevent former president Kenneth Kaunda from contesting the presidential election in Zambia conducted by the Chiluba government on the ground that Kaunda was not a Zambian citizen (it was discovered late in the day that his parents were originally from Malawi, but even Frederick Chiluba's own status as a citizen of Zambia was also contested by the opposition!). The new forms of contested citizenship resonated in some other countries as well, notably, Côte d'Ivoire, Malawi, Liberia, and Congo. The problem of the Mandingos (who are regarded by supposedly indigenous Liberians as migrants from Guinea) in Liberia and the migrant Bayanmulenges in the Democratic Republic of Congo was a major factor in the civil war that erupted in each of the two countries, with members of both groups struggling to assert their belongingness and citizenship.

The third underlying factor for the prevalence of the functional principle in Africa is the state-centered, authoritarian, and nonaccountable manner in which citizenship has been constructed within the broader framework of nation and legitimacy building. In the name of preventing fragmented states inherited from the colonial era from falling apart, power holders suppress so-called nation-threatening rival claims by members of dissatisfied (but so-called opposition) groups and pursue hegemonic and exclusionary projects that seek to reproduce the state in the image of the dominant ethnic or religious group. One-party and military regimes, which proliferated on the African political landscape in the 1960s and 1970s, provided the political hinges for authoritarian constructions of citizenship on terms that were discriminatory, unequal, exclusionary, and unjust. Of course, the policies pursued by the regimes intensified intergroup conflicts and citizenship contestations that have hallmarked national identity formation in postcolonial Africa.

The wave of democracy and democratization that swept through the continent in the closing years of the twentieth century, however, engendered new approaches to citizenship construction that have increasingly seen a movement away from the privileging of states as the sole determinants of citizenship to a more robust engagement of citizens with states. The opening up and expansion of political spaces, revitalization of civil society, and rights-based demands for inclusive, participatory, and accountable governance broadened the arena of citizenship construction. Through social movements, ethno-nationalist groups and prodemocracy organizations, minorities, and other previously excluded, dominated, and oppressed groups have challenged authoritarian structures and engaged the state in a manner that makes exclusionary citizenship now less likely—indeed, in places like Sudan and Central African Republic, where redress-seeking demands continued to be suppressed, protracted conflicts and civil war appeared to be a last resort for inclusive nation-state building, leading, in the case of Sudan, to a split into two countries: Sudan and South Sudan. To the extent that group interests and rights (and therefore the functional principle) remain crucial in the renewed citizenship struggles, it may be too early to talk of paradigm shifts in citizenship contestations and constructions in Africa, but the struggles for voice, rights, equity, and justice for members of various groups represent an important development in the search for universal citizenship.

Citizenship as a Contested Terrain

The construction of citizenship is an integral part of state and nation building. The problems of citizenship may therefore be approached from the perspective that, like the emergence of an integrated nation-state that is the end product of nation building, citizenship is not natural or given but something to be claimed and constructed. The process of constructing citizenship is two-pronged. On the one hand, it involves the construction of national identity (and allegiance as well) as the *primary identity* of members of a polity. The aim of national identity construction is to establish an overarching identity to which all other competing identities and allegiances—ethnic, racial, religious, regional—are supposed to be secondary. On the other hand, citizenship construction involves the granting or extension of civil, political, social, and economic rights to members of the state in return for the duties they render to it (allegiance, patriotism, payment of taxes, national service, and so forth). The two aspects of citizenship are theoretically linked by the fact that belongingness in the state and national identity are the basis upon which citizens lay claim to the rights and privileges provided by the state.

In reality, however, the terrain of citizenship is not as settled as the foregoing might suggest. Indeed, it is essentially contested, more so in the postcolonial states of Africa where the fatal legacies of colonialism and postcolonial authoritarian regimes have fostered citizenship hierarchies and deprived segments of populations of rights of full citizenship. In effect, contested citizenship involves the struggles by various groups, especially marginalized, excluded, minority and disadvantaged groups, to enjoy rights and benefits equal to those accorded privileged citizens by the state and to thus become full members of the state. A helpful way to understand the nature of contested citizenship is to distinguish analytically between two coexisting but opposing forces of identity formation.[12]

First is state-generated or manipulated collective identity, which typically involves the creation of a hegemonic order. Although this process of identity formation tends to be integrationist and state power holders "find it politically wiser to recognize and tolerate some forms of cultural diversity rather than impose a total uniformity by forcible means,"[13] it is often asserted through repressive means—persecution, dispossession, discrimination, exclusion, conquest, assimilation, and in extreme cases, genocide. To the extent that state power holders tend to enforce so-called common identities (as well as their component languages, cultures, and religions) as *the* legitimate identities, Peter Beilharz is right to argue that "[c]itizenship has often been used politically or systematically to integrate or modulate rather than diversify."[14] Citizens belonging to groups outside the *dominant paradigm* are generally treated as, or perceive themselves to be, excluded or marginalized. Thus, the struggles and claims by members of the latter groups for equity and justice are what lie at the core of citizenship contests.

Second, and in contradistinction to state-directed identity, there is nonstate or civil society–generated identity formation (civil society as used here refers to the nonstate segment of the public realm whose main institutional manifestation is the broad range of voluntary, nongovernmental, and community-based associations that play important roles in the process of state building). This tends to be more discerning of diversity and pluralism and offers spaces for the expression of various competing identities and rights. Civil society–led identity formation also aims at collective and integrated identity, but unlike that dictated by the state, it proceeds on the basis of inclusion, mutual exchanges, and accommodation (rather than assimilation, exclusion, or conquest), such that when a collective identity emerges, it is quite often negotiated.[15]

The identities negotiated by civil society may not have the same legal authority as those of the state, but they nevertheless present a more assured pedestal for members of disadvantaged groups to locate themselves as rights-bearing groups and engage the state, more so if civil society is regarded as the site of counterhegemonic mobilization.[16] In general, and as borne out by the experiences of several African countries, citizenship tends to be less fiercely contested where counterhegemonic claims from civil society are not suppressed and/or where civil society is able to influence or control the structuration of the state. In short, citizenship would be less contested where state-directed identity formation is informed by demands from civil society and is therefore inclusive and pluralist—as in the adoption of more than one official language, protection of cultures and religions, power-sharing arrangements that guarantee equitable access to state power and resources, the granting of political autonomy to territorial groups in a federal system, and so on, rather than where these are suppressed.

The problem mainly arises from the fact that citizenship construction is, in the final analysis, a state project because it is central to the state's legitimacy, and few states would allow a free-wheeling process of identity formation outside their control.[17] Even if civil society constituents are assumed to successfully contest, negotiate, and even mitigate grievances, the ultimate responsibility for citizenship—for granting rights and effectuating them—still lies with the state and how its power holders structure the authoritative allocation of values.[18] But even so, the location of civil society as the state of the stateless and site of counterhegemony and cogovernance makes it a key partner in the management of citizenship contestations.[19]

When we turn to the underlying reasons for contested citizenship, it becomes clear that citizenship means much more than the assumption of national identity.[20] Underlying the contestations are the competitions for scarce resources and social goods and the struggle to control political power, which is crucial to the authoritative allocation of resources and goods. In relation to citizenship, these competitions take the form of struggles to claim and assert civil, political, social, and economic rights that embody the public goods and access to them. Issa Shivji's characterization of rights as "a means of struggle . . . not a standard granted as charity from above but a standard around which people rally for struggle from below" underscores the point very well.[21]

In capitalist, liberal democratic formations, the struggle involves autonomous individuals who, under free-market conditions, compete and bargain with others to maximize benefits. The logic of this process requires that the individual be granted rights (to life, private property, free speech, association with others, nondiscrimination, and so forth) that put him or her at par with others in access and opportunities and enable them to compete equitably. Where precapitalist formations coexist with those of capitalism, as they do in most parts of Africa, the (ethnic) group by which the individual is socially and legally defined tends to be the main actor—or intermediary—in the struggle for social, economic, and political rights and relations with the state. Demands for individual and group rights are made in the context of structured inequalities, relative deprivation, discrimination, and distributive injustice in which members of aggrieved groups are disadvantaged, marginalized, or excluded from the rights and privileges available to members of other groups.

Thus, individual rights mostly demanded by groups on behalf of their members are those that promote affirmative action and social mobility—redress of imbalances in education, public sector employment, entry into the military, and so on.[22] This is because the theory of individual rights assumes equality of access and opportunities, which is possible only when action is taken to redress and reduce structural inequalities among groups.[23] In acknowledgment of this, section 8(3)a of the 1994 interim constitution of South Africa, a country where the apartheid regime had created racial hierarchies and deprived the black majority of citizenship, provided that the enforcement of fundamental human rights "shall not preclude measures designed to achieve the adequate protection and advancement of persons or groups or categories of persons disadvantaged by unfair discrimination, *in order to enable their full and equal enjoyment of all rights and freedoms*" (emphasis added).

Group rights are also demanded to protect the corporate identity and survival of the group because, it is argued, the purposes for which they are demanded (such as preservation of language, culture, religion, power sharing, local political autonomy, and assertion of the rights to self-determination and development) cannot be met by individual rights, which is why the granting of fundamental (individual) human rights has not lessened demands for group rights, especially by minority groups.[24] The case of the powerful Afrikaner minority in the period immediately following the transition from apartheid in South Africa is instructive. Although the bill of rights in the 1996 constitution is sufficiently liberal and inclusive, this did not lessen the momentum of Afrikaner demands for the right to self-determination and possibly an independent *volkstaat* and protection of Afrikaner language and culture.[25] In general, although state power holders are reluctant to grant group rights, especially those that demand political autonomy or national self-determination, because of their perceived dangers to the political order, expediency has often necessitated policies that address or lessen tensions associated with group demands and grievances.

Ethnicity and Citizenship in Africa

The basis of contested citizenship in most African states is ethnicity, which may be defined as the mobilization of ethnic identity and interests to make political demands on the state and pursue constitutive interests in competition with members of other groups. The levers of mobilization are the objective markers (language, culture, religion, myth of common origin, territory) that differentiate members of one group from others and provide the basis for forging group solidarity and collective destiny, in the process of transforming the ethnic group-in-itself into the ethnic group-for-itself. Three crucial attributes of ethnicity that are germane to its relation with citizenship need to be emphasized. The first is that ethnic identity is a collective or shared identity that merges the individual's identity with that of the group. In behavioral terms, the implication of this is that the individual as a bearer of the collective identity is representative of the group and is subject to the security/insecurity or advantages/disadvantages that that identity confers. This does not contradict the acknowledged fact that ethnicity is situational; it only means that when adopting the ethnic identity (or resource) is found to be expedient, the individual ties his or her chances in the competitive setting to the status of the group. This is in addition to the fact that in societies where the individual is defined or ranked in terms of her or his ethnic origin, as has been the case in most parts of Africa since colonial times, she or he has little or no choice.

The second attribute is that ethnicity is an interest-begotten ideology that is constructed and mobilized in pursuit of individual or group interests, and the form it takes varies from routine competition to violent conflicts. When not mobilized or politicized, ethnicity is dormant, or its existence is not troubling. But when mobilized and conflicts are provoked, ethnicity tends to become a pervasive strategy for making political demands, partly because ethnic mobilization provokes countermobilization by other ethnic groups and partly because state power holders recognize the destructive potential of ethnic conflicts and tend to take ethnic demands seriously. In general, perceived threats to the collective well-being or survival of the group (such as relative deprivation, threat of extinction of language, culture, or religion, exclusion, discrimination, persecution, and genocide) provide the most opportune setting for ethnic mobilization. Thus, although ethnic solidarity is often mobilized in pursuit of individual interests, these are disguised as constitutive interests tied to the grievances (or privileges) of the group. This is mostly done by the elites who are in the front line of the competition for socioeconomic goods and political power, but nonelites also rationally exploit the ethnic resource.[26] For ethnic mobilization to succeed, however, the mass of the people (whether rural peasants or urban proletariat) and the various subgroups have to be reasonably dissatisfied with their place in the existing system or be committed to preserving extant privileges. Where this is not the case, subethnic constituents have been known to engage in countermobilization.

Third, then, ethnic competition occurs at the intergroup as well as intragroup levels. At the latter level, subterritorial demarcations, variations in language (dialects) as well as cultural and religious practices, uneven development, and elite factionalism constitute the basis of contestations. The example of Somalia, where conflicts among clans of the same ethnic group exploded into a protracted civil war, shows that intragroup conflicts can be as serious as intergroup conflicts. The point here is that competing ethnicities are more complex than analyses that focus on only intergroup conflicts suggest. With regard to citizenship, the implication of inter- and intragroup competition and conflict is that focus should not be merely on engagements between groups and the state but also on the whole complex of horizontal engagements that involve groups not only discriminating against each other but also mobilizing to deny adversaries (outsiders, nonindigenes) citizenship rights.

Why Is Ethnicity a Basis for Contested Citizenship?

Given these attributes, especially the fact that ethnicity is constructed and involves the mobilization of collective identity/security in making political demands, we should not be surprised that it is a major basis of contested citizenship. It is by no means the only basis for contestation (race, gender, religion, class, and so on are other important bases), but it is arguably the most potent challenge to national or universal citizenship in Africa.[27] The reasons for this are well articulated in the literature on ethnicity in Africa, and they can be summarized as follows.[28]

The first reason is that ethnicity hinges on and is sustained by territory-based exclusivist and discriminatory claims. As such, it is antithetical to citizenship, which is a more egalitarian concept that assumes the formal equality of citizens across territorial boundaries within the state. The territoriality of ethnic claims makes it possible for people from outside groups to be denied citizenship rights within the same country. Perhaps the best example of this is to be found in Nigeria, where regionalism and statism have historically involved the preclusion of so-called nonindigenes (also called migrants or settlers) from citizenship rights in their places of domicile.[29] The stratification (or ranking) and inequality of ethnic groups, coupled with the fact that ethnicity thrives on competition, make politicized ethnicity dangerous for citizenship.[30]

Second, ethno-nationalism, which involves the construction of ethnic identity and solidarity for political claims, is often a counterideology to the nationalism of the (multiethnic) state, with some disaffected groups

demanding separate statehood. The history of the first decade of independence of many African states is replete with separatist agitations
and attempted secession. Attempts by Katanga in Congo and Biafra
in Nigeria to secede are most notable in this regard. The situation has
improved considerably since those heady days, with secession becoming
less fashionable and separatists now demanding greater autonomy and
access to power and resources within extant states. The examples of
the minorities of the oil-producing areas in Nigeria, Tuaregs in Niger,
Baganda in Uganda, and the Inkatha-led Zulu in South Africa readily
come to mind. There are nonetheless pockets of secessionist threats,
such as right-wing Afrikaner demands for a *volkstaat* in South Africa,
resurgent talks of ethno-regional secession (especially by elites of the
disaffected Yoruba–South West in Nigeria following the annulment of
the June 12, 1993, presidential election), and the long, drawn-out battles
of separatists of Casamance in Senegal and Southern Cameroon in
Cameroon.

Third, the highly emotive character of ethnicity makes it a powerful
ideology for mobilization, especially in cases where there is discrimination against members of the group by the state, or a genocidal threat to
the collective security or survival of the group is perceived. Its intricate
linkages to, and reinforcement by, other emotive constructs like religion and territoriality make it even more powerful. Donald Horowitz
explains the strong appeal of ethnicity in terms of the fact that "group
worth" is a focal point of both individual and group identity because
self-worth or self-esteem tends to be calculated in terms of the esteem
accorded the individual's group. Although Horowitz's conclusion that
"the sources of ethnic conflict reside, above all, in the struggle for relative group worth"[31] is somewhat exaggerated, it nevertheless helps to
explain why a threat to the group is invariably seen as a threat to the self,
which is, more often than not, the basis of the mobilization of ethnic
movements and transformation of ethnic identity into political identity.
Under the circumstances, the suppression of ethnic movements only
serves to justify further countermobilization.

Fourth, ethnic demands tend to enjoy a measure of legitimacy. The
right to self-determination, which is enshrined in most human rights
covenants and upheld by international law, legitimizes ethno-nationalism
and claims for ethnic equality and pluralism, especially where there
is open discrimination, persecution, or genocide against members of
a group. In the case of the latter, favorable international opinion and

support by international organizations and foreign powers reinforce the legitimacy of ethnic mobilization and further encourage the agitators. The case of the Ogoni minority group in Nigeria—whose struggle was placed within the larger global framework of climate change, environmental justice, and human rights and whose leader, the late Ken Saro-Wiwa, enjoyed international acclaim as a minorities' rights activist—is a good example.[32] The importance attached to other group rights like cultural, language, and religion rights and the rights of so-called indigenous peoples, as well as welfarist or distributive social and economic rights, by the United Nations and international human rights organizations has also had the same effects.

The fifth reason consists of the gross inequalities among ethnic groups in terms of population, resource endowment, political and socioeconomic advancement, and access to and actual control of political power and the public sector, which over time create ethnic hierarchies. Some of the problems in this regard are part of the fatal legacy of colonial rule in Africa. Colonial authorities' established systems of ethnic ranking elevated favored groups to superior and dominant political and economic positions, which disproportionately composed the public service, army, and police, making the latter the monopoly of so-called warrior tribes, fostered uneven socioeconomic development especially in the educational sector, and generally created a system of unequal access and opportunities among the different ethnic groups. These inequalities were maintained or even extended by exclusivist postcolonial regimes, thereby extending the terrain of competitive ethnicity and contested citizenship.

Finally, ethnic mobilization involves some form of formal or informal organization—ethnic union, hometown, cultural or linguistic association, social movement, communal self-help development union, and so forth. These not only function as interest groups, making demands in the "political arena for alteration in their status, in their economic well-being, in their civil rights, or in their educational opportunities," but they also perform shadow-state functions for members of the group, functions that entail providing social goods and services (community schools, scholarships, credit facilities, roads, and cottage industries) that the state since colonial times has failed to provide for citizens.[33] The importance of the latter functions (which propelled the emergence of what Peter Ekeh calls the primordial public, comprising ethnic welfare and development organizations)[34] lies in the fact that they encourage competition with the state. According to Claude Ake, primordial publics "became centres of resistance, means of self-affirmation against the colonizers' aggressive deculturing of the 'natives,' and also networks of survival strategies. By being all this, they became polities and essentially displaced the state, depriving it not only of legitimacy but also of a civic public. Instead of a civic public, political society was parcellized into a plurality of primordial publics framing primordial polities which are competitive with the state."[35] The failure of postindependence governments to perform better than colonial authorities in this regard, a situation that became worse with the economic decline suffered by most governments in Africa in the period beginning in the mid-1980s, ensured the survival and importance of competitive primordial publics.

The Dynamics of Ethnicity and Contested Citizenship in Africa

The contestation of citizenship along ethnic lines is both a manifestation and an aggravating factor of the festering legitimacy crisis that has rendered the nation-state fragile at best in postcolonial Africa. It shows that the processes of state and nation building are still uncompleted after many years of independence, with such fundamental issues as citizenship and ownership of the state still largely unresolved.[36] Members of several groups continue to be excluded from and denied full and equal citizenship in their states of belonging, while others who belong are subordinate and subject citizens. The aim of this section is to search for these explanations and examine how changing political, economic, and social formations and orientations since the 1960s have affected the processes.

The major explanations for protracted ethnicity-based contestations over citizenship in postcolonial Africa have to do with the authoritarian, discriminatory, and exclusivist strategies of citizenship construction that have been adopted by state power holders since the period of colonial rule. For the postindependence power holders, authoritarian strategies were ostensibly justified by the imperative of keeping together the artificial and fragile states they inherited. This approach received the support of the dominant intellectual perspectives on state and nation building at the time, which theorized nationalism as an exclusively statist ideology.[37] Strong (actually authoritarian) and charismatic father-of-the nation leaders, including military "modernizing" rulers, and limited expansion of political participation spaces were advanced as prerequisites for political stability, national integration, and economic development, which were regarded as urgent tasks of independence. In the assimilationist-centrist conception of the nation, notions of power sharing and pluralism were relatively unpopular, and rival claims to the state were perceived as threats to be suppressed or eradicated. Even countries like Nigeria (and for shorter periods Kenya, Uganda, Cameroon, Sudan, and Ethiopia) that adopted the federal solution, in which power sharing and pluralism were emphasized, approached the formula as a pragmatic means for allowing diversities to coexist peacefully "until such a time as the process of modernization resulted in a sufficient degree of national integration that would render federal structures redundant."[38]

It is against this background that the prevalence of the one-party system (and later military regimes) as instruments of nation-state (and citizenship) construction should be analyzed. The forging of national consensus through suppression of competing ethnic claims was the spearhead of this offensive. Leaders like Julius Nyerere, Modibo Keita, Jomo Kenyatta, and Kwame Nkrumah sought justification for their schemes on the basis of so-called traditional African social formations and political thought whose paradigms not only claimed the absence of class divisions and institutionalized opposition but also, more importantly, emphasized the organic solidarity of that society, the primacy of the community over the individual, and the role of the ruler as the symbol and embodiment of the unity of the "nation."

This was the context within which the totalizing tendencies of the state took root.[39] At the heart of these were the attempts to domesticate civil society and place the entire political space under state control. Nothing, including the private sector, was exempt from state intervention, and very little space was left for autonomous action. The state assumed exclusive control of national economies through nationalization, centralized planning, and unbridled expansion of the public sector. Restrictions were placed on labor unions and other civil society constituents whose demands and advocacy for human rights and good governance and close ties with opposition groups made them targets of state repression. Press freedom was in short supply, as only state-owned media that were closed to opposition elements were allowed to operate. Although many constitutions contained bills of rights, human rights were observed more in the breach. In fact, rather than rights, the obligations or duties of the citizen to the state were emphasized, as was said to be consistent with African communalism.[40] But even duties were also problematic, because of the failure of the state to reciprocate with corresponding rights. Group rights, especially the right to local self-determination, were denied. Even a federal state like Nigeria denied minority groups in the regions the right to internal political autonomy. Even ordinary and day-to-day things like popular music, personal names, clothing, and food, as well as culture and national languages, which ought to belong to the private realm, attracted government intervention, as was amply demonstrated by Mobutu's *authenticité* project in Zaire.

It is in the political sphere, however, where the full force and impact of state totalization can be more clearly seen. Opposition parties that were mostly ethnic and sectional (this was largely a response to the perceived ethnicization of the state) and their leaders were repressed or outlawed. In many cases, there was a one-party system de jure, and all public structures and organizations from the local to the national level were linked to the party—and in some countries (for example, Liberia), membership in the ruling party was compulsory for public servants. Where so-called opposition parties were allowed to function, as was the case in Botswana, Gambia, Mauritius, and Senegal, ruling parties deployed corporatist and patrimonialist strategies to co-opt the leaders and render them ineffective or physically eliminate them. Later, military regimes outlawed political associations, which they accused of being agents of division.

In all this, so-called nation-destroying ethnicity (or tribalism) was considered the chief enemy. This could not have been surprising, considering that it was perhaps the only counterstate (nationalist) ideology that escaped the totalizing process, in part because state power holders were themselves ardent players of the ethnic game—indeed, Horowitz points out that one-party regimes were "a mask for ethnic domination."[41] For members of dominated and minority groups, ethnic movements and organizations provided the vehicles of resistance to state repression. State power holders, however, tried all they could to suppress or eliminate ethnicity (opposition ethnicity, in effect), without much success. Some, like Sekou Toure of Guinea, abolished the institution of chieftaincy to arrest the growth of ethnicity, while others, like Nkrumah of Ghana and General Ironsi of Nigeria, banned ethnic associations and political organizations and discouraged ethnic political participation.[42]

Because abolition of ethnicity was impossible, some leaders were forced (by reasons of political expediency, mostly) to embrace ethnic arithmetic formulas to redress ethnic and social inequalities in the public sector and balance competing ethnicities in the composition of central government and its agencies, especially the civil service, the military, and universities. But by and large, as was consistent with the overall totalizing strategies, the emphasis continued to be placed on the deployment of the coercive apparatus of the state to deal with ethnicity and ethnic mobilization.

The foregoing summarizes the fatal foundations of nation-state and citizenship construction in postindependence Africa. By emasculating civil society's roles of cogovernance, the earlier postindependence regimes made unresolved issues of coexistence inherited from colonial rule difficult to address. The coercive and authoritarian approach to the construction of the nation-state therefore had the effect of heightening ethnic tensions and conflicts. Moreover, the inability of governments to meet the high expectations of independence, which led to the strengthening of shadow and alternative state functions performed by the primordial publics, ensured that the ethnic hold on citizenship was kept strong. The sectional and hegemonic uses to which state power was put, however, accentuated the contestation of citizenship along ethnic lines. By preserving and in some cases extending the ethnic inequalities inherited from the colonial era, by making the public sector the virtual monopoly of the president's ethnic group and precluding other groups from state power, by promoting the culture, language, and religion of that group as national symbols, and, worst of all, by making it impossible for displaced and marginalized groups to legitimately seek redress, power holders excluded large sections of the country from effective citizenship. The result was the spate of fierce contestations, separatist agitations, civil wars, and state fragility that marked the first five decades of independence.

Africa has since gone through tremendous change and transition. The period beginning in the 1990s, in particular, consisted of years of profound economic and political transformation and reforms. Democratization occasioned by constitutional and governance reforms brought with it new emphasis on the rights of individuals and groups, the dismantling of authoritarian structures and regimes, and pluralism (the opening of political space, the emergence of virile civil society, and multiparty politics). The opening up of previously closed political spaces and the growing legitimation of ethnic demands in the ferment of a global democratic revolution reinvented issues of state ownership and citizenship in a manner that called for remarkably different approaches to nation-state construction. In place of the old wisdom of authoritarian, centrist, and assimilationist strategies came the new wisdom of pluralism, power sharing, human rights, and inclusion—in short, an open and democratic approach to addressing the national question. This development has been greatly aided by new intellectual paradigms that emphasize a shift away from state-directed integration and citizenship construction to shared civil society and state-driven integration and governance.[43] A major premise of the new paradigm is the claim that "democratization is a process not of suppressing but of institutionalizing conflict."[44]

The emergence of a virile civil society emboldened previously suppressed counterhegemonic identity groups and movements to engage the state to demand inclusive citizenship. Some of the more conspicuous manifestations of this emboldening include independent mass media; rights-asserting activities of civil liberties, prodemocracy, and minority rights organizations; the reinvigoration of labor, student, women's, and professional associations seeking governance reform; and a flood of strikes, demonstrations, and other forms of protest to back political and economic demands. Given the primacy of ethnicity in the structuration of state-citizen relations, it was only to be expected that ethnic mobilization for emancipation, inclusion, equity, and justice would be a major part of the new politics of citizen movements that arose to renegotiate solidarity or belongingness. A large part of this involved the construction of spaces that empowered citizens to make self-determined choices in terms of Albert O. Hirschman's analytic categories of exit, voice, and loyalty.[45] While exit has always provided alternative sites beyond the reach of the state and has remained a redress-seeking strategy of last resort, the new politics have hinged more on the reciprocity of voice and loyalty.

The dynamics of the changing scenario of citizenship engagements are well illustrated by the experience of minority groups in Nigeria whose nationalist—in effect, citizenship—politics has moved from seeking accommodation to demanding self-determination.[46] In the northern parts of the country, where religion has been the dominant mode of domination and exclusion, minorities sought to assert their rights as non-Muslim indigenes. This pitched them against the Hausa/ Fulani, who have been at the top of the ethnic ladder since colonial times on the one hand, and on the other hand the state and federal governments from whom the minority leaders demand protection and justice. In Kaduna, Taraba, Nasarawa, and Plateau States, autonomous chiefdoms have been created to safeguard the minorities, while federal authorities have become more sensitive to reflecting the ethnic, religious, and cultural diversity of the north in the sharing of political offices and economic resources. The case of the minorities of the oil-rich Niger delta is even more interesting. There, the Ijaw, Ogoni, Urhobo, and others have exploited their location as the source of the country's oil wealth to the fullest by not only exacting a greater share of the federation's pooled revenues and increased political autonomy but also raising their levels of group worth to the point of producing the country's president (Goodluck Jonathan). Two things are particularly remarkable about the new forms of struggle from below: first, they are rights-based and aim at respecting diversity and inclusion; and second, the engagements are located within larger frameworks of governance, economic, political, and constitutional reforms involving local and global civil society and other nonstate coalitions, which makes it relatively more difficult for ethnic demands to be demonized or treated in isolation.

The new citizenship politics has been driven by (new) social movements whose demands for rights and justice dwell more on first-line participation in decision making and making the state more accountable than the old fight for formal rights. The integrated solidarity roles of the social movements have also seen the emergence of civil society and (autonomous) communities as (alternative) sites of identity and loyalty. So the notion that the state is the natural or (only) legitimate repository of integral loyalty seems to be no longer as valid as it used to be. In fact, in rethinking the state of the global South, whose chronic and endemic pathologies have stood in the way of full citizenship for all, there are those who argue that the time has come to de-privilege the state, de-construct its colonial fixation, and consider possible alternatives.[47] Cumulatively, these developments and these robust engagements have brought renewed hopes for marginalized, dominated, and excluded groups, although the continued emphasis on indigeneity remains the greatest obstacle to equal citizenship. In this regard, a lot of work still needs to be done by the state and civil society, especially in the area of reducing the gross inequalities in resources, access, and opportunities among competing groups.

One point that bears emphasizing is that the wind of change and transformation across Africa has not rendered ethnicity and therefore the functional principle less salient in the new patterns of the politics of belonging. A major explanation for this is that the structural inequalities that have historically separated the various groups and subgroups remain, a matter that the economic decline of the state has not helped. Economic decline is only one part of the state fragility variables (which include poor governance, accountability deficits, and intractable conflicts and insurrection) that have seen most governments in Africa unable to discharge the functions of effective statehood. Another explanation lies in the continued manipulations of ethnicity by incumbent political parties and governments to retain power. These manipulations, it goes without saying, ensure the retention of new ethnic hierarchies and the creation of new ones.

Concluding Notes

The emergence of a virile civil society from the throes of economic reforms and political transition as a relatively autonomous co-actor in state building, however, was a major advance in the process of resolving the national question of which citizenship is an integral part. Thus, although the structural inequalities that encourage competing ethnicities remain, and contestation of citizenship has tended to intensify in the aftermath of political and economic reforms, the chances of constructing equal or universal citizenship are now arguably brighter than they were previously.

This is not because the functional representational principle of citizenship is no longer prevalent (this will remain the case for as long as indigeneity remains the condition for citizenship) but because the new forms of citizenship engagement aim at appropriating the state, making decision making more participatory, and making the state more accountable. Within this framework, questions of group inequality and relations of domination, which need to be resolved before individuals can meaningfully become universal citizens, now stand a chance of being democratically posed and better managed, if not resolved. The increased involvement of civil society in citizenship construction makes the process more discerning of diversity and the imperatives of equitable rights and accountability, and therefore more likely to endure as a negotiated rather than a received paradigm. But this would depend to a great extent on the ability of civil society to assert itself as an autonomous co-actor in nation-state reconstruction. As John Keane puts it, "Civil society and the state must become the condition of each other's democratization."[48]

Notes

1. Reinhard Bendix, *Nation-Building and Citizenship: Studies of Our Changing Social Order* (New York: Anchor Books, 1969). The following claim by the

Benin Forum summarizes the point about group intermediation: "The Benin Forum is a sociocultural and non-political umbrella group that speaks on behalf of the Oba of Benin and the Benin ethnic group at home and in the diaspora." Benin Forum, "An Address Presented to the Governor of Edo State on 30 March 2012," Vanguard (Lagos), April 2, 2012, 14.

2. See John Rawls, *A Theory of Justice* (Cambridge, MA: Harvard University Press, 1971); Bruce A. Ackerman, *Social Justice in the Liberal State* (New Haven, CT: Yale University Press, 1980); Melissa S. Williams, "Justice toward Groups: Political not Juridical," *Political Theory* 23, no. 1 (1995): 67–91. William Alonso has noted that the notion of national citizenship as primary identity emerged only recently as part of the evolution of the modern nation-state in the West, following the French revolution; in the new states of Africa it is much more recent, dating back to the attainment of formal independence from colonial rule. Alonso, "Citizenship, Nationality and Other Identities," *Journal of International Affairs* 48, no. 2 (1995): 585–99.

3. John Ayoade, "States without Citizens," in *The Precarious Balance: State and Society in Africa*, ed. Donald Rothchild and Naomi Chazan (Boulder, CO: Westview Press, 1988), 100–120.

4. Eghosa E. Osaghae, *A State of Our Own: Second Independence, Federalism and Decolonization of the State in Africa* (Ibadan: Bookcraft, 2015).

5. Mahmood Mamdani, *Citizen and Subject: Contemporary Africa and the Legacy of Late Colonialism* (Princeton: Princeton University Press, 1996).

6. See Claude Ake, *Political Economy of Nigeria* (London: Macmillan, 1985); Ake, *Democratization of Disempowerment in Africa* (Lagos: Malthouse Press, 1994); Goran Hyden, "The Anomaly of the African Peasantry," *Development and Change* 17, no. 4 (1986): 677–705; Axel Harneit-Sievers, *Constructions of Belonging: Igbo Communities and the Nigerian State in the Twentieth Century* (Rochester: University of Rochester Press, 2006).

7. Okwudiba Nnoli, *Ethnicity and Development in Africa: Intervening Variables* (Lagos: Malthouse, 1994), 18. See also Osita C. Eze, *Human Rights in Africa: Some Selected Problems* (Lagos: Macmillan, 1984); Eghosa E. Osaghae, "Human Rights and Ethnic Conflict Management: The Case of Nigeria," *Journal of Peace Research* 33, no. 2 (1996): 171–88; and Winston P. Nagan, "The African Human Rights Process: A Contextual Policy-Oriented Approach," in *Human Rights and Governance in Africa*, ed. Ronald Cohen, Goran Hyden, and Winston P. Nagan (Gainesville: University Press of Florida, 1986), 87–110.

8. The notions of "the indigenous" and "indigeneity" in Nigeria are different from those more generally global usages as spread by the United Nations Working Group on indigenous peoples. While the latter relate to peoples who experience the consequences of historical colonization and invasion of their territories and face discrimination and possible extinction because of their distinct cultures, identities, and ways of life, *indigeneity* is used in Nigeria to refer to members of groups that claim ancestral and exclusive rights to territories of origin. That is the basis on which nonindigenes, that is, those indigenous to other territories, are treated as outsiders and discriminated against.

9. Plateau State Government, "The Position of the Executive Council of Plateau State on the Amendments of Some Sections of the Constitution," *The Nation* (Lagos), July 4, 2012.

10. In addition to being excluded from land rights, nonindigenes are denied employment, admission to public schools, and access to justice in customary (and sharia) courts and are frequently at the receiving end of ethnic violence perpetrated by indigenes.

11. Joseph E. Harris, *Africans and Their History*, rev. ed. (New York: Penguin, 1972); Devon Curtis and Gwinyayi A. Dzinesa, eds., *Peacebuilding, Power, and Politics in Africa* (Athens: Ohio University Press, 2012).

12. See Joan Cocks, "From Politics to Paralysis: Critical Intellectuals Answer the National Question," *Political Theory* 24, no. 3 (1996): 518–37.

13. Paul R. Brass, *Ethnicity and Nationalism: Theory and Comparison* (New Delhi: Sage, 1991), 21.

14. Peter Beilharz, "Citizens of Cities," *Thesis Eleven* 46, no. 1 (1996): 92.

15. Mainly for this reason, Okwudiba Nnoli advocates that nation building should be the responsibility of civil society. Nnoli, *Ethnicity and Development in Africa.*

16. Although counterhegemonic mobilization is usually thought to be antistate, Cocks points out that "the identity that rises from the bottom up [civil society] . . . is as likely to work against the established state as for it." Cocks, "From Politics to Paralysis," 519.

17. The process is not, however, as voluntary as is generally believed; enforcing the "discipline" required for effective citizenship entails a great deal of state control. See Eghosa Osaghae, "The Crisis of National Identity in Africa: Clearing the Conceptual Underbush," *Plural Societies* 19, no. 3 (1990): 116–32.

18. Krishan Kumar, "Civil Society: An Inquiry into the Usefulness of an Historical Term," *British Journal of Sociology* 44, no. 3 (1993): 375–95.

19. Eghosa E. Osaghae, "Rescuing the Post-colonial State in Africa: A Reconceptualisation of the Role of Civil Society," *International Journal of African Studies* 2, no. 1 (2000): 33–56; Eghosa E. Osaghae and Veronica A. Osaghae, "Rethinking Democratic Governance and Accountability in Africa," *Forum for Development Studies* 40, no. 2 (2013): 393–412.

20. Osaghae, "Crisis of National Identity."

21. Issa G. Shivji, *The Concept of Human Rights in Africa* (Dakar: CODESRIA, 1989), 71.

22. Myron Weiner, "The Pursuit of Ethnic Equality through Preferential Policies: A Comparative Public Policy Perspective," in *From Independence to Statehood: Managing Ethnic Conflict in Five African and Asian States*, ed. Robert B. Goldmann and A. Jeyaratnam Wilson (London: Frances Pinter, 1984), 63–81.

23. See the interesting arguments in Williams, "Justice toward Groups"; and John Kane, "Justice, Impartiality, and Equality: Why the Concept of Justice Does not Presume Equality," *Political Theory* 24, no. 3 (1996): 375–93.

24. Osaghae, "Human Rights"; Vernon Van Dyke, *Human Rights, Ethnicity and Discrimination* (Westport, CT: Greenwood, 1985); Rodolfo Stavenhagen,

"Ethnic Conflict and Human Rights: Their Interrelationship," *Bulletin of Peace Proposals* 18, no. 4 (1987): 171–88.

25. Eghosa E. Osaghae, "What Democratization Does to Minorities Displaced from Power: The Case of White Afrikaners in South Africa," *Forum for Development Studies* 29, no. 2 (2002): 293–320.

26. Eghosa E. Osaghae, "A Re-examination of the Conception of Ethnicity in Africa as an Ideology of Inter-elite Competition," *African Study Monographs* 12, no. 1 (1991): 43–61.

27. In Africa, it has been argued that "[e]thnic formations are often the most significant countervailing force to state power as well as the best defence of a separate space against the totalizing tendencies of the post-colonial state." Claude Ake, "What Is the Problem of Ethnicity in Africa?" *Transformation* 22 (1993): 7.

28. See Nelson Kasfir, *The Shrinking Political Arena: Participation and Ethnicity in African Politics, with a Case Study of Uganda* (Berkeley: University of California Press, 1976); Okwudiba Nnoli, *Ethnicity and Development in Nigeria* (Aldershot, UK: Avebury, 1995).

29. Eghosa E. Osaghae, "The Problems of Citizenship in Nigeria," *Africa: Rivista trimestale di studi e documentazione dell' Istituto italiano per l'Africa e l'Oriente* 45, no. 4 (1990): 593–611.

30. For theories and models of ethnic inequality, see Charles Hirschman, "Theories and Models of Ethnic Inequality," *Research in Race and Ethnic Relations* 2 (1980): 1–20.

31. Donald L. Horowitz, *Ethnic Groups in Conflict* (Berkeley: University of California Press, 1985), 143–50.

32. See Eghosa E. Osaghae, "The Ogoni Uprising: Oil Politics, Minority Agitation and the Future of the Nigerian State," *African Affairs* 94, no. 3 (1995): 325–44; Osaghae, "From Accommodation to Self-Determination: Minority Nationalism and the Restructuring of the Nigerian State," *Nationalism and Ethnic Politics* 7, no. 1 (2001): 1–20; Steven Cayford, "The Ogoni Uprising: Oil, Human Rights, and a Democratic Alternative in Nigeria," *Africa Today* 43, no. 2 (1996): 183–97.

33. Brass, *Ethnicity and Nationalism*, 19.

34. Peter P. Ekeh, "Colonialism and the Two Publics in Africa: A Theoretical Statement," *Comparative Studies in Society and History* 17, no. 1 (1975): 91–112.

35. Ake, "What Is the Problem," 3.

36. Eghosa E. Osaghae, "The State of Africa's Second Liberation," *Interventions: International Journal of Postcolonial Studies* 7, no. 1 (2005): 1–21; Osaghae, "Fragile States," *Development in Practice* 17, nos. 4–5 (2007): 691–99; Osaghae, *State of Our Own*.

37. Mahmood Mamdani, "Democratic Theory and Democratic Struggles," in *Democratization Processes in Africa: Problems and Prospects*, ed. Eshetu Chole and Jibrin Ibrahim (Dakar: CODESRIA, 1995), 87.

38. Roberta McKown, "Federalism in Africa," in *Centralizing and Decentralizing Trends in Federal States*, ed. C. Lloyd Brown-John (Lanham, MD:

University Press of America and Center for the Study of Federalism, 1988), 297.
See also Ladipo Adamolekun and John Kincaid, "The Federal Solution: Assessment and Prognosis for Nigeria and Africa," *Publius* 21, no. 4 (1991): 173–88.

39. Jean-François Bayart, "Civil Society in Africa: Reflections on the Limits
of Power," in *Political Domination in Africa,* ed. Patrick Chabal (Cambridge:
Cambridge University Press, 1986), 109–25; Bayart, "The Historicity of African
Societies," *Journal of International Affairs* 46, no. 2 (1992): 55–79.

40. National pledges, anthems, and other symbols of the nation-state reflected the emphasis on duties rather than rights.

41. Donald L. Horowitz, "Democracy in Divided Societies," in *Nationalism, Ethnic Conflict, and Democracy,* ed. Larry Diamond and Marc F. Plattner
(Baltimore, MD: Johns Hopkins University Press, 1994), 35–55.

42. See Kasfir, *Shrinking Political Arena.*

43. Elisa P. Reis, "The Lasting Marriage between Nation and State Despite
Globalization," *International Political Science Review* 25, no. 3 (2004): 251–57.

44. Francisco C. Weffort, "What Is a 'New Democracy'?" *International Social Science Journal,* no. 136 (1993): 250.

45. See Albert O. Hirschman, *Exit, Voice, and Loyalty: Responses to Decline in
Firms, Organizations, and States* (Cambridge, MA: Harvard University Press,
1970).

46. Osaghae, "From Accommodation to Self-Determination."

47. Martin van Creveld, *The Rise and Decline of the State* (Cambridge: Cambridge University Press, 1999).

48. John Keane, "The Limits of State Action," in *Democracy and Civil Society,* ed. John Keane (London: Verso, 1988), 15.

References

Ackerman, Bruce A. *Social Justice in the Liberal State.* New Haven, CT: Yale
University Press, 1980.

Adamolekun, Ladipo, and John Kincaid. "The Federal Solution: Assessment
and Prognosis for Nigeria and Africa." *Publius* 21, no. 4 (1991): 173–88.

Ake, Claude. *Democratization of Disempowerment in Africa.* Lagos: Malthouse
Press, 1994.

———. *Political Economy of Nigeria.* London: Macmillan, 1985.

——— "What Is the Problem of Ethnicity in Africa?" *Transformation* 22
(1993): 1–14.

Alonso, William. "Citizenship, Nationality and Other Identities." *Journal of
International Affairs* 48, no. 2 (1995): 585–99.

Ayoade, John. "States without Citizens." In *The Precarious Balance: State and
Society in Africa,* edited by Donald Rothchild and Naomi Chazan, 100–120.
Boulder, CO: Westview Press, 1988.

Bayart, Jean François. "Civil Society in Africa: Reflections on the Limits of
Power." In *Political Domination in Africa,* edited by Patrick Chabal, 109–25.
Cambridge: Cambridge University Press, 1986.

———. "The Historicity of African Societies." *Journal of International Affairs* 46, no. 1 (1992): 55–79.

Beilharz, Peter. "Citizens of Cities." *Thesis Eleven* 46, no. 1 (1996): 89–95.

Bendix, Reinhard. *Nation-Building and Citizenship: Studies of Our Changing Social Order.* New York: Anchor Books, 1969.

Bjorklund, Ulf. "Ethnicity and the Welfare State." *International Social Science Journal* 39, no. 1 (1987): 19–30.

Brass, Paul R. *Ethnicity and Nationalism: Theory and Comparison.* New Delhi: Sage, 1991.

Cayford, Steven. "The Ogoni Uprising: Oil, Human Rights, and a Democratic Alternative in Nigeria." *Africa Today* 43, no. 2 (1996): 183–97.

Cocks, Joan. "From Politics to Paralysis: Critical Intellectuals Answer the National Question." *Political Theory* 24, no. 3 (1996): 518–37.

Coleman, James S. *Nigeria: Background to Nationalism.* Berkeley: University of California Press, 1958.

Curtis, Devon, and Gwinyayi A. Dzinesa, eds. *Peacebuilding, Power, and Politics in Africa.* Athens: Ohio University Press, 2012.

Davis, Horace B. *The National Question: Selected Writings of Rosa Luxemburg.* New York: Monthly Review Press, 1976.

Doornbos, Martin R. "Some Conceptual Problems Concerning Ethnicity in Integration Analysis." *Civilizations* 22, no. 2 (1972): 263–83.

Ekeh, Peter P. "Colonialism and the Two Publics in Africa: A Theoretical Statement." *Comparative Studies in Society and History* 17, no. 1 (1975): 91–112.

Ely, John. "The Polis and 'The Political': Civic and Territorial Views of Association." *Thesis Eleven* 46 (1996): 33–65.

Eze, Osita C. *Human Rights in Africa: Some Selected Problems.* Lagos: Macmillan, 1984.

Glickman, Harvey. "Issues in the Analysis of Ethnic Conflict and Democratization Processes in Africa Today." In *Ethnic Conflict and Democratization in Africa,* edited by Harvey Glickman, 1–31. Atlanta: African Studies Association Press, 1995.

Harneit-Sievers, Axel. *Constructions of Belonging: Igbo Communities and the Nigerian State in the Twentieth Century.* Rochester: University of Rochester Press, 2006.

Harris, Joseph E. *Africans and Their History.* Rev. ed. New York: Penguin, 1972.

Hirschman, Albert O. *Exit, Voice, and Loyalty: Responses to Decline in Firms, Organizations, and States.* Cambridge, MA: Harvard University Press, 1970.

Hirschman, Charles. "Theories and Models of Ethnic Inequality." *Research in Race and Ethnic Relations* 2 (1980): 1–20.

Hogan, Trevor. "Citizenship, Australian and Global." *Thesis Eleven* 46 (1996): 97–114.

Horowitz, Donald L. "Democracy in Divided Societies." In *Nationalism, Ethnic Conflict, and Democracy,* edited by Larry Diamond and Marc F. Plattner, 35–55. Baltimore, MD: Johns Hopkins University Press, 1994.

———. *Ethnic Groups in Conflict.* Berkeley: University of California Press, 1985.

Hyden, Goran. "The Anomaly of the African Peasantry." *Development and Change* 17, no. 4 (1986): 677–705.

———. "The Challenges of Analyzing and Building Civil Society." *Africa Insight* 26, no. 2 (1996): 92–106.

Kane, John. "Justice, Impartiality, and Equality: Why the Concept of Justice Does not Presume Equality." *Political Theory* 24, no. 3 (1996): 375–93.

Kasfir, Nelson. *The Shrinking Political Arena: Participation and Ethnicity in African Politics, with a Case Study of Uganda.* Berkeley: University of California Press, 1976.

Keane, John. "The Limits of State Action." In *Democracy and Civil Society,* edited by John Keane, 1–30. London: Verso, 1988.

Kumar, Krishan. "Civil Society: An Inquiry into the Usefulness of an Historical Term." *British Journal of Sociology* 44, no. 3 (1993): 375–95.

Laski, Harold. *A Grammar of Politics.* London: Allen and Unwin, 1982.

Mamdani, Mahmood. *Citizen and Subject: Contemporary Africa and the Legacy of Late Colonialism.* Princeton: Princeton University Press, 1996.

———. "Democratic Theory and Democratic Struggles." In *Democratization Processes in Africa: Problems and Prospects,* edited by Eshetu Chole and Jibrin Ibrahim, 87–99. Dakar: CODESRIA, 1995.

Marshall, Thomas Humphrey. *Class, Citizenship and Social Development.* New York: Doubleday, 1964.

McKown, Roberta. "Federalism in Africa." In *Centralizing and Decentralizing Trends in Federal States,* edited by C. Lloyd Brown-John, 298–318. Lanham, MD: University Press of America and Center for the Study of Federalism, 1988.

Munck, Ronaldo. *The Difficult Dialogue: Marxism and Nationalism.* London: Zed, 1986.

Nagan, Winston P. "The African Human Rights Process: A Contextual Policy-Oriented Approach." In *Human Rights and Governance in Africa,* edited by Ronald Cohen, Goran Hyden, and Winston P. Nagan, 87–110. Gainesville: University Press of Florida, 1986.

Nnoli, Okwudiba. *Ethnicity and Development in Africa: Intervening Variables.* Lagos: Malthouse, 1994.

———. *Ethnicity and Development in Nigeria.* Aldershot, UK: Avebury, 1995.

Osaghae, Eghosa E. "The Crisis of National Identity in Africa: Clearing the Conceptual Underbush." *Plural Societies* 19, no. 3 (1990): 116–32.

———. "Fragile States." *Development in Practice* 17, nos. 4 and 5 (2007): 691–99.

———. "From Accommodation to Self-Determination: Minority Nationalism and the Restructuring of the Nigerian State." *Nationalism and Ethnic Politics* 7, no. 1 (2001): 1–20.

———. "Human Rights and Ethnic Conflict Management: The Case of Nigeria." *Journal of Peace Research* 33, no. 2 (1996): 171–88.

———. "The Ogoni Uprising: Oil Politics, Minority Agitation and the Future of the Nigerian State." *African Affairs* 94, no. 3 (1995): 325–44.

————. "The Problems of Citizenship in Nigeria." *Africa: Rivista trimestale di studi e documentazione dell' Istituto italiano per l'Africa e l'Oriente* 45, no. 4 (1990): 593–611.

————. "A Re-examination of the Conception of Ethnicity in Africa as an Ideology of Inter-elite Competition." *African Study Monographs* 12, no. 1 (1991): 43–61.

————. "Rescuing the Post-colonial State in Africa: A Reconceptualisation of the Role of Civil Society." *International Journal of African Studies* 2, no. 1 (2000): 33–56.

————. "The State of Africa's Second Liberation." *Interventions: International Journal of Postcolonial Studies* 7, no. 1 (2005): 1–21.

————. *A State of Our Own: Second Independence, Federalism and the Decolonisation of the State in Africa.* Inaugural lecture delivered at the University of London, April 2014. Ibadan: Bookcraft, 2015.

————. "What Democratization Does to Minorities Displaced from Power: The Case of White Afrikaners in South Africa." *Forum for Development Studies* 29, no. 2 (2002): 293–320.

Osaghae, Eghosa E., and Veronica A. Osaghae. "Rethinking Democratic Governance and Accountability in Africa." *Forum for Development Studies* 40, no. 2 (2013): 393–412.

Rawls, John. *A Theory of Justice.* Cambridge, MA: Harvard University Press, 1971.

Reis, Elisa P. "The Lasting Marriage between Nation and State Despite Globalization." *International Political Science Review* 25, no. 3 (2004): 251–57.

Shivji, Issa G. *The Concept of Human Rights in Africa.* Dakar: CODESRIA, 1989.

Smith, Anthony D. *The Ethnic Revival in the Modern World.* Cambridge: Cambridge University Press, 1989.

Stavenhagen, Rodolfo. "Ethnic Conflict and Human Rights: Their Interrelationship." *Bulletin of Peace Proposals* 18, no. 4 (1987): 171–88.

van Creveld, Martin. *The Rise and Decline of the State.* Cambridge: Cambridge University Press, 1999.

Van Dyke, Vernon. *Human Rights, Ethnicity and Discrimination.* Westport, CT: Greenwood, 1985.

Weffort, Francisco C. "What Is a 'New Democracy'?" *International Social Science Journal,* no. 136 (1993): 155–75.

Weiner, Myron. "The Pursuit of Ethnic Equality through Preferential Policies: A Comparative Public Policy Perspective." In *From Independence to Statehood: Managing Ethnic Conflict in Five African and Asian States,* edited by Robert B. Goldmann and A. Jeyaratnam Wilson, 63–81. London: Frances Pinter.

Williams, Melissa S. "Justice toward Groups: Political not Juridical." *Political Theory* 23, no. 1 (1995): 67–91.

Young, Iris Marion. "Polity and Group Difference: A Critique of the Ideal of Universal Citizenship." *Ethics* 99 (1989): 250–74.

Postscript

FREDERICK COOPER

CITIZENSHIP IS A POWERFUL CONCEPT, AND A PROTEAN ONE. IT IS above all a claim-making construct, juxtaposing people's assertion of rights against a state's assertion of obligations. Citizenship both presumes and fosters a sense of belonging, of membership in a collectivity, and therefore it simultaneously includes and excludes. Citizenship is a focus of claims and counterclaims in today's Africa, as it has been in the past—within African colonies and independent countries, across colonial empires, in reference to a variety of diasporically and territorially defined collectivities. One of the virtues of this volume is that it gives as much attention to the variety of meanings of citizenship as to the importance of the category. It is all to the good that some of the contributors to this volume disagree with others over how the concept should be used. And it is also to the good that several of them write about the future of citizenship claims with passion, not just analytic precision.

Much of the controversy lies in how one is to conceive of the relationship between citizenship and colonialism and how to assess the impact of colonial patterns on contemporary Africa in the long run. Colonization, one argument goes, produced subjects, not citizens.[1] But does this conception give too much weight to colonizers' perceptions of their own power to define categories, when the realities were more ambiguous than that? As Emma Hunter points out in her introduction to this volume, so-called subjects engaged with colonial legal structures in different ways.[2] And they had their own conceptions of what political belonging might mean. The question is how much we want to consider colonial empires to be contested spheres, in which—for all the extremes of inequality—struggle mattered. In chapter 2 of this volume, Nicole Ulrich points to the complexities of struggle as long ago as the eighteenth-century Cape.

Khoesan, slaves of Southeast Asian origin, and lower-level Dutch in varying ways sought either to distance themselves—literally or figuratively—
from the Dutch East India Company administration or to use the
state's own legal mechanisms to claim at least a slightly better situation
within it. After the British takeover from the Dutch, the status of *subject*
of the king became itself a basis for making claims. As Ulrich shows,
"the incorporation of Khoesan . . . into the category of 'British subject'"
allowed workers to claim basic legal protections. There is no need to
exaggerate the effectiveness of such claim making across much of the
history of European colonization in Africa, but we can avoid the trap of
having to choose between conceptions of absolute subjectification and a
view of power relations as "negotiated."

Even the idea of an imperial "subject" presumes some form of incorporation into a polity, and empires deployed a range of mechanisms to
make sure that subjects understood both their subordination and their
incorporation. They at times needed loyalty—even military service—
from their subjects, and command and exemplary violence were not
necessarily sufficient to enforce loyalty on a daily basis, let alone in circumstances when imperial power could be very much in question. That
is why the category of "subject" could hardly be a stable one. Colonial
regimes went to considerable effort to police their boundaries precisely
because of the ambiguity of imperial power. People in the categories
of subject and citizen knew—or at least some of them knew—about
the other and moved between social fields characterized by each. As
Cherry Leonardi and Chris Vaughan (chapter 3, this volume) put it,
"multiple registers of political language were being spoken simultaneously or alternately" and the "rhetoric of rights and citizenship was
intertwined with older discourses of genealogy, personalized and paternalist rule, and patrimonial obligation." Citizenship, for many Africans
in the colonial period, was something they knew about but could not
have. It was therefore the focus of demands, complaints, petitions, and
mobilizations.

Colonial governments were confronted both with the fragility of
their own mechanisms of control and with the ambivalence of elites in
and out of government about the simultaneous imperatives of imperial
inclusion and the maintenance of boundaries. Even in the paradigmatic
case of French Algeria—where the juridical basis of the subject-citizen
distinction was worked out and the separate system of "justice" for noncitizens was enshrined—influential members of the French political

establishment repeatedly questioned the legitimacy and practicality of such distinctions until they were formally repudiated in the Constitution of 1946.[3]

If the association of subjecthood with colonization turns out to be complex, the association of citizenship with the "nation" is problematic as well. Citizenship has a long history—much longer than notions of "the nation-state" or "popular sovereignty." At times—such as Rome in the era of the Republic (509–27 BC)—it implied that the people of Rome had a political voice, and its selective extension became a tool of Roman elites for incorporating a portion of conquered people. In AD 212 the emperor Caracalla declared all nonenslaved male inhabitants of the Roman Empire to be citizens, with the right, among other things, to have any legal cases involving them to be heard in a Roman court. Here was the model for imperial citizenship: defining membership in a vast, culturally diverse system whose unity was created by the power of a state. When the possibility of extending citizenship to the subjects of the French empire was being debated in 1946, proponents and opponents alike referred to the proposal as a new "edict of Caracalla." The arguments—in political mobilizations in Africa as much as in the legislature in Paris—were vigorous and uncertain in outcome or significance, because both government leaders and African activists wanted to give juridical weight to concepts of belonging: one to insist on loyalty and obligations, the other to claim rights and resources.[4]

In historical terms—in 1946 as much as 212—the location of citizenship was not predetermined. Empire could be a meaningful unit of political belonging, a claim on the patronage of the king or the parliament, an assertion of rights within a large, diverse, resource-rich political entity. Or monarchs could insist that they were the source of rights, which they could allocate differentially to groups within their realms. Such a ruler was not entirely free to *not* grant rights, however, without risk to his legitimacy and authority.[5]

When the idea that rights originated in "the people" entered political discourse, the stakes of deciding who constituted the people became higher. No sooner had the declaration of the rights of man and of the citizen emerged in the Paris assemblies in 1789 than the question of whether they applied in the colonies as well as in metropolitan France came to the fore. The revolutionary assemblies at first temporized, but after the revolution in Saint-Domingue broke out in 1791 they decided for pragmatic as much as principled reasons to include free people of color within the realm of citizenship, then to free and make citizens of the slaves. But the restrictive vision came back when Napoleon tried to reinstate slavery, succeeding in most of France's colonies but provoking the exit of Saint-Domingue from the empire.[6] The question of imperial citizenship would be debated periodically from then on. The exclusion of colonized people from citizenship was not a notion that could be taken for granted.

Imperial citizenship was a focus of demands in the British as well as the French empire in most of the nineteenth and twentieth centuries. About the same time as France passed its new edict of Caracalla, the British Parliament (1948) passed its Nationality Act, which granted a superposed British citizenship to citizens of Canada, Australia, and the other dominions—and the colonies as well.[7] But if the domain of citizenship could be wider than the territorially defined nation, it could also be smaller. In early modern Spain, citizenship had much more to do with cities than with kingdoms; the institutions of urban society defined what membership in a political entity signified.[8] The ambiguous locality of citizenship—which is neither new nor specific to Africa—is quite relevant to the problems that are central to the chapters in this volume. Is the existence of sentiments of belonging at the level of a linguistically or culturally defined community—a moral community, to use John Lonsdale's term—compatible with citizenship in a state-centered conception?[9]

Hunter argues in the introduction to this volume that notions of belonging can exist simultaneously at different levels and that one function of the state can be to foster and protect the diversity of its population. In principle, she is right, but things do not always work out that way. As Jean Marie Allman showed in regard to British West Africa in the 1950s, the form and rhetoric of "Asante" nationalism could be quite similar to that of "Ghanaian" nationalism. And the two engaged in bitter conflict, precisely because they saw that locating the nation at one level diminished power at the other.[10]

Indeed, the very conception that one sort of citizenship can be considered "national" while another is "ethnic" flattens the historical process that defines units of political action and subjective belonging. Asante was itself an empire that forcibly incorporated people into its institutions, assimilating them to varying degrees and maintaining distinctions to varying extents. John Lonsdale (chapter 1) warns against treating the forms of incorporation or belonging in different African societies (centralized or otherwise) as a specifically African form of citizenship that could be used as a model today. What might today appear as fundamental units of belonging have been shaped at various times by migration, the flexibility of kinship structures, adaptation to new environments, cultural interaction, religious conversion and invention, and the power of elites to forcibly incorporate some people and violently exclude others. Colonial regimes—*pace* Mahmood Mamdani—fostered both a theory that reified ethnic boundaries and practices that blurred them. As V. Adefemi Isumonah argues for Nigeria in chapter 8 of this volume, the argument for ethnically defined group rights "presumes that the question of subgroup or major group membership is settled. Every ethnic group membership is frozen."

One has, nevertheless, to be careful about going too far in emphasizing the variability and changeability of the citizenship construct. The power of the citizenship construct does not lie in its fluidity. States take claims seriously when they have a social and political basis. People's sense of belonging is not fixed in time, but it is not transitory either. Affinity may or may not crystallize in group membership, that is, in the notion of belonging to a bounded collectivity, to which one either belongs or does not.[11] And group membership may or may not translate into the capacity to allocate resources with authority. To talk about citizenship is to talk about the relationship of units of belonging to units of power. That means, as several of the authors in this volume make clear, that discussion of citizenship entails analysis of how states resist claims as much as how they respond to them.

Demands for cultural recognition or defense of local or regional interests are one form of claim making but not the only alternative to a nation-state-centered view of power. People can organize on the basis of class, gender, and generation. They demand many different things of states. The question is not so much whether states should recognize cultural particularity as whether they respond to a wide variety of collective mobilizations and what categories of people and what categories of political actions states can exclude from the political arena. Several contributors to this volume point to the dangers of privileging the principle of "indigeneity."[12] Isumonah, for example, sees ethnic representation as privileging certain power brokers over others. Eghosa E. Osaghae (chapter 10) sees such a politics as not only promoting conflict but also "disenabling" claims to equality among all citizens. Solomon M. Gofie (chapter 9) shows that even a state—post-1991 Ethiopia—willing to vest a degree of power in regions and to promote an "ethnic federalism" put in place a "formal recognition of multiple identities" while avoiding crucial issues of human rights. Henri-Michel Yéré (chapter 5) reports that even as powerful a figure as Félix Houphouët-Boigny could not get elite Ivorians to accept flexible concepts of nationality, setting off the escalation of claims for a true *ivoirité* that excluded people with a historic pattern of cross-border connections that had contributed to the prosperity of Ivory Coast. The very fact of privileging "ethnic citizenship" allows state officials the possibility of playing off ethnic groups against each other and against other demands for social and economic justice. Osaghae powerfully criticizes the "state-centered, authoritarian, and nonaccountable manner in which citizenship has been constructed within the broader framework of nation and legitimacy building." And Aidan Russell (chapter 4) describes an especially insidious instance of a state that promoted a sharp line between the included and the excluded, while denying even the included "space to express the slightest hint of independent political thought." The ethnicization of politics is as much the consequence of such state politics as ethnic differentiation is the cause of political conflict.

In both colonial and postcolonial times, the assertion of rights implied more than one kind of demand at a given time. The quest for citizenship was not just a demand for recognition as a "nation" or for a political voice in running that nation: It was part of a quest for a chance for a better life in a world in which states are essential actors. It was a quest for dignity. Different movements put the accent on different places, and the tensions between different levels—between local or regional collectivities and the state, between demands for equality with a privileged group and autonomy from that group—are tellingly described in the chapters of this book.

Is the citizenship construct a "Western" import, a particular form of relationship to the state that excludes others? Yes and no.[13] Africa is rich in the variety of forms of belonging, of affinity, of a relationship of political authority to people. Citizenship can be defined to include all such methods (incorporation into "networks of authority," as Hunter puts it), but then one will have to invent a new term to focus on a particular—and particularly powerful—form. Citizenship is so important as a form of claim making because it posits a collective body of equivalent citizens who have a common relationship to the state. That Africans need to come to grips with the state—and specific forms, territorially defined, of the state—is a product of history, in which the place of colonization looms large. But it is not a history of a simple imposition. Citizenship enables people to push on the form, as well as the actions, of the state.

One can distinguish the horizontal nature of the citizenry from the vertical relationship characteristic of patrimonial systems, including African kingdoms and European empires—which discourage relationships among equivalents and foster relationships of patron to client, of king to subject, of emperor to subordinate rulers. In such terms, citizenship presumes a certain kind of state, one that recognizes a "population" that is both the object of state power and—in democratic theory—the ultimate source of state power. Critics of liberal governance postulate that such a state form reduces complex social and political relationships to a one-to-one relationship of individual to state.

The actual politics of citizenship is not so simple—in France, Great Britain, or the United States as much as in any African country. People bring their various connections among themselves to their connection to the state. Citizens are not, in practice, equivalent in resources and influence. Some are more "in" than others. But the citizenship ideal is an important claim-making tool, an assertion of equivalence that, if effectively made, limits the vertical structures of power. In the aftermath of the constitutional innovations that made his constituents into French citizens, Léopold Sédar Senghor developed a theory of political action that was quite explicit on this point. He called for two forms of solidarity: "horizontal solidarity," among African citizens of France; and "vertical solidarity," between European and African France. His metaphor of vertical solidarity acknowledged the reality of inequality—in wealth, education, access to media—that colonization had produced, while turning the vertical connection into an African claim on the superior resources of European France.[14]

Senghor's generation of political leaders was building movements out of potential citizens as they actually were—with their kinship networks, cultural practices, patronage relations, and village or urban communities. Recognizing that the generalization of citizenship brought to the voting booth largely rural Senegalese, Senghor sought to build a constituency by working through regional elites—the marabouts associated with the major Islamic brotherhoods. The political movement he fashioned thus linked the particular social organization of rural Senegal to the institution of voting, organized in the 1950s on a French model. Here and elsewhere, the politics of citizenship was relational, drawing on complex and dynamic affinities in rural and urban Africa. Such politics is typical of much of the world where citizens vote.[15]

That last point is a critical one, for the social dynamics of citizenship can degenerate into a divisive form of patron-client relations if not subjected to the discipline of elections. The horizontal solidarity that an open and fair election embodies can turn into an entirely vertical relationship, in which the population as a whole has no check on the activities of elites and patrons mobilize rival sets of clients, leading to a political arena that is not only undemocratic but also divided. As Lonsdale points out, population growth shifts the power in patron-client relations toward the patrons. Even where elections continue to be held, the extremes of vertical authority can undermine the making of claims in the name of the equivalence of citizens. But, as such events as the popular mobilizations that drove Blaise Compaoré out of Burkina Faso in 2014 demonstrate, citizens acting together, outside of elections, can challenge a person who holds the power of patronage, state authority, and armed henchmen.

Now, the framework for such conflicts is the territorial state. In former French Africa, this situation results from the fact that Senghor lost one of his most important battles: over the location of citizenship. He fought for, and for a time seemed to be getting his way, in creating a multilayered conception of citizenship, recognizing people as both French and African. His starting point was citizenship in an empire—French citizenship—but he wanted to inflect it to acknowledge the diversity of the peoples that made up the French empire. The Constitution of 1946, written by an assembly of which Senghor was a member, made French subjects into citizens without forcing them to give up their personal status under Islamic or "customary" law. In important ways, the citizenship they won was diluted. Ultimate power rested in a national assembly in which Africans were underrepresented. But citizenship was also a basis for claiming rights at the level of the individual territory, in French Africa as a whole, and in the entire French Union (as the empire was renamed). Senghor wanted basic rights—freedom of speech and assembly, for example—to be guaranteed at the broadest level, for he feared that local political interests would tempt leaders to undermine the rights of citizens. He wanted Africans to be able to take their rights with them, whether at home, in another African territory, or in European France. And he wanted French Africans to unite among themselves in a federation of African territories, an expression of "horizontal" solidarity that was distinctly African. As Yéré explains in this volume, a broad conception of citizenship was shared in other parts of French Africa, but some, like Houphouët-Boigny, rejected the idea of an African federation and sought a direct relationship of each French African territory to a French federation in which all would be citizens.

These disagreements, as well as France's reluctance to face the social and economic costs that demands for the equivalence of citizens would have produced, led to a separation of citizenships instead of one of the various forms of federalism that most West African politicians had sought. France's West African territories ended up in 1960 as eight nation-states, most small, most poor, most with limited resources to promote education and health services. The most important asset their leaders had was sovereignty, and they guarded it jealously. Senghor himself ended up in the trap he had predicted would ensue from what he called the "balkanization" of Africa: regarding power within the territorially bounded state as a zero-sum game, he proved willing to trample on the political rights of Senegalese citizens to retain it.

The "unit" question was thus a critical dimension of the history of citizenship in the time of decolonization. Basil Davidson has referred to the nation-state as a "curse"—not because the state is an evil thing or because nation is not a genuine focus of sentiment, but because seeing the two as inexorably linked draws stark boundaries around a territorially defined space and presumes homogeneity and singularity within it, making political control into an all-or-nothing affair.[16]

Perhaps the layered notion of citizenship that seemed a real possibility in the 1950s might have proven less brittle than the resolutely national citizenship with which African states ended up—making leaders reluctant to cede some of their power to a more inclusive (federal or confederal) African entity or to smaller (regional, ethnic) units within the territorial state. Perhaps not. But citizenship politics did not end there. There was still the question of—to use Lahra Smith's expression—how "meaningful" citizenship within newly independent states could be?[17]

More useful than the dualism of subject-citizen or western-nonwestern citizenships is another notion mentioned in some of the chapters of this book and in some of the scholarly literature on citizenship: between "thick" and "thin" citizenship. Is citizenship merely a formal expression of membership in a political unit, be it imperial, national, or otherwise? Or does citizenship convey something more: voting rights, eligibility for office, protection against government abuses, the right to education, to health services, to possibilities for collective action? Is citizenship a matter of the relationships and associations that people construct for themselves, outside of but in relation to state institutions? Rather than operating as a static dualism, this distinction enables us to focus on processes of "thickening" or "thinning." Might one conceptualize the politics of the late 1940s and 1950s in French Africa as a "thickening" of the formal status that was constitutionally granted, after much contestation, in 1946, as trade unions demanded equality of wages and as African politicians operating at territorial, Africa-wide, and empire-wide levels kept pushing for political, social, and economic reforms?

And did the first generation of African rulers, well aware of the volatility of citizenship claims from their own experience of the 1950s and equally aware of the limited capacity of their governments to meet the demands of citizens for social and economic justice, try to thin out citizenship? Might the demands coming from citizens close to the seat of power for a thicker citizenship for themselves have something to do with the tendencies in such countries as Ivory Coast to take an increasingly exclusionary view of citizenship, to define categories of people out of it, and hence out of the possibility of making claims?

Thinking about the varying levels at which citizenship discourse and practices exist helps us understand the changing spatial and juridical world that Africans have had to navigate since the middle of the twentieth century—and the bitterness brought about by some of these changes. For a time after World War II, British and French Africans had the legal right to travel to and settle in parts of their respective empires, including the British Isles and metropolitan France, and they could do so as rights-bearing citizens. Such possibilities—however harsh the conditions of life that intraempire migrants experienced—shaped an African presence in European cities and movements of people, money, and cultural practices between Africa and other parts of the world. Independence entailed the separation of citizenships, softened by treaties and other arrangements that for a time made it easier for people from the ex-colonies to move to Britain or France and in some cases to establish or have recognized their British or French nationality. But in France, where French citizens in Africa had once had a political voice, the power to decide the rules of access to citizenship was transferred to metropolitan hands. When the French government decided in 1974 to restrict immigration, including that of its pre-1960 citizens, it was within its power to impose its rules. Britain likewise tightened its restrictions on the movement of people from its former dependencies in Asia and Africa to the British Isles in the 1960s, drastically so in the 1970s. So if an ambiguous imperial citizenship was pushed into national containers in independent African countries, Britain and France also adapted more national, more exclusionary, definitions of citizenship, vis-à-vis the descendants of people whom they had once tried to keep within their imperial embrace.

But citizenship is more complicated—and more controversial—than a neat line between those who have it and those who don't. Citizenship has not been an indivisible construct. Postwar social policy in European states linked certain rights to work status and residence, not nationality, at a time when migration within and beyond Europe was extensive: these rights included wage and benefits legislation, access of children to schools, medical care, participation in trade unions, and access to courts administering labor law. In some cases, people could vote in local elections in their country of residence, even if they were not citizens. Some scholars, such as Yasemin Nuhoğlu Soysal, who have studied this phenomenon perceptively, refer to this situation as "post-national citizenship." But the "post" presumes a chronological priority to "national" citizenship. In fact, the postnational citizenship Soysal describes resembles the imperial citizenship of the French Union after World War II.[18] More recently, the advent of the European Union has set out a supranational, European citizenship, which is inscribed on people's passports, while the Schengen process has bumped to a European level the control of movement and identification that is often regarded as intrinsically national.[19]

But this inclusivity is specifically European (and its future, at this point, cannot be taken for granted). To many Africans, Europe as a whole is surrounded by a barrier, and people risk their lives in crossing in leaky boats between Africa and the Canary Islands or Sicily in an attempt to cross it. The politics of the "sans papiers" has become a political issue in France, in which memories of a previous citizenship regime—and the contributions of African subjects and citizens to the defense and prosperity of France—are invoked against the exclusionary nature of the current regime.

Can African governments devise their own equivalent of the Schengen system? There were waves of expulsions of nonnationals from a number of African countries in the 1960s, and in this volume, Russell, Yéré, and Samantha Balaton-Chrimes (chapter 6) all describe exclusionary practices of African states vis-à-vis each other.[20] Yet the founding treaty of the Economic Community of West African States (1975) and subsequent protocols look toward a "community citizenship" derivative of citizenship in the member states and "the abolition of obstacles to free movement of persons, services and capital."[21] But the restrictions on movement remain tighter than those of Schengen. Two Nigerian law professors describe these provisions as "a Greek gift, giving rights with the right hand and taking them back with the left," as national governments stick to their own forms of regulation.[22] African leaders and scholars are aware of alternative models of citizenship, of the possibilities for their citizens and the dangers to their power, of more flexible and inclusive citizenship regimes.

Looking within and beyond the state-citizenship nexus in Africa, we are left with multiple questions. Can African states move toward notions of citizenship that are thick and inclusive rather than thin and exclusive? Can states be responsive to the multiple forms of affinity among their populations and the multiple forms of mobilization of their citizens, not just affinity and mobilization based on putative linguistic or cultural commonality? Can wealthy countries that depend on cross-border movements of workers recognize how much the welfare of the entire population depends on people with different relations to the state and to each other?

Citizenship claims shook up colonial regimes just when they thought their top-down programs of economic development and gradual and controlled extension of political participation would give colonial rule a new lease on life. They threatened the leaders of independent states enough to thin out or even suppress recently won citizenship rights and at times led African rulers to dismiss the very notion of rights as a neocolonialist idea. But in different African countries at different times, citizens have reasserted their right to claim rights, to equal treatment before the law, to a determining voice in public affairs, to respect for human dignity and welfare. One period when such tendencies are evident in numerous African countries is the present. Osaghae, for example, points to "rights-asserting activities of civil liberties, prodemocracy, and minority rights organizations; the reinvigoration of labor, student, women's, and professional associations seeking governance reform; and a flood of strikes, demonstrations, and other forms of protest." The politics of citizenship, as this volume makes clear, has a present and a future as well as a past.

Notes

1. Mahmood Mamdani's *Citizen and Subject: Contemporary Africa and the Legacy of Late Colonialism* (Princeton: Princeton University Press, 1996) has much to say about subjecthood but little about citizenship. For a critical discussion of Mamdani's book, see the section "Autour d'un livre" in *Politique Africaine* 73 (1999): 193–211, with commentaries by Ralph Austen, Frederick Cooper, Jean Copans, and Mariane Ferme and Mamdani's response, as well as differing commentaries in this volume.

2. A similar point has been made about indigenous people's use of the legal institutions of colonizing powers in a collection of studies edited by Saliha Belmessous titled *Native Claims: Indigenous Law against Empire, 1500–1920* (New York: Oxford University Press, 2011).

3. Emmanuelle Saada, *Empire's Children: Race, Filiation, and Citizenship in the French Colonies*, trans. Arthur Goldhammer (Chicago: University of Chicago Press, 2012); Laure Blévis, "Sociologie d'un droit colonial: Citoyenneté et nationalité en Algérie (1865–1947); Une exception républicaine?" (PhD diss., Institut d'Etudes Politiques, Aix-en-Provence, 2004); Alix Héricord-Gorre, "Eléments pour une histoire de l'administration des colonisés de l'Empire français: Le 'régime de l'indigénat' et son fonctionnement depuis sa matrice algérienne (1881–c. 1920)" (PhD diss., European University Institute, 2008).

4. Frederick Cooper, *Citizenship between Empire and Nation: Remaking France and French Africa, 1945–1960* (Princeton: Princeton University Press, 2014); Jane Burbank and Frederick Cooper, "Empire, droits et citoyenneté, de 212 à 1946." *Annales: Histoire, Sciences Sociales* 63, no. 3 (2008): 495–531.

5. Jane Burbank, "An Imperial Rights Regime: Law and Citizenship in the Russian Empire," *Kritika: Explorations in Russian and Eurasian History* 7 (2006): 397–431.

6. See the classic text of C. L. R. James, *The Black Jacobins: Toussaint L'Ouverture and the San Domingo Revolution*, 2nd ed. (New York: Vintage, 1963; orig. pub. 1938); and the more recent books of Laurent Dubois, *Avengers of the New World: The Story of the Haitian Revolution* (Cambridge, MA: Harvard University Press, 2004) and *A Colony of Citizens: Revolution and Slave Emancipation in the French Caribbean, 1787–1804* (Chapel Hill: University of North Carolina Press, 2004).

7. Sukanya Banerjee, *Becoming Imperial Citizens: Indians in the Late-Victorian Empire* (Durham, NC: Duke University Press, 2010); Daniel Gorman, *Imperial Citizenship: Empire and the Question of Belonging* (Manchester: Manchester University Press, 2006); Kathleen Paul, *Whitewashing Britain: Race and Citizenship in the Postwar Era* (Ithaca, NY: Cornell University Press, 1997).

8. Tamar Herzog, *Defining Nations: Immigrants and Citizens in Early Modern Spain and Spanish America* (New Haven, CT: Yale University Press, 2003)

9. John Lonsdale, "The Moral Economy of Mau Mau," in Bruce Berman and John Lonsdale, *Unhappy Valley: Conflict in Kenya and Africa* (Athens: Ohio University Press, 1992), chaps. 11 and 12.

10. Jean Marie Allman, *The Quills of the Porcupine: Asante Nationalism in an Emergent Ghana* (Madison: University of Wisconsin Press, 1993).

11. Rogers Brubaker, *Ethnicity without Groups* (Cambridge, MA: Harvard University Press, 2004).

12. On these issues, see also Peter Geschiere, *The Perils of Belonging: Autochthony, Citizenship, and Exclusion in Africa and Europe* (Chicago: University of Chicago Press, 2009).

13. Ramola Ramtohul (chap. 7, this volume) sees the "Western" notion of citizenship as having "little relevance for African nations." The latter see citizenship as a matter of descent: one is a citizen of the homeland of one's ancestors, regardless of where one lives. V. Adefemi Isumonah (chap. 8, this volume) acknowledges the force of such an argument but sees it as self-serving for the elites and in the end divisive. He argues that a focus on individual citizenship, with flexible notions of belonging, offers the "possibility of building a Nigerian political community or national belonging."

14. Léopold Sédar Senghor spelled out these notions in numerous forums in the late 1940s and 1950s. One of the first was in his newspaper *La condition humaine*, July 11, 1948. For a more detailed analysis, see Cooper, *Citizenship*, 187–89, 203, 446–47.

15. In a pioneering study of how African political parties mobilized people, Aristide Zolberg portrayed them not as mass parties in the Leninist sense but as machines that aggregated different social categories. They were, in this sense, similar to the political machines of twentieth-century American cities, which worked through brokers to line up immigrant communities of different ethnic origin as well as other interest groups. Zolberg, *Creating Political Order: The Party States of West Africa* (Chicago: Rand-McNally, 1966).

16. Basil Davidson, *The Black Man's Burden: Africa and the Curse of the Nation-State* (London: James Currey, 1992).

17. Lahra Smith, *Making Citizens in Africa: Ethnicity, Gender, and National Identity in Ethiopia* (Cambridge: Cambridge University Press, 2013).

18. Yasemin Nuhoğlu Soysal, *Limits of Citizenship: Migrants and Postnational Membership in Europe* (Chicago: University of Chicago Press, 1994).

19. Some "Europeans," however, are more "in" than others. Roma, most notably, are marked in a special way in France, Italy, and elsewhere.

20. The tensions behind xenophobic tendencies appeared in Ivory Coast in 1958 in riots instigated in Abidjan against Dahomean and Togolese residents, even though at the time they shared a common citizenship. See Henri-Michel Yéré's chapter (chap. 5) in this volume. For another view of exclusionary practices in contemporary Africa, see Laurent Fourchard and Aurelia Segatti, "Of Xenophobia and Citizenship: The Everyday Politics of Exclusion and Inclusion in Africa," *Africa* 85 (2015): 2–12.

21. Quoted in Protocol A/p.1/5/79, "Relating to Free Movement of Persons, Residence and Establishment," May 29, 1979, www.comm.ecowas.int/sec/index.php?id=apo10579.

22. Michael P. Okom and J. A. Dada, "ECOWAS Citizenship: A Critical Review," *American Journal of Social Issues and Humanities* 2, no. 3 (2012): 115.

References

Allman, Jean Marie. *The Quills of the Porcupine: Asante Nationalism in an Emergent Ghana.* Madison: University of Wisconsin Press, 1993.

Banerjee, Sukanya. *Becoming Imperial Citizens: Indians in the Late-Victorian Empire.* Durham, NC: Duke University Press, 2010.

Belmessous, Saliha. *Native Claims: Indigenous Law against Empire, 1500–1920.* New York: Oxford University Press, 2011.

Blévis, Laure. "Sociologie d'un droit colonial: Citoyenneté et nationalité en Algérie (1865–1947); Une exception républicaine?" PhD diss., Institut d'Etudes Politiques, Aix-en-Provence, 2004.

Brubaker, Rogers. *Ethnicity without Groups.* Cambridge, MA: Harvard University Press, 2004.

Burbank, Jane. "An Imperial Rights Regime: Law and Citizenship in the Russian Empire." *Kritika: Explorations in Russian and Eurasian History* 7 (2006): 397–431.

Burbank, Jane, and Frederick Cooper. "Empire, droits et citoyenneté, de 212 à 1946." *Annales: Histoire, Sciences Sociales* 63, no. 3 (2008): 495–531.

Cooper, Frederick. *Citizenship between Empire and Nation: Remaking France and French Africa, 1945–1960.* Princeton: Princeton University Press, 2014.

Davidson, Basil. *The Black Man's Burden: Africa and the Curse of the Nation-State.* London: James Currey, 1992.

Dubois, Laurent. *Avengers of the New World: The Story of the Haitian Revolution.* Cambridge, MA: Harvard University Press, 2004.

———. *A Colony of Citizens: Revolution and Slave Emancipation in the French Caribbean, 1787–1804.* Chapel Hill: University of North Carolina Press, 2004.

Fourchard, Laurent, and Aurelia Segatti. "Of Xenophobia and Citizenship: The Everyday Politics of Exclusion and Inclusion in Africa." *Africa* 85 (2015): 2–12.

Geschiere, Peter. *The Perils of Belonging: Autochthony, Citizenship, and Exclusion in Africa and Europe.* Chicago: University of Chicago Press, 2009.

Gorman, Daniel. *Imperial Citizenship: Empire and the Question of Belonging.* Manchester: Manchester University Press, 2006.

Héricord-Gorre, Alix. "Eléments pour une histoire de l'administration des colonisés de l'Empire français: Le 'régime de l'indigénat' et son fonctionnement depuis sa matrice algérienne (1881–c. 1920)." PhD diss., European University Institute, 2008.

Herzog, Tamar. *Defining Nations: Immigrants and Citizens in Early Modern Spain and Spanish America.* New Haven, CT: Yale University Press, 2003.

James, C. L. R. *The Black Jacobins: Toussaint L'Ouverture and the San Domingo Revolution.* 2nd ed. New York: Vintage, 1963. Originally published 1938.

Lonsdale, John. "The Moral Economy of Mau Mau." In *Unhappy Valley: Conflict in Kenya and Africa,* by Bruce Berman and John Lonsdale, chaps. 11 and 12. Athens: Ohio University Press, 1992.

Mamdani, Mahmood. *Citizen and Subject: Contemporary Africa and the Legacy of Late Colonialism.* Princeton: Princeton University Press, 1996.

Nuhoğlu Soysal, Yasemin. *Limits of Citizenship: Migrants and Postnational Membership in Europe.* Chicago: University of Chicago Press, 1994.

Okom, Michael A., and J. A. Dada. "ECOWAS Citizenship: A Critical Review." *American Journal of Social Issues and Humanities* 2, no. 3 (2012): 100–116.

Paul, Kathleen. *Whitewashing Britain: Race and Citizenship in the Postwar Era.* Ithaca, NY: Cornell University Press, 1997.

Saada, Emmanuelle. *Empire's Children: Race, Filiation, and Citizenship in the French Colonies.* Translated by Arthur Goldhammer. Chicago: University of Chicago Press, 2012.

Smith, Lahra. *Making Citizens in Africa: Ethnicity, Gender, and National Identity in Ethiopia.* Cambridge: Cambridge University Press, 2013.

Zolberg, Aristide. *Creating Political Order: The Party States of West Africa.* Chicago: Rand-McNally, 1966.

Contributors

SAMANTHA BALATON-CHRIMES is a lecturer in international studies in the School of Humanities and Social Sciences at Deakin University, Melbourne, Australia. Her research is interdisciplinary in nature, cutting across politics and political theory, development studies, and anthropology. Her research explores political formations and processes that seek to address social, political, and economic inequalities in contexts of development, with special concern to understand the ongoing effects of the historical contexts of such inequalities. Her work deals with both empirical and theoretical issues and focuses on the context of postcolonial communities. Sam holds a PhD in politics from Monash University. She is author of *Ethnicity, Democracy and Citizenship in Africa: Political Marginalisation of Kenya's Nubians* (Ashgate, 2015).

FREDERICK COOPER is a professor of history at New York University and a specialist in the history of Africa, empires, and decolonization. Among his books are *Decolonization and African Society: The Labor Question in French and British Africa* (Cambridge University Press, 1996), *Tensions of Empire: Colonial Cultures in a Bourgeois World* ([coedited with Ann Stoler] University of California Press, 1997), *Beyond Slavery: Explorations of Race, Labor, and Citizenship in Post-Emancipation Societies* ([with Thomas Holt and Rebecca Scott] University of North Carolina Press, 2000), *Colonialism in Question: Theory, Knowledge, History* (University of California Press, 2005), *Empires in World History: Power and the Politics of Difference* ([with Jane Burbank] Princeton University Press, 2010), *Citizenship between Empire and Nation: Remaking France and French Africa, 1945–1960* (Princeton University Press, 2014), and *Africa in the World: Capitalism, Empire, Nation-State* (Harvard University Press, 2014).

SOLOMON M. GOFIE is an assistant professor at the Department of Political Science and International Relations, Addis Ababa University, where he also served as the chair of the department (2009–11). Human rights, migration and transnationalism, transnational involvement, conflict resolution and peace building, citizenship and political communities in the Horn of Africa are his areas of research. He was a visiting scholar at the University of California, Berkeley, Research Fellow at University of Cambridge, and held a visiting assistant professor position at the Department of Political Science, University of Montana, Missoula. His PhD is in Political Science, University of Manchester, United Kingdom, and he holds an MA in Human Rights from the University of Oslo, Norway.

EMMA HUNTER is a lecturer in history at the University of Edinburgh. Previously, she taught at the University of Cambridge and coordinated the CAS/Leverhulme 2011/12 visiting fellowship program on the theme of "Citizenship, Belonging, and Political Community in Africa." She is the author of *Political Thought and the Public Sphere in Tanzania: Freedom, Democracy and Citizenship in the Era of Decolonization* (Cambridge University Press, 2015) and "Dutiful Subjects, Patriotic Citizens and the Concept of Good Citizenship in Twentieth-Century Tanzania," *Historical Journal* (2013).

V. ADEFEMI ISUMONAH is a professor of political science at the University of Ibadan, Nigeria. He was a Cambridge/Africa Collaborative Research Fellow, University of Cambridge, October 2011–March 2012 and the 2005/2006 Bank of Ireland Nelson Mandela Fellow at the Irish Centre for Human Rights, National University of Ireland, Galway, Republic of Ireland. His main research interests are in the fields of citizenship, ethnicity, and minority rights. His recent published works are "Imperial Presidency and Democratic Consolidation in Nigeria," *Africa Today* (2012); "Armed Society in the Niger Delta," *Armed Forces and Society* (2013); (with F. O. Egwaikhide) "Federal Presence in Higher Institutions in Nigeria and the North/South Dichotomy," *Regional and Federal Studies* (2013); and "Minority Political Mobilization in the Struggle for Resource Control in Nigeria," *Extractive Industries and Society*, doi:10.1016/j.exis.2015.04.011.

CHERRY LEONARDI is a senior lecturer in history at Durham University. She is the author of *Dealing with Government in South Sudan: Histories of Chiefship, Community and State* (J. Currey, 2013).

JOHN LONSDALE is an emeritus professor of modern African history at the University of Cambridge. He is a coauthor of the two-volume

Unhappy Valley: Conflict in Kenya and Africa ([with Bruce Berman] Ohio University Press, 1992); a coeditor of *Mau Mau and Nationhood* ([with E. S. Atieno Odhiambo] J. Currey, 2003), *Writing for Kenya: The Life and Work of Henry Muoria* ([with Wangari Muoria-Sal, Bodil Folke Frederiksen, and Derek Peterson] Brill, 2009), *Ethnic Diversity and Economic Instability in Africa: Interdisciplinary Perspectives* ([with Hiroyuki Hino, Gustav Ranis, and Frances Stewart] Cambridge University Press, 2012); and the editor of *Colonial Kenya Observed: British Rule, Mau Mau and the Wind of Change* ([by S. H. Fazan] 2015).

EGHOSA E. OSAGHAE is a tenured professor of comparative politics at the University of Ibadan and is the vice chancellor of Igbinedion University Okada, Nigeria. He was the Emeka Anyaoku Chair of Commonwealth Studies at the University of London for 2013/2014 and gave the chair's inaugural lecture, "A State of Our Own: Second Independence, Federalism and the Decolonisation of the State in Africa," in April 2014. Professor Osaghae's academic specialization is in the areas of ethnicity, conflict management, and federalism. He has published extensively on these subjects in books and journals and sits on the editorial boards of several leading journals. He served as the chair of the Panel on Quality Assurance Assessment, United Nations Economic Commission for Africa, 2011–12, and as a consultant to the African Development Bank's Country Mission to Zambia, in which capacity he produced the country's Governance Profile in 2002.

RAMOLA RAMTOHUL is a senior lecturer in the Sociology Unit of the Department of Social Studies at the University of Mauritius. She is also a collaborative member at the Centre of African Studies at the University of Cambridge. Her research interests are in gender politics and citizenship in multicultural contexts, and privatization in the African higher-education sector. Her publications include "Intersectionality and Women's Political Citizenship: The Case of Mauritius," *Journal of Contemporary African Studies* (2015); the coedited volume *Gender and Citizenship in the Global Age* ([with Laroussi Amri] CODESRIA, 2014); "Gender and Politicized Religion in Mauritius," *Sociedad y Religión* (2014); "Fractured Sisterhood: The Historical Evolution of the Women's Movement in Mauritius," *Afrika Zamani* (2013); and "Academic Freedom in a State Sponsored African University: The Case of the University of Mauritius," *American Association of University Professors Journal of*

Academic Freedom (2012). She has received research fellowships from the University of Cape Town, American Association of University Women, University of Cambridge, and University of Pretoria.

AIDAN RUSSELL is an assistant professor in international history at the Graduate Institute of International and Development Studies, Geneva, and a Title A Fellow of Trinity College, Cambridge.

NICOLE ULRICH is a senior lecturer in history at Rhodes University, South Africa. She researches and has published on the radically democratic forms of organization that emerged among organized workers in South Africa in the 1970s. In addition, she has published a number of journal articles on the solidarities and broader transnational connections forged by the poor and laboring classes in the eighteenth-century colonial Cape. She was a Cambridge/Africa Collaborative Research Fellow, University of Cambridge, October 2011–March 2012.

CHRIS VAUGHAN is currently a lecturer in African history at Liverpool John Moores University. Previously, he taught at the Universities of Durham, Leeds, Liverpool, and Edinburgh. His articles have appeared in the *Journal of African History* and the *Journal of Imperial and Commonwealth History*. He is also the coeditor of *The Borderlands of South Sudan* ([with Lotje De Vries and Mareike Schomerus] Palgrave, 2013) and has advised the African Union on border disputes between Sudan and South Sudan.

HENRI-MICHEL YÉRÉ is currently an engagement partner for diversity and inclusion at the Novartis Institutes for Biomedical Research (NIBR). His PhD thesis, "Citizenship, Nationality and History in Cote d'Ivoire, 1929–1999," was successfully defended at the University of Basel in 2010.

Index

—

www.ingramcontent.com/pod-product-compliance
Lightning Source LLC
Chambersburg PA
CBHW072052020426
42334CB00017B/1485